From Startup to Unicorn

Anil Sethi

From Startup to Unicorn

An Essential Guide to Build, Scale and Sustain Value for Platform and Tech Startups

Anil Sethi
Russikon, Switzerland

All visuals in the book belong to Anil Sethi.

ISBN 978-3-031-53893-3   ISBN 978-3-031-53894-0 (eBook)
https://doi.org/10.1007/978-3-031-53894-0

© The Editor(s) (if applicable) and The Author(s), under exclusive license to Springer Nature Switzerland AG 2024

This work is subject to copyright. All rights are solely and exclusively licensed by the Publisher, whether the whole or part of the material is concerned, specifically the rights of translation, reprinting, reuse of illustrations, recitation, broadcasting, reproduction on microfilms or in any other physical way, and transmission or information storage and retrieval, electronic adaptation, computer software, or by similar or dissimilar methodology now known or hereafter developed.

The use of general descriptive names, registered names, trademarks, service marks, etc. in this publication does not imply, even in the absence of a specific statement, that such names are exempt from the relevant protective laws and regulations and therefore free for general use.

The publisher, the authors, and the editors are safe to assume that the advice and information in this book are believed to be true and accurate at the date of publication. Neither the publisher nor the authors or the editors give a warranty, expressed or implied, with respect to the material contained herein or for any errors or omissions that may have been made. The publisher remains neutral with regard to jurisdictional claims in published maps and institutional affiliations.

This Springer imprint is published by the registered company Springer Nature Switzerland AG
The registered company address is: Gewerbestrasse 11, 6330 Cham, Switzerland

If disposing of this product, please recycle the paper.

Acknowledgements

This book is primarily meant for entrepreneurs, aspiring entrepreneurs and family-run businesses that want to focus on sustaining value. A sequel to 'From Science to Startup', this takes the readers a step further into the real world of leading their startups towards becoming billion-dollar startups.

I am deeply grateful to the entrepreneurs who I've had the privilege of advising over the past decades. Their passion, resilience, and belief in the reason for having undertaken their journeys have not only inspired me, but have also enriched the content of this book. Their real-world experiences have provided invaluable insights into the challenges and opportunities for creating tomorrow's unicorns.

I've had the honour to teach entrepreneurs and aspiring entrepreneurs at some of the top research institutions of the world including ETH Zurich. I've also had meaningful conversations with government entities in countries including Finland and Poland on how to institutionalise entrepreneurship as a way to drive sustainable growth. The book provides experiences distilled from those learnings through my teaching and mentoring over a thousand entrepreneurs in different stages of their journey. There have been many individuals who have played a key role in my journey so far—and I'd like to thank my many students, who have allowed me to be a small part of their entrepreneurial journeys. Often, my work has been to help them recognise who they're meant to be. You know who you are, and my doors are always open for our next coffee conversation.

The book is about inclusive entrepreneurship. It is not 'us' vs 'the other'. Our ability to generate value depends on building bridges rather than walls. As Richard Bach wrote in 'Jonathan Livingston Seagull', 'If our friendship depends on things like space and time, then when we finally overcome space and time, we've destroyed our own brotherhood! But overcome space, and all we have left is Here. Overcome time, and all we have left is Now. And in the middle of Here and Now, don't you think that we might see each other once or twice?'

I'm grateful to many individuals who have played an important part in my journey. Andros Payne has provided many insights over multiple conversations. Silvio Bonaccio has been an active supporter of my journey as an entrepreneur, teacher and enabler. The concept and insights regarding sustaining value in large family-run businesses have been made real and richer through talks with Nils Wagner, among others. Friends who are in the process of building something meaningful and globally relevant include Bea Knecht, who founded the world's largest TV streaming app Zattoo, and Konrad Bergstrom, whose companies include XShore, Zound and Soeder. Entrepreneurs and mentors who have enriched my insights include Nicolas Berg, Christian Peters and Manish Srivastava. Robert Wolcott provided an American perspective of entrepreneurship. Sandip Das has seen me evolve over the past decades and someone I could always count on to do what's right. Poonam and Harsh Dhanwatey have inspired me by their tireless efforts to save the tigers and the very nature that sustains us, for over three decades, working on this important topic before it became fashionable and increasingly important for sustainability of forest land.

Writing this book was far more enjoyable than I anticipated. I do hope the reader shares this experience while reading it, too. I realised how much I have learnt when I began writing. And how much I have to give.

Tomorrow belongs to those who ask the right question. The future will be created by those who are not scared of asking the Ultimate Question of Life, The Universe, and Everything. I hope the book enables the entrepreneurs to ask the one question that really matters.

I would like to acknowledge the Springer publishing team led by Prashanth Mahagaonkar and Ruth Milewski in helping me transitioning my manuscript into an insightful book.

My wife Aradhna who challenges me to visit and revisit some of my opinions from her point of view as a journalist, wife and friend. My children Aakash and Aanya help me remain curious and see the world with fresh eyes full of hope. It was Aanya who coined the title 'From Startup to Unicorn' to reflect on my own journey. Their constant distractions have been my joy and reason.

This book is a reflection of my own journey of finding my purpose. It will have served its purpose if it helps the readers to find their own.

Contents

1 **The Power of Entrepreneurship** ... 1
  Subverting National Sovereignty ... 5
  Are You Meant To Be an Entrepreneur? ... 6
  Takeaway: Vision Is Key. Everything Else Can Be Hired ... 8
  Why Entrepreneurship? ... 8
  References ... 10

2 **The Entrepreneurial Mindset…** ... 11
  What's the Best Background to Become an Entrepreneur? ... 11
  Different Kinds of Startups ... 14
    Technology Startups ... 14
    Startups Driven by Pain ... 14
    Platform or Route-to-Market Startups ... 15
  Technology Startups ... 16
  Startups That Start with the Pain ... 17
  Platform Startups ... 19
  How to Start a Technology Startup ... 21
  Transitioning Tech to Manufacturing in a Tech Startup ... 22
    Takeaway: To Scale your Technology, Freeze the Tech,
      Work the Manufacturing ... 23
  How to Start a Platform Startup ... 24
    Software-Driven ... 25
    Investor Ecosystem ... 26
  Milestone Planning in a Startup ... 30

vii

	Can You Sustain the Competitive Advantage of an Existing Business?	31
	Annex 1	33
	Reference	35
3	**Pitching to Investors: Conveying the Essential Aspects of Technology Startups**	**37**
	Technology	39
	Team	40
	Loyalty	41
	Vision Aligned	41
	Fully Onboard	41
	Gaps and How to Address Them	42
	Balance	42
	Market	42
	Vertical Focus	43
	Requirement Gap	48
	Manufacturability	49
	IP	50
	Competition	55
	Gap Defined	56
	Monetisable	57
	Size, Growth and Stickiness of Competitors	57
	Market Evolution	58
4	**Go-To-Market Strategies, Investor Options and Tracking Value**	**61**
	Go-To-Market	61
	Value Vs Volume	61
	Turnkey Vs Customisation	62
	Partner Strategy	63
	Value Capture Across Supply Chain	65
	Beachhead Market Traction	66
	Pilot Customer and Distribution Channels	66
	Horizontal Vs Vertical	67
	Reference Points	68
	Investors and Funding	69
	Own	70
	Awards	70
	Customer Funding	72
	Angel Investors	72
	Family Offices	73

	Foundations	74
	Angel Funds	76
	VCs	77
	Strategic Investors	77
	VC Vs Strategic Investors	79
	Where's the Value?	82
5	**Technology Startups: Machinery and Manufacturing**	87
	Technology Leadership	87
	Machine Customisation	89
	Custom Components	89
	Guarantees	90
	Machine Building Bottleneck	91
	Custom Process	92
	Revenue for Inaction	93
	For Tech's Sake	94
	Certification	95
	Replication	96
	Asset Lock	96
	Dilution	97
	Milestone Plan	99
	Manufacturing	101
	Mindset of Manufacturability	101
6	**Technology Startups: Maximising Product Value, from the Customer's Perspective**	103
	Logistics	103
	Component Vs Solution	103
	Internal Component	104
	Internal Solution	105
	Sell-Through Component	106
	Sell-Through Solution	107
	Manufacturability	108
	Mindset	111
	Reaching Scale	115
	Multiplier Effect of Money	117
	Outsourcing	120
	Standards	121
	Cost Optimisation Vs Value Capture	123
	Hardware Vs Software (Pricing, Scale, Replicability)	124
	Lab Market	127

7	**Technology Startups: Value Transition, Pre-Empting Risks and Sustaining Relevance**	129
	Stability	129
	Timeline of Technology	130
	Tech as Competitive Advantage	131
	Tech as Revenue Driver	132
	Technology Capturing Value in a Declining Market	132
	Exception 1: Health	133
	Exception 2: National Security	134
	New Business Models in Mature Markets	138
	Facebook and LinkedIn	139
	Ring	140
	Tesla	140
	Fitbit	141
	Genome Startups	142
	Apple iWatch	142
	Tech Convergence into a Platform	144
8	**Platform Startups: Foundation**	145
	Really Tiny Vertical	146
	Are you Addressing the User's Work or Leisure?	146
	What Segment Are You Replacing?	147
	Addressing Pain	148
	Tech ≠ Platform	149
	Enable a Conversation	149
	Unicorns Over the Decades	150
	Leveraging Weaknesses of Incumbents	155
	Capability to Scale	156
	Cold Start Problem	158
	Investor Commitment	159
	Team Alignment	160
	Ecosystem	163
9	**Platform startups: Pre-Empting Challenges and Identifying Opportunities**	167
	Tech-Agnostic	167
	User Networking Effect	169
	Evolving Business Models	171
	Goods and Services	171
	Eyeballs	172
	Online Personal Info	173

	Platforms to Enable Business	173
	Platform with Its Own Branded Content	174
	User Personal Information	175
	Platform Looking for a Slice of the User's World	177
	Platform Productising the User	177
	User-Driven Network	177
	Platform Tracking Users' Interest	178
	The User Assumes Platform Ownership	179
	Pre-Empting Health Conditions Based on Big Data	180
	Platforms Looking at Genetic Information	181
	Platform Looking for a Slice of the User's Time	183
	Platform Enabling Users to Share Experiences Within the Network	184
	Leveraging the User's Leisure	184
	Enjoyment Driving User Stickiness	185
10	**Sustaining Platform Value**	187
	Tapping the User's Emotions or Stay Mad, Stay Tuned	187
	Platform Owns User	190
	Partially Closed Loop	191
	Fully Closed Platform	194
	R Value	197
11	**Waves of Value Transition**	203
	The First Wave: Risk	203
	The Second Wave: Credit	204
	The Third Wave: Extractive	205
	The Fourth Wave: Transactional	206
	The Fifth Wave: Pre-Emptive	207
	The Next Wave: Generational	207
	The Final Wave: Convergence	209
12	**Identifying the Right Investors**	219
	Obsession	220
	Communication	221
	Can you Sell?	221
	Gel	222
	Who Will You Hire to Report to?	222
	Bootstrap	223
	What Is Your Priority?	223
	What Are You Making Better?	224

Being Great	224
Easy Money	225
Milestones	225
Technology Risks	226
Manufacturing Risks	227
Commercial Risks	227
Lock-In	228
Existing Entrepreneurs in the Mix	229
Once Investors Are Onboard	230
IPO and Implications	230
First-Time Investors and Their Mistakes	231
Angels	231
FOMO	231
Emotional Investment	232
Timeline	232
Future Funding	232
Competence	233
Sole Investor	233
No Clarity	234
Financial Oversight	234
Different Objectives	234
First-Time Strategic Investors	235
Executive Sponsorship	235
Size of Investment	235
Future Funding	235
Other Investors in Future Rounds	236
Rights and Obligations	236
Timeline to Scale	236
Future Strategy (Scale or Exit)	237
Inclusive or Exclusive	237
Reason for Investment	238
Payment for Buying or Investing and Startup Founder Lock-In	238
13 All About Equity	**241**
Startup Valuation	250
Looking Inwards	252
Valuation to Close Deals	253
Anti-Dilution	253
Veto	254

	Initial Funding Size	255
	Convertible Loans	255
	Priority Rights	256
	Valuation with Future Funding for Strategic Investors	257
	Earn-Up	257
	Participating Preferred	258
	Drawing Them In	258
14	**Scale or Sale**	261
	Factors That Help Decide Whether to Scale or Sell	261
	Founders	262
	Technology	262
	Funding to Scale	263
	Financial Investors	263
	Strategic Investors	265
	Risks with Strategic Investors	265
	Risk Mitigation	267
	Bridge Funding	269
	Non-dilutive Funding	270
	Lean	270
	Funding from Customers	270
	Risks	271
	Mitigation	272
	Irrelevance	273
	How Can You Maximise Exit Valuation?	280
	Standard	280
	Platform	281
	Transitioning Value	281
	Stakes of Stakeholders	282
	Strategic Investors	282
	Reverse Exclusivity	283
	Investment Rounds	283
	Own Vertical	283
	Long-Term Contracts	284
	Multiyear Service Agreements	285
	Ecosystems	285
	Exclusivity with Strategic Customers	286
	Partial Exit	286
	Institutionalisation: Why Startups Need to Institutionalise	288

xiv   Contents

15	**Why Entrepreneurs Fail**	293
	Long-Term Liabilities Tracking Short-Term Revenue	307
	No Beachhead in Platform Startup	307
16	**Does Geography Matter?**	311
	The US Perspective	311
	View from Europe	312
	The Asian Perspective	314
	View from the UK	315
	The Swiss Perspective	317
	Technology	317
	Incubators	318
	Inclusive Environment	318
	Open Ecosystem	319
	Manufacturing Skills	320
	Hiring Good People	321
	Funding and Investors	322
17	**Purpose**	325

About the Author

Anil Sethi is based in the heart of rural Switzerland, where he has created his own little piece of heaven, together with his wife Aradhna, children Aakash and Aanya, and other animals including his dog Whisky, cats and bees.

Driven by joy and impact, he has taught some of the brightest minds at ETH Zurich and other universities in Switzerland. He has also mentored start-ups from other countries at the behest of the European Union. His other pursuits include making beer and gin, and the aspiration to eventually make sake.

Having co-founded over 10 technology startups, he is well regarded as a person of note in the world of entrepreneurship. His mother, Mrs. Suresh Sethi, is still hopeful that he'll eventually get a job.

1

The Power of Entrepreneurship

A long time ago, in a world that had no plastic whatsoever, an ape descended from the branches of a large tree to take tentative steps on his two hind legs.

Many moons later, the Portuguese, who began to explore West Africa, started the slave trade. This was driven by the need for a workforce to work in plantations on Caribbean islands. The ship owners and the merchants led this and became incredibly wealthy as a result.

At about the same time, the Spanish Armada, which made Spain one of the wealthiest empires in the middle ages, was led by men who risked everything in search of new worlds.

Fast forward to the twentieth century, which brought forth the industrial revolution. This changed the agrarian way of living, which had remained static for over 2000 years. Henry Ford institutionalised manufacturing, bringing the Ford Model T, where he is famously reported to have said, 'you can have any colour, as long as it's black', and in the process, did not only bring forth a new product but completely reinvented transportation.

More recently, Silicon Valley became a thing. It was the driver, while at the same time becoming a product of its own making: institutionalising innovation & creating incredible wealth for both entrepreneurs and their investors.

Looking into tomorrow may be done with new eyes, by vision augmentation done by companies such as Apple and Meta.

Woven within all these stories is our own story of evolution & progress. However, each example is different and has very different implications for the larger ecosystem.

The reason for writing this book is twofold. The first is to explore how truly successful startups can be created. The second is to understand how the positive impact of these startups can benefit the larger society, creating in the process a more sustainable ecosystem for more innovation, which in turn can drive the creation, sustainability and inclusiveness of future wealth.

Let us look at each of the snapshots from history one more time.

The ape recognised that walking on his two hind legs left his hands free, with this ability being the basis for innovation. This enabled him and his ilk to use their newly found capability to create tools. These tools in turn enabled him to magnify impact. Since the key driver was hunting or foraging for food, two free hands enabled him to hunt more effectively, particularly with the newly created tools. He realised that he could obtain the same energy by consuming meat once or twice per day that he would otherwise obtain by consuming fruits and berries all day or maximising food output by growing food instead of constantly moving on. Over time, this created a clear definition of work between hunting and farming, and societies began to form. The ape's first steps on his hind legs were then the precursor to the evolution for the entire human race that followed.

The slave trade started by the Portuguese had an enormous impact in the pre-industrial world by driving volume output from plantations in the Caribbean. This provided a showcase of the benefits of global trade. It was also valuable for the Portuguese and eventually to many other countries in Europe since it provided a blueprint to leveraging an inexpensive workforce from Africa to Europe and eventually to the Americas. However, the impact on Africa was disastrous and left many communities completely decimated. This was one of the first examples of an extractive industry on an institutional scale spanning generations. To provide context, an extractive industry is one where a small group benefits at the expense of a larger majority that work to create value that does not benefit them proportionately. An inclusive industry, on the other hand, is one where all groups involved in creating value benefit more or less equally.

The Spanish Armada sailed to far-away lands, including much of South America, starting in 1516, when Spanish navigator Juan Díaz de Solís sailed into the estuary joining Uruguay and Argentina. He, and those who followed, encountered the local people there. The interaction was not friendly; the indigenous people were enslaved and worked to death in the silver mines. The slave trade further supported this mining work and was one of the first instances of an institutionalised extractive industry (Acemoglu & Robinson, 2012).

In 1519, Cortéz landed with 550 men on the beach of Mexico. He asked for a meeting with the Aztec ruler, Montezuma II. The local population did not know how to react, and after all, they felt they had little to fear from a mere few hundred strangers when their own population was in the millions.

Cortéz and his men were taken to meet the Emperor. At a signal, his men, who were armed with guns, took the Emperor prisoner by overpowering his bodyguards, who were only armed with wooden clubs and stone blades. This was the beginning of the conquest of the Americas, and within a century, the local population had been decimated by 90% (Harari, 2014).

Henry Ford is commonly recognised as one of the pioneers who spearheaded the automobile revolution and, in the process, forever changed American life. Ford innovated rapid manufacture, where the focus of manufacture moved from fully customised work to creating standards that provided dramatic efficiency increases due to replicability. This scale provided sustainability to the enterprise, which in turn provided stability to its workers and resulted in a sustained era of prosperity for society and the emergence of a middle class. The replicability also reduced the price paid by the customer, enabling society to access the car and consequent improvement in quality of life. Beyond this, it can be argued that Ford model T, which was simple to operate, affordable and durable, made the automobile accessible for the average consumer, giving rise to 'suburbia' and helping redefine how we all work and live.

Silicon Valley is the place where they build tomorrow. Some of the most innovative products and services around us, worn by you or tracking where you were last night, are from Silicon Valley. Soon, they'll also be able to determine precisely what you did. It begins to get a bit more 'big brother' when they're able to pre-empt what you're likely to do. Silicon Valley deals with information, which is the new currency. More importantly, this enables those who crunch this information to know precisely what we do, what we're thinking or what drives us. An easy example of the possible pervasiveness of this technology is to talk about something, anything at all, when your Instagram app is on. You don't have to be using Instagram at the time. You may begin to notice ads relating to the same thing within a few hours on your Instagram feed. What's interesting is that you don't even need to search for the term, be it Lagavulin or lingerie. The audio is simply picked up by the Instagram app. Silicon Valley also gave rise to the social media phenomenon, which has now become all-pervasive. This limits our network to others who think like us. This risks isolation and not being able to appreciate a different perspective. This is more insidious than is obvious, since instead of appreciating other perspectives and the reasons why, those of a similar view come together and build walls to keep the 'others' out.

The ability of companies to control what you see through their AR/VR glasses implies that they may be able to see your reaction to what you see by way of pupil dilation and magnify divisions to create stickiness or monetisation. This may be the most dangerous of all. More about this later.

My motivation for writing this book is twofold.

The first reason is to identify the causes by which startups become unicorns. This also implies the identification of decisions that stop startups from scaling or being able to sustain value. This is from the perspective of both technology startups and platform startups.

Technology startups are those that create a specific technology that becomes the basis for the startup. More importantly, the market perceives the value of the startup based on the technology. Such startups create their own competitive advantage on account of their intellectual property based on their technology. These companies have a high survival rate but often struggle to scale and take a long time (often multiple years) to take the step out from the lab to prototype and over time to scale.

Platform startups, on the other hand, are those that create a platform that enables users to create, share or transact information, products or services. Over time, these startups eventually end up owning the entire ecosystem of which they are a part. Therefore, although they start as being a product of the ecosystem, they eventually end up owning the entire ecosystem. Therefore, even as a number of startups address a particular market, over time, one startup ends up owning the entire market. This is because every new user joins the startup with the largest number of users, enabling the startup to capture more value, as value for the users increases proportionally to the number of users. The other startups simply lose relevance over time.

The second reason is to highlight the relevance and capacity of unicorn startups to sustain inclusive ecosystems. This implies that the startups not only gain significant value, achieving unicorn status & beyond, but in doing so, create positive ecosystems and pockets of sustainable wealth for the larger society within which they have been created. In the ideal scenario, this initiates a virtuous cycle where new startups that can retain, sustain and scale this value can be created. This is as relevant for large companies to help them retain their competitive advantage, since most technologies risk becoming automated, commoditised or outsourced over time.

The above examples across history show that entrepreneurial activity has been the basis of moving society forward. Entrepreneurs have also been the chief drivers in the creation of incredible wealth for society at large or certain segments thereof. However, this has sometimes been at the cost of not only destroying entire ecosystems but also decimating civilisations in the erroneous belief that simply because certain societies are not aligned to a given definition of 'civilised', they are not deserving of consideration or protection or the opportunity to coexist and thrive.

Subverting National Sovereignty

It is not a given that wealth creation by entrepreneurs may also benefit the ecosystem. In fact, the incredible power of startups that were created two or three decades ago, including Amazon, Facebook & Google, in many ways far exceeds the destructive power of entire countries in the pre-industrial era. This is particularly relevant with the global reach and the power to influence or subvert democracy itself in the most powerful nations, on account of platform startups backed by rogue extranational actors knowingly or otherwise by the startups. The question regarding whether governments should actively work to protect their entrepreneur-driven ecosystems to sustain value within the country that has helped create or incubate it will become seminal to avoid value extraction on an institutional scale.

Awareness of the factors that influence scaling and sustaining value can mitigate the risk of a nation becoming digitally subservient. The ways in which value is created in nations, from access to raw materials, the capability to convert these into value-added products, to information about and access to social networks, and finally information that can positively impact our health, increase progressively and exponentially. However, as value creation moves more towards information and greater personalisation, there is an ever-increasing risk of abusing not only where the value is captured but indeed using this information to create a wedge in the fragile foundations that underpin democracy across the world.

There will be those who argue that their mandate as entrepreneurs is to focus on wealth creation for their company by creating value for customers, and it is the responsibility of the state to cater to the development of an ecosystem that may enable future startups to grow and thrive. This is akin to those who decide not to have children and rue the fact that their tax dollars also go towards the upkeep of schools.

It is important to recognise that by disavowing this responsibility, startups do not just ignore the creation of new startups and a sustainable ecosystem driven by innovation. Ignoring this also risks creating a society split along the lines of 0.1% incredibly wealthy and the remaining 99.9%. The disparity between extreme gaps in relative wealth is unable to sustain a stable society. The argument that when there is adequate wealth to go around, it will benefit all segments of society equally is also fallacious. A good example is the USA, where the pure capitalistic approach towards addressing diabetes with insulin has resulted in the price of insulin per month being close to $1000, compared to a mere $35 in Canada. The wealthy are thus in a position to motivate lawmakers such as the US Congress to retain the extractive laws and regulations that enable them to keep making super profits at the cost of those whose lives depend on it.

Thus, by ignoring the sustainable development of ecosystems, we risk much more than simply concentrating wealth in the hands of a few unicorn entrepreneurs. We risk the sustainability of society over time, since the benefit of wealth creation cannot be sustained over time if it excludes the weakest sections of society.

Before we delve into scalability and sustaining this value, it is important to address questions that prospective entrepreneurs have, but either don't ask or are unable to answer.

Are You Meant To Be an Entrepreneur?

Perhaps the most fundamental question you can ask about entrepreneurship is whether you're meant to be one. This is because true entrepreneurship starts from the mindset of the entrepreneur. The question that is often asked is whether entrepreneurs are born or made. However, from experience distilled from conversations with hundreds of entrepreneurs, it appears that entrepreneurs often begin by identifying a gap in the market and a belief that they may be able to address this gap. Entrepreneurs can also begin by achieving technology excellence in a specific area and finding a market that they can impact. This latter often takes longer than they anticipate, since customers don't buy technology, but what it can do for them. Customers buy the impact that any given technology has on their business. This product-market fit takes longer than technology entrepreneurs expect, and it is due to this uncertainty that many give up or run out of resources to continue and scale.

One of the constants in the life of an entrepreneur is uncertainty. This pertains to the maturing of the technology and extends to identifying customer needs. The uncertainty also impacts the revenue of the startup. Revenue options can range from one-off product sale revenue to on-going revenue. Since revenue opportunities evolve over time depending on the change in the value of the product for the customer, this also results in uncertainty over revenue capture over time. As the startup begins scaling, the entrepreneur cannot be as hands-on with the product development and has to focus more on developing the management team.

My first startup entailed working with a group of scientists to commercialise their breakthrough innovation where they held a number of world records. As a sign of my commitment, I left my executive position at a large company to drive commercialisation, fundraising, etc. They, on the other hand, said they would consider moving to the startup if and when enough funding came through to enable them to transition with equivalent salaries *and* transfer their outstanding holidays to boot. I was simply more comfortable with uncertainty. Entrepreneurship is not about dipping your toe into the water, but jumping right in, since from an investor or customer's perspective, if you don't have enough trust in your own vision, why should they believe in it.

As you progress with creating your own startup, you will come across potential team members who either fall into the former or latter category. You will recognise them when you see them. The former team members will share your motivation to create impact and risk everything to do so. The latter will focus on reducing their own risk, rather than betting everything on the success of the startup. In the same way that it's important to know the risk that you're comfortable with, it's as important to perceive the risk that your various team members can deal with. Some of us deal with stress and uncertainty better than others, and it's good to know who's who, before you begin your journey. Those who focus on reducing their own risk are key in balancing the total risk that the startup takes since they provide a reality check that is often missing in the exuberance of the startup team, including ensuring a timeline to revenue and survival.

An often-asked question is whether entrepreneurship is the best way to attain wealth. It is true that entrepreneurs create incredible wealth, as well as the way they are able to make the future in their image. However, this is not because they start with the idea of creating wealth. Their vision more often is to create an enormous impact, or an exciting future, full of promise and the opportunity to reach for the sky, such as Elon Musk's aptly named 'SpaceX'. Your personal wealth accumulation is only a reflection of the value you create. Capturing this wealth and its monetisation are key subjects that are covered elsewhere in this book. By this measure, your odds of becoming fabulously wealthy are much higher by becoming an entrepreneur than virtually any other activity you may undertake. You may not make it in the first time, but there are few other ethical or strictly legal ways of getting there.

Someone once asked me what motivated me to become an entrepreneur. Those who ask this question will never understand the answer. However, if you're reading this, it's very likely that you also feel something in your gut like

I did. Something that tells you that you're meant for bigger things and to build the future that you'd like to live in.

Often, this feeling of wanting to do something bigger and more significant is almost overpowering. The clearest way of knowing if you're right for this is to ask yourself if you'd be happy to work on your vision if you had to do it for free. Often, what keeps us from becoming entrepreneurs is the fear that there's something special about entrepreneurs that we may not have. However, there's one thing that all entrepreneurs have and that's vision, or the belief that they can create something better than what exists today. So long as you're absolutely clear about the difference that you can make to your selected market, that's enough to get started.

Takeaway: Vision Is Key. Everything Else Can Be Hired

Vision is also critical when the going gets tough. When you approach investors and they keep slamming the door at your face or you don't have the money to pay your employees, it's the vision that keeps your people motivated. It's an overarching goal that you can believe in, when things are hitting the fan.

As you progress in your own journey of creating the future in your own image as an entrepreneur, you will invariably take the steps necessary to identify your business idea, validate its relevance, identify the market, figure out how to get investors, increase the perceived value so that you give away as little equity as possible for investment and to help you become an entrepreneur.

As Yoda said to Luke Skywalker, '*Do, or Do Not. There is no Try*'.

Why Entrepreneurship?

You're at the cusp of becoming an entrepreneur. You have an idea and have validated the customer gap, to the best of your knowledge. The team, to the extent it is onboard, seems to be well balanced and aligned with the long-term vision of the startup. It's a real opportunity. It appears to be a *go*.

You still see yourself plagued by the implications of the prospect of moving into a world of uncertainty. It's at this time that you recognise what it is that entrepreneurship gives you, since we often tend to forget what we have when we only focus on what we don't. The greatest privilege that entrepreneurship affords you is the opportunity to create something that's bigger than yourself. Steve Jobs called it the opportunity to make a dent in the universe. While most of us simply live lives based on structures created by others, being an entrepreneur enables you to envision and create some of these structures. I call it the opportunity to create the future based on your vision. Ask yourself if your footsteps are that different from those of individuals who were simply driven by their own conviction, in the face of conventional and prevailing wisdom. Vision is simple and easy to recognise, as when Steve said let's aspire to create something beautiful, when Mark said let's be social again, or indeed, when Elon decided that the only future of humanity was to become a multi-planetary species.

The journey of entrepreneurship is the journey into the unknown since you're charting a path that has not been trodden before. However, this uncertainty is on your own terms and your success or failure is directly related to your own effort, with a modicum of luck thrown in. This is unlike working in a big organisation, where you're working to fulfil the vision of the entrepreneur who started *that* company.

In my own journey as an entrepreneur, I recognised that there was a great deal of uncertainty relating to my work schedule, since this was driven by investor discussions. I would spend time waiting for investors to revert with questions after sending them the information. Conversely, I realised that these same investors would send a brief request for information on a Friday afternoon, effectively putting paid to my weekend. I decided to maximise this time by spending an incredible amount of quality time with my very young children, something unfathomable for my peers in banking or consulting.

Another element that entrepreneurship provides is the freedom to build on your dream. Most of us simply work to fit into a box created by a big company and do what's needed to meet its objectives. It is indeed rare that you have the opportunity to dream about the future and mould it into your own image. Being an entrepreneur means you imagine how the future of humanity will be and begin building it, brick by brick.

As mortals, we are all limited in our time. As Confucius, the Chinese philosopher, said in 550 BC, 'we have two lives; the second begins when we realise we only have one'. Entrepreneurship is one of the few things that can enable you to reach for immortality. At some point in each of our lives, we all realise that more than half the sand in our own hourglass has passed. However, as the amount of sand that is left decreases, we also develop the ability to more easily recognise the gems in the sand that remain. When we look back at what we leave behind that may remain once we are gone, most of us don't have an easy answer. The gems in the sand are only relevant if they are used to create something that creates impact on others before they too pass through the hourglass. Entrepreneurship is the opportunity to create something that institutionalises our vision and enables us to create something in our image that can live beyond us.

If the measure of our lives is not simply the money we have made but our impact to creating a better tomorrow that lives beyond us, it's entrepreneurship. Within entrepreneurship, speed is nothing without direction.

As you begin your own journey of entrepreneurship towards scale and sustainability of value, I wish you comfortable shoes.

References

Acemoglu, D., & Robinson, J. A. (2012). *Why nations fail.*
Harari, Y. N. (2014). *Sapiens: A brief history of humankind.* Random House.

2

The Entrepreneurial Mindset…

What's the Best Background to Become an Entrepreneur?

Going by the buzz you hear, you'd be forgiven if you believe that to be a successful entrepreneur, you need to be in your early 20s, get admission in Harvard or Stanford and quit before finishing your education.

The reality could not be more different. The average age of entrepreneurs is over 40. It is at this age that most people realise that they know enough about any given market and that most people are just winging it as they go along. By this time, they have a network and are taken seriously. They do not always come from the Ivy League institutions. One might assume that a majority of them come from the world of technology. The reality is quite different, since one of the greatest limitations of technologists is seeing the world through the eyes of the technology or solution capability rather than its impact as a source of competitive advantage. Additionally, technologists working in research institutions tend to operate in their own zone of comfort, where they do not have to deal with uncertainty other than what the output of their next experiments might be. This makes a majority of them unsuitable to delve into the world of uncertainty, where you have to promise a future vision to your investors based on the needs of your pilot customers that may only be a mirage, at a price point that you hope is high enough to warrant a healthy and sustainable super profit, for a cost where you wonder if you've omitted any critical expense items, in a time frame that you desperately hope will not get delayed too much. In addition, when you've done all that, you still have to find lots of other customers who also want the same thing, and you pray that you've been able to get all the kinks out of the system to ensure that you can replicate what you've done, and it lasts long enough to help you consolidate some kind of reputation and fix the initial flaws which are inevitable. If you're trying to be an entrepreneur, you feel I've overstated the challenges grossly, simply to dissuade you from your endeavour. If you're already one, you assume I'm telling *your* story even as you're currently trying to sort out one or the other challenges stated above.

With the uncertainties mentioned above, the majority of entrepreneurs come from the world of business, where their chief qualification is simply curiosity. They realise that they need a solution to a problem they experience that simply isn't available. Their curiosity leads them to question whether this problem is also experienced by others. If they can find a simple solution to the problem, the next step is to see if this can be scaled up and if the solution can also be provided to others. This is often how the greatest entrepreneurs begin.

More often than not, naivety is also a key attribute of entrepreneurs. It is this that provides a purity of purpose that entrepreneurs often have. Entrepreneurs often start with identifying a gap in the marketplace between what exists and what customers *would* want, whether such customers exist or not at the given point in time.

Of the entrepreneurs who come from the world of technology, the majority are in the process of completing their education, be it their Masters or PhD. This is truly the sweet spot for technology entrepreneurs. This is because, having done their undergrad, they have adequate understanding of the given technology and its impact on its commercialisation. Someone who has just finished his (or her) PhD and has not yet joined the tenure track in a university or research institution also has less to lose by moving into entrepreneurship. The longer someone stays in research post-PhD, the more difficult it becomes to become an entrepreneur, because not only do they give up more effort put in to further their academic career, but they also have to unlearn behaviour patterns that are appropriate for research and academia but anathema for entrepreneurs.

There are two exceptions to the above. The first exception is young technology students who decide to start platform startups or startups that do not have technology excellence as part of their core competence as the key value proposition of the startup. Such startups are technology-agnostic, and a rudimentary knowledge of technology such as website tools enables the building of the startup. The second exception is professors who have deep knowledge about a given area of technology. In the latter case, these tenured professors bring technology excellence into the technology startup and sometimes participate as cofounders of startups but do not become active founders. The link of a technology startup that is a spin-off from a professor's research provides many advantages that provide a source of competitive advantage if the sensitivities are recognised early on and managed well. If they are not, the startup just blows up in your face, technological excellence notwithstanding. These are addressed in more detail later in the book.

Those from the world of technology who desire to commercialise their technology and pursue entrepreneurship suffer from a disadvantage: they seldom know anything about anything not related to technology. However, in order to commercialise successfully, you have to be able to see the world through the eyes of your customer, and to get investors to invest, you have to be able to see the world the way they see it, and ultimately, from the perspective of the entity that may buy the startup, in order to identify the source of sustainable value for the buyer. Technology teams see it only through the lens of technology. Therein lies the nub.

This affords a unique opportunity to someone doing his MBA or a freshly minted one to become involved with the technology team to cofound the startup. Often, when a nontechnical person starts a startup, it tends to be technology-agnostic. The disadvantage of this is that the barriers to entry are low to non-existent. Therefore, despite his best efforts to become an entrepreneur, the management student has an enormous barrier to coming up with an idea that can be defended against copycats en route to market. Joining hands with a technology team helps him find a technology that can be protected and is not trivial to copy for competitors. For the technology team, the benefit of getting someone with a business mindset helps them address their weakness of addressing the world's challenges with their technology, since the business driver will help in clearly defining customer focus and is able to identify the perception of value for customers. He may also be able to align the business case to what investors look for. In short, he may be able to make the technology startup investible. This is a great opportunity to become part of a startup.

One of the most important elements of becoming an entrepreneur is patience. This is because everything invariably takes longer than you expect, right from doing your website and business card design to ensuring replicability and stability of your solution, and in case of a platform startup, determining how to transition 'interest' from customers to getting them onboard.

The first step towards becoming an entrepreneur is not to see how you can become one but to identify a need. Then, using your industry knowledge, validate if this truly exists. Becoming an entrepreneur is in essence taking it upon yourself to address this need. It's the point where you begin to see problems as challenges and opportunities. It is when you define your value proposition based on the perceived value that you may be able to bring to address these challenges and how you may be able to capture a certain component of this perceived value created in the form of revenue. It's when you do this that you've truly taken the first step towards becoming an entrepreneur.

Everything after this is simply semantics.

Different Kinds of Startups

Once you've decided to become an entrepreneur, the next question is how you go about with starting something. The answer is similar to the question of how to become rich. You don't go after the money. You focus on value creation. The money just follows.

To start a startup, the first step is to determine your value proposition and what market it can benefit. In this sense, the startup is a result rather than the starting point.

There are multiple kinds of startups. I've put them in three broad categories. They are platform startups, startups driven by pain and technology startups.

Technology Startups

These are the first category of startups. These normally come out of research entities and universities. Tech startups are often backed by patents and are the traditional form of startups. Despite the glamour associated with platform startups, tech startups are the most likely to be successful.

Examples of tech startups include Cisco. Google is another example of a tech startup, although it became a platform as it scaled up.

Startups Driven by Pain

These are the second category. I define these are startups that arise from a pain that you may have experienced when you're looking for a solution that does not exist. People often see these as problems. Entrepreneurs see them as opportunities.

Platform or Route-to-Market Startups

These are those where you create a platform and buyers and sellers populate it. This can also be a platform where users populate their information and you sell the user information to your customers. Platform companies include Facebook, eBay and Amazon. They are not defined by technology leadership but by user-friendliness. There is a very important element to keep in mind with platform companies. There's only one winner. The stronger one platform becomes, the more irrelevant other platforms competing for the same space become. Thus, route-to-market is key to success.

Let us look at the differences between the three kinds of startups in more detail (Fig. 2.1).

The visual above showcases the key characteristics of the different kinds of startups as well as the key success factors to create and sustain the success of these startups.

What is important is that companies such as Google, Uber and Facebook began as technology startups but were perceived by users as platforms since they enabled users to obtain information about the world through them or connect people to services or to each other. Therefore, how a startup begins is often very different from how it is perceived. OpenAI began as a technology startup and was perceived as such. However, over time, it's possible that it may

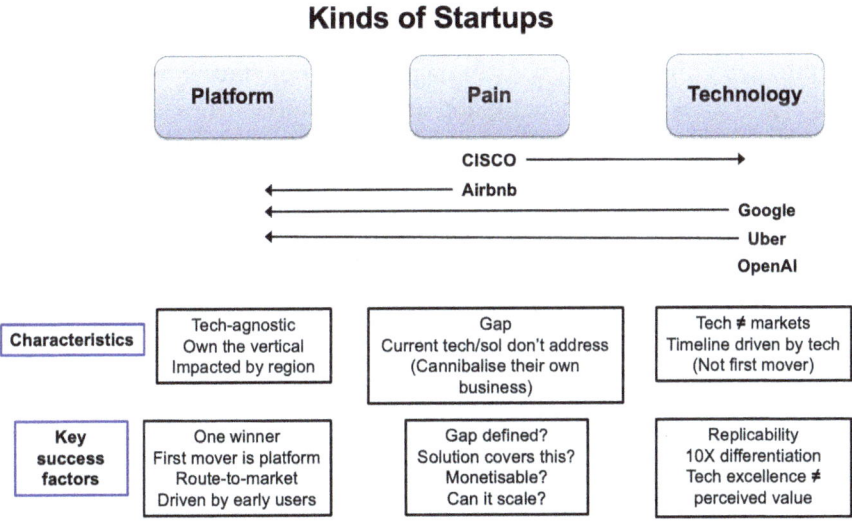

Fig. 2.1 Different kinds of startups

transition from being a technology resource to becoming a platform bringing resources and requirement together.

The various kinds of startups and how they are perceived are discussed below in more detail.

Technology Startups

Tech startups normally come out of research institutions and technology universities. One of their criteria is that they are often very strong on technology and have reams of peer-reviewed articles (if you know what this is, it's very likely that you're creating a technology startup). These startups are also very strong on IP, whether captured as patents or simply kept as process know-how.

More often than not, technology startups have great technology but lack clarity regarding customer focus. This is not because the technology cannot drive value in a particular customer segment; it can add value in multiple segments. As shown in the visual, technology does not automatically result in market relevance or leadership.

To respond to the question pertaining to customer focus, the tech startup needs to define whether it wants to play in cost-plus or value-added segments as well as whether the perceived benefit from its solution is incremental or revolutionary.

There is a difference between technology startups coming from the USA (and, to an extent, the UK) and those from Continental Europe. The ones from the USA often have very early-stage technology since it is so easy to raise funding with a well-articulated vision and a slick deck. Thus, investors invest in startups that are little more than an idea. In the case of platform startups, that is a reasonable approach. However, for technology-driven companies, it is imperative that the technology should not only exist beyond theoretical first principles but also have demonstrated impact via a replicable prototype.

Nanosolar is a great example of a typical US tech company. It raised over $400 million, while changing technology, not once, but several times, towards commercialisation. The company was able to raise funding due to the network of serial entrepreneur and founder, Martin Roscheisen. But the main challenge of technology startups is that raising money is only the enabler. The technology needs to work. Ultimately, the company could not fight gravity too long and folded in 2013 (From Science to Startup).

In Continental Europe, on the other hand, the conservative approach of scientists and researchers results in technologies that are often in the lab far longer than they should have been before they decide to commercialise. The benefit of this approach is that the technology is robust. However, despite global technology excellence, there is a risk of commercial obsolescence due to an inferior technology having gone-to-market or having created critical mass via relationships with strategic partnerships. The greater risk is that the inferior technology, but the one that is first-to-market, becomes the market standard.

Another risk of technologies emerging from Continental Europe is that the researchers often do not have the mindset of commercialisation needed for transitioning any technology towards the market. This results in them delaying the manufacture entirely too long, impacting timelines and scale-up. European researchers often have an approach of managing challenges in-house to their own detriment, implying insourcing manufacturing equipment needed to manufacture. This prioritisation of cost over time is often the reason that European technology startups remain niche or become technology-licensing entities.

Factors that make the difference between success or bust include the level of customisation needed to commercialise. If off-the-shelf equipment to manufacture the product is available, this dramatically reduces risk. However, customised equipment and a custom-designed process can multiply complexity.

A common theme of technology startups is the relevance of replicability. This is less important for software companies but critical for hardware-based tech startups. Delay in replicability is the chief factor for delayed milestones and ultimately the funding well running dry.

Startups That Start with the Pain

In the world that we live in, entrepreneurship is defined by and glorified via startups that became large global behemoths owning entire sectors. These are platform startups. As discussed earlier, although they are the most valuable success stories, the percentage of startups in a particular vertical that actually make it is remarkably small and is always in single digits. However, for state intervention and geopolitical security considerations, there would perhaps be only one per platform.

However, it is important to keep in mind that the most significant entities in the past have mostly been startups that started with the pain. Most companies that started prior to the industrial revolution tended to be of this nature. These startups proliferate in times when the technology is static or where technology is not linked to the capability to transition it to commercialisation. Prior to the industrial revolution, there was very little mass manufacturing capability. Automated replication capability, which is a primary driver of transitioning technology innovations into solutions of commercial relevance, was at this time even further into the future.

Let me begin by putting something out there that every entrepreneur already knows. It is challenging and painful to start and run a startup. Any startup. What keeps you going is the vision of the difference you can make to customers, to institutionalise it so that it lives beyond you and the money!

Pain startups start with a basic stated or unstated need. You start by requiring a product or service that doesn't exist. The gap is as obvious to you as it is not, to everyone else. As Laxmi Mittal once said when he was asked about his vision for steel and why he felt there was value in acquiring distressed steel-producing assets, when entire governments were trying to get rid of them; 'I can see what others cannot see'. In addition, he was a mere millionaire when he said it, rather than a multibillionaire that he is today, as a result of this belief.

The only reason to do a startup is that you see a gap between what customers need and what's available, and you take it upon yourself to bridge that gap. There's also the temptation to put a dent in the universe, as Steve Jobs said. A common misconception is that to succeed, one needs to have well-rounded skills. However, being slightly good at multiple things may not result in excellence in any. One or two sharp edges as a result of extreme competence may in fact improve your chances of making a dent. Steve Jobs, like Elon Musk, was not considered to be an easy person to work for due to his extremely high standards. However, his clarity of perception of what the future would look like enabled him to not only create a dent but also create global leadership in multiple industries. A startup that starts with the pain implies that you have a requirement that cannot be addressed by existing technology. Once you come up with a solution, you may realise that others also have a similar requirement. You have now identified a customer segment. It can be significant, as the example below illustrates.

In 1981, Sandy Lerner and Leonard Boasch graduated from Stanford. Eventually, in 1984, Sandy became the director of computer facilities at the MBA school at Stanford, while Leonard was responsible for computers at the Department of Computer Science at Stanford University in San Francisco. Their computers were on different systems and could not communicate with each other. Leonard found a way to get their computer systems to talk to each other so they could send messages to each other, by way of a device they called the router. This became the basis of Cisco, short for Francisco. In essence, the reason for Cisco's existence was because Sandy and Leonard worked in different buildings that used different computer systems that could not communicate with each other. In 2000, Cisco briefly became the most valuable company

in the world, with a valuation of over USD 500 billion, and continues to be an important foundation of the internet.

There are several points that need to be addressed before you jump headlong into such a startup. The first question is whether the gap is clearly defined and the value of your proposed solution demonstrable. The greater the clarity is, the better the chances of the initial potential customers being converted. These will be your chief proponents, so they are the ones who need to know what the value is. You need to ensure that the value that you expect to bring to customers can be monetisable. To take an example, if you had brought an instant and totally reliable communication service in 1990, users would have been willing to pay a significant sum per use, since this was the time when you had to post letters and it took weeks to get to another country. However, after the advent of e-mail for free, a better e-mail solution can only be given for free since 'free' is now the reference point.

Scale is critical. You need to ensure that the addressable market is large enough. Otherwise, this becomes a limiting factor, and investors simply won't bite (much more about this later).

Reconcile what you're bringing to the table vs what your customers are taking away. In a discussion with NATO officials regarding flexible solar modules with my first startup, I highlighted the high efficiency, whereas they were mostly interested in the different colour options. On my inquiring why this was important, I was told that this was because they often operated in conflict zones, so modules that stuck out from the ambient colours posed a risk from fringe factions.

Once you've answered these questions, or at the very least, are aware of what the questions are, you simply need to go ahead and begin.

Platform Startups

Platform startups have certain characteristics. They are most often the startups that people talk and know about. They are the ones that create billionaires. You've probably heard of them in passing. They include YouTube, Facebook (now META) and Twitter (now 'X').

However, one of the major limitations of platform startups is that there is only one winner in a segment. Let's take fax machines. One fax machine is useless. However, two fax machines can talk to each other if they are on the same platform. If there are 100 fax machines, the 101st machine has to be on the same platform so that it can talk to the first 100 fax machines. Therefore, although there are many entrants in any given sector, only the one that gets to the threshold customers first and continues to scale from there wins and ends up with a large majority of the market, effectively going towards 100%. All the others simply don't survive. A few who are able to capture small subsegments of the market are acquired (which is a good exit strategy for the founders) if their timing is right.

There are three questions to ask to ensure you're building the right value:

1. Who will buy your startup in 3 years?
2. What exactly will they buy?
3. How are you building the value they'll buy?

The answer to the three questions helps startups recognise the ultimate value that will be sustained over time. Everything else is either transactional, will become automated or will become commoditised.

Uber is a good example of a platform startup. They scaled up truly fast, and at last count, were still bleeding massive buckets of money. However, their competitor Lyft could not scale fast enough and build market share. They are now shopping for someone to acquire them, and it is likely that as the window shortens with Uber getting ever more market share, the Lyft sale is likely to happen at a more modest valuation than $5B, which they were once offered. Uber is likely to be upstaged, not by a superior technology or a more efficient solution. It is likely to be outcompeted by an entirely superior business model. This could be one where cars do not need drivers but are self-driven or autonomous. Millions of privately owned cars enter the market as taxis, given that a majority of cars are used only 5–10% of the time. Makes sense for the car owners, since it would give them a revenue stream for an asset that just sits there for over 90% of the time. Unlike Airbnb, a car is less personal than your house, so the barrier to car owners becoming comfortable with strangers being in their car has already fallen.

If you're selecting the kind of startup you'd like to start or get involved in, the platform startup seems perhaps the most tempting. However, it has the greatest risk since there is only one winner. Your chance of betting on that winner is as much down to strategy as it is to luck. Often, startups that are in a platform space focus on technology, since tech seems to be more under their control. The question to ask is whether the customers care. Tech is only useful if it provides you with a competitive advantage. However, if the only competitive advantage is getting more customers, improving tech is like looking for your keys where the light is best, rather than where you lost them.

How to Start a Technology Startup

You're at the cusp of starting a technology startup. There are a few things that you need to keep in mind when you begin this journey. We consider two options regarding your background and provide a view regarding your box. Based on this, you'll realise how to think outside it. It is only when you realise that technology people think very differently from business people or investors that you can have a balanced judgement. The first option is that you're a scientist and from the world of research. You've been working on the technology for a few years and have likely discovered or invented something that's the first in the world. Excellent! The question is now how do you commercialise?

One of the things to keep in mind is that commercialisation is different from inventing something. Inventing involves going to the lab and trying to do something different every day, in the hope that one of your results will convert lead into gold, rather than blowing the place up. Commercialisation, on the other hand, implies being able to do the same thing again and again, a million times, or even a hundred million times a year. Year after year. An important element of starting a technology company is trying to figure out the market you'll address. If your answer is that your technology can address several markets, including (but now only limited to) healthcare, mobile telecom, education and security, you're very deep inside the tech box. Getting out of this box will be challenging and yet imperative to commercialise successfully. This is because each of these markets has a different degree of urgency, motivation to obtain a new solution, speed or timeline, certification requirements and pushbacks from their existing stakeholders who are aligned with the existing ecosystem.

An important consideration towards successful commercialisation is how much customisation is needed. This is not only for the product being sold to the customer but also for the machinery needed to make it. As a tech person, your answer is likely that this is trivial. In fact, it is precisely for this reason that tech startups slip up on their manufacturing milestones. In addition to custom machinery that may be needed to produce the product, another question to address is that the process may need to be designed from scratch to fit the custom machine. This is far from trivial and almost always results in significant delays. The second option is that you're from the world of business and see a market opportunity for which you see a technology that fits. Here, your key advantage is that you have clarity regarding the market and the gap, as well as the potential value that the given technology can bring.

One of the most important considerations is that technology with the technology team is seldom of any value. The only exception is when large companies buy portfolios of thousands of patents, and this is for an entirely different reason, the freedom to operate, or FTO.

At the same time, one of the biggest liabilities with technologies is that they sometimes come with the tech team as a package. This is not a problem for any other reason but for the fact that tech people think very differently. For example, tech teams often cannot relate to profit or time-to-revenue. Cash flow, the holy grail of any startup, is another of those things. As an extreme example, you could be faced with tech founders asking for an exit as soon as investors invest. However, we're not there yet, and will cover this in more detail when we discuss investors.

In summary, to start a technology company, you need clarity regarding the market that the tech will address, the gap that potential customers perceive the tech will fill and the time to commercialisation. The level of customisation of the machines needed to make the solution and the process that needs to be designed will also determine the timeline to market.

Transitioning Tech to Manufacturing in a Tech Startup

Let me start with the good news. For all startups that are started, technology startups have a far greater chance of surviving 5 years after they are founded. In Switzerland, for example, approximately 50% of startups survive 5 years after they are founded. However, in the case of technology startups emerging from ETH Zurich, over 90% are still around after 5 years.

The bad news is that there are many problems that can result in the company failing, but which result in the ultimate failure getting dragged out by years, rather than a swift demise, as is the case with platform startups. Some of these problems are discussed below.

One of the most common challenges of tech that is transitioning to manufacturing is that it is led by tech people. This correctly implies that the thinking driving this is tech-focused in nature. To be aware of this thinking may enable you as a tech person to recognise the box you're in. As a non-tech person, this helps you to recognise how tech persons think early enough to take steps.

Tech teams often tinker in their labs for much longer than needed and definitely longer than they can afford, particularly after funding comes through. The mindset of tech teams is that they go to their labs every morning and expect to do something different. Manufacturing, on the other hand, focuses on doing the same thing a million times or even a billion times, without any variation.

Takeaway: To Scale your Technology, Freeze the Tech, Work the Manufacturing

Tech teams have a dangerous predisposition to try and save money by designing and making the machine needed for producing products in-house. To complicate things further, their view is to create the process by writing the software on the custom-designed machine. This is like saying that instead of getting a coffee machine, you start with a metal box, and put containers for coffee bean and water, and for good measure, add the software needed to control how much water at what temperature is pushed through the nozzle through the coffee, which in turn is ground based on another software instruction.

The manufacturing mindset is to outsource as much as is possible and definitely get the suppliers to provide guarantees. They correctly recognise that the important element is to focus on the core competence and outsource everything that is off-the-shelf. This is because it is the core element that captures the value-added. Everything else is a commodity and cost-plus. In the coffee example, Nespresso recognised this early on. They realised that the main value would be in consumable capsules. They outsourced the machines and only focused on selling the coffee capsules, providing healthy and sustainable revenue.

Tech founders often delay entirely too much to obtain a manufacturing mindset in the game. All the tech founders I have spoken to over the past decade recognise this delay when looking back. The only exception is software companies, where the focus is to perform the solution once since replicability is seamless.

In summary, the one simple advantage of manufacturing thinking over the tech mindset can be eloquently summarised: *Done is better than perfect.*

How to Start a Platform Startup

Since the beginning of the industrial revolution, the greatest revolution of our times has been the Internet revolution. This has completely revolutionised the way we live and work, in a way that was only done once in the past 2000 years, with the advent of the industrial revolution over a century ago. The industrial revolution heralded the rapid manufacturing of all products, including consumer commodities that we today take for granted, including motorised transportation from horse-driven carriages to manufacturing processes that not only enabled consumer products but were principally the basis for the term consumerism.

In the same way, the internet revolution provided dramatic efficiencies in communication, which is the basis for all e-commerce. Beyond this, the internet revolution provided the greatest leap in the quality of life of individuals since the industrial revolution.

In the same way that the industrial revolution enabled workers to live further and further from the places of work resulting in suburbia, which combined urban work opportunities and access to space and affordable housing previously available only in rural environments, the internet revolution provided opportunities to disassociate work from the place of work.

The ability to work as efficiently on a computer irrespective of location also gave rise to the concept of the Home Office, which became part of public consciousness from 2020 to 2022 due to the global COVID-19 lockdown. The Internet revolution also gave rise to more millionaires than ever before, at a pace only comparable to the first oil explorers at the cusp of the Industrial Revolution. Microsoft created over twelve thousand millionaires when it went public. Apple created thousands more.

However, although these were companies that came into being due to the technology innovation that heralded the internet revolution, their value was directly proportional to the effort they put in developing products and selling them to customers. However, over time, something remarkable happened. The new generation of companies that subsequently became gorillas and took over the mantle of creating enormous numbers of millionaires and becoming billion-dollar unicorns was because they created platforms rather than creating products and selling to customers. These platforms in turn facilitated users to interact or transact with products, services or their own personal information. The value of these startups transitioned from the sum of products produced and sold to the value of the user information or that of the commission from the goods and services transacted between users. These are the poster

children of our generation. These include Facebook, Amazon, WhatsApp, Snapchat, Alibaba and Flipkart.

The biggest challenge with platform startups is that there is often only one company that wins and ultimately defines the platform for any given platform and a majority of the potential user base. For this reason, these platform startups become valued so highly. This implies a systemic downside. There are countless users for any given startup that comes to nominate a platform category. There is also a challenge for new entrants that aspire to address an existing and therefore attractive platform dominated by an incumbent gorilla. This is that any vertical that exists with any kind of market traction is already taken. Thus, for a startup to aspire to dominate any platform, it has to begin working towards it before the platform comes into public consciousness and effectively gives rise to and own the platform as it scales.

However, even with such challenging odds, there are cornerstones that can help create startups that can become successful platforms and own their category.

Software-Driven

One thing that defines platforms is that they are almost exclusively software-driven. This does not imply that they do not have any hardware components. In contrast, hardware provides ownership of the supply chain and creates a further barrier for users to shift due to the investment made. The investment may be money- or time-based. Uber is an example of an online taxi platform. To the end-users, it is an app-based taxi service. However, in reality, it is a platform backed by a robust tech backbone that links demand and supply. The demand is your need to go from point A to point B. The supply is in the form of the taxi drivers who get a customer and share a percentage of the proceeds for the privilege. Furthermore, Uber is able to ensure greater ownership of that supply, viz., the taxi drivers, by providing them with hardware to be installed in the taxes that provide location information. Uber also controls the payment channel, since users pay Uber electronically. Uber in turn pays the taxi driver after deducting the hefty commission. This provides for traction with customers since they are loath to share sensitive credit card information with too many supply channels if one channel provides adequate service.

The key benefit of being software-driven is that once the solution begins to gain traction with the user base, it is seamless to scale it up. Another benefit of being a software platform is that it is much easier to pivot if the user base shows a higher perceived value for a particular component of the service or simply needs something else. The software platform enables you to pivot or simply roll out an update.

The greatest risk of failure arises from getting locked into the technology rather than simply using it as a backend support mechanism. Since software platforms are often started by tech founders, there is a propensity to lock into the technology that you, as the founder, has tried so hard to create. The legacy asset then becomes the liability that hinders the ability of the startup to pivot. What happens when the startup faces challenges in the market is that it tries to address it with technology instead of focusing on the need of the market, which may simply be a user interface or a better user experience.

Investor Ecosystem

A reality that startups simply need to recognise is that the investor community is a core element of platform startups. To obtain initial funding, platform startups require a certain kind of investor. Normally, investors look for technology and an existing market where size and growth can be demonstrated. However, since platform startups start with a view to bring a new kind of platform into existence, they fulfil neither of the two elements that most investors look for as a precondition to investment. Therefore, the kind of investors who invest in platform startups are investors who all have previously started and scaled their own platform startups or investors who are used to seeing platform startups start, scale and succeed.

Platform investors tend to be based in certain parts of the world. Silicon Valley is where the majority of such investors are located. Other platform investors tend to be on the east coast of the USA. The reason that most of them are based in the USA is because the USA is a large market with high cultural uniformity and the same language. Thus, a platform startup has more opportunity to scale and find customers with the same offering. This is very different from continental Europe, which is split into multiple languages and distinct cultures. Therefore, platform companies such as Facebook or Uber would not have become global success stories if they had started in Europe.

Recognising the limitations of the existing investor community is an important element to help a prospective platform startup align its search to find appropriate investors or to consider relocating to a more investor-friendly jurisdiction.

One of the greatest challenges of platform startups that are in the early stages of evolution is determining how to hold on to customers who are already onboard. The importance of this cannot be overstated, since not only the revenue streams but indeed the entire survival of the platform startup depends on its ability to sustain traction with its users. The primary focus of platform startups is then to own their customers that have come onboard. This can be for a tiny slice of the potential customers available, since platforms are inherently global. The reason for creating stickiness of those who have come onboard is that this can convert into a stable revenue stream and a powerful reference point for investors. In addition, as any entrepreneur who has ever been grilled by investors knows all too well, vision reflects idealism, addressable markets give hope and milestone plans may give confidence, but revenue is gold.

The explosive growth and proliferation of private taxi platforms is a case in point. Taxi services have been platforms for a long time. One can argue that they became platforms before the term was so coined. They did this locally and by way of having a common phone number for a given city, so that users needed to remember only that number. This was of value for frequent travellers, by providing them with certainty regarding the kind of car they could get if they flew into a new town. Beyond this, there was also a sense of security by ensuring that the travellers were not duped on landing in a new city by relying on a local taxi. London, for example, has had minicabs since forever. This has plugged the gap between the high-priced taxes of London and the abysmal public transport system, which, being one of oldest in the world, is truly creaking at the seams. Minicabs provide a service by combining the convenience of a private taxi, albeit a modest one, at an affordable price point.

I recall travelling to Amsterdam in 2005 and finding private taxi services where the drivers were immaculately attired and drove high-end cars. The first time I used this service was on the advice of a colleague. I was pleasantly surprised when on landing at the airport, the driver, who was dressed in a suit, escorted me to a brand-new Jaguar. He appeared to be quite well educated and articulate. It transpired that he was previously a software professional but found the work too stressful and had decided to move to running a private taxi, since it afforded him peace of mind, stress-free working hours and sporadically, interesting people he could speak to. Clearly, the platform was alive and well, albeit on a local level even before the Internet recognised it as such.

Once realisation dawned that taxi services were a ripe area for disruption due to the existence of local solutions and the behaviour patterns necessary for building traction and a minimum level of customer loyalty, this became a thing. Funds from the largest players on Sand Hill Road in Silicon Valley began to see this as the next big platform play.

In a relatively short period of time, there was a proliferation of startups addressing this market. The question for many other startups that evolved in different parts of the world was how to gain traction with the user base that initially came onboard as early adapters. Lower traction meant ease of migration to a slightly more user-friendly new player. This was imperative to ensure consistent revenue and create a barrier for a subsequent entrant. This was particularly pronounced as realisation dawned that there was no requirement to actually own the taxis but only an app for the customers' smartphones and the link of individual taxi drivers.

The USA, arguably the biggest market for startups at the time of writing, saw the emergence of Uber and Lyft. Uber began first and was considered a service for 'ballers'; those who wanted to be seen coming in a limousine. Lyft, on the other hand, had a very relaxed approach. It was not uncommon to have drivers 'high-fiving' the passengers. They thus split the market along lines of different expectations, as Uber was considered to provide the more formal experience and Lyft had drivers very similar to the profile of the initial users.

The business model, which by this time had become well-entrenched across the board, was to extend the stickiness of having hardware on the taxi of the driver instead of simply having an app on his smartphone. The taxi platform startups further locked in the drivers by not providing them with the flexibility to use taxis for rides outside the platform. The drivers were not allowed to look for private passengers and could only accept them based on the algorithm generated by the taxi startups, taking into account the proximity of taxis from the passengers. Finally, the drivers were controlled by way of the payment channel and were paid only after the commission was deducted directly by the taxi startups.

Cumulatively, these measures played a very important role. They ensured that there was a barrier for the supply, i.e., the taxi drivers, to move out of the system. They tried to provide personalised services to their customers to gain additional traction. This went beyond prompt taxi service to recognise users by their number so that the user did not need to provide information about their most commonly used addresses to the startups. The startups did all this at prices that compared favourably with conventional taxis. A multi-country footprint also provided comfort to frequent travellers that they would not be duped by unscrupulous taxis. This is rife in countries across the world, from Delhi, where it is not uncommon to take a taxi from point A to point B, and after a harrowing 2 h journey, realise that the distance could have been covered in the 10-min leisurely walk, to Rome, where the sleight of hand of taxi drivers is so swift and that if you give €50 to settle a bill of €5, you only get five euros in return and the driver shows you the €10 you gave him. 'Resistance', as someone once said on a spaceship, 'is useless'.

Over time, the platform solutions moved towards consolidation. However, something interesting happened along the way. Unlike in normal software platforms where there is only one winner to the detriment of all other players in the flat global market, this did not occur in the case of taxi startups. The reason was the presence of hardware in the taxis, which in effect created a barrier in the supply side of the market. Regional players were thus able to establish fiefdoms and sustain their shares of the market. In the entity that was the first to obtain a particular threshold of taxi drivers onboard for a given city, it was simply able to provide better service to customers. This was due to the greater presence of taxis, which resulted in shorter waiting times. This helped push brand recognition locally, helping the startup to further consolidate its position as the incumbent. Over time, the change in the underlying technology will make the hardware irrelevant in taxi wars, and the lock-in will move only to the app. At this point, there will be another shake-out in the industry. This may result in another wave of innovation and create space for new startups to emerge.

MySpace Vs Facebook

The taxi platform strategy provides valuable insights into software platforms such as MySpace, which, although it had 16 million monthly users when Facebook was much smaller and was acquired for $580 m, simply could not cope with the popularity of Facebook and eventually disappeared after being absorbed by a corporation that saw its value but failed to recognise how fleeting the perceived value of a platform startup can be before consolidation occurs. What Myspace failed to recognise in the early days was the premium paid by users for trust. While Myspace enabled users to come onboard simply with pseudonyms, Facebook needed real names and e-mail addresses. On account of this, while Myspace got users who wanted to hide their real identities, Facebook got real people, who in turn were trying to establish real networks. This network effect in turn created more stickiness due to on-going memories that were captured and became a reference point for the future.

The taxi platform strategy recognised the value of creating traction and a barrier to the exit of taxi drivers by integrating hardware and user data to provide personalised services, as well as the opportunity to create a more compelling value proposition for users. Facebook showed how networks can help sustain users. We will discuss how startups can use this as a strategy to create a more sustainable competitive advantage in more detail later.

Milestone Planning in a Startup

You're in the thick of your startup at this time and trying to figure out what needs to be done. Every time you get a pen and paper out to get an overview of the things you need to accomplish, you realise that something urgent needs to get done. In the process, your grandiose plans of having milestones and a timeframe attached to them take a back seat (again). So what *is* the point of doing milestones, when you can either not keep up with them or they simply take second priority to the urgent stuff.

As US president Eisenhower once said, 'Plans are useless, but planning is indispensable'. The reason for doing milestones for your startup is that this forces you to take a step back from the operational chaos and see the big picture. As the founder, it is not only your job to have an overview of the day-to-day stuff, but to ensure that this stuff contributes to creating the big picture. The operational people in your startup don't have the overview, that's why they're operational.

An important element that milestone planning does is ensuring that you are starting with the end in mind. This is because milestones, while not being as esoteric as your vision, are the steps that take you towards your deliverable, whether this is a revenue, prototype or go-to-market objective. Activities within startups slip through the cracks (read 'excuses why stuff can't be done on time, within budget or done at all), since the point of your startup is to do something that hasn't been done before or deliver customer value that hasn't been delivered before. Otherwise, you'd be a department of a big corporate replicating what's already been done before.

By starting with the end in mind, you begin to try to understand what users truly want. This is the crux of a successful startup since larger corporate solutions are often built incrementally and fail to deliver the evolving value that users want, for which they would ultimately pay a premium. As the founder, the various things that you need to balance include customer acquisition, current customer requirements, suppliers, investors, your own people, resource planning, cash flow and operational objectives and hiring great new people, to name a few. Having milestones ensures that you don't miss out on any of the critical ones. It also does not hurt that investors care only about the deliverables or milestones, rather than the operational steps that get you there. A sample milestone plan is provided in the Annexure at the end of this chapter.

The milestone plan provided in the Annexure is more focused on milestones for a technology and manufacturing startup. Although the granularity seems semantic, the reason for this is twofold. The first reason for an overview milestone plan is to ensure that while you're tracking the most sensitive elements, you're not missing other administrative elements that also need to get done in order to progress the startup. These include steps such as certification, without which customers may not be able to buy in commercial volumes. The second and the more pragmatic reason for the comprehensive milestone steps is that investors track startups based on the milestones they achieve after they invest. If the startup only states two critical milestones and fails to achieve one, the investors can punish the startup by way of reducing the valuation for the next round of funding. However, if the startup has 200 milestones, most of which are noncritical, and fails to achieve one of them, the underachievement is only 0.5%. This expectation management is important since most startups need to go to their current investors for the next round of funding or for a bridge round, as the next round often takes longer than expected.

Can You Sustain the Competitive Advantage of an Existing Business?

The great challenge with any existing business, as any successful first-generation entrepreneur knows, is the challenge of sustaining it. There is good reason for this concern. In over 50% of ultrahigh net-worth families, all wealth is lost by the end of the second generation. The decline seems to accelerate over time, since in over 90% of such families, all wealth is lost by the end of the third generation.

There are two main reasons why this happens. The first is that the next generation does not do anything to protect the wealth that has been created. The second is that the next generation does something. Let us delve deeper into these two reasons why wealth dissipates and options to stop this decline.

Often, the next generation does not do anything to change the business that has enabled wealth generation. However, in such cases, if the business entails hardware products, the business risks become commoditised over time. This is due to improvements in manufacturing technologies. The case of complex watches is a case in point. When tourbillon watches were invented in 1795, they were considered to be a marvel of microengineering. However, today, it's possible to buy a Chinese made tourbillon watch for a few hundred dollars. This is in spite of the fact that Patek Philippe watches with the same complication sell for $0.5 million onwards. However, we'll come back to this.

In case the wealth has been created via software, the big risk of not doing anything by the next generation is that over time, software tends to become automated due to dramatic improvements in chip performance and the ability of AI to learn. The second factor is that software behemoths including Google, Facebook and the like consider providing this capability for free, since their business model is driven by the number of users and time spent by these users, rather than direct revenue per user.

However, the second option of doing something poses far more risks.

Often, the next generation decides to find the next big thing to showcase their entrepreneurial mindset. They do this in two ways. Either they try to extend the business or they try and begin a new one. When the next generation plans an aggressive expansion of the business, they often look at the example of the Patek Philippe with the $0.5 m price point. What they fail to appreciate is that when wealth is created in B2B sectors, value is commoditised as technology goes off-patent and becomes commonly available. It is only B2C brands that sustain value over time. Furthermore, value is captured in products that are closest to the end customer even as their components lose gross margins over time. The more attractive the business segment and the higher the growth, the greater the risk of cost-competitive competitors emerging.

The greatest risk occurs when the next generation tries to begin a new business. The risks range from technology to manufacturing to route-to-market, and these risks are covered comprehensively in the next chapter. However, the major risk centres around the interest of the customer to buy, as well as the criticality and duration of the customer's problem being addressed. What the next generation does not appreciate is that customers never buy technology, but what the technology does for them. Either it enables them to gain a competitive advantage, increase revenue or reduce costs. Each of these provides opportunities and entails risks for the new business.

The new business also needs to identify not only the potential customers that may have interest to buy but also validate and quantify this. Validation implies getting active confirmation of the potential customers' keenness to buy. Quantification is getting the customers to define the scope of the problem or pain that the new business solution resolves. Quantification of the pain in monetary terms equals the revenue potential. The duration to which the new product resolves the pain is the period of time for which the revenue stream can be sustained.

In summary, it is possible to sustain the relevance of an existing business. However, key questions need to be addressed and validated with the customer, including the customer's problem that the product resolves. Finally, the timeline of the customer's problem that the product or solution provides is the extent of the sustainability of the business.

Annex 1

Milestone	Q1*	Q2	Q3	Q4	Q5	Q6
HR/Admin						
Contracts of key team members / employees finalised	■					
Team transition to startup	■					
Tax-optimised ESOP put in place for key employees (if relevant)	■					
Hiring of key personnel with production and industrial experience (prospective candidates identified and offers given)	■					
Putting management and business development team (and personnel) in place		■				
Government approval process for material and disposal (in alignment with machine specs and material waste)			■			
Key personnel with production and industrial experience joined team			■			
Certifications required to getting product to the market are identified		**				
Certifications required to getting product to the market are obtained (dependency)			**			
Hiring of personnel with relevant expertise (logistics and supply chain, finance, marketing)			■			
Hiring of personnel (including marketing and communications, business development)			■			
IP/Tech.						
***Technology transfer (IP license agreement)	■					
Define patent opportunity on specific components		■				
Apply for patents including design patents (and strengthen IP portfolio)			■			
Funding						
Initial startup setup	***					
Initial funding (and any 'friends, family & fools' investment at different valuation)	***					
External funding (from investor)				****		
External funding from external investors presented						■
Advance from customer(s) against products (particularly if limited exclusivity provided. This will mitigate dilution)			■			
Consider external non-dilutive support (include soft loans and grants). This minimises equity dilution, and creates perception of arms-length from beach-head customer				■		
Go-to-market						
Branding strategy defined			■			
Key partners for go-to-market identified			■			
Key customer relationships in the market established			■			
Agreements (including limited exclusivity based on time, region or product vertical) defined			■			

Task	1	2	3	4	5	6	7
Customer (go-to-market partners) testing completed			✓				
Marketing and communications strategy in place			✓				
Prototype products from the existing equipment to strategic customers for establishing relationships			✓				
Manufacturing							
Initiate discussions with equipment manufacturers / & outsourcing partners	✓						
Discussions on location of manufacturing plant finalised		✓					
Manufacturing equipment and concept finalised to order		✓					
Equipment manufacturing partners selected, with negotiation on design exclusivity, ongoing support & guarantees			✓				
Cleanroom specs defined (ensure this is aligned with machine & access into cleanroom			✓				
Quality testing equipment specs defined (aligned with manufacturing process and expected yield)			✓				
Quality testing equipment ordered			✓				
Preliminary tests of equipment done at the location of equipment supplier			✓				
Equipment delivered and installed				**			
Testing of individual manufacturing to ensure output (yield, throughput)					**		
Logistics and material handling supply chain defined			✓				
Scale-up for second facility or modular design defined						✓	
Start building the infrastructure needed for housing the manufacturing plant			✓				
Start building the key components of the supply chain				✓			
Testing of individual manufacturing to ensure output (yield, throughput)						✓	
Define standard and freeze manufacturing design to ensure output aligned with future scaling						✓	
Process monitoring and control equipment ordered for purchase				✓			
Process monitoring and control equipment delivered & installed						✓	
Equipment for measurement of performance ordered				✓			
Product packaging specifics defined and machine ordered				✓			
Product packaging specifics defined and machine delivered and installed						✓	
Simulations for components and processes repeatedly tested for reliability/reproducibility						✓	
Start of volume production and de-bugging complete							✓

* Considered to begin from when funding is transferred
** Signifies dependency
*** Signifies dependency on investor(s) to achieve milestone
**** Signifies dependency on strategic investor(s) to achieve milestone

Reference

'From Science to Startup'.

3

Pitching to Investors: Conveying the Essential Aspects of Technology Startups

As an entrepreneur, your opportunity is the gap between the market need and what's available. Your challenge is bridging the gap between the perceived market need and your tech excellence. The visual below helps to identify the market with the maximum value over time (Fig. 3.1).

The visual above shows how to identify the customers who provide the highest value. There are three points to consider.

1. We always start with the criticality of the need. An example is if a customer asks for water, there is a difference between whether he may otherwise die of thirst or whether he simply wants bottled sparkling water. In the case of the former, the customer may be willing to pay anything for water. For the latter, he may only pay a couple of dollars.
2. The second question to consider is whether the need has been stated by the customer and whether the customer is losing revenue due to the absence of such a solution. This is not always the case. Petroleum-based cars require frequent servicing. Instead of making the cars better, the car companies realised that they could continue making money by servicing these cars. The end-user paid more, so the car companies did not own the problem. Thus, they had no motivation to improve their cars, as it would have negatively impacted their revenue stream. Till Tesla came along, with 90% fewer moving parts and dramatically lower servicing costs. They are only motivated to change due to the obsolescence of their technology and the emergence of the new technology.

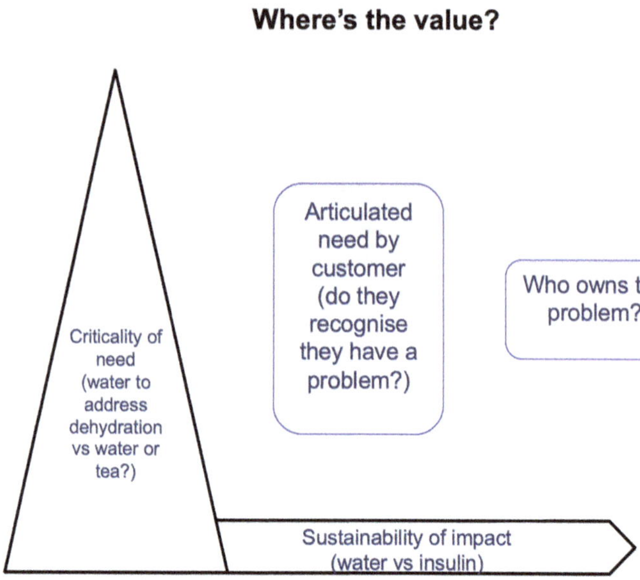

Where's the value?

Diagram showing: "Criticality of need (water to address dehydration vs water or tea?)" on vertical axis; "Articulated need by customer (do they recognise they have a problem?)"; "Who owns the problem?"; and "Sustainability of impact (water vs insulin)" on horizontal axis.

Fig. 3.1 Identifying sustainable value

3. The sustainability of the impact shows how long the customer will need the solution or have dependence on the solution. In the example of the critical need for water, this need would disappear once the customer had drunk the water. However, for a customer who wants insulin, the need is likely to persist as long as the person lives. A longer sustainability of need thus ensures the highest monetisable value over time.

Before we look at how a technology startup can be truly scaled, it is important to identify the attributes and steps that are needed to transition science to a successful startup. We term this the journey of moving from technology to a successful startup.

These topics serve to demystify the steps needed to convert a technology into a successful startup. Along the way, they help technology entrepreneurs recognise the box defining their world view by providing them with a perspective from outside it. These also help in identifying gaps in the team, customers and timeline to revenue, which are particularly useful during investor negotiations. Along the way, the vision is for these steps to serve the technology entrepreneurs to recognise what needs to be done and why this is important,

3 Pitching to Investors: Conveying the Essential Aspects...

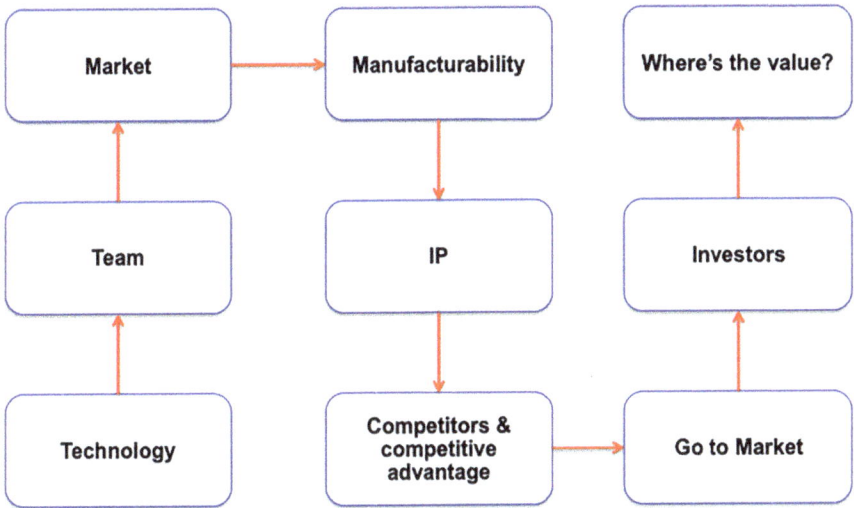

Fig. 3.2 Steps to validate maturity of technology startup

and with this clarity, have the conviction to say no to things that seem interesting but either risk distracting them from their vision or risk diluting their focus towards successful commercialisation.

The steps discussed below will not enable a technology startup to get to a unicorn status; that comes later. These steps do something far more important—they help ensure the startup's survival over time. The steps below are also part of the due diligence that a smart investor does to assess the capability and risks of the startup and its eventual ability to scale becoming a unicorn. This storyboard is shown in the visual below (Fig. 3.2).

Technology

Since technology startups invariably start with the technology as a basis, we begin by trying to address the key attributes needed in the technology.

Impact: Technology teams assume that breakthrough technology will immediately gain customer traction. However, the reality is that customers never buy technology. Customers buy a solution to a problem they have, and more importantly, a problem they think they have. Therefore, when a technology tries to respond to 'impact', it needs to answer the following three questions:

1. Who are the customers?
2. What does the technology do for customers?
3. Why should they care?

Customers either buy something that can increase revenue, reduce costs or provide them with a competitive advantage.

Revolutionary or Evolutionary: Startups often assume that a small percentage change in technology is adequate to create market impact. The reality is that the technology needs to normally be approximately 10 times better than existing technology available in the market. This is because by the time the technology goes through the prototyping, pilot and final commercialisation, it has already been several years. The time needed increases further in case there is customisation needed in machine design or process integration. In the meantime, the incumbent technology also improves. If this improvement is 10% per year, it is 50% better or cheaper than it was in the time it took for the startup to enter the market. However, incumbent players have strong relationships with customers as well as ecosystems to support their businesses. This makes it even more difficult for a customer to provide justification for moving to the new technology. The one reason it is possible to move to the new technology is if it does something more than the incumbent players in addressing a customer issue not yet addressed. In this case, the new startup has an advantage, since it does not need to support its ecosystem, unlike the incumbent players, who have deep investments in their existing asset base and need to ensure utilisation to cover maintenance costs. However, in every other case, it is imperative that the startup either has something that the incumbents do not or starts with a significant reduction in cost. It is important to consider that if lower cost is the only source of competitive advantage, it is a race down to the bottom, since ultimately, sustainability of business will be at the cost of ever eroding margins, and finally, it is impossible to compete with wages per hour in China.

Team

Universities around the world are full of technologies with potential. Much of this is in the IP licensing department of universities. The reason most of this does not see the light of day isn't because it's not good—it's because you can't convert a technology into a business without a team driving it forward.

There are some critical attributes that are needed in a team to convert a technology into a successful startup.

Loyalty

The team needs to have the same priorities. Unless the team succeeds or fails together, the team will have different responses to decision points. If a team member holds another position where he is likely to face a conflict of interest, this puts him at odds with the rest of the team. For instance, if a cofounder happens to be a scientist with a research entity, he may face a decision regarding government funding that he may drive towards the startup or the research. This needs to be flagged out and avoided since it can easily imperil the survival of the startup or the motivation of the team.

Vision Aligned

The team needs to have the same vision of commercialisation. If some team members want to continue with the status quo in equity ownership or obtain organic growth, this could very quickly result in a divergence that becomes more starker with new customers and growth opportunities. If you've invented the technology, you may not want investors to come in and take your ownership or control away, due to your lack of trust regarding how they may use it. On the other hand, the reality of investors coming in is that the focus of the technology moves towards market relevance. Technology for the sake of technology is then only relevant so far as it provides scope for future advances that in turn provide future IP.

Fully Onboard

Cofounders often delay the time when they expect to get fully onboard. This is the result of a perceived degree of risk of the startup compared to being employed by the research institute. Since there is always some amount of risk in the startup, it is important to define clear decision points and timelines when the cofounders come onboard, in the absence of which they have to return their equity to the remaining cofounders. It is also important to get noncompete agreements signed between the cofounders so that no one is motivated to leave and join another competing startup. These noncompete agreements sometimes are not valid, depending on jurisdictions, but serve their purpose of making the competing startup less attractive for investors due to impending lawsuits, which no investor wants to deal with.

Gaps and How to Address Them

Successful tech startups need more than just tech geeks doing fancy research; otherwise, they are called labs. It is important to recognise the capabilities that are needed to convert the tech to a product, whether this requires manufacturing, sales, business development or experienced entrepreneurs in the mix. The risk of belly gazing is real, where tech entrepreneurs only look at their innovation in exclusion rather than from the perspective of customer relevance. It is thus absolutely critical to identify the customer impact of the innovation and identify the skills that are needed to get there.

Balance

It is not enough to have the various skills onboard; it is important to recognise the different opinions. In the absence of this, there is always a risk that the nontechnical team members are subservient to the tech team. This translates to the mindset of the startup remaining tech-driven, which emphasises tech excellence rather than market relevance and research funding rather than customer references. In the absence of this, it becomes difficult to raise the next round of funding from investors to continue commercialisation.

Market

This is the most obvious raison d'être for any startup to exist. Unfortunately, tech startups do not often recognise the relevance of this and tend to proceed with the assumption that as long as the technology has global excellence, the market will obviously appreciate and pay for it. However, absence to validate the market can turn into a survival risk, particularly if the tech entrepreneurs are more comfortable with tech and use assumptions rather than real conversations with potential customers about their potential requirements.

For any startup, the opportunity is the gap between the customer requirements and the solutions being provided by competitors. The main challenge of startups is the gap between where their capability is and where they need to begin addressing customer requirements. The points below serve to objectify the market need and replace assumptions with reality.

Pain: In most conditions, the market only exists if there is a gap between the market need and what is already available. This is the market potential. Furthermore, customers need to perceive this gap, and it should result in a quantifiable pain, since the quantification of the need is converted into monetisation potential. Clear articulation of pain by a customer can also help a startup in soft funding to develop a solution to address this need.

Vertical Focus

It is important for the startup to identify the verticals that it wants to focus on. This point is obviously relevant for only those startups whose technology can have relevance across multiple industries. Interestingly, most tech startups do have cross-industrial relevance, so this point needs to be considered carefully, since it is very difficult to move to a different vertical once you commit to one. This can also help startups make the best decision regarding the vertical to focus on, depending on how the customers see them.

There are three levels of relevance from customers for any startup's solution. These are the reasons why a customer would consider buying a product. These are competitive advantage, profit maximisation or cost optimisation.

As discussed above, if the startup focuses on customer needs that are based on the customer obtaining a competitive advantage, it is much more likely that the customer may be willing to pay a lot more for the privilege of being the only one to have the solution. The benefit of providing an exclusivity to a customer is that this enables the startup to obtain its solution to the market and create reference points for future customers. The challenge for the startup is to ensure that it limits the scope of the exclusivity that it provides to initial customers so that it is not restricted from approaching future customers. This exclusivity may be limited by region, vertical or time.

For instance, a startup focusing on a next-generation substitute for concrete that has better insulation properties than existing solutions may find traction with one of the largest cement manufacturers in the world, such as LafargeHolcim. This collaboration would make sense for the startup since it would provide credibility. However, LafargeHolcim would probably want an exclusivity from the startup that provides it with a competitive advantage. The startup's option would then be to limit this exclusivity so that it is for a limited period of time (say 2 or 3 years), for a specific region (only the region where LafargeHolcim is the market leader) and only for a specific vertical (in this case, cement) so that the startup is able to address other customer verticals down the supply chain like construction companies directly. At this time, creating a strong footprint also provides the startup with an opportunity to become the reference point for the evolving market, which can provide future revenue opportunities.

Market Growth: The team needs to consider market growth when addressing customers. A growing market implies that customers are open to considering new solutions and technologies to capture part of this growing market. A rising tide lifts all boats. However, a market that is contracting implies that customers may only be looking for solutions that help in cost reduction.

Consolidation and Flux: The startup needs to consider the level of consolidation of the market. Greater fragmentation implies that there are many customers with small market shares. This provides a good opportunity to access the market. If the market does not have too many players and is concentrated, this may imply that the customers are locked in by competitors. In spite of consolidation, if there is flux in the market or where the customers owning the largest market shares have changed over the recent past, it implies that the market is highly competitive.

The startup then needs to identify the factors that drive up market ownership. One factor may be technology: to take an example of healthcare, if a new market leader develops a new molecule or successfully addresses a significant health issue. Another factor is also based on route-to-market, as when Didi Chuxing of China acquired the operations of Uber in China, providing it with a significantly larger footprint in China. A third factor could be based on competitive pricing, as when Apple began the relationship with Foxconn for manufacturing the iPhone. This risk is lower if there is flux, where competitors' positions have evolved and customers are open to new solutions.

Standards and Certifications: This is one of the least explored barriers to accessing the market. Startups often ignore the need for certifications before customers are allowed to integrate a new technology into their products before they bring them to market. Depending on the sensitivity of the solution, this may have different thresholds. Each certification takes time and money to obtain, and the absence of this implies that at best, the startup may only be able to sell to the research departments of customers. The startup needs to also check if there are standards to adhere to, in order to sell to the market. Furthermore, this may imply that royalties may need to be paid to get a licence to be on the given standard, which in turn can change not only access to the market but also financial projections.

On the other hand, if there are no standards, the startup has an opportunity to create its own standard. This can take up to 3 years, since new standards are subject to a vote by over 140 countries and take multiple steps and approvals. However, if the startup is able to go through the process and obtain its own solution certified as a standard, it becomes a reference point. Although this takes time and patience to achieve, it is a very enviable position to be in, since all other competitors have to certify against the startup's reference point. There is also an opportunity to gain royalties from competitors who want to licence the startup's technology. The startup thus also has an opportunity to partake in revenue from markets that it does not enter directly due to royalty revenue.

Size: It is commonly understood that the total market size needs to be over a billion dollars for the startup to truly scale since it is clear that the startup will be unable to capture more than a certain percentage of the total market. This also has implications for being able to attract investors. However, it is far more important to address a smaller market where the startup is able to gain a majority share and become the dominant player. This enables it to create references and subsequently begin addressing the larger market. Initial revenue also provides confidence to investors since investors always look for something more than simply outstanding technology, and customers provide confidence regarding the team's ability to deliver value as well as a validation of a market need.

Cost-plus or Value-added: It is important to know if the market considers the solution to be cost-plus or value-added. A cost-plus solution is one that addresses a need at a lower cost. The driving force is the cost, implying that there will always be pressure to further reduce cost. This position is clearly not attractive to customers. A value-added product addresses new value that customers appreciate compared to their other alternatives. This translates to higher profits for the startup and, more importantly, results in enduring profits over a longer period of time. This further enables the startup to use the super profits to invest in research and innovation and continue the cycle of providing more value-added products in the future.

Solution or Component: The distribution of value is not equal along the supply chain. If the startup's solution is considered an end solution by the customer, the startup is able to capture all the value perceived by the customer. However, if the startup's solution is considered a component in a product, the value that the startup is able to capture decreases. This is because the customer captures some of the benefits from the component when the end product is provided to *their* customers. In essence, Tesla may obtain super profits from selling its cars, partly due to the strength of its brand. However, any battery component that is provided by a supplier of Tesla may not have a proportional share in the super profit due to the absence of brand recognition. A sub-supplier to the battery supplier that may be providing capacitors may only end up making a market-standard profit percentage of 15–20% or be able to sell on a cost-plus basis (Fig. 3.3).

The above visual demonstrates how the startup is able to capture more value when it knows how its solution is perceived by the customer. The options and impact on the startup's pricing are discussed below.

1. Component vs product: If the customer sees the solution as a component, the startup's capability to monetise is limited, as it is not easy for the customer to define the value of each component. If the customer sees it as a product, the perceived value is higher and much easier to monetise.
2. Internal use vs sell-through: If the customer uses the product for internal purposes, it is imperative for the startup to know the replacement value or what internal problem it addresses. If the produce is sold further by the customer, it is easier for the startup to charge more depending on how the customer showcases the product to *its* customers.
3. Competitive advantage vs driving revenue vs optimising costs: It is imperative for the startup to know why the customer buys its solution. If it is a competitive advantage, the startup can generate very high revenue. If it helps the customer to drive more revenue, the startup can negotiate a slice of the customer's revenue as a part of its own revenue. If the customer reduces its cost by using the startup's solution, the revenue may continue to decrease, and the startup is at the highest risk. This is discussed in more detail later under the topic 'underlying technology risk'.
4. Data conversion into competitive advantage: The startup needs to understand if its solution can be used to capture data. If so, this can be converted into actionable intelligence, which can help it sustain and scale revenue over a longer period of time.

Existing Ecosystems: Startups often assume that markets operate independently. However, more often than not, products operate in ecosystems, some obvious, others less so. For the startup to try and replace a solution with its own, it is important to recognise the ecosystem that also needs to be either replaced or where the startup's solution fits seamlessly. Uber became successful largely because it used the smartphone of taxi drivers rather than trying to roll out its own hardware before creating hardware to create stickiness. All the

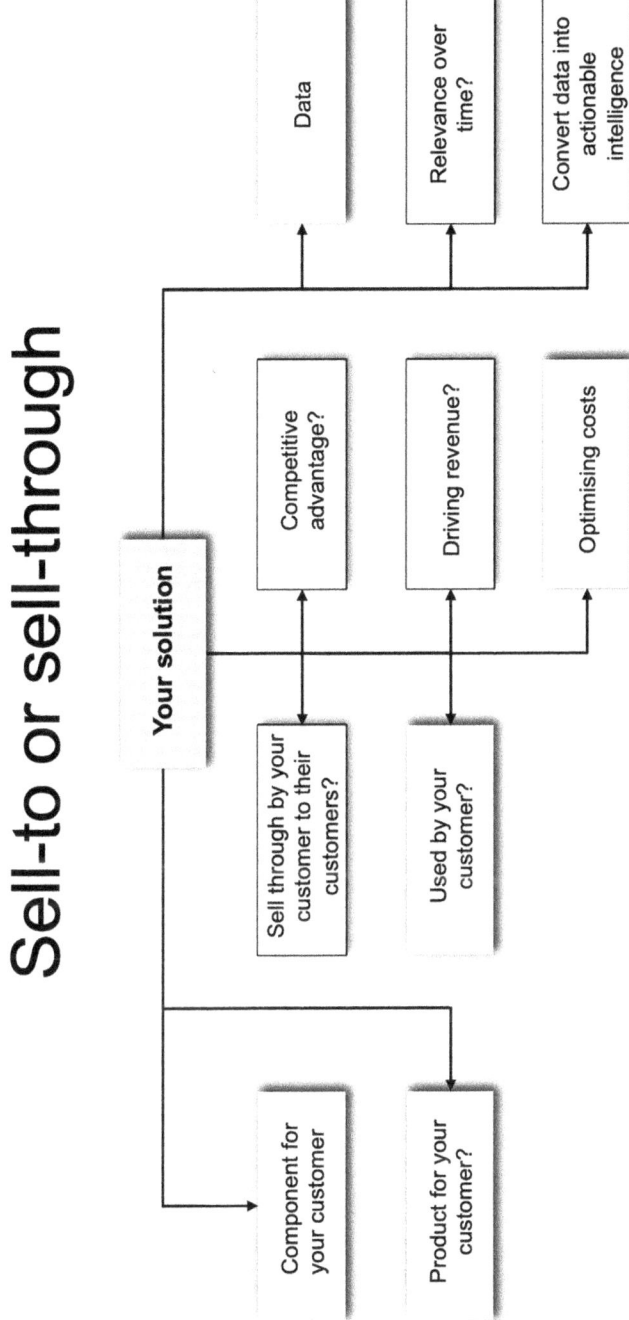

Fig. 3.3 How is your solution perceived by your customer

drivers had to download the Uber app, and they were ready to go. This enabled it to scale dramatically. Ultimately, this may also be its greatest weakness, as we discuss later.

Political Sensitivities: Although markets often seem egalitarian, they often have political considerations. This provides stickiness and protection to incumbents and can often limit access to others. Google could only access the Chinese market by limiting access to content deemed sensitive to Chinese authorities. Due to the uncertainty of information sharing via networks, Facebook is still restricted from operating in China. This has provided an opportunity for Chinese companies to develop and cross a certain threshold, which enables them to sustain their market position even if Facebook is allowed in the future. The car market is fraught with these sensitivities, due to which incumbents were not provided financial incentives from governments to develop electric vehicles on account of political pressure from entities such as OPEC. Awareness of such sensitivities can enable the startup to reap benefits if competitors are in geographies that are locked out of the market and can lead to an opportunity to provide solutions to customers at premium prices.

Requirement Gap

Tech startups often find interest from customers rather than an urgent need. This needs to be carefully considered since customers often do not have the luxury to buy from suppliers based only on 'interest'. Even solutions that are likely to have more potential for the future are often shelved when the quarterly performance of customers comes under pressure. Another challenge for the startup is the requirement gap, which pertains to the gap between the solution needed by customers and the maturity of the prototype developed by the startup. Whereas startups often focus on the innovation of their products, customers are more keen on stability and performance within strict guidelines. For customers, innovation is often subservient to 'boring'. This is similar to the patient with a pacemaker, who simply wants it to function exactly as it should for exactly as long as it should without any surprises and airlines want solutions that are no better and no worse than expected. Even better performance can be penalised by customers. A supercapacitor that is more efficient than indicated may put pressure on the battery. If this battery is put on a mobile phone carried by a user in his chest pocket, there is a risk of battery explosion due to the higher than expected performance of the supercapacitor.

Manufacturability

One of the greatest challenges of tech startups is that they are particularly focussed on tech—to the exclusion of anything else. This largely pertains to manufacturing, because scientists often consider manufacturing as low-end, since it does not entail any innovation or creation of breakthrough knowledge, but simply replicating the given product without any modification. However, without the core question of whether it is possible to manufacture or its viability, the technology often remains a technology without any viable route-to-market.

The following questions need to be answered to address the manufacturability of hardware technology.

Replicability: Manufacturing implies replicating the results obtained in the lab or the prototype that has been created. Although a prototype can enable technology startups to obtain access to customers and generate their interest, it truly is the capability to replicate the product that enables them to convert this interest into revenue. Even if this replicability initially results in modest output requiring highly skilled personnel to have constant oversight, this serves the critical purpose of providing initial references of strategic customers. The replicability has to ultimately result in high-throughput manufacturing, since to address the larger market, it is important to design high-volume manufacturing early on.

Stability: Stability in manufacturing means being sure that the machines work for a designated period of time to provide replicable output. However, the replicability of the output is not worth much if the machines that are designed to create this output are unable to provide stable performance. My first company had a focus on flexible and lightweight solar cells, with a large market in mobile phones. Since this was prior to the advent of the iPhone, we had a discussion with the management of Nokia, the global leader at the time. Their interest was driven by the ability of the highly efficient solar cells, which added approximately 2 g to the weight of the phone, to increase talk time by 10 min for 30 min of exposure to the sun. We proudly mentioned that although we had indicated an efficiency of 12%, it increased to 14% in certain solar modules. Their immediate response was completely negative, which came as a surprise. Higher efficiency risked overcharging the batteries of the mobile phone, which in turn risked their exploding. Given that many people carry their mobiles in their breast pocket, or approximately 5 cm from their vital organs, this entailed a very high risk for Nokia. This was far from theoretical, as it turned out with Samsung. In its rush to take its Galaxy Note 7 mobile phone to the market, Samsung omitted its robust testing, resulting in some batteries overheating and catching fire. It was estimated that Samsung lost $17 billion in revenue due to this issue.

This risk of lack of stability lies with every industry, and the highest value-added sectors, including healthcare and industrial manufacturing, require extremely high degrees of confidence in the stability of the product or components that are used by them, since this can not only result in lower costs or mitigate disruptions in the manufacturing line but can also adversely impact lives.

Scalability: When technology teams set up manufacturing, they assume that their competence automatically extends to machine manufacturing. However, the real challenge begins when things go well. When the team is able to showcase replicability from their pilot machine, they have to replicate the machine to scale production. Machine design standardisation becomes critical to enable this replicability. A higher degree of customisation is inversely proportional to ease of machine replicability, since nonstandard parts, customised process integration and testing limit scalability.

IP

Intellectual property, or IP, is often the bedrock underpinning technology startups. This enables the startup to protect its own technology from others as well as ensure that other competitors cannot block it from taking its solution to the market. It is imperative for the startup to put a patent strategy in place that addresses considerations relating to investors, customers, partners and competitors. This patent strategy has two elements: the first enables it to capture, protect and defend its own knowledge created (or block others), while the second element helps it ensure that it has freedom to operate (or ensure others do not block the startup).

FTO and Investors: One of the most important reasons for patents in startups is to create value perception. Investors are the first customers of a startup since they are the ones that provide the initial funding that enables the startup to realise its vision. Given this realisation, the most important value that they can hold on to in early stages of technology startups are patents, since the startup is too early-stage to have demonstrated manufacturing stability or customer lock-in. Patents provide perceived value by converting knowledge excellence into a tangible asset.

Investors can invest as much as 40% of their efforts in the IP validation of technology startups prior to investing. Part of the due diligence is focused on the startup's patents and their relevance, but a significant area of focus is towards whether the startup has freedom to operate, or FTO. This is because for any investor, the worst-case scenario is not that the investee company does not succeed—that happens for 6–8 out of any 10 investments. The worst-case scenario is when the startup does everything right with technology including setting up manufacturing and being able to replicate it all and gets traction with customers, but a competitor has a patent that stops the startup from bringing the solution to market. This is far from uncommon even for large companies. In fact, at the time of writing, there are on-going legal disputes regarding FTO between Apple and Samsung, the two Goliaths of our time in mobile telephony, even as Samsung continues to be one of Apple's key suppliers.

However, a startup can prepare for FTO and address future investor concerns. Assume that a competitor has a patent that may overlap with the technology used by the startup. This is where the defence strategy kicks in. The focus is to demonstrate to the investors why the startup's innovation and route-to-market cannot be stopped in the event of competing patents. The startup has to identify all patents in its domain where there is a risk of competing patents that may stop its ability to commercialise. It then needs to prepare arguments stating why these patents do not *exactly* overlap with its own technology. If any patent from a competitor does overlap, the date of the filing of the original patent needs to be checked to verify if the patent has expired. If the patent has not expired, it could pose a real risk to the startup's capability to commercialise and may stop the investors from investing. In such a scenario, prior art and the public domain come into play. The startup needs to check if the information captured in the competing patent that risks blocking it was ever in the public domain prior to the competing patent. This is critical because it shows why the competing patent was invalid in the first place. The information previously available is called prior art. The reason prior art is important is because patents can only be filed if the innovation is new and not if it was known earlier, irrespective of whether it was filed as a patent or not. This prior art in the public domain helps the startup eliminate the risk that a competitor's patent might block the startup. The public domain includes scientific journals or being presented in research symposiums.

Technology Patents: There are a number of different kinds of patents that a startup can file to protect its innovation. The most important one is the technology patent. This identifies an innovation that is a result of a unique process, design, combination of materials or a combination thereof. This normally protects the startup for 20 years, but the comprehensive protection comes at a price. The patent does not automatically grant protection across the world but needs to be filed separately in different countries or groups of countries. Since the filing and renewal fees can cumulatively exceed $100 K, it is important to consider the countries where this is filed. A good rule of thumb is to cover countries with the most likely markets for products, as well as the countries where the manufacturing base is likely to be located.

To determine whether an innovation should be converted into a patent, the startup needs to verify whether the innovation leaves a signature of uniqueness in the end product. The patent should only be filed if there is an end signature on the product. This is because since a patent involves capturing the precise uniqueness and steps used to create the innovation, it provides all information about how to replicate the innovation to competitors. It is thus imperative to ensure that the patent can be policed from those who may want to copy and replicate the knowledge, which can only be done if the end product can be tested for the unique signature. Without the means to police the patent from competitors copying it, it is better to keep it as a trade secret.

Design Patent: This is often used to augment technology patents. This is very specific to a design, and due to this, it is easier and significantly cheaper to obtain. The lifetime of this patent is often 25 years. The combination of a technology patent with a design patent strengthens the overall coverage of the unique knowledge created. For instance, a technology patent may be created to capture unique knowledge. However, a design patent may ensure that customers are limited to specific consumables that are needed to use the technology.

Nespresso created the coffee capsules, which kept the flavour intact and brought in convenience for relatively good coffee. The uniqueness was the coffee ground capsules. By augmenting technology patents with design patents, Nespresso was able to ensure that no other company was able to substitute their capsules and bring cheaper capsules into the market. They recognised that the real money was in the consumables, which were capsules. Therefore, they decided not to make the coffee machines that used their capsules but only to focus on the capsules.

However, Nespresso failed in two important elements. They had no way of knowing when a coffee drinker had consumed all the capsules. They also failed to pre-empt the emergence of competitors with copycat capsules as their patents expired. The result was that over time, other companies began to manufacture capsules that fit into the Nespresso machines. Since users often simply exhausted the capsules and had to wait for 3–4 days before the ordered capsules were delivered by Nespresso, they would simply go to their nearest store and find the store-branded capsules, which would also fit in the Nespresso machines but were much cheaper. Over time, users began to realise that the store-branded capsules delivered a similar coffee experience, resulting in Nespresso losing customers. The only solution was to ensure that the machine did not accept non-Nespresso capsules while at the same time knowing when the users were close to consuming all the capsules. As a result, Nespresso came up with Vertuo capsules, which had a barcode. This served two purposes. They provided information to Nespresso regarding the coffee habits of the customers, and more importantly, the Vertuo machines did not accept any capsules that did not have the Nespresso barcode. The new strategy of Nespresso covers multiple elements and includes a new design, protected by a design patent, the barcode, which stops coffee machines from using capsules without barcodes, and information about the coffee consumed by users, to pre-empt ordering and delivery of additional capsules.

Process Know-How: When the innovation results in a signature on the end product, it is easy to capture it as a patent, as discussed above. However, if the know-how is in the process without any signature on the end device, filing a patent would risk showing the unique knowledge created to competitors without the ability to police it, enabling them to copy it. In such cases, the best option for the startup is to capture it as a trade secret. The benefit of this is that there is no time limitation or expiry of this know-how, unlike for patents. An excellent example is Coca Cola, which has kept the special formula as a trade secret for over 100 years. This does limit the ability of the startup to outsource manufacture or to sublicense the manufacture to customers. For this reason, it is important to consider the business case as it evolves and creates strategic lock-ins with suppliers and customers where it can foresee a long-term relationship.

Algorithms: There is a common perception that algorithms are a form of patentable IP. Although they could certainly be considered IP, the main challenge with patenting them is that it is relatively easy to make small modifications in the code and show that the patent is not being contravened. Algorithms are often patented in the USA due to the strong litigative environment in the country but are seldom performed in Europe or elsewhere. In this scenario, the best option is to keep the secret algorithms secret by keeping them in the startup's own servers and only allowing customers or users to access the impact after putting in their specific data.

Exclusive Licence of IP: IP, in the form of patents, is often held by universities and research institutions. It is important to have a strong licensing agreement that enables the startup to progress with commercialisation without the risk that another competitor may also obtain the licence. Thus, it is imperative that the licence be exclusive. Beyond this, the licence ideally should cover all industries, since it is difficult to estimate the market in which the startup finds traction. It is also important to combine sublicensing since the startup may decide not to sell the product but sell the machine used to make the product instead. This would imply that the patent is being sublicensed by the startup.

The perspective of the research institution must be kept in mind when negotiating the licence agreement. Unless research institutions are owned or funded by corporations or otherwise have an affiliate relationship with for-profit companies, their main motivation is largely to ensure that the research finds its way to the market and creates impact. If the universities are based in the USA, they have stronger motivation to share in the commercial upsides, since they are not funded by the government. European universities are much more pliable due to such funding support. Nordic universities are often so lacking that companies from China and elsewhere such as Huawei have set up bases within the universities to identify and transition the technology out of the countries so that commercialisation may be done in other countries, to the detriment of the Nordic countries.

The great risk for startups when negotiating with the universities on spinoff agreements is not knowing what they want or the implications of giving something away. In addition to not asking for overall exclusivity of the patent licence or inclusion of sublicensing, startups need to address the issue of how the licensor is compensated. The three options are equity, percentage of revenue and percentage of profits. Equity is a reasonable option if it is given without any strings attached by the university and is fully dilutable, as for all other equity holders. The percentage of profits can benefit the startup since startups can postpone profitability indefinitely. The riskiest option then is the percentage of revenue since this can make the startup less competitive over time. In the last case, it is important for the startup to agree on net revenues pertaining only to the patent to avoid a catch-all payment on total revenue.

Startups often start their go-to-market by addressing customers who are willing to pay more, which translates to super profits for the startup. However, over time, the startup broadens its focus to address customers with lower price points, squeezing its profit margins. In this scenario, if the startup's profits are 10% of its revenue and it has to pay 5% of its revenue as licensing fees, this translates to 50% of its total profits. Beyond this, the startup needs to clarify how the percentage evolves if it is acquired by a strategic investor. In the absence of this, the risk is that the agreement implies that the strategic investor also pays a similar percentage of *their* revenue or profit, which is completely untenable.

Capturing Ancillary Ideas: As part of a comprehensive IP strategy, startups need to consider not only core ideas, which they can capture as technology patents, design patents, keep as process know-how or get via technology licensing. They also need to consider ideas that may have potential but are not yet known as being fundamental to the future business of the company. These ideas may be options that the startup may need to consider in the future without investing management time and money to create patents, or they may simply be areas where the startup may consider keeping its freedom to operate. It is important to consider such ideas and how to address them since there are many pivots in the journey towards successful commercialisation. The best option is to simply publish these so they are considered prior art, mitigating the risk of any competitor filing patents in these areas.

Competition

Once the startup is clear about the customer vertical to be addressed, the startup's value proposition is the gap between customer requirements and what is available. This is where having clarity about competition comes in.

It is not simply what competitors provide that is important. More important is what the customers perceive they are getting from competitors. When a customer buys something from IBM, he's not buying an IT solution; he's buying peace of mind. Even though IBM is likely to be more expensive than a similar solution provided by a startup, in the customer's eyes, IBM stands for certainty (at the time of writing). If he's unclear about what his requirements are (and many customers fall in this category because most decisions are made with a degree of uncertainty of information available), no one from senior management is likely to ask questions when he goes for IBM.

Specific areas that need to be kept in mind relating to competitions are discussed below.

Cost or Value Advantage: Startups often look at the price that a competitor is charging the customers and find it incredible how high this price is. However, in doing so, they don't fully appreciate what customers pay for. Take Starbucks. Most competitors would look at the price of a cup of coffee at Starbucks and find it amazing that customers pay it. For instance, Starbucks coffee costs $8 in Zurich. However, they don't recognise what the product is. The common perception is that people go to Starbucks for the coffee. However, when you visit Starbucks in the late afternoon and see the women congregating with their prams, you realise that it truly stands for 'escape'.

The second danger of going for the 'cheaper than' competitive advantage is that even if you're able to compete on price, it's a battle to the bottom of the barrel, since there's always someone willing to make the product cheaper. While you may assume that the main competition comes from China due to their incredible manufacturing acumen, the real competition may arise from a completely different source. This may be from companies that have a different business model, where their revenue streams are driven from services or even personal information, which they can use for advertising. In such cases, the real risk is that they may simply provide the product for free. Take Spotify. The company is based on the premise that it is simply easier to stream music than have it in your hard drive, since by paying a fixed amount each month, you simply get access to all the new music without having to buy it each time. Apple may outcompete them by providing music for free, since millions of people have their iPhones. In such cases, a new business model of Apple could be to let people listen to a certain number of ads to listen to music for free.

It is much more attractive to compete on value by providing something that the competition does not have and something that addresses a key requirement of the customer. Tesla may be able to outcompete the other car manufacturers in servicing. Whereas conventional car companies may have a strong footprint across different geographies that car owners may be able to go to in order to get their car serviced, Tesla may be able to pre-empt a problem in the car even before the car owner becomes aware of it. They may then simply be able to contact the car owner and service the car at the owner's location at a time convenient for the owner. Beyond convenience, the incredible user experience may become a key selling point for potential car buyers still on the fence.

Gap Defined

A startup always has one advantage against incumbent competitors: the absence of any existing legacy assets. Therefore, the startup has freedom to look for the best possible solution for the customer without having to ensure that the existing assets are optimally used or having to cover the cost of servicing the legacy assets when pricing a solution for a customer. At the same time, startups often go wrong with reading the signs during customer discussions. Keywords have very different meanings for the customers than for the startup. The risk arises when the startup simply assumes that technology superiority compared to what the customer currently has is enough reason for the customer to buy their solution. The startup may say 'innovative' and mean this as a competitive advantage, but a customer may hear 'untested'. Communication with the customer is critical and is often not done adequately to validate the gap between customer needs and what is available. In fact, it is this gap that becomes the starting point of being able to outcompete competitors and begin creating reference revenue.

Monetisable

As a startup, you may have identified the gap between what the customer may want and what the competitors can provide. You may also have received confirmation from the customer that this is a pain. However, unless the customer confirms that it would be willing to pay money to resolve this gap, it is simply not monetisable.

The startup can validate the value of addressing the pain early on. It can do this in two ways. The first scenario is if the startup's solution is cheaper than the competing solution. In such cases, the startup can simply calculate part of the savings of the customer, and this becomes its revenue opportunity. As discussed earlier, this puts revenue pressure on the startup each time another competitor does it cheaper. In the second case, the customer is able to use the startup's solution to do something more than was possible with competing solutions. This offers the startup the opportunity to lock in the customer and protect itself from competitors for much longer due to IP.

Size, Growth and Stickiness of Competitors

Given a large and growing market, the percentage ownership of the market held by competitors showcases the distribution of the competition and the relative monopolistic power held by them. If a very small number of competitors hold majority stakes in a global market, it becomes clear that the market is relatively static and rigid. If these competitors have not changed over time and have kept their relative positions of revenue and footprint, it becomes clear that it is likely to be very difficult to dislodge them. This is not simply due to their superior solutions but also due to their deep ecosystems integrated within existing customers. A good example is SAP, which is so deeply integrated into customers that a significant percentage of the IT staff of the customers are dedicated to the upkeep and on-going integration of SAP solutions into the customer workflows.

In such cases, it does not make sense for the startup to address the competitor head-on; the investment needed to change the perception of large customers combined with motivating customers to shift their investments from incumbent competitors would simply be too much. This can be effectively addressed with guerrilla marketing. A good strategy would then be to address new customers instead of the large existing players, or ones who have yet to get onboard with the equivalent of SAP. Since SAP is focused on large companies due to the extensive nature of the solution, an effective access point is to start with small and mid-sized companies or with startups. This provides very little competition since SAP would have no on-going traction with the customers. Furthermore, as these companies grow, the startup has the opportunity to grow with them. A further sharpening of focus would be to address one or two segments, since it is easier to become a major player in a small segment such as biotech and 3D printing, rather than trying and being everywhere. This strategy also insulates a startup from commoditisation due to specific sector-specific insights and data relevance. This in turn provides ever more relevance for new customers from the same sector who look for a solution that provides actionable intelligence.

If no competitor has a majority or if no new competitors have gained market leadership in the recent past, it implies that ecosystems pertaining to specific competitors do not yet exist within customer domains and customers are still looking to competitors to provide innovation. This is a good sign for the startup and indicates that its innovation may gain traction with customers.

The second consideration is the growth of competitors. This indicates whether the market is growing and whether customers are investing in innovation or cost reduction. If the focus is innovation, it implies that customers have not yet invested in creating internal ecosystems to support this and may be open to new solutions. However, if the market is focusing on cost reduction, it indicates that new innovation may hold very little value since the decisions are made by the CFO and are directly focused on cost reduction. The perceived value of an innovation is then limited and ever-shrinking.

Market Evolution

Market leadership is often a function of finding competitive advantage when others are simply trying to keep their lights on. Google is an excellent example of this. It could be argued that Yahoo had largely invented search in the mid-1990s by hiring hundreds and eventually thousands of people to simply search for new websites and put them in folders that made the information easy to find online. Over time, Yahoo perceived search to be so commoditised that it outsourced this function to Google and moved its focus to new strategic initiatives. Google, on the other hand, looked into the crystal ball of how online information was likely to explode, as it became ever easier for not only small and medium companies but even individuals to create websites. Google focused on search as its core competence. By creating a search engine that scoured the web for new websites and information, prioritising them by way of now only the external nodes (or hyperlinks) they connected to, but how many external nodes connected back to them, Google was able to make sense of search in a world of ever-expanding information. In the process of converting data into meaningful information, Google was able to create trend information about virtually any topic imaginable but also deep personal insights about its individual users.

The ability of the startup to pre-empt and address the concerns relating to the various topics discussed above not only improves its chances of getting smart investors onboard but also to get on the path to scaling.

small and medium companies but even individuals to create websites. Google focused on search as its core competence. By creating a search engine that scoured the web for new websites and information, prioritising them by way of now only the external nodes (or hyperlinks) they connected to, but how many external nodes connected back to them, Google was able to make sense of search in a world of ever-expanding information. In the process of converting data into meaningful information, Google was able to create trend information about virtually any topic imaginable but also deep personal insights about its individual users.

The ability of the startup to pre-empt and address the concerns relating to the various topics discussed above not only improves its chances of getting smart investors onboard but also to get on the path to scaling.

4

Go-To-Market Strategies, Investor Options and Tracking Value

Following from the earlier chapter, technology startups have multiple options relating to defining their go-to-market strategy and how it may evolve over time, depending on the perceived value for their customers. Together, these help them make a better assessment of their funding needs and timeline for scale. This in turn helps to find the right investors. These are discussed in more detail below.

Go-To-Market

Once a startup has defined the product that will drive its destiny (until the next pivot), the go-to-market strategy becomes pivotal. This is about how the product or service will be provided to the user and who the user in this context actually is.

There is often a gap between why the startup perceives the customer buys their solution and why the customers truly buy it. The ability to bridge this gap enables the startup to scale up and sustain its value.

Value Vs Volume

One of the first things that a startup has to consider in its marketing strategy is whether to focus on the value of the innovation in defining a pricing strategy or to drive volume sales. The benefit of value-based pricing is that it enables the innovation to be considered a high-end product that is able to command premiums. The risk of this pricing, on the other hand, is that unless the high-end product can sustain its aura of excellence or is able to convert it into a brand, other players eventually catch up and are able to replicate this. Rolex was able to convert its micromanufacturing excellence and capability to perform high-precision components into a brand. It is able to retain its aura of exclusivity despite selling close to 800,000 watches (only known because Rolex has its movements certified by the official Swiss Chronometer Control Centre, COSC, and their numbers are public).

By being perceived as high value and by maintaining premium pricing, the startup risks a delay in take-up by customers. This delay puts pressure on the cash flow of the startup. Furthermore, if the solution provided is an industrial solution or one that has to align with internationally recognised standards, a brand has much less relevance and consequently a lower premium.

Sputnik Engineering was a company based in Switzerland and manufacturing inverters under the brand name of SolarMax. In the early 2000s, photovoltaic (PV) solutions had a dramatic growth spurt due to a combination of awareness of CO_2 and climate impact of conventional energy sources and a reduction in the cost of PV. Sputnik rode the wave and was soon ranked number four globally in inverters, which are used to convert direct current into alternating current. However, Sputnik products always had premium pricing. The company assumed that customers would be willing to pay a premium for their solutions since they were made in Switzerland. At approximately the same time, private equity firms began circling Sputnik for a slice of the action to help the company grow further and push more economies of scale. However, recognising that this would result in outsourcing of the manufacturing or loss of control, Sputnik refused to get them onboard. At the same time, Chinese manufacturers were also scaling up their manufacture since they recognised that they could address the global market if they could meet international certification norms. Over time, customers began to put increasing pressure on Sputnik to compete on cost, since the only requirement of the inverters was that they adhere to international standards since these standards measured performance over time. Finally, in December 2014, Sputnik fired all their employees and closed their doors. This was a dramatic fall for a company with one shareholder/owner, which may have been valued at close to a billion dollars only a few years prior to dramatic commoditisation.

Turnkey Vs Customisation

Startups that predominantly have tech cofounders often have a deep bench of technical capability. This means that they are often very comfortable with addressing customer requirements even if they are nonstandard. In fact, they often take it up as a challenge. This results in nonstandard equipment and custom-designed processes. This comes without warranties, and in case of increased customer requirements, the startup struggles to replicate the effort. In essence, revenue increase entails a proportional increase of highly skilled people needed to custom-design the solution.

In contrast, when a startup consciously decides to use off-the-shelf equipment to create its solution, it makes scale-up seamless since replication is much easier. In case some degree of customisation is needed, the startup can convert this from a limitation into an opportunity. This is also the step where the startup can get other partners involved in the delivery of the solution for customers. These partners do the custom work needed in exchange for sharing some of the customer revenue. However, in the process, the startup is able to scale rapidly. At the same time, the partners become stakeholders and interested in the on-going success of the startup since it drives their own revenue. Getting partners to invest in building machinery also provides a second benefit for the startup. Since the startup does not invest in the raw materials, machine components and manpower needed to create the machines, it does not need to raise this additional funding from investors. This results in lower dilution for founders, so that they are able to hold on to a larger slice of their startup.

Partner Strategy

A strong partner strategy is an indispensable part of an effective go-to-market strategy. This is because strategic partners, particularly those who commit to working exclusively with the startup, extend their credibility to the startup and provide confidence to customers. It needs to be reiterated that one of the greatest concerns that customers have with a startup's solution is whether the startup will continue to exist over time. A strong partner mitigates this risk for the customer.

There are other benefits for the startup. To obtain these benefits, the startup needs to ensure that it has executive visibility with the corporation. Disney is a great example of this. In spite of being over a century-old company, Disney has instituted an incubator programme. This is as much to drive innovation jointly with the next generation of startups as it is to forge strategic relationships with them for future collaborations. One such relationship was with Sphero, a startup created by cofounders who met at Techstars in 2010 and started the company with a singular focus—to redefine creative play experiences with the original Sphero app-enabled robotic ball. Sphero joined Disney's 3-month accelerator programme. This led to a joint collaboration that led to the creation of the BB-8 droid, a robot that starred in Disney's *Star Wars: The Force Awakens*. Sphero was also able to obtain an investment of $120 K from Disney and Disney CEO Bob Igor as mentor (https://tech.co/news/big-brands-partnering-with-startups-2015-11).

In turn, the corporation also gains a tremendous amount from the startup. This is because over time, large companies become inwards looking. Therefore, they risk losing their competitive advantage and market leadership position. When this occurs, the innovative spirit is replaced by a focus on process optimisation. A partnership with a startup offers the corporation an opportunity to reignite the spark of entrepreneurship. For the corporation, this is driven by another need—the need for talent. By some estimates, 90% of millennials today would rather work in a startup than in a corporate giant (http://fortune.com/2015/04/26/startups-inside-giant-companies/). There is thus an enormous war for talent, and unless corporations become more entrepreneurial, they risk missing out on the brightest young talent. In 2013, GE wanted to kickstart its entrepreneurial drive, and over the following 15 months, it had funded over 500 internal projects.

When defining a partner strategy, the startup also needs to recognise the risks of the business case of the corporate partner. There are two scenarios. Let us illustrate this with the help of the car industry.

If the startup has battery technology, the three options would be Tesla, the existing car companies and a battery provider, say Northvolt. The advantage of going with Tesla is that this would directly impact the acceleration or the range. Since the company's focus is driven by these two objectives, the traction is likely to be driven by strategic considerations and top-down considerations. The startup's key risk is that Tesla may want exclusivity, which may limit the rollout of the technology. If the startup goes with any of the existing car companies, the battery technology may be limited to their nascent electric car divisions, which may be a knee-jerk reaction to Tesla. Beyond this, the startup may encounter pushback from the deep-rooted existing ecosystems that still support petroleum cars. If the startup were to go with Northvolt, which has raised hundreds of millions of dollars within 2 years since it was founded, it would encounter a larger startup that is trying to juggle the establishment of a large-scale manufacturing system while at the same time trying to integrate into the ecosystems of existing car companies that are in the process of tentatively moving into electric vehicles. It would encounter three uncertainties. The first would be of the relevance of its technology into Northvolt and commensurate revenue for this recognition. The second would be of Northvolt's revenue relevance with its customers: the car companies. The third and final uncertainty would be the car companies' strategy towards moving to electric. A good indicator for a startup is to minimise variables and limit them to those they can control. In the last case with Northvolt, the startup may encounter too many variables that are outside its control but that can still limit its rollout or relevance.

Value Capture Across Supply Chain

A technology startup often has relevance across multiple points in the supply chain. It is important to recognise this, since value is not captured consistently across the supply chain.

My first company created flexible solar cells using machines and processes custom-designed by the team. Since we had innovated the entire supply chain, we had the option of whether to sell machines or solar modules. The market for machines was relatively rarified since few companies around the world had the capability to build these complex machines with built-in processes. Solar modules, on the other hand, became commoditised over time, since many companies, including Chinese companies competing on price, entered this market. Another advantage of making machines over making modules was that customers paid you 40% of the total price of the machine upfront, which largely covered the cost of building the machine. As a machine producer, you were able to operate with a reasonable cash flow situation. On the other hand, making modules entailed investing in machines, paying for them, installing them and initiating module manufacturing and selling modules to customers, and getting paid 3 months after delivery of modules. This was an adverse cash flow situation to work with.

Some companies went further to identify opportunities to capture value. First Solar, a US company producing cadmium telluride solar modules, realised that many countries had restrictions in cadmium, due to the perception of toxicity surrounding it. Since First Solar realised that there was no risk of toxicity due to the strong molecular bond between cadmium and tellurium, it decided to lease out the modules while still retaining ownership. This innovative model of rollout also ensured that First Solar was able to qualify for the subsidies provided by governments on energy generation, providing a secondary revenue opportunity.

GE Capital was formed in 1933 when GE realised that its customers struggled to obtain financing to buy its appliances. Since GE knew its customers and their risk profiles, it decided to start offering financing on machines. In this way, its customers did not have to delay investing in their machines. Over time, GE realised that the financing business was able to not only capture customers but also became increasingly profitable due to the attractive interest rates and the regular revenue flows. In the mid-1980s, GE capital contributed to a significant proportion of the total profits of GE, despite being a relatively small part of GE. Thus, GE was able to convert a customer limitation into not only a way to attract and keep customers but also created a new profit stream in the process by going down the supply chain to capture value that others did not know existed.

Beachhead Market Traction

Startups often make the mistake of going for several markets at a time, in the assumption that at least one of the markets will gain traction. This is a cardinal error, since what often ends up happening is that almost all the markets find the startup's solution interesting. At the same time, the startup realises that all the markets need more work to convert to revenue and need specific customisation. What began as a risk mitigation strategy ends up sucking up all the oxygen from the room, leaving the startup bereft of any time to focus on one.

It is far better to validate the market options and focus on one that desperately needs a solution, is willing to pay for it, has a scale opportunity and finally can be provided to customers in a reasonable period of time. The time period for providing the solution to customers is important since it provides confidence to investors. This additional confidence translates to greater traction with investors and increased pre-money valuation.

Pilot Customer and Distribution Channels

Once a specific beachhead market has been chosen, a pilot customer is the next key decision in the go-to-market strategy. A good pilot customer should ideally provide funding that can be used not only for products but also in developing them. This then becomes a codevelopment effort, and the customer invests in the development of a solution that can help it address its own needs. Beyond this, the pilot customer also becomes a strong reference case for the startup to address other customers. The startup needs to be careful how other future customers perceive this pilot customer relationship, since if it is perceived to be strategic, they may assume that the pilot customer may have access to better technology from the startup. In such cases, they will look for alternative solutions instead of becoming customers of the startup.

The pilot customer can also become a distribution channel to customers further downstream, thus eliminating the need for the startup to set up logistics capability early on. The startup has to ensure that it is able to capture the appropriate value when using the logistics capability of the pilot customer and retains the freedom to set up parallel distribution chains to avoid exclusivity lock-in.

A Swiss startup Touchless Automation developed the capability to move very tiny objects using microfluidics principles to levitate and manipulate them. The startup found that this could be of relevance for mechanical watch manufacturers. It looked at the existing solutions available and realised that this capability was lacking since conventional suppliers used mechanical touch to move tiny components. However, due to the fragile nature of these components, any contact could risk damaging them, many weighing as little as 0.0001 g. It found interest from one of the suppliers, which decided to invest and allowed the startup to use their facilities and skilled people to design machines to showcase this. Beyond this, the supplier also became a customer for the machines and integrated the startup's machines in its own solutions to the watch industry. This helped the startup demonstrate market relevance and initial traction for its solutions. Although the solution was relevant in multiple industries, including biotechnology and electronics, the narrow focus helped the touchless automation transition from tech excellence to industry relevance.

Horizontal Vs Vertical

Technology startups often have solutions with relevance across multiple industries. Often, entrepreneurs see the world through the lenses of technology rather than relevance or impact. With several billion-dollar markets across different sectors, entrepreneurs often substitute a decision with a nondecision. Instead of deciding on one market, they simply decide to continue discussions with customers across multiple markets since they always have the fear of missing out (or FOMO) on a billion-dollar market. This can be considered a horizontal market focus since the startup provides a solution that may have relevance across multiple industries. The challenge with this is that the startup's effort becomes completely diluted across sectors and geographies.

The vertical market approach, on the other hand, identifies a specific market so that the startup obtains customer validation and then puts effort into opportunities in the specific sector. The startup can then focus on different points in the same market segment. It is important to note that costs, revenue opportunities, competitors and competitive advantage are likely to be very different for different levels in the supply chain. The startup could thus decide between licensing its technology, which is relatively low risk. Alternatively, it could focus on producing and selling machines that produce its product. It could go further downstream and let others produce machines on which the startup creates and sells its own product. Alternatively, it could create a brand or a user experience with its product. Its decision needs to be based on where the value is likely to transition to in the future.

Let us illustrate the difference by way of a startup that provides quantum computing. The horizontal go-to-market strategy is to put this computing capability in servers and allow customers from across all sectors to access it. The startup thus ends up with customers who want to research the origins of the universe, perform computational modelling of new molecules to address cancer, and customers who want to make cryptocurrency trading more seamless, among others. The challenge of the startup is that each of the verticals has a different kind of value for customers. Without knowing what the ultimate value for specific customer groups is, the only option for the startup is to charge by time and server capacity used. The second problem is that as soon as another startup develops a slightly cheaper way to perform computations at the same speed, the first startup will have to reduce its cost to remain competitive and retain its customers.

If the same startup with the quantum computing solution were to focus on one sector, say cancer, it would be able to begin capturing insights into the factors that cause cancer, and over time, crunch big data to identify specific precursors for people from specific backgrounds which may result in greater risk. Over time, this solution by the startup could help flag high-risk individuals and catch cancer at an earlier stage, making it easier to treat and much less expensive for individuals, their employers and insurance companies paying for treatment.

Reference Points

The right go-to-market strategy is about creating reference points. In the same way that the most memorable journeys are about moments, not days, and life is measured best by experiences, not decades, the best go-to-market strategy is about identifying specific reference points that help to keep track of the transition of technology into market rollout. This crystallises the focus on impact and at the same time helps in looking back at the deliverables achieved.

One weakness that often plagues startups that begin from tech excellence is that they quickly devolve towards their own competences at the cost of doing what needs to be done to commercialise successfully. They forget that what got them to a specific point is very different from what needs to be done to get to the next point. This is a bit like the ironman triathlon, where excellence in swimming will only get you across the 3.9 km distance across the lake, and you then need to change your style and speed completely to complete the 180 km of cycling, after which you again need to pivot completely to complete the 42.1 km marathon at the end.

By focussing actively on reference points in defining the go-to-market strategy, the startup recognises when it needs to pivot from doing things better to doing different things. What gets a startup to a customer pilot is innovation, whereas going towards commercial scaleup entails stability, replicability and certification.

Investors and Funding

For any technology to scale up, it is important to consider funding. However, for many tech startups where the founders may have invented the tech, sharing ownership is anathema. They thus focus on organic growth to ensure full ownership of the company. What these startups miss is that organic growth without investor funding invariably results in a delay in the go-to-market and eventually gets overtaken by competitors. This finally results in market irrelevance since the startup can simply not scale up fast enough to cater to the market need.

Very seldom can tech startups commercialise without funding. Hardware startups always need this funding unless they want to limit themselves to creating patents and IP licensing. Even software startups need funding, not to develop the software but to obtain market visibility and create a footprint with strategic partners to ensure adequate traction to ensure relevance. Perhaps the only business cases that do not warrant external funding are those that cannot scale faster with additional funding. A prime example of this is advisory on consulting services. This is limited by the time of the people involved, so if 10 people equate to $1 million, 100 people will get $10 million. Investors do not consider investments in these entities precisely because they do not scale.

There are various options for obtaining funding. These are discussed below.

Own

A company normally starts with funding from the founders. It is important that the founders limit their own funding to the founding, rather than trying to cover the seed funding as well. The seed funding may be $20 k to $500 k. By assuming that this too will be covered by them, the founders often assume an optimistic business case or focus on what they like to do rather than what needs to be done to convert the tech into a business case. It is not uncommon for founders to be forced to provide additional funding if they are unable to attract external funding, but if this becomes absolutely necessary, it at least forces them to recognise the gaps in the business case or to determine that the startup does not have legs.

The implications of remaining here are that often startups simply decide to remain with their own funding, recognising that investors entail strings and external duress to grow, capture market share and scale. If this is done because cofounders feel that they need their independence and full control over the destiny of their startup, this is a reasonable decision. However, sometimes startups feel that they may be able to scale without external funding, but only by using their revenue generated by their customers. This does not work for a number of reasons. First, their customers' payment cycles are longer than they anticipate. Two: they have far less leverage in negotiations with their customers, due to which they end up making significantly less revenue than their incumbent competitors that they are planning to replace, since their customers argue that the startup does not have credibility or references. There is another risk that the startup needs to be aware of if it goes for organic growth without external funding. This is that even though it may have a solution that is superior to competing solutions, the paucity of funding will stymie growth and provide competitors with technically inferior solutions to capture the market. This will leave the startup to cater to niche markets and risk eventual irrelevance.

Awards

Once the founders have defined the impact of the tech on specific end-users, the next funding option becomes possible. It is imperative that the founders pivot from talking about tech excellence to talking about the possible impact. The reason this can be particularly challenging is that it forces founders to change their mindsets. The education and the backgrounds of the founders often result in them only committing to anything if they have already done it or if they absolutely know it can be done. However, the pivot forces them to now go into a world of uncertainty, where they now have to envision and evangelise an uncertain future with no clarity about their ability to achieve it or even know if it may be possible. However, it is this that helps in connecting them with foundations that have the mandate of selecting startups based on specific areas of impact. This recognition from awards provides several advantages to the startup. They provide early funds since these awards are often accompanied by cash. They also provide credibility, visibility and access to a network, elements that any startup needs and something that is often missing in the founder team. Most importantly, pitching the vision of impact makes founders recognise the value of what drives positive decisions from external stakeholders. This learning will ultimately pay off multifold, whether it pertains to strategic customers, suppliers, corporate partners or investors.

Although some recognition via awards is good, there are implications of trying to apply for too many. When I started my first company in 2005, we had a very strong technology and our focus was on the clean energy market, since we had innovated a flexible solar cell with a thickness of less than a human hair with world record efficiency. Within a year, there was a wave of alternative energy, and we got a lot of visibility. Therefore, we swept all the awards in every competition we entered, amassing thousands of dollars in award money and press visibility. At one point, I met Neil Rimer, partner at Index Ventures, while they were discussing a term sheet with us. Now Index Ventures is one of the most venerated VC firms in the world, having backed startups such as Skype. When I told him that we had been recognised with the seventh award in 2006, he candidly asked me if we had any time to do the actual work of developing the company. I realised that we were getting so lost in the adulation of the visibility that we were not focussing enough on what needed to be done to progress the business. That was the last competition we entered.

The learning was that it is of value to apply for a few awards and competitions since this helps the startup obtain initial funding and press. However, there is a clear law of diminishing returns, and over time, there is a very real risk of the team becoming distracted from the real business of making it happen. Additionally, no serious investor ever invests in a startup because it has won a few awards, but on how strong the business case is by looking at customer interest, traction and sustainability.

Customer Funding

One of the best options for obtaining funding for startups is to obtain funding from customers. While this may seem obvious, the challenge occurs when the startup is unable to provide a product because it is not yet ready. Obtaining funding from customers without providing products can be done in a number of ways. The most obvious one is for joint development. This provides the customer with a perception of creating new IP, which is similar to outsourcing R&D. Here, it is important to define it as development rather than R&D, since if it is the latter, the customer may rightfully want to have co-ownership of the IP created. However, in the case of joint development, any IP created is likely to be a design patent, which is much less likely to inhibit the startup's future options compared to a technology patent, if shared with the customer. For clarification, a design patent only captures the exact shape and precise design, whereas a technology patent captures a product, design or process that provides a unique and innovative output.

The other advantage of joint development is the option to use the equipment and the capabilities of the customer for free. This can be a substantial advantage, given the limited resources of the startup. Another advantage of joint development is the lower risk in case things simply do not work, since the customer is fully engaged. It is much easier to pivot or to minimise negative reputational repercussions if milestones are not achieved if the customer team is also involved in the milestone effort.

Another option for funding from customers is by way of an advance. This is much more onerous than development funding since it implies clear deliverables and specified timelines, as well as a potential penalty if the startup is unable to meet demonstrable timelines. However, as long as the startup does whatever is necessary to mitigate this risk, this funding option comes with no other strings attached, such as interest, equity dilution or interference in the company strategy via the board.

Angel Investors

This is normally the first proper funding done by a startup, beyond the founder funds. This is relatively easy to obtain and often comes without too many strings attached. The founders can access angel investors via credible professional entities in their network, including banks and accounting firms. It is important to keep the funding semantics simple. While the main focus of the entrepreneur tends to be on the valuation, this is much less important

4 Go-To-Market Strategies, Investor Options and Tracking Value

than other elements. Even if the valuation is slightly lower than what the entrepreneur hopes for, the long-term impact of giving away 15% vs 12% at a slightly lower valuation is not material. Far more important are the conditions of the investment.

For instance, it is more important to ensure that the angel investor obtains normal equity rather than preference shares. This is because preference shares come with several rights, such as dividends and first rights, as well as others, including board seats, priority and veto. It is wise for the entrepreneur to postpone these onerous terms to a future round, since future investors investing in round A or B will invariably require this. By then, the entrepreneur is likely to be much better prepared to deal with such conditions and recognise the implications of accepting them and has put the startup on a more sustainable path towards commercialisation.

One advantage of angel investors is that they invest their own money. Thus, they do not have any specific pressure regarding the timeline for return or exit. This is very different from other investors, as we shall see shortly. The proximity to the startup also makes it likely that they may invest in future rounds and tap their networks for future funding rounds.

A risk in dealing with angel investors is when the startup gets them too deeply integrated into its operations. While this appears tempting due to access to free skills, it often becomes a hinderance since the startups end with two reporting and decision structures. Additionally, as the investment made by angels is a significant part of their wealth, they often second-guess the founders when founders try to invest in equipment to de-risk their own investment. Since the founders almost never have certainty regarding whether a specific equipment investment is the right one, this secondary reporting and need for justification ends up hindering the work of the startup. Second, since angel investors seldom have an understanding of how value is likely to transition in the future, as their own wealth creation may have been from traditional industries, their advice may be dated as best and often completely misdirected.

Family Offices

Family offices are very similar to angel investors. The key distinction is in the size of the fund available for investment. Whereas angel investors have between $1 m and $5 m available for investments, it is not uncommon for family offices to have in excess of $ 100 m to $ 500 m and often much more available for investment.

Unlike angel investors, family offices are much more visible. Therefore, family offices are often managed by financial managers to ensconce wealthy individuals, also called principals, from day-to-day administration. This implies that conventional access points such as banks or audit firms are not adequate to gain access to such family offices. While they may provide introductions, banks or audit firms do not provide the credibility necessary to gain visibility. It thus becomes important to have advisors who have market credibility and networks.

Legal advisors can be a powerful source of gaining access to these entities since partners in reputed law firms are often trusted by wealthy families.

Family funds offer good investment stability and often provide future funds for growth, while at the same time having minimum formal requirements of showcasing milestones and aggressive scalability. This makes them solid partners for a startup if it can get them onboard. They, however, have very little to offer by way of market access or helping the startup prepare for future funding rounds from external investors. This risks making the startups feel comfortable and slackening their pace of scaling. If the startup realises that it needs to continue being aggressive in achieving the necessary milestones to retain relevance or have their own networks to attract the next round of funding, this is a good investor to have.

Foundations

Foundations, or 'Stiftung', as they are known in the German speaking part of the world, are family offices where the wealth creator has died, leaving the money with clear mandates regarding how it might be spent. These thus support causes rather than technologies. This has a profound impact on startups and their pitch. While angel investors or family offices normally invest based on the business case combined with their familiarity with the technology or the market, foundations only look at what the trial impact is on the chosen end markets. This means the entrepreneur needs to begin talking about not only what markets the tech focuses on but also the impact that the tech creates for the customer. This tends to be outside the zone of comfort or competence of most tech entrepreneurs. The gap between the messages of the tech entrepreneur of tech excellence is very different from the impact, which is what the foundation understands. The entrepreneurs who are able to make the bridge between tech excellence and final impact while articulating its relevance find access to funding that comes with very few strings attached. The attractiveness of this funding is due to its substantial size but also because it is often given as a grant rather than against equity, without future priority or veto rights.

When startups do obtain funding from foundations, they risk becoming truly comfortable since there are very few reporting mechanisms and often no board representation by the foundation. This can be risky since it is easy for startups to feel that there will be more soft money available when the cash flow position becomes tenuous. However, the strict regulations of foundations often restrict them from additional investment, and without external guidance, the startup often continues to work on technology rather than getting closer to the market. Therefore, it often has difficulties obtaining the next round of funding from professional investors. Additionally, the lack of guidance on the board or strategic level on what needs to be done to be ready for future funding means the startup is ill prepared for future investors, where it competes with other aggressive startups vying for the same investor pool. This is similar to the reason why startups that are founded during recessions have a better survival rate than those founded during economic growth. Startups that are founded in recessions are very lean and focus on a powerful story, immediate customer traction and initial revenue, whereas startups founded during economic growth find relative ease of raising funding. Due to the easy availability of funding, these startups continue to work on what they have been doing rather than what needs to be done to obtain future funding. Since funding rounds operate on the premise of 'what got you here is not what will get you to the next level', the startups are simply not ready to become lean when the economic cycle turns negative and when investors have to make choices regarding which startups they will continue to support and which will be let go. It's also this reason due to which startups in the USA that raise hundreds of millions of dollars run into cash flow problems if they can't continue to get ever-increasing funding rounds. Getting a large round of funding is not a good thing for two reasons. One is that the startup creates on-going liabilities such as hiring too many people, which need to be paid every month. Second, large funding often comes with more aggressive timelines and pressure from the investor, which reduces the flexibility of the startup to pivot. Startups from other countries often wonder how US startups get funding, which is often 100 times more than they do, and still end up going bust. In my first startup in Switzerland, we were negotiating with a Swiss cantonal bank, and they suggested a soft loan of $0.5 m. This was for a manufacturing facility for flexible solar cells. At the same time, our competitors in the USA, including Nanosolar & Solyndra, were negotiating soft loans exceeding $100 m to $500 m. When we were raising our round A of slightly more than $10 m, these companies had individually raised over half a billion in soft loans by 2010. We would look at these funding amounts with incredulity and feel that with this level of funding, it was inevitable that they would end up being the global standard for thin-film photovoltaics. It thus came as a shock to us when shortly after, both these companies filed for bankruptcy. Solyndra had become so bloated due to multiple funding rounds that finally totalled to over $1.2 billion that when it started missing milestones, it became easier to file for bankruptcy than to dramatically cut the fat.

Angel Funds

With ever more angel investors interested in investing in startups on one side and a proliferation of startups on the other, a new funding entity has gained relevance in recent years. These entities enable prospective investors to invest smaller sums within the same shareholder agreement. The benefit for the startup is that it now has access to funding options from angel investors without having to deal with different investor conditions and idiosyncrasies. It must be noted that different angel investors often have different timelines and definitions of startup success and consequential exit. It thus becomes an enormous challenge for a startup to manage investor expectations once they come onboard. Contrary to the expectation of startups that the main problem is to get angel investors onboard, the reality is that managing expectations after funding is absolutely critical to avoid a decision freeze. These decisions can pertain to future funding rounds, funding size and valuation of potential exit options. Those angel investors who have interest in future funding rounds have an interest in keeping the valuation low. Investors who perceive a risk of losing their board seat or dilution may also push back on future funding, particularly if the startup is operationally in the black.

Angel funds mitigate these concerns by enabling startups to obtain long-term funding on soft conditions. Angel investors come onboard within one shareholder agreement and have one or two representatives on the board. Future funding rounds are also much easier since different investors with varying viewpoints counterbalance extreme opinions or one investor asks for exclusivity to the market. All this augurs well for the founders since fairness can never be a given in relationships with investors.

Angel funds can also be beneficial for small angel investors, who otherwise simply do not have the resources to validate an investment opportunity or do proper due diligence. Due to this, first-time angels often end up losing money, or worse, getting swindled out of it. Angel funds enable these small angels to get in with a low ticket size, typically starting $10 K, and do not have to worry about the fairness of investment terms or valuation. They are thus able to focus on the sector of their comfort and find a broad swath of opportunities with varying degrees of maturity, size and horizon timelines.

VCs

Venture capitalists are another source of funding. It can be argued that VCs were the original investors of startups. However, they may have become a victim of their own success. Over time, the stellar return on their more successful investments, including Google & Facebook, has resulted in VCs being able to raise funds exceeding a billion dollars. Therefore, there is intense pressure to invest in larger rounds.

Tech startups have longer gestation periods and often plateau at valuations of $100 m to $500 m, whereas platform startups that survive tend to have a much greater chance of becoming unicorns and do so in a much shorter period of time since they can scale faster due to the absence of technology-based limitations. On the other hand, VCs are always under time pressure to provide returns to their investors. Although the survival rate of platform startups tends to be very low due to the low barrier to entry, those that survive also have a higher propensity to become unicorns and do so in a relatively short period of time. Due to these factors, VCs are often not always the best fit for technology startups and find platform startups more appealing.

Strategic Investors

These have always been a stable investment option for startups. Those are investors who are in the same business as the startup or are directly in the supply chain. Thus, these investors are often likely to be customers of the startup's product.

The dual relationship of being investors and customers is fraught with risk, which stems from the difference between things that are important for the investor and for the startup. While the startup prioritises selling to as many customers as possible for as high a price as possible, the strategic investor's interest may be to have exclusive access to the startup's solution at the lowest price possible. The strategic investor may also be able to exert influence favouring itself in the next round of funding, particularly relating to priority and veto rights. Furthermore, this is perhaps the most important, the strategic customer's interest is to buy the rest of the startup that it does it already own at as low a price as possible, whereas the founders of the startup naturally want to have the option but not the obligation to sell at the highest price possible. When the strategic investor is on the board, it has the capability to exert influence for its own benefit and is detrimental to the founders.

It is important for the startup to recognise these risks before it signs the legal document of the investment. One way to mitigate these risks is to get financial investors before the strategic investors come onboard. Since financial investors are more aware of the risks and conflicts relating to strategic investors, they can help mitigate these risks as they try to protect their own interest to exit at the highest valuation possible. Alternatively, if strategic investors are the first or indeed the only investment option for the startup, a sound strategy is to obtain multiple strategic investors at the same time. This ensures that one investor counterbalances the onerous conditions of the second while also giving the founders the option to exit at a reasonable timeline.

In case getting more than one strategic investor onboard is not possible, the founders need to capture their own exit strategy in the investor documents. These include the option but not the obligation to sell their shares (and obliging the investor to buy these shares) at a defined timeline for a clearly stated price on achievable and demonstrable milestones, which the strategic investor does not have the capability to modify unilaterally. This is also where good legal support pays off. Any gap or ambiguity in the terms obliging the strategic investor to buy shares of the founders will be used as an excuse by the strategic investor to not buy shares. As a consequence, the founders may end up being locked in for perpetuity with no option of exit and become glorified employees of the strategic investor until the time when their technology is fully absorbed by the investor, at which time the investor may simply cease to provide on-going financial support to sustain the operations of the startup. At this time, the startup simply closes down.

It is important for the startup to recognise these risks before it signs the legal document of the investment. One way to mitigate these risks is to get financial investors before the strategic investors come onboard. Since financial investors are more aware of the risks and conflicts relating to strategic investors, they can help mitigate these risks. Alternatively, if strategic investors are the first or indeed the only investment option for the startup, a sound strategy is to onboard multiple strategic investors at the same time. This ensures that one investor counterbalances the onerous conditions of the second, such as lock-in or exclusivity, while also giving the founders the option to exit at a reasonable timeline.

VC Vs Strategic Investors

Since startups often receive interest from two major types of investors who have the funding and the capability to help them scale, it is important to compare the two investor groups, viz., VC and strategic investors.

Timeline to funds: As a young pre-revenue startup, your clock is already ticking. In such cases, VCs are likely to provide you with funding first, since they are also under a timeline to provide returns to *their* investors. It doesn't hurt to sign on some strategic customers for your pilot, as this helps your negotiations with VCs.

Timeline to exit: This is one of the major differences between VCs and strategic investors. VCs invest for a fixed timeline, at the end of which they need to exit and make their money. They are in it for the money. Strategic investors, on the other hand, do not plan to exit unless the investment turns out to be dud. They consider investments as outsourcing their R&D.

Valuation: VCs try to minimise their valuation when they invest, but once they do, their motivation is to maximise their valuation for future investors. Strategic investors, on the other hand, are not *that* concerned with the valuation at initial investment. However, since they expect to buy the rest of your company as commercialisation progresses, they try to minimise your future valuation in future rounds.

Exclusivity: VCs operate on the premise that since they have no idea what technology will succeed in a given sector, it makes sense to invest in multiple startups with different technologies or routes-to-market. They will thus not only not provide exclusivity to the startup but also consciously and aggressively invest in multiple startups with different technologies to address the same customer vertical. They also encourage cannibalism across their investments (since their focus is on money maximisation, rather than soft factors such as emotions, as mentioned above). Strategic investors, on the other hand, are loyal creatures. Thus, once they invest in a startup, it is likely that they would sign a noncompete where they refrain from investing in similar technologies or even across multiple technologies addressing the same market. A startup should consider obtaining such exclusivity from the strategic investor without providing reciprocal exclusivity to keep its own options open.

Future funding: With VCs, future funding is not a given. It depends on their funding cycle and if the buzz is still there. With strategic investors, the opportunity for future funding is extremely large, since they consider you as an extension of their own business. In the case of strategic investors, founders should consider obtaining partial exits in the case of future funding, since over time, exits become increasingly difficult due to management changes or product cycle-based obsolescence.

Market buzz: VCs often invest based on market buzz. If you happen to have the market buzz in your pitch, your chances of funding (or at least getting the opportunity to pitch, which is almost half the battle) with the VC increase dramatically. Since strategic Investors are more focussed on their business, and they happen to know exactly what it is, the advantage of a buzz tends to be limited (unless the strategic investor happens to be a new technology company (e.g., social media).

Executive sponsor: VCs normally have a partner driving the business with clear oversight, driven towards milestones and eventual exit at a healthy multiple. Strategic investors, on the other hand, do not always have executive sponsors, particularly for large conglomerates, which often have turnovers exceeding $100 billion. It is important to keep in mind that their R&D expense runs into billions of dollars.

For decisions to invest up to a few million dollars into the startup, a manager on the venture team may have sign-off authority. Combined, the average time a manager spends in his role in a corporation is 3 years. This risks the startup becoming an orphan, since as it grows and requires future funding for which board clearance may be needed, no one from executive management wants to sign off on new technology. At the same time, it is also not easy for management to write off the investment and hive it off if it becomes successful in the future. The result is homeostasis at the corporate level, due to which the startup eventually withers off. This is in spite of a viable business value proposition. For a startup, it is key to identify an executive sponsor within a strategic investor so that the investment is already considered a strategic initiative from the perspective of the strategic investor.

Fund cycle: VCs have fund cycles, which imply that at the end of this, they have to return the funds to *their* investors. The fund cycle often tends to be approximately 7–10 years. The startup needs to know if the investors are towards the beginning or end of their cycle since this will also determine when the investors need to exit. Strategic investors do not have this limitation and invest based on requirements, so long as they have an executive sponsor or the board has already signed off the amount.

Customers: VCs normally want the startup to address all customers possible to capture maximum value. The good ones will also strive to open doors to their strategic relationships to enable this. Strategic investors, on the other hand, deter others from becoming customers since potential customers assume that strategic investors have priority in obtaining the latest release or the best solution that ultimately provides a competitive advantage to the strategic investor compared to other customers. This is the most significant and underestimated risk of getting strategic investors in the mix.

Level of certainty: The greater the level of certainty of revenue is, the greater the logic of obtaining VCs. This is because VCs will help in maximising the value of the company once revenue begins for future fundraising or exit. If the level of certainty of getting to revenue or achieving milestones is less, it is better to go with strategic investors, since they are more patient and more willing to invest more money, since their focus is not financial return but the option to have a business solution that provides a future competitive advantage.

In addition, there are several other classes of investors that become relevant as the startup matures. These include sovereign funds or private equity. Sporadically, other funding options have also come up over the past years but have not been able to sustain their relevance or have been unable to institutionalise, in part because they have been plagued by pilferage. These include crowd funding or initial coin offerings, also called ICOs. In these, the startup raising funds issue its own virtual coins, which in theory have a basis in its own valuation. However, the investors that ICOs attract are often those who already hold crypto assets and are generally high-risk individuals. Given the uncertainty of being able to raise funds in this way, combined with the uncertain value of the base cryptocurrency that investors invest with, this seems to have largely collapsed as a means of fundraising.

However, the basic premise of enabling a startup to obtain a number of micro investors to fund initial development holds relevance, particularly if these investors have no special rights or presence on the board of the startup. One hurdle is regulation, since in many countries, if a startup has more than a specified number of shareholders, it is deemed to be a public company and is subject to regulations and administration accordingly. However, given the motivation of smaller investors to consider investments in young companies as an alternative to other asset classes, ICOs linked to virtual currencies such as Libra, floated by Facebook and backed by real assets, may find a resurgence as a viable form of fundraising.

You're all geared up as a startup to commercialise your idea and you've got the idea, IP and customer gap under your belt. Perhaps you've also got some initial customer feedback to bolster your business case. However, you really need the funding to make it happen, to avoid irrelevance.

A summary for the evaluation of startups is provided in Fig. 4.1.

As the evaluation chart above illustrates, if any of the criteria above is not fulfilled, it creates risk for the startup. The risk can relate to the ability to protect the startup's IP, manufacture in volume or find traction with customers.

Base criteria	Secondary criteria	Scoring
Technology	1. New (Invention) 2. Improved (Innovation)	
Team	1. Two or more 2. Previous startup 3. All-in 4. Aligned on timeline and exit	
Market	1. Vertical clear 2. Need articulated 3. Criticality of need 4. Sustainability of need 5. Initial contact	
Manufacturability	1. Tested 2. Replicable 3. Stable 4. Certified (if needed) 5. (Custom design - custom M/c)	
IP	1. Have tech & design patent 2. Have tech patent 3. Licenced patent (exclusive) 4. Nonexclusive patent 5. Freedom to operate	
Competitive advantage	1. Customer lock-in 2. Increase over time (from tech to data dependence	
Go-to-market	1. Product (not component) 2. Addressing sustainable need 3. Data capture opportunity	
Customer	1. Institutional 2. References 3. Value-added (not cost-plus) 4. Has customer provided funding for pilot (without IP rights)	
Total score		

Fig. 4.1 Evaluation of market readiness and gaps in technology startups

Where's the Value?

This is one of the critical questions that a startup needs to ask itself. By starting with the end in mind, the founders could go down a very different path from if they had started on whatever path seemed easiest. Your own path towards becoming an entrepreneur was driven by key decisions where your choosing the alternative would have led to a corporate career and following someone else's vision. In the same way, if the startup starts with the vision of creating impact and sustaining the value of the impact, it makes decisions that are in line with sustaining relevance.

This question is far from trivial. Even large companies find it challenging to survive if they move away from the DNA that was their basis for being created and ultimate success. A good way to address this is for the founders to ask what impact the company expects to stand for in 20 years or longer, compared to where they expect to be in 2 years. In the absence of this fundamental question, it is likely that the founders of the company will make decisions that have quarterly or annual impact rather than long-term sustainability.

Outsourcing is an excellent example. Companies across the USA and UK have outsourced manufacturing to China as a mode of saving costs in manufacturing. Since executives in the US companies remain at the helm for only a few years before moving on with their golden parachute, their focus is to improve the bottom line within their tenure to benefit from company performance. However, this upside is purely temporary since the company loses manufacturing jobs in the country of origin. Beyond this, the company also loses future innovation, since innovation often arises when R&D meets manufacturing in addressing the evolving requirements of customers. Thus, although the company shows improved bottom line numbers for 2–3 years, it is unable to sustain super profits that enable it to compete on value and devolve to competing on price. Since price-based competition is very seldom sustainable in a developed country, over time, the company becomes irrelevant.

This is also seen in family businesses. Small and Medium Enterprises (SMEs) in Switzerland are often privately owned companies. They are run as a generational business. Often, the generations following the entrepreneur who built the business manage it, not as entrepreneurs but as managers. Over time, this results in the company focusing on replicable manufacturing rather than innovation. As a consequence, thousands of SMEs go bankrupt in Switzerland since their value generated is unable to sustain the extremely high salaries of their workers. The health of the entrepreneurial ecosystem is measured not only in how many companies go bankrupt but also in the number of new startups that are established to replace them. In 2021, over 50,000 startups were created in Switzerland. Over 400,000 people are employed by companies founded in the past 10 years (https://www.s-ge.com/en/article/news/20221-ranking-new-start-ups). The high cost of doing business in Switzerland due to some of the highest average salaries ($80–100 K per year), combined with the presence of some of the world's best technology universities, which are funded by the government, means that the startups are largely value-driven, rather than providing slightly suboptimal solutions for a lower cost. This value-driven approach provides a strong barrier from competitors who try to provide a cheaper solution since customers focus more on quality and price is not a decision driver.

Apple faced this early in its evolution to becoming a trillion-dollar company. Apple was founded with a view to being different. In 1984, Steve Jobs was unceremoniously forced out of Apple. In the following years, Apple lost its way and its reason for existing so completely that in 1996, instead of producing world-class products, Apple was selling not only computers but also digital cameras, video consoles, TV appliances and CD players and was precipitously close to bankruptcy. Propitiously, Apple acquired Jobs' new company NeXT, which focused on designing and building high-end workstations for use in academia. This software was so effective that it was this software that Tim Berners-Lee worked on when he created the World Wide Web, while at CERN (https://www.macworld.co.uk/feature/apple/history-of-apple-steve-jobs-mac-3606104/)

When Jobs returned, he realised that the company he had founded had strayed from its DNA, providing an amazing experience to the end-user. He decided to stop all products other than the core that Apple had started with, the computer. Although over time, Apple has expanded to other products, it has stayed true to its initial focus of providing beautiful products that provide amazing experiences to end-users.

To have a startup that not only scales but also continues to hold on to the market it creates begins with the vision of the founders. This is easy to ignore when you're starting up, when your main objective is to get the first angel investment and the first paid pilot. It's as easy to ignore when you look at the startups that have become unicorns, because retrospective vision is always 20:20. When you look at the startups that have scaled successfully *after* they have done so, it's more difficult to remember the times when they almost didn't make it, or at the colossal errors of judgement that subsequently become propitious pivots of good fortune.

However, there must be some cornerstones that can help the entrepreneur scale seamlessly or avoid errors of judgement that can ultimately doom the future of her (or sometimes, his) startup. In this book, we address the most important ones and capture insights that are early indicators of what founders need to do, or more importantly, avoid doing, to convert their idea into a billion-dollar company.

Whether you're an entrepreneur starting a technology startup or platform startup, the following chapters will enable you to ask critical questions that will help you to have more clarity regarding what your solution is worth to your customers, how to increase stickiness, how to scale and finally, how to sustain value.

5

Technology Startups: Machinery and Manufacturing

Converting a technology startup into a billion-dollar company is very different from doing so to a platform startup. With a platform startup, the important steps, as articulated in the previous chapter, involve doing certain things to capture user traction. In the case of a technology startup, this deals with what not to do.

Technology Leadership

A technology team considers commercialisation when the technology has achieved global technology leadership. However, in certain cases, the team begins with a perception of value that the market would appreciate. While this is a perfectly appropriate and even a preferred strategy in the case of platform startups (covered separately), it does not always bode well for tech startups. This is because unlike a platform startup, a tech startup's success depends on much more than simply finding a market gap or being able to showcase the perception of value in a given customer segment. Although these are crucial, it is the startup's capability to deliver products that determine its success.

It is perfectly okay for a platform startup to be tech-agnostic. It would not be advantageous to lock itself to any given technology since end-users do not care about the technology used but only the user experience. If a platform startup finds a better technology that serves its needs or enables it to provide a better or more stable user experience, it needs to retain the flexibility to make the switch. In contrast, technology startups need to ensure that the technology works. When serial entrepreneurs who have prior experience with platform startups start a technology startup, they tend to focus on the market need and address this gap. They often forget that unlike platform startups, technology startups cannot be, by definition, technology-agnostic. This cardinal error of ignoring the capability of the technology to become commercialisable is what often dooms tech startups.

The route to becoming a unicorn deals as much with what the startup should do as it does with what the startup should not. Technology startups take specific steps to transition this technology from the lab towards commercialisation. Let us look at these steps and how they impact their ability to scale (Fig. 5.1).

Fig. 5.1 Overview of considerations to scale and sustain value in technology startups

We now delve deeper into the factors that determine the capability of technology startups to scale, as well as their actions that ultimately limit scaling into a unicorn.

Machine Customisation

When a tech startup begins the process of commercialisation, the cofounders are often fully capable of creating not only the product but also the machine and the software needed to make it work. Since they emerge from the research domain, they often have the baggage of trying to optimise output with limited funding. This is because of the funding challenges during research, their inability to afford professional machines and being forced to create one from spare parts. This results in creating prototype machines that do the job but are often notorious for their lack of stability. These machines also need someone with a PhD to ensure that they run. The greater challenge is the team's false assessment that this is the correct strategy to commercialise.

With a direct comparison between the prices of commercially available machines and machines built by them, the team's opinion regarding building their machines gets further crystallised. This is because the commercial machines seem far more expensive, whereas the technology team obtains gratification from having created yet another innovative machine capable of running a proprietary process. This, however, leads to some problems that limit scale or become hurdles in doing so. These factors and their impact on the startup's agility are covered below (Fig. 5.2).

Custom Components

By building its own machines, the team invariably veers towards nonstandard or custom components. Although this seems logical to the team having done this during research, it becomes an enormous challenge to ensure that these parts continue to be available in the future. Thus, what begins by being a matter of convenience and cost optimisation becomes an enormous hurdle, since component specifications, thresholds and tolerances are not only not thought through, but the weakest tolerances often become the major bottleneck. During scale-up, this results in the team spending ever-increasing efforts to make the machine perform on a stable basis and deliver consistent performance at 99% uptime, which is often the minimum requirement by the customer.

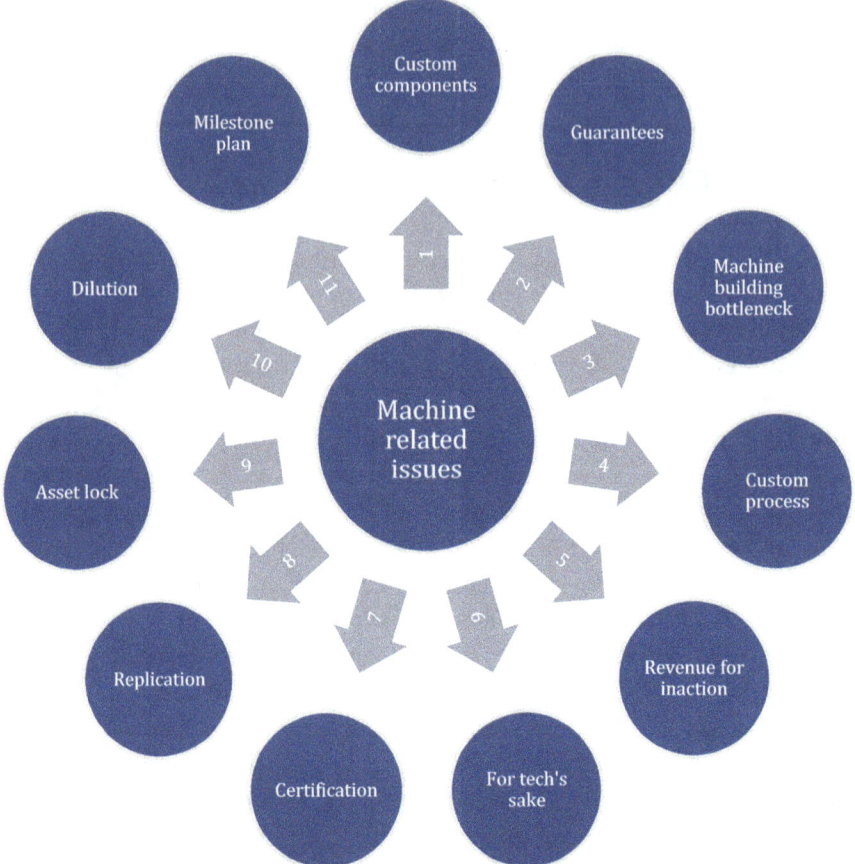

Fig. 5.2 Overview of machine 'make or buy' decision

Guarantees

Since the team creates their own machines from spare components, the main focus is to build a prototype machine that works and provides output that the team has innovated. This is an important step since it helps the team ascertain whether their technology can transition from pure research to the first pilot machines. The reason this is important is because many scientific results cannot be replicated outside the lab due to variables specific to the lab equipment.

Therein lies the risk. The challenge with using spare components is that they are nonstandard. The tolerances of the various components also differ based on their expected use and built-in obsolescence date. This results in a situation where the entire machine is as stable as the least stable components.

Beyond this, components, particularly electronic ones, have an irksome habit of becoming obsolete just as you figure out how to make them work. Since it is likely that the components used by the team to build the prototype machine are those that are just lying around as spare parts, they are likely to be closer to obsolescence than to just having been innovated.

As the startup begins to scale and replicate its machines, it runs into the problem of being unable to easily acquire components as they are scaled out and quality issues since the least robust components determine the stability of the entire machinery. Due to the time invested in developing and customising the technology with suboptimal machines, it becomes very difficult for the startup to recover from or avoid a down round due to the paucity of funds and missed milestones related to performance and stability.

Machine Building Bottleneck

The capability to build the pilot machine often addresses a completely wrong problem, which is: is it imperative to build it in the first place. Startups often underestimate the expertise needed to build in scale. Therefore, the primary focus tends to be innovation. When these startups look at commercial machine manufacturers, they often see only the high price of these machines compared to one that they might design and that might 'do' what the expensive machines promise. They fail to see the focus on using standards that these machine manufacturers have and the seamless supply chain. They also completely underestimate the service and support available when the machines do not work from day one. Technology entrepreneurs also fail to recognise that just because you can build something does not mean it has the same high value as your technology innovation. Value, after all, is what is perceived by the customer. This perception is driven as much by the technology as it is by the utilisation. If the customer is able to find alternatives in the market that do the same things, he is likely to compare the equipment on price rather than the value as perceived by the tech entrepreneur. The second thing that drives value is utilisation. One can easily imagine the perceived difference in value for a delicate silicone valve that makes a coffee machine work from a similar machine that is inside a pacemaker, since one makes slightly better coffee and the other extends life.

Custom Process

When technology entrepreneurs transition from the lab to the startup, their confidence in being able to create new solutions to address the marketplace is based on the technology as well as their own proprietary process. In turn, the process is frequently based on steps that are not patentable but provide the special output that differentiates them from existing solutions.

The main problem with custom processes is that they limit the replicability of the solution. Thus, if the startup wishes to provide the technology with the integrated process as a solution, it is limited in its capability to outsource. Therefore, the startup can only source components and integrate the process before creating the final solution. Thus, no turnkey solutions are possible, limiting the capability of the startup to leverage the manufacturing capability of ancillary equipment manufacturing firms. Another challenge is that since the custom process is not protected under patent protection, there is always a risk of knowledge proliferation. This can happen if key employees leave, on during collaborations with research entities, or via equipment suppliers.

Finally, the startup needs to ask an important question: is there relevance of the custom process in the mind of the customer? If there is, the incremental value for the customer needs to be equated against the risks inherent to the custom process, as discussed above. Often, there isn't. One example of this was Optotune.

Manuel Ashwanden, the founder of Optotune, was researching new ways of creating tuneable lenses during his PhD at ETH in the early 2000s. This was just before the first iPhone came out, so the market was still not accustomed to a smartphone. He had innovated a lens that could change its focus on the basis of an electric current, compared to the existing solution, where two lenses would require a motor to constantly change their focus by moving one lens back and forth. Although the market was not driven by B2C digital camera solutions, the B2B market was already enormous, right from mobile scanners to scanners scanning the price code at departmental stores.

This addressed an enormous market need, since the existing solutions had a lifetime of focussing up to five million times due to the constant motor movement, whereas Manuel's solution could go on for over two billion times due to the absence of mechanical moving parts. However, his innovation needed customised equipment and was complex to manufacture. He looked for existing solutions that had similar functionality to bridge the long time between technology innovation and market need. He realised that headphone speakers had used technology that used oscillating electric current, which in turn vibrates the diaphragm, causing sound waves to create sound. Furthermore, this was a completely mature technology, and the equipment needed to manufacture it was commercially available without the need to licence patents or the risk of FTO being blocked. Therefore, despite having innovated a complex technology to create tuneable lenses, Manuel decided to use the existing technology to create innovative lenses. The technology that had enabled him to identify a market need was in effect not needed to address it. With close to 400 people today, most of them are highly qualified and specialised, servicing ever-growing customer needs due to lightweight cameras with high-speed focusing requirements. Optotune is successful and scalable. All this was only possible because Manuel looked at existing manufacturing to address a market need rather than innovating from the ground up.

Revenue for Inaction

A technology entrepreneur innovated LiDAR technology for specific applications. As background, LiDAR (*light detection and ranging*) helps to evaluate distance from an object by shining a laser and calculating the time for it to be reflected, as well as the wavelengths reflected, to calculate the distance and create 3-D representations of the object. His question was how to define market focus. With the assumption that the market in 2025 for LiDAR was likely to be approximately $2.5 billion, that was significant enough to be interesting. However, as any technology entrepreneur will recognise, customers do not buy technology. They buy solutions to the problems they have, whether it is gaining a competitive advantage, driving up revenue or bringing down costs. It is also clear that different customer groups have different scopes of criticality of the problems they expect to address. The higher the criticality, the more they are willing to pay for the solution. The longer the criticality exists, the longer they are likely to keep paying.

The last point is particularly relevant for startups. The longer the criticality exists, the longer the startup has the opportunity to obtain revenue from the customer. However, if we take this one step further, we also realise that by capturing the customer's data generated to enable better responses or decisions, the startup can strengthen its lock-in with the customer. The lock-in enables the startup to outcompete future competitors or even commoditization or automation of the technology.

Returning to the entrepreneur's question regarding what market to address, it is important to keep in mind that markets pay for the perception of risk. He had identified two market segments. One was logistics, where LiDAR could be integrated into drones and robots for moving materials within large warehousing facilities. The second was village communities in mountain areas, where the risk of avalanches was likely to become more significant over time due to the impact of climate change on permafrost. In logistics, the pricing of LiDAR was likely to be based on the activity it enabled. Therefore, the cost was always likely to be under pressure, since if a better or cheaper solution came along, the startup's solution would likely be replaced. In the case of the village communities, the LiDAR solution was meant to provide an early warning regarding the possibility of an avalanche. Additionally, the solution's capability to provide risk assessment in case of an avalanche to livestock, assets and homes, as well as human lives, would make it more valuable over time.

The basis for revenue of the LiDAR solution for logistics was what it enabled or for action. The revenue basis in village communities was for inaction since inaction provided safety to the community. Beyond this, identifying community risk provided a lock-in with insurance companies as downstream customers. Since customers pay most and for the longest periods of time to mitigate the perception of risk, addressing this question early helped the startup to sustain value and avoid commoditization for much longer, while increasing data relevance made it more attractive as an acquisition opportunity and an exit opportunity for the founders.

For Tech's Sake

Many entrepreneurs build startups for the sake of the technology. This is more prevalent in Continental Europe than in the USA. While it is common to find tech startups in the USA doing funding rounds and building manufacturing factory layouts as well as a sales network without having finalised the technology, this would be not only shocking in Europe but absolutely impossible to achieve because no investor would fund this. However, starting with the technology risks locking the startup in what might be seen as an inefficient process or one that does not scale well.

The great challenge is that these entrepreneurs are often in love with the technology, rather than by its capability to create impact. Where this becomes a problem is when these entrepreneurs realise that the impact is not clearly articulated or is not addressing a pain point for the customer and ignore it! They then continue to try and find revenue sources where the technology can showcase relevance. Since the only customer segment that still values technology for the sake of technology is research within universities, the startup finds a small and static market there. This can provide adequate revenue to keep the startup alive on an operational level, just about covering the salaries of the founders, particularly if this is augmented by additional state or multigovernmental support such as EU funding programmes. Over a period of time, it becomes increasingly difficult to scale these technologies, and they ultimately become completely commercially irrelevant and disappear over a period of time.

Certification

Markets never require technology; they need solutions. When a startup has prowess in custom-designing machines to manufacture its products, it fails to recognise its own strength, which is in breakthrough technology. By designing and creating its own machines, the startup removes of its area of competence into an area where breakthrough technology competence is replaced by adherence to standards and guaranteeing that if business scales and more machines are needed, the team has the capability to deliver. While breakthrough technology is able to produce breakthrough output, the focus of machine manufacture is to ensure 'boring'. 'Boring' implies that the machine has the necessary certifications, clearly defined uptime, servicing schedule and ease of servicing and replacement of consumables.

I began my first company for the manufacture of flexible solar cells using a semiconductor based on copper-indium-gallium-selenium. The various materials had to be evaporated between 700 °C and 1300 °C to achieve multiple layers of the right thickness, the thinnest being 30 nanometres and the total thickness being 2.5 microns (for reference, a human hair is 100 microns, and there are 1000 nanometres in a micron). The technology team's competence also extended to creating the machine, since they had innovated the technology in the lab using custom machines. When we created the first pre-pilot machines, the team simply extended the evaporation sources needed without any consideration to the replenishment of the materials consumed. Over time, we realised that the material consumption took less than a week, at which point the machines needed to be fully opened and reset. The reset or reconfiguration took 3–4 days due to the precise nature of the desired semiconductor layers. Beyond this, opening the machines also meant that there was a risk of contamination and minor impurities. This forced us to build an expensive clean room, costing significant money and time, all of which could have been avoided if we had gotten the machine built to our specifications. All in all, a rather expensive and time-consuming cost and time optimisation exercise.

Replication

One of the greatest challenges of technology companies trying to take tech out of the lab is replicability. The challenge stems from research itself, since machines are often custom-designed and modified on an on-going basis to obtain different results, with the ultimate goal of obtaining results that are superior to whatever exists. In this way, it is very similar to the evolution of life, where there has been constant evolution, which continues to this day. Ultimately, the aim of evolution is to modify the species to make it more fit to survive in a continuously evolving world. In the same way that one of the greatest strengths of our ancestors who evolved in Africa was the ability to run incredible distances, in order to hunt animals including horses to the point where the animals simply collapsed with exhaustion, our future generations may have specially evolved thumbs for continuous scrolling on smartphones, at the cost of distance vision, since a large part of the waking day is today spent gazing at a mobile screen.

The challenge in research is that the main focus is not how to replicate the results but how to obtain different results each time with a view towards constant improvement. Beyond the physical attributes of the research, the mindset of the researchers is that innovation is the most highly regarded activity and engineering is simply plebeian. However, transitioning from a technology to a startup implies the ability to supply products to customers. This entails an early focus on high-throughput replicability, where the output has built-in stability. To focus on replication, the tech entrepreneurs have to focus on machine redesign, moving away from the innovative mindset to focussing on standardisation of machine design that enables replicability.

Asset Lock

Any technology startup has to consider two things when taking tech to the market: successful tech transition from lab to the market and minimisation of dilution. Let us look at these in more detail.

The process of technology transition from lab to large-scale production is fraught with risks in the form of key decision points. Whatever manufacturing equipment the startup invests in may end up being suboptimal, since over time, the design evolves to increase efficiency. The output is seldom planned in the beginning since it is impossible to properly gauge the market traction. The team often focuses on manufacturing flexibility rather than streamlining output when the pilot manufacturing facility is designed. Therefore, flexibility is always at the cost of manufacturing optimisation. Finally, setting up in-house manufacturing risk customisation becomes a hurdle when scale-up or subsequent outsourcing needs to be considered. As we observe, a wrong decision in any of these areas risks limiting the scale of the startup for a long period of time.

In fact, the best strategy regarding acquiring manufacturing assets is to keep them as industry standard as possible, rather than having a specific strategic alignment with a machine manufacturer, particularly if this is a mature technology. This will eliminate any risk that the machine manufacturer uses this lock-in as a negotiation tactic to capture greater profit or for the tech startup to be competitively disadvantaged on account of a machine manufacturer that is less competitive due to build- and design-quality, stability or throughput.

Dilution

Dilution occurs either when investors come in with a large amount of investment at an early stage when the company value is low or when investors include future valuation caps for future rounds of funding or a higher conversion multiple when their preference shares are converted into equity. Here, we discuss the impact of obtaining a large amount of investment early.

There are sound arguments for raising as much money as you possibly can, since investors may change their minds or find another dalliance tomorrow. Even large companies can do this to stave financial uncertainty. Few in the US car industry can forget the auto company crisis of 2008.

On November 29, 2006, the Ford CEO Alan Mulally invited top bankers to a packed ballroom in a New York hotel and made a simple proposition; he wanted to raise money by mortgaging all of Ford's assets. Given that Ford was not in dire straits, this sent a ripple in the leading automakers, and Ford was derided for this decision. However, Mulally was able to raise $23.6 billion in loans. By doing so, he was not only ensconcing Ford from future recessions or other unexpected events or market slowdowns. He also recognised that cash provided the means to build a future competitive advantage since all existing assets risked becoming liabilities and a drag on Ford's flexibility to respond if the demand dynamics evolved dynamically (https://www.cnbc.com/id/30134908).

Soon after Ford got its loan, the market dropped off a cliff due to the housing crisis less than a year later. The auto market collapsed, and the other two Detroit majors, GM and Chrysler, had to both go to the markets, begging bowls in hand, looking for white knights, to stave bankruptcy. GM found one in the form of Fiat and is now a subsidiary of Fiat, whereas Chrysler is now part of Germany's Daimler group. Ultimately, it was Fiat that lived to see another day, and of the big three from Detroit, it continues to be the only surviving independent car maker.

One of the largest competitive advantages that a startup has against large incumbent players is that it does not have any existing asset base that needs to be utilised due to the enormous investment that has gone into building and maintaining it. It is important for the startup to maintain this advantage for as long as possible. This is because over a period of time, any legacy assets become a liability since they take away the entity's flexibility to cater to evolving demands with equal flexibility in supply. Startups often fail to realise that the pilot plant is not meant to get the startup to the black. It's only meant to show the route to getting there and help the startup in raising a larger round of funding (at a much higher valuation) to getting there. Only once product maturity has been achieved can the startup consider insourcing the manufacturing to further drive product throughput and optimise product cost.

There is one good reason why a tech startup should consider doing manufacturing in-house. This is if the core IP in the form of process know-how resides in the manufacturing process itself. This is the scenario where the manufacturing does translate to a multiplier effect of funding. Scrona is one such company.

Scrona makes print heads. These are similar to the print heads used in household printers but for two key differences. First, they are up to a million times smaller in volume than inkjet droplets. Second, they function not by pushing the material to be printed but by pulling the material from the tip of the print head due to ionisation, called electrostatic droplet actuation. This enables the size of the droplet to be dramatically smaller than the tip of the nozzle. The markets include touchscreens with resolutions beyond anything that is available, ultra-secure identity cards or even micro-LEDs. In your reading this book on a flexible ultrathin display or on your AR/VR headset, it's entirely possible that you're seeing the impact of Scrona's technology. The technology of creating print heads enables tens of thousands of nozzles in a square cm of space. Based on this, it is clear that although the company could progress to the market faster by outsourcing some of the process steps and minimising the machine investment cost, this would risk IP proliferation.

Based on the above example, it is clear that for an early-stage technology that may have multiple application areas for the future, there are more opportunities for IP capture, both for technology and design, and it is wise for the startup to keep manufacture in-house.

Milestone Plan

Most technology entrepreneurs assume that their customer is their first customer. Counterintuitive as it may be, this is often not the case. If we assume that the customer is the one who gives the money, the first customer of the startup is actually the investor. The customer merely demonstrates the future viability of the business to the investor.

To showcase the steps towards achieving its viability and full potential, the startup needs to prepare a milestone plan. This does two things. First, it takes the steps from where the technology is to where it needs to be to demonstrate the first product rollout or show initial market relevance. Second, it links the funding asked for with the milestones planned. It is important to keep in mind that investors do not fully understand operational challenges. It is also fair to say that for the most part, investors do not really care about operational milestones such as hiring people or setting up machines. What they do care about are the milestones that the startup achieves in the time it promises. This is also what they measure the startup against. The reason for this is that each milestone achieved reduces risk, beginning with technology risk, then manufacturing risk and finally commercial risk via scale. In turn, each milestone increases the value of the startup, making it more attractive for future rounds of investors. Ultimately, for financial investors looking for a financial return on their investment, metrics that show how the value of their investment increases are key to getting them onboard. The milestone plan provides them with this comfort and keeps the team's focus on transitioning the technology to the market, rather than technology improvement in isolation.

The milestone plan looks backwards as well. It begins by looking back to when everything began and captures the highlights of achievements pertaining to the technology, team and initial market development and validation. The milestones already achieved provide confidence to investors about the competence of the team. This translates to strengthening the pre-money valuation during investor negotiations. This is pertinent even if the startup addresses existing investors. By highlighting the milestones achieved, the startup is able to increase the value at which existing investors invest again, or at the very least, limit the reduction of valuation, in case no new investors can be found for the upcoming round of funding.

As the startup progresses, it does not just address larger investors. Investors are intrinsically different and look for different things. In other words, the specific elements that may have enabled the startup to raise an earlier round may not be the conditions that the next round of investors look at.

Zurich Cantonal Bank (ZKB) is a Swiss regional bank focusing on supporting businesses in the Zurich region. Beyond the focus on profitability, it also provides an extension of the fiscal policy of the Swiss National Bank, in a way that international banks such as UBS do not. One of the activities of ZKB has been to support startups that often come from ETH Zurich. This is by way of proving a soft loan of approximately $ 0.5 m, based on strong technology. After providing this for over 100 startups, ZKB realised that most of the startups were unable to progress towards the next round of funding. It turned out that since the startups received funding based on technology excellence and there was very little oversight after the loan was granted, the startups continued to work on improving the technology. The reason this became a problem was that the investors who evaluated the startup for the next round of funding expected an articulation of the market need and initial steps in getting market traction, rather than simply further improvement in the technology. In the absence of the business case, the startups were unable to attract future investors. Furthermore, as ZKB was unable to provide any follow-up funding, the startups often ended up going bust. Since the startups were led by technology founders, they felt most comfortable doing research. The only time they contacted ZKB was when they had funds for 2–3 months remaining, and at this time, it was simply too late to begin getting traction in the market or hitting the milestones needed by the next round of investors.

The milestone plan thus needs to encapsulate not only the operational steps that the team needs to take but also address the three risks that afflict any technology startup: the technology risk, the manufacturing risk and finally the commercial risk. Initial investors invest based on the excellence of the technology. However, as the startup advances and prepares for future investors and larger rounds, it needs to begin addressing risks around manufacturing, including outsourcing and getting partners onboard. Whatever the focus of the startup, and whatever the geography, it is imperative for the startup to recognise that as it advances with funding rounds, it needs to address fundamentally different risks in its milestone plan with the investors' funds at each stage of funding. It is thus not adequate to address challenges effectively, but the recognition of the problems that need addressing. This is the basis of ensuring relevance for the next round of investors or being attractive for a potential acquirer.

Manufacturing

In principle, manufacturing always denotes stability since a complex manufacturing process entails substantial investment. It also deters competitors, who, in addition to having no credibility in the given market and for the given customer base, also need deep enough pockets to develop and stabilise. This was, after all, the basis of the industrial revolution: the capability to manufacture on a large scale.

While this served the large industrial giants well, particularly during low-tech churn and stable and long industrial cycles, it becomes a severe limiting factor if tech evolves at a rapid pace. In such cases, any established manufacturing system risks becoming a white elephant if the company changes the complete manufacturing line to address evolving customer needs. It is thus forced to use the existing infrastructure; however, it might be suboptimal for next-generation products. It is exactly this element that over time weakens incumbents in any industry. While new entrants try to determine end-user challenges and the best possible solution that may address this, incumbents begin by looking at their spare manufacturing capacity. The seeds of obsolescence, as seen from this, lie within the DNA of each company.

Mindset of Manufacturability

Startups often underestimate the criticality of having a mindset of manufacturability. This does not imply focussing on manufacturing. Quite the contrary. To scale, the startup needs to get out of the tech mentality at the earliest. What it does imply is that the startup recognises that standardisation of the manufacturing process be put in place.

A common problem of tech startups is that they focus on the tech, to the exclusion of rapid manufacture. The tendency to try and do everything in-house and customise their way out of problems that arise becomes an enormous hurdle as the startup begins scaling.

Standardising and looking at ways to automate manufacturing enables rapid scale-up. Beyond this, the next step in the mindset of manufacturing entails identifying entities that have existing capabilities to manufacture components that can be easily integrated to make the product. This does two things. It frees up capital of the startup so that it needs to raise less capital, thereby keeping equity dilution low. The capital the startup raises can then be used to focus on building market relationships. As the startup does not know what the optimal size of the manufacturing facility will be, it does not need to block funds into developing manufacturing facilities of suboptimal size. The second is that a supplier ecosystem gets more entities onboard who have a vested interest in the success of the startup. Furthermore, getting a manufacturing entity onboard ensures that if there are challenges in getting everything to work, the experience of the manufacturing entity becomes a source of free and valuable advice. If all else fails, the manufacturing entities often provide guarantees so that they take the onus of ensuring that stuff works. These manufacturing entities are often far more clued into evolving standards as well as knowing what components are nearing obsolescence. For a startup to know that its effort is using components that will continue to be available is critical and often determines the face of startups.

Startups often begin with doing everything in-house. Their mindset of manufacturing is driven by three assumptions. To begin with, because they can. In addition, then, because it's far cheaper. In addition, finally, because it's faster. However, beyond the initial prototype, focusing on rapid manufacturability frees them to focus on standardisation in manufacturing. This is very different from the initial mindset of research-driven startups, which focus on doing something new every day and rapid and varied prototyping. By outsourcing manufacturing, the startup is able to look for the areas where value resides.

These are the initial set of tools and reference points to help in determining how technology scales and the hurdles that stop them from doing so.

6

Technology Startups: Maximising Product Value, from the Customer's Perspective

The second set of challenges that limit technical startups from scaling are discussed below.

Logistics

One of the least appreciated elements of scaling up for hardware-based tech startups is the value of logistics and the supply chain. This is driven by the early stages of the startup's evolution, when the focus is on creating the product and showcasing it to customers. However, as soon as the startup delivers something that is acceptable to customers, the latter begin to request it in increasingly larger quantities.

This gap between supply and demand is endemic for tech startups. Often, the main difference between success and failure is how fast the startup is able to determine its delivery challenges. The assumption is that the startup is not manufacturing everything in-house. This is an important assumption, since as discussed earlier, all components are very seldom value-added. For the cost-driven or commoditised components, it is critical for the startup to outsource them. Outsourcing as many components as possible also helps the startup scale faster by remaining lean. However, this requires expertise in a supply chain that scales, right from component ordering to validating quality, all the way through to getting the product in the hands of the customer. By putting the right system in place early, the startup can mitigate future challenges that otherwise hinder scale.

Component Vs Solution

Startups often have such an all-consuming focus on their solution that they omit connecting this with the market need. There are several factors that impact the value of the solution to the customer. Having insights about this can enable the startup to not only charge more money for their solution but also to make money for longer, which is far more pertinent. The factors to consider are whether the startup's product is considered a solution or a component and whether it is for the customer's in-house consumption or for sell-through.

Internal Component

Condis began in Switzerland in 1903 as Fabrique Suisse de Condensateurs. It sells medium- and high-voltage solutions, including capacitors, to utilities around the world. Its first large breakthrough was in 1908, when it sold a 110,000 V battery to the Eiffel Tower. Held as a privately owned company for close to a century, it was sold to Maxwell in 2003. Over time, Condis management realised that US culture was very different from the Swiss style of management. The Swiss culture was more geared towards sustainability and generational stability, whereas the US work style was more transactional. Therefore, the Condis management realised that Maxwell would ultimately move production to a lower-cost country such as China from Switzerland due to the short-term cost benefits on account of the dramatically lower salary costs. The transactional approach of US management meant that in the short-term, the manufacturing cost would indeed decrease, although over time, the quality would likely degrade, and the innovations would plateau. However, in the meantime, the US company would have already exited from the business with a trade sale. In 2018, Condis brought its own freedom from Maxwell by way of a management buy-out by getting Swiss investors onboard. As it transpired, the Condis management was right, as soon after the management buy-out, Maxwell itself was sold to Tesla.

The products sold by Condis are considered components by utilities for their own use in the transmission of electricity. Thus, the capacity of Condis to drive super profits is limited. Since the risk of commoditisation always looms, Condis needs to consciously showcase reliability based on decades of experience and Swiss standards of quality. Pivoting customers' attention to the risk of failure of a national power line and the consequent domino effect on national security and on industries is an effective lever to retain customers while continuing to sell at a premium rather than simply trying to compete on cost with competitors. Decision-makers within customers are willing to pay more to avoid the risk of failure, particularly if this failure happens in their watch. By highlighting the internal component's ability to mitigate the risk of this failure, it is possible to get customers to sign off, particularly if there is a likelihood of the failure occurring in the foreseeable future.

Internal Solution

Fanuk is a world leader in industrial robots for manufacturing. Their focus is productivity to improve performance and profitability and optimisation of high-precision processes. These are largely complete solutions, and customers largely know their value in precision manufacturing.

Fanuk has a challenge. This is because it provides a solution that is better than existing solutions. In other words, Fanuk helps its customers do exactly what its competitors do, but does it better or more precisely. This implies that the super profits of Fanuk are a percentage of the improvements that it enables in its customers compared to its competitors. This can be a limiting factor for Fanuk because as its competitors improve their technology or reliability, Fanuk's profits risk going down to industry levels and will put pressure on its premium pricing. As technology to build robots becomes increasingly automated, it risks becoming commoditised. However, beyond this, the real risk is that new technology may make the incumbent technology obsolete, as we begin to see the advent of soft robotics, made of silicon with joints driven by air pressure rather than heavy motors.

One way to mitigate the risk of competitive pressure is to extend the value for customers. Thus, instead of simply enabling customers to perform more precision manufacturing, additional value could include the capability to inform customers if there is likely to be a failure point in the manufacturing. This would imply that the robot goes beyond analysing its own health and begins to analyse the health of the external environment to pre-empt risks or enable better manufacturing decisions. This could be done by analysing manufacturing patterns and highlighting anomalies. Over time, additional information could enable Fanuk to provide more precise diagnostic information to customers that could have an impact on quality, throughput or yield, thus increasing its perceived value and stickiness.

Interestingly, Fanuk has begun integrating IOT solutions into its robots. The question of how it will continue to compete as the entire vertical becomes commoditised and is superseded by new technology is yet to be answered.

ANYbotics is a Swiss startup doing robotic solutions. Their robot is able to climb steps and walk in a predefined route. It could be argued that this can be done by other commoditised robots. However, the focus of ANYbotics is industrial inspection, and in the markets that this solution addresses, trust in data is critical to pre-empt and identify possible risks. These markets include offshore oil and gas, chemical plants and mining. The ANYbotics robot 'ANYmal' is able to capture heat signatures and gas leaks using sensors. Furthermore, by analysing the risks posed by a combination of these factors changing in concert, the ANYmal is able to identify possible risks. For instance, a gas leak from a high-pressure gas line in an electricity utility may not be a reason to worry, but if the gas is inflammable and is in proximity to an electrical line or motor that overheats, it could risk an explosion, resulting in loss of life and breakdown of energy supply. The ANYmal is thus able to provide this information on an on-going basis to the machine operator. Furthermore, it may be possible to suggest optimal running conditions by using the data from other similar equipment installed in other facilities and the ideal servicing schedule. Thus, over time, the value of the ANYmal solution is not only in the data it captures to ensure safety but also in the pre-emptive assessment of risk optimisation and reduction of service-based downtime. This enables increased stickiness with customers even if other lower-cost robots emerge in the future.

Sell-Through Component

More often than not, the product provided by the startup is not a complete solution but a component for a larger solution sold further by the corporation.

Bharat Forge is one of India's leading companies and is led by its chairman Baba Kalyani. His aim was to provide a superlative product with a focus on quality as a basis for inspiring trust. With a deeply loyal workforce, Kalyani began to produce axels for the car industry. The quality of their solution was demonstrated by the fact that at the time of my meeting him in 2015, they were supplying axels for over 60% of all cars in the USA. Discussing the greatest challenges that lay ahead for him, Kalyani confided that it was two things. The first was that the axel, although a core part of the car's foundation, was still a component of the final solution. Therefore, his ability to charge super profits for this component was limited.

The second was the timeline to obsolescence. This implied that the greatest risk for Bharat Forge was not that a competitor would begin building better or cheaper axels but that axels would ultimately become unnecessary for cars. Given the emergence of Tesla into the mainstream, Kalyani's concerns were indeed propitious.

Sell-Through Solution

Intel makes chips. For the most part, the end-users do not know exactly what they do, but there is a clear perception that they make computers faster. Therefore, although most people would not recognise an Intel chip if it was augmented in them to boost their intelligence, they are quite willing to pay a premium for the privilege of buying a computer that has *Intel Inside*.

This is partially a result of sustained marketing by Intel to highlight how their chips are superior to others such as AMD. Beyond this, Intel has been able to recognise that most consumers have limited understanding and even more limited bandwidth to track features of computers. Since most users simply want to trust their decision about something they will buy perhaps once every few years, given the plethora of tech jargon, Intel becomes an easy way to gauge quality. Becoming a reference point for quality and a reason for the purchase has enabled Intel to sustain its high margins with computer manufacturers.

Although the Intel chip should be considered a component within the larger solution provided by its customer to end-users, it has been able to pivot being perceived as the most valuable part of the solution and indeed the one part that drives value. This is a critical pivot driven by capturing and becoming the value driver of the solution, effectively commoditising the other components of the solution.

If the startup has a solution that is being sold further as a solution by the customer, rather than as a component, the startup has a much greater opportunity to capture value. Startups often struggle to identify the correct price point for both internal components and internal solutions. A good way to recognise the appropriate price is to validate whether the customer uses the product of the startup to address existing challenges more efficiently or whether the product is being used to do something that the customer was previously unable to do. If the startup's product addresses better efficiencies, the product will always be under price pressure. Beyond this, the product risks becoming commoditised in the eyes of the customer if it does not provide new value.

The startup needs to actively pivot towards being recognised for providing a solution that enables the customer to create new value. Doing so ensures that the startup is able to sustain higher profits for longer even as it increases its footprint to scale.

Manufacturability

Most tech startups have best-in-class knowledge about the tech. Their competence around the tech is so deep that when they need machines to take the tech from the lab to the first level pilot, they simply go ahead and create the necessary machines to produce the product. While this showcases the capability of the team and often enables them to get an angel investor onboard, it does not ease the transition towards commercialisation.

Instead, the customised machine completely limits the scale-up of the startup. This is because when the customised machine is put together, the team often does it with whatever components that can find. Two things happen. The first is that the components are often nonstandard. Some of them are the latest innovations, whereas others are reaching the end of their lives, soon to be replaced by the next-generation tech. Thus, when the team decides to replicate the machine to scale the output, they are unable to find the components originally used to create the first machine. The second is that there is no guarantee for a machine created from spare parts, unlike a machine ordered from a machine manufacturer. Since the original machine is put together by the team using components that have varying levels of quality standards, the final machine is only as good as the component with the lowest quality threshold.

Beyond this, any customised machine always needs process control to provide the desired output. This implies writing and integrating software to make the machine actually do anything.

Take a coffee machine. Even if you put the coffee grain grinder, the water pump and electricals together, you don't automatically begin getting great coffee. No, for that to happen, you have to tell each component what to do. In addition, for this to happen, you need to write software that tells the machine how much coffee beans to grind, how fine the grind should be, the temperature and pressure of the water as it passes through the ground, the time that the water is in contact with the ground and finally, how to ensure that the coffee machine can do this for 20 cups of coffee a day for years on end, so that it can be serviced just before it stops working. In addition, this is just for a cup of coffee.

To mitigate all these failure points, it is imperative that the startup team put on-going tech developments on ice when they move them towards manufacturability. They then need to look at commercial machine options on which their product can be manufactured. This does not make the transition from research to pilot research easy. Quite the contrary. However, once the team is able to align commercial machines to produce their product, the scale-up becomes dramatically easier. Closer alignment with customers is also important at this stage since the customers will tell you what components they care about and, consequently, will pay money for. It is possible that the commercial or off-the-shelf machine may not provide the exact specifications or capabilities in the product. In such cases, this is an opportunity for the startup team to obtain feedback from their customers on the criticality of the missing attributes of the product manufactured from the commercially sourced machine. This helps the team to know if their customers' challenges are sufficiently addressed with their product from an externally sourced machine. Not surprisingly, this is most often the case. Rather than revealing their ability to create complex machines that create unique and not easily replicable products, the team should focus on rapidly scaling up to address a growing market need.

As the visual below shows, the more technical complexity the startup decides to own rather than outsource, the more the cost (more investment needed = further equity dilution) before the startup even knows if it will successfully be able to transition its technology into a fully replicable solution that can be manufactured in scale. This is before the commercial viability and sustainability of the solution can be demonstrated. This is called the timeline of uncertainty (Fig. 6.1).

For any startup, having a shorter timeline of uncertainty enables it to identify route to scaling, relevance and revenue with the minimum time and funding. The challenge that any startup has to address based on

1. If the startup plans to be a platform simply enabling conversations or transactions between two parties, it knows within a matter of months if it will work. This is like Facebook, which went viral by facilitating conversations.
2. If the startup wants to have its own content in addition to enabling conversations, it takes more effort since the content needs to be relevant, focussed and updated. Knowing whether this will succeed takes longer. Apple's iTunes store creates its own apps in addition to letting app developers put them online.
3. Startups often create their own software with off-the-shelf hardware. The software development takes time and often is considered risky by corporate customers due to integration challenges and security issues. It, however, enables strong lock-in due to hardware integrated with its software.
4. If the startup wants to create software with customised hardware product, the money required is significantly more, and it takes longer to find out if it will work. This is due to uncertainty for customers as well as the startup's

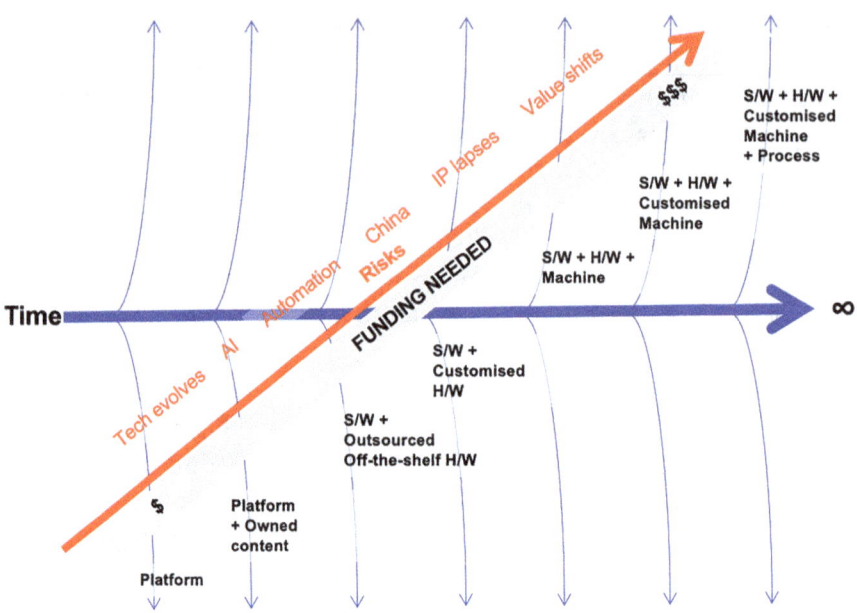

Fig. 6.1 Timeline before a startup knows if it will succeed

capability to manufacture. Most technology startups do this since it provides them with more control.

5. If the startup creates software and customised hardware and further, customises the machine on which the customised software runs and the custom hardware product is made, the money and time take is much more before the startup can even know if it will work. Deep-tech founders often try to do this. But unless there are compelling reasons and very deep pockets, this is a very high-risk strategy. In my first company we created our own machines and custom process in order to create unique products. Eventually, we tried to simplify manufacturing by getting industry-standard components, we lost valuable time and investor money to learn this. Although our initial estimate of total funding was about $15 m, it took over ten times that much, before we finally had our exit. We still failed to make it to unicorn. Although early entrepreneurs would consider raising this level of funding an accomplishment, it actually seemed like a betrayal towards investors, since they believe your vision and you effectively force them to keep investing. With close to 20 years from initial investment to exit, as a startup, it could be considered a failure.

6. The most challenging work that a startup can undertake is to create its own software that runs on custom-designed machines to create innovative and new products with a built-to-purpose process. Process innovation is far from trivial. Take a coffee machine. The process involves the time and temperature of the roast, the grind size of the bean, the pressure and precise temperature of the water that flows through the ground, and the duration for which the water interacts with the ground. All this for a cup of coffee. And as customers, we take it for granted, only recognising if the coffee is a bit off. The level of complexity means all the variables have to work before the startup can even know if it is likely to be successful. This entails high amounts of funding, often in the tens if not in the millions of dollars, and investors are loath to come onboard for this reason. Elon Musk did this with SpaceX. Although it may change the course of humanity by enabling us to go to Mars and beyond, it came perilously close to going bankrupt. The first three flights of SpaceX between 2006 and 2008 resulted in failures, almost bankrupting the company. The fourth flight was able to reach orbit, and the fifth flight was able to successfully launch a satellite into orbit.

Each additional variable increases the time and money required before the startup can demonstrate that it will succeed. We call this the timeline of uncertainty. With the long timeline, there is a risk that the external environment may change. This is driven by changes in software technology, AI, patent expiry and change in market relevance in the eyes of end-users. OpenAI is an example of how new technology completely renders the existing technology redundant. OpenAI's ChatGPT is capable of generating full code for a variety of purposes on a simple prompt. This work used to previously be done by highly qualified and highly paid software professionals.

It's imperative for the entrepreneur to assess the timeline of uncertainty and align with his cofounders, investors and customers. Misalignment of this timeline is one of the main reasons why startups fail, since they run out of time or money even though their value proposition is valid.

Mindset

Technology entrepreneurs often walk into entrepreneurship, expecting it to be like research. This attitude implies an expectation that the market should appreciate technology innovation. What they fail to realise is that investors see technology excellence every day and often several times per day. This does not impress them for good reasons: technology excellence does not always translate to commercial success. In continental Europe, for example, due to conservative attitudes relating to entrepreneurship, R&D goes on much longer than needed to bring a product to market. While many may consider this to be a good thing, the reality is that this often results in commercial obsolescence, since inferior technology identifies a market gap and forges ahead to address it.

Technology entrepreneurs often tend to overestimate their own relative importance and fail to consider the relevance of other skills that are as important to commercial success. By not recognising the criticality of other capabilities, they omit giving them a seat at the decision table. Contrary to their own view of keeping the same mindset in their startup, the technology entrepreneurs do themselves a disservice, since the research mindset is mostly top-down and research excellence oriented.

Top-down implies that decision-making is research focussed, which is done by the professor and communicated down. This is contrary to an inclusive environment, where ideas are not considered for their intellectual quotient but for a more pragmatic conversion to market. In fact, some of the most successful companies recognise the market need and pivot the technology to address it. ANT is one such company.

The ANT Group did not start as a conventional startup, with a technology trying to look for a market. It was in fact a solution to a problem that Jack Ma, the founder of Alibaba, had a lack of customer trust with existing payment mechanisms, which in turn impeded the growth of Alibaba's business. Weak consumer protection laws combined with quality control issues for goods online were key hurdles for people trying to buy goods online. As a response to this lack of trust, Jack Ma established Alipay to act as an intermediary, which would keep the buyer's money in escrow until satisfactory delivery was made, after which the money would be transferred to the seller.

By the end of 2006, over 300,000 merchants accepted Alipay as a recognised intermediary, largely driven by the credibility of Alibaba. However, this trust enabled it to spread beyond servicing Alibaba, and it began to attract and be the platform of choice for all kinds of product and service providers online. With government endorsement in 2010, its growth accelerated further. Today, it has in excess of 1.3 billion users, including over 300 million outside China, and made transactions of over USD 33 trillion in 2019. Based on the central position that it occupies in all transactions performed by an increasing number of users, it is likely that ANT is just getting started (https://marker.medium.com/how-ant-group-became-the-biggest-fintech-company-in-the-world-7afae29ec1d3).

Technology entrepreneurs often lack an understanding of what entrepreneurship entails. Indeed, they may already expect a reward for transitioning the technology into a startup. They then expect a cash-out simply for creating the startup and funding it with the first investors.

Beyond this, even if technology entrepreneurs decide to commercialise, they often want to be cautious and not overestimate, even if they do not achieve their stated goal. More critically, tech entrepreneurs often have aversion to sharing their 'baby' with external investors, for fear it might get taken away from them. This fear, together with their confidence in being able to generate modest revenue, makes them question the need to get investors while giving something they have created and being taken out of their comfort zone. Technology entrepreneurs often pride themselves in their ability to multitask or work on different technologies in parallel. However, as any successful investor knows, drive comes from focus. In addition, always having a plan B simply implies that you're not willing to give it your all to make it work.

Technology entrepreneurs are often unsure about market relevance. This leads them to address multiple markets or even to address any customer who comes along. This results in not being able to build a robust number of references in a given market segment. This forces them to expend valuable time and bandwidth in customisation for markets. Since this customisation effort cannot be used in other markets, this progressively puts them in a position of competitive disadvantage. While initial market testing and validation are necessary, it is important to focus on one to drive references, revenue, relevance and, ultimately, industry leadership.

Another challenge relating to mindset is being satisfied with less. Often, technology entrepreneurs focus on being in a niche, high-value sector where they are able to drive consistent revenue. However, this often plateaus off at a modest number, without the benefit of providing the startup with a buffer for future innovation. By not getting investors onboard, the startup also misses the opportunity to have successful and networked stakeholders rooted in its success and willingness to step in to bridge a funding, headcount or expertise gap.

Ultimately, this focus on 'niche' markets is a misnomer, since over time, competitors who may have begun by addressing a low-value high-volume market segment build capabilities. We saw this in the computer industry in the early 1980s. There were three categories of computers: supercomputers, midsize computers and desktops. Over time, desktops became increasingly powerful, partly due to Moore's law as well as due to economies of scale. Over time, the specific market for midsize computers simply got taken by desktops. This was also observed in countries over the past five decades. In the 1960s and 1970s, 'Made in Japan' was code for cheap and low quality. Today, Japanese goods compete with some of the most high-quality products anywhere. More recently, China took over that mantle, but over the past years, even China's quality has evolved, enabling it to compete for higher quality products, both in consumer and industrial segments. This is to the detriment of Western countries, which decided to outsource to China and are now finding that China is slowly outcompeting them with no recourse other than protectionism from Chinese products. This in turn is detrimental to customer choice and simply pushes higher costs or lower efficiencies and quality to the final customers. This is because once you outsource in the interest of short-term gain, you lose manufacturing capabilities that in turn drive economies of scale. On a national level, by deciding to insource, a country brings these inefficiencies to end customers in the form of price increases. By trying to make products after having lost its manufacturing capabilities on a national level, its own products are more expensive than competing products available elsewhere. This drives inflation, as seen in the UK post-BREXIT. This was the result of decades of outsourcing manufacturing, due to which experienced manufacturing knowledge was lost over time as people retired, young people did not choose to pursue engineering as there were no jobs in this sector, and manufacturing innovation had no place to thrive.

The mindset of technology entrepreneurs needs to rapidly transition technology to the market, with customer focus as the basis to achieve scale. Alignment between the cofounders is critical to leading in uncertainty. The importance of this is often underestimated. Even simple words such as 'success', 'scale', 'exit' or 'timeline' mean very different things to different cofounders. Words such as 'designation' add further complexity.

Teams often have very different perceptions of what timeline implies. 'Long-term' is 1.5 years in US startups since they often focus on platforms, and the market evolves incredibly fast. In Continental Europe, on the other hand, technology startups that have come from research that has taken 20–25 years in the lab consider 1 year to be short-term. In case they are in health care, the short-term is even longer, and the long-term can exceed 15 years. Similarly, 'success' for an entrepreneur from the USA may imply the ability to scale the solution to 20 countries in 5 years, whereas for his more conservative European counterpart, it may imply having 12 people and setting up a sales office in one or two countries outside the home country. Without early alignment and bringing potential areas of conflict to the fore, founders risk inability to make decisions that would enable them to scale or provide them the funding to do so.

In summary, mindset is as much about wanting to scale as it is with letting go of certain core tenets centred around research to begin to look at the world through the eyes of the customer. In addition, being able to see the world the customer sees it is the first step in getting him onboard, since he recognises that you're both going in the same direction.

Reaching Scale

Skiing entails standing on two unwieldy sticks that are almost your body length, with boots that are a couple of kilos each. These skis make it next to impossible to walk, as anyone who's learning how to ski attests. Once you've worn the skis, you get to a baby slope and try to ski down without falling too much. The next thing you learn is how to brake. You do this by bringing the front of your skis together keeping the back as far apart as possible. In addition, this is how you brake. Till it isn't.

As you graduate from the baby slope, you go to the blue slope, which is also very gradual like the baby slope, but much longer. Once you're comfortable skiing down the blue slope, you progress to the red slope, which is a lot steeper and you go a lot faster. You naturally brake the way you've learnt, but after doing this a few times, you begin to feel the pressure on your knees. In addition, skiing, which was fun till this point, begins to be less fun due to the persistent knee pain. At this point, if you have to graduate to the next braking technique, which is to keep your skis parallel and angled against the direction of the slope by taking a small jump as you're skiing down. At this point, skiing becomes effortless and fun again. Now, if you're so inclined, you could decide to proceed to the black slope, which is even steeper and narrower as well. You could easily go up to 125 km per hour on this slope. At this speed, if you were to brake using the original braking technique you had learned on the baby slope of putting your ski tips together, you have a fair chance of dislocating your knee or worse.

Thus, what you learn to begin skiing needs to be consciously unlearned to go faster. What got started is very different from what helps you go truly fast.

This is an important lesson that applies to startups. Tech startups start with knowing how to create the technology. However, as soon as you are able to link your technology competence to customer relevance, these same customers often see the technology as a competitive advantage or as a revenue driver. When this happens, the customers' demand for product increases dramatically and outstrips the startup's capability to deliver.

On the other hand, investors, who are invariably onboard by this time, are beginning to put increasing pressure on the startup to hit key milestones to attract new funding and ensure that the value of the equity held by the initial investors increases via a bump in the startup's valuation. The startup then proceeds to simply do what it has done to get to this point and continues organic growth rather than taking a hiatus to transition all its technology to a commercially available manufacturing setup. At this time, the startup addresses three problems.

1. Addressing ever-growing customer requirements and obtaining volume output to them of the same consistent quantity.
2. Organically building and scaling larger equipment to facilitate this output.
3. Managing investor expectations since this time, milestones have begun slipping on account of the challenges of transitioning technology to larger-scale manufacturing.

And as investor milestones slip, the startup gets ever more focussed on getting the machine together organically. All this while the startup may be missing the most important element, which is to own the impact of its own product, and thereby the value. More about the last one later.

However, the cardinal rule of startups is to address one problem at a time and select the one that is most critical. Furthermore, if the customer is the one who pays the startup, this is the investor in the initial stage. The customer is only to help the startup validate its market relevance rather than for revenue. Showcasing traction with the end customer is only to validate the business case and obtain the best terms possible with the investor. In the same way, the startup must already recognise the challenge that will determine its ultimate value in the market, that is, to reach volumes seamlessly once the solution has been proven. Early outsourcing becomes critical to scaling, since even when the startup scales, the startup has limited time to capture this value before the value transitions out of the product and into the user experience.

The team needs to have a realistic assessment of the maximum potential of the startup. The reality is that every startup cannot scale, and every business case or technology is not sustainable over a longer period of time. The risk of the team is that it falls in love with the idea of running the startup, rather than looking at it objectively. However, the best opportunity to sell the startup, if the team so desires, is when there is hope in the market about the potential rollout. A typical example is Apple. Each year in September, when Apple is about to announce the new iPhone, the price goes up in expectation. However, as soon as the iPhone is announced, the price dips, since the reality simply cannot keep up with all the expectations in the market and the actual product updates that happen have already been priced in.

The team will always be the first to know if their entire business is at risk of ultimate commoditisation. In such cases, a good strategy is to exit and sell when the market has future hope. This is discussed in more detail in the chapter on 'scale or sale'. However, if the company truly has value that will be sustained over time, the team must consciously stop doing certain things such as organic manufacturing scale-up and use off-the-shelf professional machines to ensure standardisation. Only then can the startup focus on not only scaling faster but also tracking the value transition as perceived by the customer. Startups that are able to capture this value transition are able to sustain value even as they scale.

Multiplier Effect of Money

This is one of the least appreciated elements of capturing value for founders when building a startup. When you raise a round of funding from investors, one of the main things to consider is how the value of the startup can increase. The main premise of using investor funds to drive up the value of their startup is that higher valuation results in lower dilution for the founders for their *next* round of funding. Investing in those areas that increase the startup's value by the highest amount results in minimising dilution with future funds, thus retaining the maximum equity possible with the founders.

However, the allocation of funds in different activities does not increase the value of the startup in a proportional manner. It is thus important for the startup to evaluate the fund allocation based on not only the operational activities but also how it helps the startup to increase valuation. This is because higher valuation of the startup during the next funding round would not only reduce the dilution of the founders but also enable them to negotiate more attractive conditions for funding.

Let us consider the multiplier effect with the example that you are dealing with at any point in time with your startup. When you raise a round of funding, this is allocated to various elements of the business. These include hiring people, doing pilots, including customisation for initial customers, setting up manufacturing, marketing activities and certification. Although each of these activities requires funds, the impact of the activities in increasing the value of the startup when you plan the next round of funding is not equal. The hiring of people, so long as this helps strengthen the team and fill in gaps, definitely helps. For example, a technical team focusing on manufacturing to hire a senior manufacturing or supply chain expert adds value to the startup. Pilots with customers provide references and the possibility of data. These in turn showcase the market relevance of the technology and drive the valuation. If you're able to get exclusivity from the pilot customers without giving it to them, this helps drive up the valuation further. Customisation, on the other hand, does not help and ties resources. Therefore, unless this customisation results in a customer lock-in, it is wise to consider outsourcing this.

Some of the decisions that founders face at the early stages of the startup include whether to insource manufacturing or focus on customer needs and soft factors such as data and personalisation. Since tech founders are most comfortable with technology, they often decide to keep all their manufacturing in-house. In doing so, they end up investing a lot of their investor funds in manufacturing that largely ends up being suboptimal compared to getting it done by a commercial supplier. Therefore, if the startup does all manufacturing instead of outsourcing parts of it, it ends up reinventing the wheel instead of using the knowledge available in the market. It also increases the cost of the product since it is never going to be as cost-efficient as the commoditised elements already available in the market. However, often, most parts of the manufacturing are possible with external entities. Outsourcing thus frees up resources for focusing on customer experience or customer data lock-in. In fact, setting up manufacturing is almost never a turnkey project and entails hiring people to manage the machinery, servicing the machinery and finally trying to obtain an output of the appropriate quality. It only makes sense to do this if there is IP around the machines or if the process is inextricably linked to the manufacture. If not, manufacture can truly hurt the increase in the valuation. Marketing activity is also an easy way to burn cash. Unless you're a social media startup or one focussing on B2C markets, marketing often provides a modest increase in valuation. Getting customers onboard, on the other hand, always increases valuation. Certification can make the difference between having R&D departments as customers and becoming mainstream if your sector focus is one that requires certification to be used by customers. Based on this, it is easy to see how looking at the multiplier effect, or working backwords from the drivers of valuation in the next round of funding, helps focus the startup on what matters. Interestingly, the same multipliers matter even if the startup considers a sale.

In fact, when money raised from investors is **not** put into areas that can have a multiplier effect in driving up valuation, it ultimately destroys company value. This happens because startups raise funding based on a given valuation. This valuation depends on a number of factors, including the articulated market need. In such cases, the utilisation of funding becomes important to ensure a multiplier effect, since future funding and valuation at which this happens depends on customer references and future traction in the larger market opportunity.

Entrepreneurs normally focus on the more urgent activities and activities that are within their core competence rather than those that the next round of investors measure them on.

As the visual shows, entrepreneurs do not just have to do what they have done better to attract the next round of investors and ensure a higher valuation but actually change what needs to be achieved.

Each funding round normally entails approximately one third of the company being given to the new round of investors. If the company raises USD one million, the investors are not as concerned about the areas where the company invests the money as they are about the milestones that the startup achieves. This is because the achievement of key milestones helps the startup raise more money at a higher valuation, giving a paper upside to the earlier investors. However, when the startup spends money on setting up suboptimal manufacturing, this becomes capital intensive. This high capital outlay is not only due to the machine cost but also due to the investment in the location, including clean rooms and hiring manufacturing people to manage and service the machine. If the startup outsources the noncritical part of this manufacturing, it would have the option to use a significant part of the investor funds to work more closely with customers and define the requirements, as well as focus on capturing the future value generated by providing the product to the customers. The funds used to drive customer pilots may have a multiplier of 5X. The manufacturing investment may only have a multiplier of 1.5X, as part of the manufacturing may be cost-driven or commoditisable (more about this later).

If the startup raises $1 m from investors at a post-money of $3 million and puts 70% of its funds into manufacturing and 30% into creating customer references, the post-investment value of the startup becomes $ 7.65 million ($3 m*0.7*1.5X + $3 m*0.3*5X).

Instead, if the startup uses 70% of the funds raised for creating customer references and 30% for manufacturing (including outsourcing), the post-investment value of the startup becomes $ 11.85 million ($3 m*0.7*5X + $3 m*0.3*1.5X).

Money is more than just money from the founders' perspective. If entrepreneurs see the money being spent as a percentage of the startup's valuation at the time, they would suddenly see the value in outsourcing any activity that does not increase the value of the startup. Thus, if the price of buying a noncritical machine is USD 500 K out of $ 1 m of funding raised from investors for which the startup has given away 30% equity, the effective cost of the machine is 15% of the company. This is equity that will never return to the founders. If the founders now recognise that their personal wealth at the time of the company sale is the equity they hold at that time, it is clear that the founders' wealth will be 15% less due to the machine investment.

This can be illustrated in what we call $1000 pencils. Startups often focus so much on their first funding round that when this finally happens, they do not prioritise where the money should be spent. If the startup then spends money on nonessentials such as buying extra pencils when the valuation is low, the equivalent price of the pencils in % equity terms when the valuation increases will be dramatically higher. As an example, if Mark Zuckerberg had spent 500 dollars of the funds he had first raised to buy a colour printer when the valuation of Facebook was a million dollars, this would have been 0.05% of Facebook's value. Given that its value is 800 billion dollars at the time of writing, that printer would have cost 400 million dollars.

For founders, it is important to see things from this perspective, since equity is all you've got by way of potential wealth. In addition, once you've spent it or given it away, the value accrues to someone else.

The startup thus needs to be acutely aware of the investment in noncritical assets with its early investments. This will maximise the founders' equity and, at the same time, help the startup scale faster by being asset light.

Outsourcing

Startups often set up their own manufacturing when they transition their tech. This is simply because they have the capability of designing and setting up their own manufacturing. The motivation becomes particularly pronounced when they perceive the risk of IP proliferation during outsourcing. This can be a cardinal error, since keeping all manufacturing in-house forces them to address the manufacturing challenges and try and optimise manufacturing when they should be trying to find customer traction and testing business cases to sustain and scale their relevance and revenue over time.

Outsourcing manufacturing is often one of the best decisions that a startup can make. In other words, all manufacturing should not be outsourced. In fact, the startup needs to evaluate specifically what components of their solution help them to capture and sustain value with customers. Asking this question forces the startup to address customer interest rather than technology exclusivity. The startup may have begun with technology excellence, but customer relevance is what ultimately drives revenue and sustains value.

Unless there is something very specific in the process that the startup has innovated, a large part of the tech components can indeed be eventually outsourced. To clarity, the tech components may not be capable of outsourcing outright, but that is exactly the point. They may need to be simplified so that they can be outsourced or standardised to the extent where off-the-shelf components can be found. Simplifying production is an important step in order to achieve scale. The more components of the solution the startup outsources, the easier it is for the startup to pivot if customer needs change, since the startup is not locked in with the manufacturing assets.

The second reason for outsourcing in the initial stages of commercialisation is that any size of manufacturing that the startup does may end up being suboptimal. Whereas the startup team assumes that the pilot manufacturing setup will enable them to obtain revenues, the output simply goes to showcase the capability to customers and provides a level of comfort to customers that this product fits their requirements. At this point, the startup has to scale up to meet customer requirements as well as bring down prices.

Responses change dramatically if the questions are posed differently. Instead of asking what should be outsourced, the team needs to ask itself what absolutely needs to be kept in-house. It also needs to provide a reasoning why any activity kept in-house captures critical value and increases customer relevance over time. Linking in-house manufacturing with dilution of the startup is a good way to force a good decision, since more in-house manufacturing requires more funding, and this implies giving away more of the company to investors.

Standards

Being part of a new standard or even creating a new standard is an incredible source of sustained competitive advantage for any startup. This can help sustain value and enable the startup's solution to become a reference point for customers.

Instaheat is a tiny startup. The founders did something simple and elegant. They determined how to heat water directly with electricity. They did this using a technology called ohmic heating.

Why is this unique, given that we all have boilers that help us boil water, from kettles to boilers for getting hot water for your shower? The uniqueness is because electricity normally heats a metal coil, which in turn heats the water. The problem of heating water directly with electricity is twofold: electricity flows with water and risks electrocuting the person, and electricity can split water into hydrogen and oxygen, resulting in an explosion on account of the dramatic volume expansion.

Instaheat cracked both these challenges. Others had done this, but the Instaheat team was able to reduce the size of the electric component dramatically to the point where it could become part of a tap. The team also determined the flow so that the technology could increase water from 20 °C to 99.9 °C instantly and sustain a flow of approximately a litre per minute. Because the water was heated at the tap itself, the solution could sustain hot water with a flow rate of a litre per minute continuously.

The market was enormous. In Europe, the total energy wasted each year on account of keeping water hot in boilers in homes and commercial establishments was in excess of €36 billion on account of heat radiating out. However, to take small steps to address the market, Instaheat decided to address the coffee market for machines used in commercial establishments. These coffee machines were priced at over $10,000 and had the problem of not being able to address water to a consistent temperature and calcium formation when the boiled water was stored in the machine. It received traction from 5 of the 7 companies operating in this market segment globally and received an advance from one of these companies (even before the startup was established) and a few machines that the founders could open and begin testing. As a matter of procedure, the team then decided to validate that their technology was in alignment with the necessary certifications so that they would not have any bottlenecks regarding safety. This turned out to be as far from procedural as was possible.

The team found that there was in fact no standard at all for an electric device that was within an electrical system where the components of the electrical device also served as an insulator. This was because no one had even innovated this technology or perceived the need to ask for approvals to create this standard since the technology did not exist. The easy way would have been to pivot and only address the markets where this electrical system within another electrical product was not a requirement. The team, however, decided to take the far more difficult route since their conviction was that the real opportunity to create sustainable impact was to go the route of creating a new global standard.

The process of creating a global standard was not only nontrivial; it was also intensely political. The first step was to obtain approval from the Swiss government entity responsible for standards. After convincing them of the uniqueness and safety of their solution, they were introduced to the team responsible for the European contingent. The team went through the same procedure and was then permitted to present to the global standards committee for a brief informal awareness session. This was to gauge the mood and make them aware that a new request for a standard in electricity was forthcoming. This was an opportunity to gauge the mood of the key players as well as their concerns so that he could begin working on the formal proposal to be submitted the following summer. However, prior to the formal application, the team had to submit the proposal informally to key players in half a dozen countries so that they could pre-empt the thorniest concerns and assuage them early on. The formal proposal after addressing the concerns of the small coterie was then submitted in the summer of the following year to be proposed in the formal plenary. Additional issues that were raised were then addressed by the team and submitted to the standards authority for consideration for the following year. The total time for the process is ~4 years.

This isn't exactly startup-paced. However, for Instaheat and for startups that go through all the steps and emerge from the other side with a new standard, it is an enviable competitive advantage where competitors have to align their solution to the standards set by the startup and then content with the patent filed by the startup before taking their solution to the market.

Cost Optimisation Vs Value Capture

Tech startups sell to customers based on their calculation of how much it costs to create the solution and add a profit margin on top. This assumes pilot production, with affiliated costs that are not optimised for scale; in summary, it assumes suboptimal or high cost. It also risks leaving a lot of money on the table.

This way of calculating product price is disingenuous for several reasons.

The first is that in the beginning of the pilot setup, the output is low, and the associated costs are very high. This may make the product unattractive to the customers that are most important for the startup, to showcase traction in the market to prospective investors and because these initial customers become a reference for future customers. This is often combined with in-house manufacturing, which also increases manufacturing cost, as discussed earlier.

Another element that results in a pushback from customers is that the solution is unproven. They are thus unwilling to commit more resources or long-term purchase commitment. If the startup's solution is strategic in nature, the associated service requirements also deter customers from a more extensive rollout without adequate testing.

However, the most important element for a startup to consider is whether its solution is able to capture data that enable the customer to make better decisions over time. In this way, tech startups need to think like platform startups, which provide a platform where users can exchange information or can transact goods and services. The first step for a tech startup is to identify a customer vertical for whom the solution provided by the startup is able to capture value that enables the customer to make better decisions over time. Once this is done, the startup can customise the pricing model that makes it easy for the customer to buy and integrate the solution.

CLEMAP is a company based in Ticino in Southern Switzerland close to the Italian border, providing a hardware solution for energy metering. Their business model was to provide their hardware solution to electric utilities. The startup's revenue model was to sell their solution and try to capture a given profit margin upfront. Manufacturing was partly performed in Italy, and the rest were in Ticino. After getting pushed from their customers and after realising that they were unable to get traction in the market, the startup realised that the solution was too expensive for their customers, as they were trying to load up the entire cost upfront with customers instead of showcasing these customers as references. They also realised that electric utilities may be agnostic to the value of their solution or might even compete with their own business models for the future. Since CLEMAP's solution could also pinpoint excess electricity usage for various electricity-consuming products within homes, the solution was definitely going to increase in relevance over time as it captured and analysed more consumption pattern data over time. The company also pivoted to customers who were actively motivated to sell or distribute its solution to users because this would help them in driving their own business cases.

By pivoting to customers whose business case was further bolstered by using the platform and remaking their revenue plan on a subscription basis rather than upfront pricing, CLEMAP was able to address the issues that limit most tech startups, sustaining and scaling value over time.

Hardware Vs Software (Pricing, Scale, Replicability)

Tech startups that have solutions that require both hardware and software often have a conundrum. Hardware limits scalability, particularly if the startup decides to do this in-house. On the other hand, simply doing software minimises customer stickiness. It is customer stickiness that can sustain revenue over long periods.

The first question that such startups must address is to identify customer verticals where the value relevance increases over time, while the product value appears to plummet. Canon is an excellent example of this.

Canon makes high-end cameras and has been a market leader in this segment. However, it has been plagued by two challenges. One is that most users only use the most rudimentary functions of a camera. The second is the advent of ubiquitous smartphones. In spite of Canon's effort to highlight the specific functionalities and tech superiority of its cameras, the unfortunate reality is that most users simply do not care. While there is little that buyers would find attractive in a professional camera compared to a smartphone of 2020, the relevance of images has not reduced. Quite the contrary. However, not everywhere, as we'll observe.

Ring.com is an excellent example of how this value transitions and how it is in fact possible to capture and increase relevance over time. Rather than selling the camera upfront, Ring realised that the value for users for images and videos would likely increase over time. Therefore, Ring decided to make their solution subscription-based. Beyond this, Ring is able to capture something of potential sustainable value by having a permanent position at the main access points of homes and an app that many users visit multiple times each day. This physical presence creates a barrier for any other competing solution. Thus, Ring will always be the first platform that users will choose in the future when any new innovation relating to home security emerges, even though other apps or solutions may be first-to-market or marginally better because they already have the Ring hardware installed.

However, coming back to Canon, a strategy to focus on highlighting its tech excellence or to use their influencers to show Canon in a good light may be addressing the wrong problem. This would be akin to determining which direction to point the Titanic after it had sprung a leak. The value has moved to the relative value of images, rather than on the pixel density or the dynamic range on image quality of photos.

The strategy of Canon with their cameras appears to be to sell them, get the money, and run. However, this fails to appreciate the relative value of images over time by different kinds of users. For a company tasked with ensuring the safety of reinforcing walls on a mountainside, identifying a 0.2 mm movement overnight that is not related to the coefficient of heat may imply that the foundation is at risk, with a potential mud slide and potential loss of life. For an eye hospital where eye images are captured and compared over time, a comparison may help identify someone with the early stages of eye cancer, with a potential risk of losing vision or worse. To a social influencer, on the other hand, the relative value of an image is driven by the ease of selfies.

For the first two examples above, the relative value of images over time (and the high-quality camera that captures them) may be life-saving. The last example of the social media influencer, on the other hand, may not be worth fighting for since Canon may never be able to integrate Instagram, so it is essential in the toolbox of any self-respecting influencer. If Canon were to market the camera to all three groups, its entire effort is likely to be wasted. However, if it were to pivot from simply selling the camera to providing image relevance over time, the first two markets may be willing to pay a lot more over time, whereas the third market would not be worth wasting time on.

Stickiness: An important thing happens if Canon were to pivot from selling cameras upfront to capturing images and converting them to revenue based on end-user relevance. Over time, the relative value of these images would increase. Therefore, instead of competing more and more on price as Chinese camera manufacturers catch up with Canon's technology, it would become more valuable to end-users due to the relevance of images over time, with the physical camera only becoming the hardware lock-in. This stickiness would persist so long as the underlying technology is not overtaken by a new technology.

Over time, the pivot from being hardware driven to software focused enables scalability and replicability. Hardware provides a lock-in to the customer and is able to own specific real estate in the same way that Apple watch owns your wrist and Ring owns the access to your home. The hardware enables this ownership, which makes it difficult for users to move away. The software enables value capture via this hardware access point. The most basic solutions enable comparison. An example of this is if Cannon captures images of mountain walls over time and red-flags movement by comparison of images over time. A more advanced capability may be to analyse these images and foretell the risk of collapse and a subsequent mountain-slide or the potential impact of climate change. The more Canon can move towards showcasing pre-emptive risks or impact that helps a specific customer vertical in better decision-making, whether it is a risk of mountain-slide or eye cancer, the more its value can increase over time by sustaining and scaling relevance to its end-users.

In summary, hardware-only solutions are always subject to commoditization over time if the market is large enough due to the propensity and capability of countries such as China to copy. Moving from hardware-centric to hardware and software is the first step in mitigating commoditization risk so long as the underlying technology stays the same. If the startup is able to pre-empt risks of users and improve its ability to provide better actionable intelligence to users with increasing data points, the startup can scale its value over time. Furthermore, by transitioning to end-user relevance, the startup can better position itself to sustain value over time.

Lab Market

One of the easiest markets for tech startups to address is the lab and research market. However, this is also the riskiest for two reasons. One: it doesn't scale, because even if the research facility loves your product, there is no scale factor, since all they'll buy is one device. Two: labs are known for being able to work with products that are still half-baked, with wires sticking out, and devoid of any kind of stability. This is because they're manned by PhDs who enjoy tinkering and love a challenge.

Going to the lab market in fact delays your time-to-relevance. Relevance in turn is driven by identifying a market that has a desperate problem. The lab market provides a broad customer focus for the startup (read 'no focus'). The lab market props up the startup, but due to the challenge with scaling, it is not particularly attractive for smart investors.

A good way to leverage the lab market is to access data, since labs often do not have the same perception of the value of data and are not focused on using data as a revenue driver. This bolsters the value of the startup, since technology is only the enabler, whereas data relevance showcases the impact. The data capture also strengthens the startup's negotiation position with investors even as it begins to address commercial business verticals.

Another advantage of addressing labs is the potential for access to equipment. As any tech startup knows, equipment costs a lot of money, at a point where without the necessary machines, the startup is unable to showcase value. As discussed elsewhere, equipment investment does not have the same value multiplier effect when planning the utilisation of investor funds.

As long as the startup focuses on the lab market, it delays identifying the commercial market that will drive scalability. The earlier the startup begins addressing this, the earlier it can begin driving larger relevance. As Claude Honegger, Group CIO of Credit Suisse, said when we discussed challenges, startups fail to obtain initial traction with large corporations: 'The average CXO of a global corporate receives over 250 e-mails a day. Approximately 10% of these are from companies trying to sell something. They're the first to be deleted. If you truly want to sell something to the corporation and contact the CXO, you only have two options. Either solve his problem, or make him shine'.

These are the second set of criteria that limit technology startups from scaling. The next chapter captures the concluding set of criteria that limit technology startups from scaling.

7

Technology Startups: Value Transition, Pre-Empting Risks and Sustaining Relevance

This chapter provides the concluding cornerstones that highlight challenges and decisions that ultimately limit the scaling or sustainable value capture of technology startups.

Stability

If there is one word that defines a tech startup's capability to scale, it is stable. Tech startups go to the market with innovation, whereas corporate customers are looking for something else entirely. For them, a startup entails risk. If the startup has a software component (and almost all do), the great risk for the corporate customer is the challenge in integration. The corporate CIO has seen enough great products from external vendors that are amazing as stand-alone products, but the integration with the customer's existing software platform entails risk. As a result, corporate customers often prefer to buy solutions that may be suboptimal but integrate fully or seamlessly with existing infrastructure.

On the hardware side, tech startups begin with innovation. Since they are often founded by entrepreneurs with a science or technology background, they have a mindset of excellence and simply continue innovating. This means that as the startup removes of the lab and into the first manual pilot, largely funded by angel investors, it continues to use the machines that it has assembled or created to constantly change variables to modify output to improve the product. In certain cases, the startup decides to focus on this improvement before going to customers with the product. This often becomes an inwards-looking cycle, since the quest for excellence implies that there is always scope for improvement. These startups then completely miss out on creating customer relevance and traction. In turn, since customer reference is often the one thing that helps the startup raise the next round of funding, tech startups often run of money at this point.

When this product is provided to customers, they test it to evaluate how it fits their requirements. Often, this product becomes part of a larger solution. If the startup is striving for constant improvement, in effect, this implies that the product is constantly changing. However, corporate customers thrive in providing boring and replicable solutions that provide exactly the functionality promised. No less and no more. Today's technology has many dependencies, and electronic components are finely tuned. This means they need to operate within very tight thresholds and require tight tolerances. A tech startup that is constantly innovating fails to provide replicability. Without this, it becomes very unlikely that corporate customers will come onboard.

When corporate customers buy from a startup, the startup assumes that the customers are onboard for the long term, and it is only a matter of scaling sales. However, these small sale volumes are often for R&D and testing. The corporation does not negotiate pricing since the quantities are very small. Furthermore, for testing, the corporation does not need the certifications that would be mandated to get the product to the market. All of these factors make stability critical for the startup. What differentiates a tech startup from research is that in research, the scientists start each day with a view to creating something different in the hope that it will get better. However, a startup has to focus on creating the same product time after time. When researchers become entrepreneurs, the right way to look at innovation is to freeze the product specs while doing the research separately in a research facility such as a university in a joint development programme. It is only when the updated innovation has proven stability and the startup knows precisely how the machine design can be modified and scaled up should the startup roll out the new innovation. Even here, it is wise to inform and obtain feedback from customers, since a new innovation may entail rolling out training to their after-sales tech support to manage, service and maintain the innovation.

Timeline of Technology

All tech startups are based on an underlying tech. This underlying tech always has a timeline, from innovation through to obsolescence. By understanding how customers perceive tech innovation, tech startups are better able to position themselves to plan exclusivity, revenue maximisation or a timeline to exit. We discuss this in more detail below.

The visual below shows the technology cycle underlying any technology innovation. The life cycle of a technology follows the path of innovation to obsolescence. Knowing how customers perceive it is critical to formulate the appropriate route-to-market, maximise revenue and sustain lock-in (Fig. 7.1).

Tech as Competitive Advantage

This tech timeline begins with any new technology that comes to the market. As the visual shows, when any technology comes to the market, customers consider this to be a competitive advantage. This implies that customers would buy this but would prefer exclusivity. This exclusivity in turn means that a customer who buys this would try to limit access of the tech to other competitors. As long as the startup can limit the scope of this exclusivity by time, region or customer vertical, this is an excellent opportunity for a startup to capture high revenue. The startup can also use this opportunity to become the global standard or reference point, which provides future opportunities to capture revenue. Common examples of this include AR/VR technology for

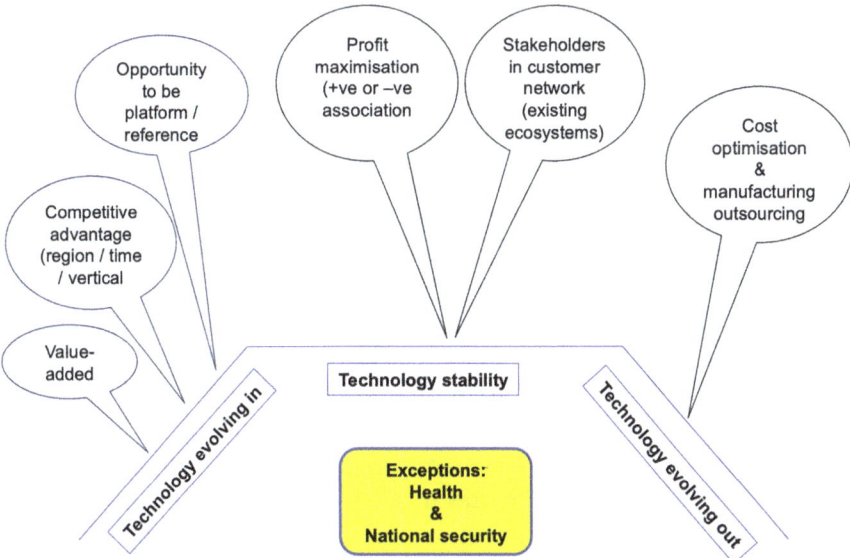

Fig. 7.1 Life cycle of technology for tech startups

identifying diseases using an AI database (at the time of writing) or blockchain for CRISPR to create and uniquely identify designer babies (ethical considerations notwithstanding). It is important to recognise that this window is very brief and that there is a high risk of other players in the new and evolving supply chain capturing this value.

Tech as Revenue Driver

Once the underlying technology reaches key players in the market, customers buy this because of its ability to boost their revenues on profit margins. An example of this would be wireless headphones such as Apple's AirPods. Many such solutions are in the market, which is growing rapidly and expected to do so for the foreseeable future. If a startup has a solution that can provide a specific value such as being able to pick up the heartbeat of the person wearing the headphones and identify irregular beat or problems stemming therefrom, this would definitely make the headphones more sticky and withstand future competitors with a better hardware design. The clearer the startup providing this heartbeat solution is in demonstrating revenue increase for the headphone manufacturer, the more it may be able to link its own revenue with the increased revenue of the headphone manufacturer. In addition, the startup may be able to benefit from the existing networks established by the customer to further accelerate its footprint.

Technology Capturing Value in a Declining Market

Over time, the market for any technology plateaus as the technology itself becomes commonly available. At this point, the product competes on price rather than on innovation. Take desktop computers. Anyone buying these computers is not looking for or expecting breakthrough tech innovations. They simply expect them to work and select one based on the lowest price. A startup that provides a solution to a company manufacturing and selling desktop computers now needs to recognise that the customer will consider its solution through the lens of cost optimisation rather than as a way to gain competitive advantage or even as a driver of super profits.

Another issue for a startup providing innovative solutions in a declining market is pushback. Although the marketplace is declining and is likely becoming replaced by a new ecosystem, the incumbent marketplace still has the headcount to service and maintain the existing ecosystem, both on the side of the customer and lower down the value chain. When the startup tries to focus on cost reduction, there is a strong pushback from the people who are likely to be displaced as part of the cost reduction. Thus, instead of finding a market that is amenable to cost reduction, the startup often finds a customer who is antagonistic and wants to protect its ever-declining market and sees the startup as creating redundancies.

Although addressing a market that is fully mature, declining and driven by price is not an attractive one to address, it offers opportunities for a startup. It is much easier to create references if the startup keeps the price for its solution competitive. It is clear that this would not cover the cost of providing this solution. However, this is not the point. The point is to create a customer reference and capture data points and use these to provide a value-added solution similar to the 'freemium' model used by mobile apps. The initial reference also becomes a stepping stone to accelerating the customer footprint as the customer transitions to the emerging technology.

Exception 1: Health

There are two markets that do not follow the conventional innovation-to-obsolescence curve shown above. One market is health. For technology startups addressing health, technology innovations are only the access points to eventually capture customer data. Take an example of a tech startup addressing patients with muscle degradation diseases. Although the startup may provide a solution that helps those with Alzheimer and track their muscle effectiveness or show reminders for medicines, the real opportunity for the startup may be to capture data for specific patents over time, including the specific medicines, lifestyle choices or exercises that delay the onset of symptoms or result in further muscle degradation. These data collation for subgroups may reflect in some lifestyle charges that are more effective in delaying muscle degradation in people of Asian background, as compared to Anglo Saxons. Furthermore, someone who has worked as a mason all his life may react differently to a specific kind of therapy than a business executive with a desk job. Another person who suffers from obesity may react differently to specific therapies or may be at risk of another health problem emerging from a specific therapy. A startup that captures such patient data over time will only become more relevant in converting this into future revenue opportunities as well as becoming an attractive acquisition target.

The insurance business is largely commoditised. It is well recognised that a majority of individuals select their insurance provider based on the monthly premiums that need to be paid. A tech startup that develops an algorithm to pre-empt the health challenges of insured people to highlight health risks may struggle to scale revenue with the insurance company. Instead of focussing on aggressively driving the best revenue deal with the insurance company, it may be far more attractive for the startup for the long term if it negotiated on being able to use patient data. This would then enable the startup to make more meaningful forecasts regarding the health risks of individuals with the benefit of a large number of data points of individuals. Furthermore, as the startup collects data points for the same individual over a longer period, it gains the ability to better assess how a health risk for the given individual worsens or gets better over time. Ultimately, even as the underlying technology is finally replaced with a new technology, the relevance of end-user data often sustains over time. This then becomes the equivalent of Ring.com, but instead of providing access for a home (as discussed earlier), this provides ownership to the health of the individual. Thus, even as a particular market is becoming commoditised, there are opportunities for startups to capture and sustain value. This may also provide an effective exit strategy for the startup.

Exception 2: National Security

The second area that does not follow the conventional curve relates to national security. If a startup solution brings value to national security, the first customer is unlikely to stop the startup from providing its solution to other customers. The customer often benefits if the solution is rolled out to other customers.

Arktis Detectors is a company that has created extremely sensitive sensors that can detect tiny radiation signatures. Their solution is an innovative neutron and gamma detection system and includes isotope categorisation to distinguish dangerous radioactive sources from benign sources. One of the most practical applications of the technology is in identifying nuclear material that could be used to make a dirty bomb.

For reference, there are over two million radioactive sources in circulation today. Each time there is a regime change in countries that have access to nuclear materials, whether as bombs or from nuclear power plants, there is risk of pilferage. Furthermore, several of the regions that split from the Soviet Union when it transitioned to Russia in 1991 had nuclear missiles. Many of these were stolen and disappeared. Since 1986, approximately 60% of these lost and stolen sources have never been located. This risk continues to increase to the present day. During the Russia Ukraine conflict, when the head of the

Wagner Group Prigozhin made a coup attempt in Moscow and suddenly stopped 200 km from Moscow, he did so after he captured a silo where some of Russia's nuclear bombs were stored. Perhaps Moscow wasn't his destination after all, and the bombs provided safe passage and his ticket to untold wealth and freedom to continue the plunder of countries in Africa and other conflict-torn countries. Till his plane inexplicably fell from the sky. From this, it becomes unsettlingly clear that the world is not a perfectly safe place. It also means that if you felt at risk when you were walking down a dark alley, you may have had reason to worry.

Soon after the company began, they received support from DARPA due to practical applications in the field of border security. With this reference, they were soon able to roll out their solutions to airports, including multiple locations in the USA as well as in European cities. Although their solution was innovative, no country or airport authority requested exclusivity, since the more airports there were, the safer the entire region became. Beyond this, the fact that the solution addressed national security meant that customers never negotiated on the cost of the solution. The risk of a dirty bomb slipping into a country and the consequence made a price negotiation largely irrelevant. Finally, this solution was economic-cycle proof and was completely insulated from GDP growth if the country was in recession. Thus, the greater the global uncertainty and conflicts, the more relevant this solution became for national security.

To put the timeline of tech in a broader perspective, we can consider the example of telecom, since this is literally closest to your heart. Although the technology may be driven by innovation, innovation is not always a good thing. Since new and innovative mobile batteries are not always stable, like any new and emerging technology, it is useful if they are boring and simply work as they are meant to, since they are on average two inches from your vital organs.

Let us look at the mobile timeline to technology obsolescence.

In the early 1990s, Yahoo was the company that for most people defined the magic of the Internet. I recall when I first experienced the Internet at the office of Sun Microsystems, when I first saw the sparkling new computers at their office in Bangalore in India. I asked the manager what I could use the Internet for, and he guided me to the Yahoo website. 'Search for anything', he said. I found folder upon folder of information about everything and links to where I could get more information. The world became dramatically accessible at that point because for the first time, I was able to get instantaneous information about anything in those innumerable folders, from photography to fishing, two of my passions, where for the former, I caught several good ones, and for the latter, I may catch my first any moment now.

This is not too dissimilar to the first experience of those of us who grew up in the 90 s and experienced the Internet for the first time. The search was easy in those days, and Yahoo was able to systematically put information in its folders, using hundreds of people to do so. However, like for any technology, if you can't increase efficiencies when you scale, your business plan is likely to plateau off. Yahoo experienced this when the Internet became increasingly egalitarian. As the number of entities that came online with their own websites proliferated, it became increasingly difficult for Yahoo to keep up. At this time, in the late 1990s, Google came up with its search engine. For a period of time, Yahoo believed that the value driver was the footprint with end-users. Therefore, it decided to outsource the search to Google, its ultimate nemesis. The search was still just that, with no specific revenue stream other than a licence fee from entities such as Yahoo that were using it. However, over time, the value transitioned since users were not as sticky to Yahoo as they were to an efficient search engine. In addition, in the lack of any exclusivity, Google was simply able to provide this better cleaner experience. It was, in a word, all about search. However, Google's business case was different from that of Yahoo, which was trying to capture value from obtaining sensible information about business websites. Google was playing the long game. It did not want to charge the entities that had websites or even users doing these searches. Google wanted to capture advertising dollars. To do this most effectively, it realised that it now had the ability to capture the location, interests and challenges of users searching for specific information. Over time, it was able to capture the personal information and interests of users, as well as how they evolved over time. This in turn enabled it to very precisely target hundreds to thousands of users with personalised advertising linked to their specific searches as well as past interests in a user base of over several billion users and counting. Moreover, but linking the interests of users with targeted advertising, Google was able to demonstrate a far greater rate of stickiness of users, as users found more meaningful information during their search (Fig. 7.2).

In the late 1990s, mobile phones were introduced. By the early 2000s, they were in the process of becoming ubiquitous. The business model of mobile operators was to have last-mile ownership with us, the consumers. In turn, they purchased mobile phones from mobile phone manufacturers such as Nokia and Ericsson. They made part of their revenue from the 24-month subscription, but their super profits came by selling frills such as ringtones. Some of you are old enough to remember this. You know who you are.

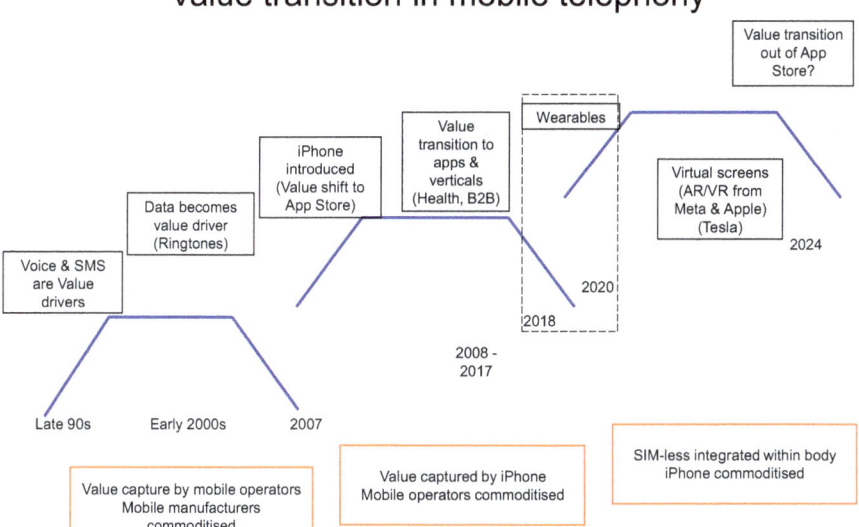

Fig. 7.2 Value transition due to technology obsolescence

By 2006, the mobile operators were raking in the money. In addition, then 2007 happened. This is when Steve Jobs introduced the iPhone. In addition, like everything Apple does, they changed one small thing, which completely where and how value was captured. They created the App Store. Effectively, this created the direct relationship between Apple and the end consumers. The last-mile relationship pivoted the super profits from the sale of apps directly to Apple. Over time, regular mobile calling and SMS became only two uses of mobile phones. However, beyond this, their relevance decreased over time as apps that were able to do the same thing using data emerged.

Apple thus created a business model that made the old one driven by mobile operators completely obsolete. Within years of the iPhone introduction, the mobile operators moved from capturing value to being parts of the supply chain, where value was captured by the platforms that had the apps. Over time, companies such as Samsung caught up with Apple's ecosystem, together with the software platform backed by Google to create a competing ecosystem. The value had at this point moved firmly to the ecosystem, with the mobile operators left to compete on cost. The only revenue driver with the mobile operators was the data since networked apps used data to access the internet.

Over time, Apple has lost its competitive advantage based on the value of the ecosystem. It has, however, extended this via its EarPods, since it helps Apple to own another sensory element, that of hearing. This may extend its competitive advantage for a period of time. However, the next challenge is when the markets move completely to wearables. The mobile screen is in the process of being replaced by spectacles with augmented reality and a virtual screen, the AR/VR glasses. This, like objects seen from the rear-view mirror of your Tesla, may be closer than you think. Apple's iPhone will then have become commoditised and replaced by devices that are wearable and able to provide a more personalised experience. This may include personalised information based on augmented reality, as relevant to each user. Furthermore, this may also provide 24/7 tracking of health and go further than the iWatch. At this time, the value based on the underlying tech would have transitioned to the next technology. The assumption is that this technology based on augmented reality will at some point in the coming decades again be supplemented by a technology that further integrates augmented reality from spectacles to contact lenses, where the backup memory is not for the device but of the individual wearing it. At such time, the technology will likely identify health risks based not only on personal health but also by pre-empting this by way of genetic risks. This will be the ultimate level of user stickiness due to the extreme difficulty in replacing this hardware, particularly if you assume that devices such as AR-based contact lenses are only interfaces and that the hardware is the human body. Tomorrow's trillion-dollar companies will likely emerge in this area.

New Business Models in Mature Markets

Insurance is a relatively mature market. The premise is simple: identify risks in any activity and pay a premium to someone to take over the risk. The risk in any enterprise is binary: 0 or 1. However, increasing the number of activities changes this from a binary to a percentage risk. Taking the example of an ocean voyage, a binary risk implies that either the ship will succeed in its journey or it will sink. However, if you increase this to a thousand shipping journeys, the risk can be calculated as a percentage, based on past experience. The greater or more precise this information is, the better the risk calculation. The premium can then be spread over the thousand journeys so that it covers any one ship sinking while still providing a profit to the entity insuring this risk.

This has been done for a few hundred years. What is interesting is that it has not changed much in this time. Even today, insurance consists of insurance companies getting a premium from every insured person and paying for those who get sick (excluding the USA, which curiously cannot seem to make this work). Although the amount of premium collected from individuals does not vary much, the insurance companies end up paying a majority of the payout each year to a tiny percentage of those insured. Beyond this, traditional insurance companies have not truly used personal data available to more precisely pinpoint risks.

Generali of Italy is one of the world's largest insurance companies and provides health insurance and real estate. Today, Generali's revenue from health insurance entails receiving regular premiums from insured persons. If these persons have health challenges, Generali covers the cost of the treatment. However, for a large number of these insured people, Generali does not even know the e-mail address or contact numbers, let alone other personal data, since this is held by agents. For its auto insurance, the company knows about the accidents that its clients have had and can modify its insurance policy accordingly. With regard to real estate that it owns, the company repairs the real estate sporadically or when the buildings show signs of wear and tear. Generali, like most insurance companies around the world, has not changed how they calculate the risks across multiple verticals, such as health insurance, auto insurance and home insurance. They compete among themselves for a slice of the same pie.

Let us see if unbundling the risks can help new startups or companies from other sectors identify pockets of opportunity and outcompete incumbents.

Facebook and LinkedIn

Facebook is able to determine if you're depressed based on your activity on the site. So does LinkedIn, since it knows about your relative motivation at your workplace or your desperation for a new job, or whether you've been stuck in the same designation compared to your peers. While these may not by themselves seem critical data points, depression is the precursor to eating disorders, which in turn can give rise to diabetes, blood pressure, cardiovascular diseases and multiple cancers. Depression can also result in increased smoking, which results in lung cancer. Incumbent insurance companies simply don't capture this.

If Facebook or LinkedIn, to name but two social media platforms, decides to get into health insurance, their focus on being able to identify depression as a precursor to many preventable diseases will help them run rings around the incumbent insurance players.

Amazon is even more pervasive. Based on the buying patterns of over a billion users and the time and duration that the users spend on the site, as well as the times of the day (or night) that the users log on, Amazon may have the capability to identify with some certainty if women are pregnant *before* they become aware of this. This may be due to the changes in the sleep patterns driven by hormonal changes in the body upon becoming pregnant. This changes the risk profiles of the users, and Amazon would be the first to know. Additionally, if a user orders a book on yoga and another one for relieving back pain, Amazon knows that the user has a back problem and is looking at alternative therapy. Over time, if the users buy (or browse) TRX equipment to strengthen the back, Amazon knows that the user is getting better. All of these help Amazon specify the health risk for each user and outcompete traditional health insurance companies. Aside from this, Amazon is already in the insurance business, since it insures parcels and guarantees the quality of many of the articles delivered. To this extent, this business has already been disaggregated and is out of the scope of traditional insurance companies.

Ring

Ring provides a video doorbell. It enables people to know who is at their door. This is done by Ring providing the video when someone rings the bell and showing it to the users via an app. If a user decides to pay a subscription fee, Ring also enables the user to playback the recordings of movements captured via motion detection sensors. This then enables Ring to obtain deep insights into risks in the neighbourhood. This risk analysis can help Ring to quantify the risk of break-ins and property damage as well as the risk of thefts for specific neighbourhoods as well as facial recognition to help identify the perpetuators. Again, this is far from the existing domain or capability of traditional insurance companies. In addition, as an aside, Ring is owned by Amazon.

Tesla

Tesla makes cars. It does this rather well. So well, in fact, that it's been able to not only become profitable without any kind of subsidy by governments or that provided by oil companies in the form of soft loans to the car companies to keep them afloat and continue producing oil-guzzling cars, but because it's been able to get potential car buyers to fall in love with its cars. So much so that most global car manufacturers now have a strategy to move to electric. Getting end-users to fall in love with your product doesn't happen often. Users will recognise this between the difference in owning a computer by IBM (or by any other brand) and that owned by Apple. While the computers using Microsoft seldom had users excited or emotional, virtually every buyer of Apple computers seemed to have an emotional relationship with the Mac, which this persevering author included. The result is evident in where Apple is compared to any other company in the world. Tesla elicits the same emotions.

However, beyond waxing eloquent about Tesla, it has done something interesting with risk. The company knows exactly how drivers drive its cars. Therefore, if it decides to get into car insurance, it would be able to do so seamlessly, with far better assessment of the risk of accidents due to the driver. Beyond this, the car itself is able to capture video in case of accidents so that liability can be more easily passed to the other driver's insurance provider if the Tesla driver is not at fault. However, this is only the first step. Due to the capability of the car to capture information and share with Tesla, ostensibly to keep the car safer, the next step could easily be to have sensors in the steering wheel of the car to monitor the health of the driver. This would enable Tesla to gauge any health risk and provide a personalised insurance premium to the driver. The mobile app can help track the steps and rate of motion of the user when on foot, further providing information about the level of fitness of the driver. Sensors in seats could provide an indication of the weight of the driver, as well as change over time. Since the seat can be customised to the various drivers, Tesla could get an idea about the health over time of multiple people driving the car. All of these data points over time can help Tesla capture an ever-growing segment of the premium insurance market, since in the beginning, more affluent and conscientious people bought cars.

Fitbit

Fitbit has caught the imagination of users around the world. Users check their steps every day to try and hit the holy grail of ten thousand. In turn, Fitbit provides them with updates on their health measurements, including heartbeat. In most of their devices, it is not yet possible to activate location due to the absence of a GPS chip. However, what it misses in GPS capabilities is more than compensated for with the long battery life. This means that the Fitbit can be worn for up to a week before charging. This provides an unprecedented look at the health of users even when they are asleep. This simple focus on health tracking enables them to know how the users are and, more importantly, how their health changes over time. As users upload more personal information, including their food consumed, Fitbit builds more comprehensive individual user profiles. All these can become effective tools to quantify health risks to users. It is interesting to note that at the time of writing, almost none of the conventional insurance companies tracked the health of users or used them to pre-empt health risks.

Fitbit is in turn owned by Google, which purchased it in November 2019 for $2.1 billion. Google has reams of information about users, which includes user profiles, their location, interests and locations of travel (based on entries in Google calendar). This information can enable Google to target travel insurance, taking the itinerary, personal profile of the user and potential risks of the region of travel. This is a profitable segment of the total insurance market, and users providing the greatest profit opportunity could very easily slip away from the traditional insurance companies, leaving them with the users with higher risk as calculated by Google but still unknown to the insurance companies and consequently the highest payout.

Genome Startups

The startups that collect our genome and provide us with our medical risks, such as 23AndMe or Ancestry, have even more comprehensive information about personal health risks. This would enable them to simply select the lowest-risk individuals, and as and when they get bought over by a large tech company that also has a wearable health tracking solution, fine-tune their model further, to take the behaviour of specific individuals into consideration to further assess health risks. For instance, a genome of someone may show a predisposition to diabetes if the person leads a sedentary lifestyle. However, if the wearable device shows an active lifestyle, the overall risk of the person may be much lower than average, leading to a much lower insurance payout and a very attractive business model to address personalised health insurance.

Apple iWatch

The Apple iWatch enables users to track steps as well as their health parameters. In addition, the health app also encourages users to put in their specific health data, ostensibly to obtain more precise and relevant information. This enables Apple to gain insight into the specific health conditions of each individual. More importantly, Apple is able to track the daily activity of users, such as the steps taken. More importantly, by aligning geo-locations, the apple is able to identify the fitness levels of individuals. Here's how it can be done. If you go up a long flight of steps or walk up a road that has a steep incline, Apple can calculate your speed and your heart rate when you started as well as when you reached the top. Over time, comparing this for the same individual can help Apple track the rate of change of health. This can provide insights into your average health compared to that of others. Combining parameters such as your genome data and your specific background can further enable Apple to identify health risks, either because you may have a predisposition to specific ailments or because you may be immune to them.

The above examples cover individual health insurance and show how this market may be ripe for disruption. However, insurance also covers property. Here is how this market could be disrupted with new technology.

The real estate assets owned by Generali at the end of 2019 were close to € 500 billion. Having enormous asset holdings is not uncommon for insurance companies and banks. These entities often own tens of thousands of buildings. Switzerland has approximately two million homes. With home ownership at approximately 40%, this means that 1.2 million homes are owned by entities such as banks. Like any other insurance company holding real estate assets, their main focus is to ensure that the assets are maintained well and provide a return by being rented out. However, this entails several risks.

The first risk pertains to managing assets. Today, asset management companies repair their assets when they show signs of wear and tear. Sporadically, assets are broken down and rebuilt when it is assumed that they have reached the end of their lives. However, they do not often track the health of their assets, which results in accelerated wear and tear, such as humidity, which can degrade the steel in the structure. However, the challenge is that some assets degrade on the inside while still seeming in reasonable condition from the exterior. This risks collapse, and the resultant costs include loss of lives. Other assets continue to be stable and usable for several more years, so tearing them down becomes an unnecessary cost. New technologies and startups can track the health of these assets, either when they are built or by testing to check for degradation, and significantly reduce the costs of maintaining the buildings or flag risks, thus enabling better decisions on repair or replacement.

However, there are more important opportunities with assets, and the existing asset managers are not tapping these. These pertain to leveraging assets. Beyond the asset itself, future revenue opportunities arise from what they can enable. Wireless LAN enables information flow, which is increasingly important as individuals spend increasing amounts of their leisure time in digital media. Solutions such as Ring's doorbell solution provide security to the assets. Beyond this, tracking the health of individuals who reside in these assets provides enormous opportunities to monetise. Interesting enough, this plays directly into the business of insurance companies, so is currently an opportunity lost. This is only the surface of the opportunities that are possible when these assets are leveraged, particularly if asset leveraging addresses the personal risks of individuals. Companies that are able to identify, capture, monetise and scale will drive value. All the others, including many of the incumbent players, will be left holding the cost elements and ultimately become insolvent or bolstered by tax-payer dollars.

Tech Convergence into a Platform

In the book 'WHERE IS EVERYBODY', where Stephen Webb delves into the absence of signals from any extra-terrestrial civilisation, he speaks of evolutionary convergence. Although the different animal species diverged over 300 million years ago, they have been able to create similar sensory mechanisms to maximise their chances of survival. Our sense of sight seems obvious to us, but Webb's research shows that there are over 30 kinds of eyes that exist in the animal kingdom. Therefore, although there was complete divergence in the evolution of different animals, their sensory capabilities to see the world converged to provide them with a competitive advantage geared towards survival.

Ultimately, true scaling of technology implies bridging the gap between being perceived as a technology and becoming a platform. To achieve this, the technology needs to address all the challenges addressed above, including avoiding lock-in into manufacturing, customisation and seeing the technology as a competitive advantage. Over time, the focus on technology needs to transition towards addressing customer needs. Furthermore, if the company is able to pre-empt customer requirements by way of customer data, it further sustains the customer lock-in. Finally, if the customer data enable the company to highlight pre-emptive risk, it further transitions towards sustained customer dependence, while at the same time getting other stakeholders who have much to gain by coming onboard. Sustaining value over time is thus the ability to enable customers to sustain their competitive advantage.

8

Platform Startups: Foundation

Platform startups are all about the user experience. The perceived (and real) value of the startup depends on the number of people onboard. The key asset of the startup begins with the service or interaction you provide, since this is what keeps them coming back but soon transitions to the personal data of the users. This is because the users' personal data is what helps you target them more effectively. It should be noted that although we refer to the platform users as customers, they are often the product, particularly if their personal data are shared with advertisers. In such cases, it is the advertisers who are the customers. Facebook is a prime example of platform startups. Although we as users assume that we are its customers, we don't actually pay anything to Facebook. The advertisers do this, and in turn, Facebook tries to find a good fit between the users that advertisers are trying to target and our personal interests. These personal interests may be those we search for, what we share with our friends, or sometimes, what we say.

The true value of the startup is the amount of time that these customers spend on your platform. The sustainability of its relevance depends on how long you can keep getting these customers to return to your platform. Startups do not like to highlight this benchmark for investors for two reasons. The first reason is that it appears nonintuitive since the basis for most platforms is consistent customer acquisition and usage by customers, which in turn translates to pushing ads through to them and using these ads as a source of revenue. The second and more pertinent reason is that they risk providing too much information if this information shows a levelling off over time, or even worse, a high drop-off rate, which in turn negatively impacts their own valuation.

With customers having a constantly increasing number of apps, social media activities and platforms vying for their time, it is very rare that a new platform is able to drive ownership of a certain part of the users' day on a daily basis. The ones that are able to do this become the billion-dollar companies that we see today. The question is how to get there.

While there is no obvious answer and it is a given that you need a large amount of luck, it pays off to heed certain cornerstones to create a successful platform startup. These assume that you have a limited amount of funding and that you do need to showcase some degree of relevance, traction or stickiness in order to raise the next and significantly larger round of funding. These are discussed below.

Really Tiny Vertical

Most platform startups aim big. It is good to remember that although Facebook today has significantly over two billion users, it started with one school in the USA. Harvard. Once it had traction with the user community there, it went to other schools. Only once it recognised user requirements and how it could make its platform relevant for these users did it open the platform to people beyond this core community.

The risk of going too large too quickly is twofold. The first risk is that the startup spreads itself too thin over multiple sectors and is unable to obtain traction or establish key relationships necessary to own the vertical. The second is that it loses control of the narrative. By being everywhere, the startup is already in the public domain. Any failures thus play out in public view, risking opening flanks for competitors and degrading much-needed credibility with users and corporate clients alike. Typical risks include security lapses, due to which user information is leaked out.

Are you Addressing the User's Work or Leisure?

Since the idea behind platforms is to gain traction with the time of the user, it is important to step back and define what time slice you are addressing. Is this work-related or related to leisure? In case it is work-related, it is unlikely that you will be able to push ads as a key source of revenue. In such cases, the revenue needs to be identified early on. In case of leisure, something like a game unfortunately doesn't cut it anymore. Here, it is useful to take a step back and recognise that the Apple app store has over two million apps, as does the Android app store. Apps that are successful are tiny slivers of the universe of apps that exist. A platform that focuses on and owns a tiny market segment by providing value addressing an existing problem or urgent need is far more likely to gain and sustain traction. Here, it's not enough to know how you'll find them; it's as important to know how they'll find you and why.

China has had the steepest learning curve so far as social apps are concerned. This is due to two factors. One is that the Chinese government actively blocked American platforms from accessing the market. Second, the Chinese market was large enough to help local Chinese apps scale and obtain millions of users, whether they were addressing 30-year-old or older single people or young teen girls. In fact, the 'Singles Day', created by Alibaba, had the largest 1-day turnover in 2021 of over $84 billion. This compares with approximately $10 billion done by Amazon on its Black Friday sale in the same year. This is a sign that markets outside the USA may be where growth opportunities lie.

What Segment Are You Replacing?

Just as important as the users' time that you're addressing is to ask the question about the users' existing segment that you're replacing.

This pertains to the users' time segment and, by implication, to the users' experience that the platform plans to replace. You do need to ask whether the value you're trying to replace is information, transaction, network or leisure. For example, you are unlikely to replace the user's time spent on Facebook if you try to replace the information that it provides, if the user goes to Facebook to get validation of their world view. This was highlighted by how US President Trump exploited the perceptions of risks of the conservative right-wing segment of the US population and put himself forward as their validation and voice.

Users have ever-limited time due to the proliferation of platforms for both business and leisure, vying for their time. For a platform to become relevant in this crowded market of the users' mind-space, it is far easier to address the changing interests, needs, desires or concerns of users and address this change. It is much easier to get users onboard if you become their voice.

The process of vertical identification can be performed in two ways. The first is to provide a solution that exists but where you can provide a significantly superior experience. Here, the startup's challenge has the opportunity to be tried by the user. In a world where users often have app fatigue, this is a significant barrier. The second can be to identify an urgent problem to which a solution does not exist. Difficult as it sounds, the real opportunities may lie in this direction. The opportunities may be beyond conventional apps and in addressing industrial sectors, which often use technology that is several decades old. Since this area is also much larger by volume, with market sizes in excess of several hundred billion dollars, a tiny market share can equate to a very healthy revenue opportunity. A good example is Ethon AI, which was the result of researchers observing the challenges in identifying errors in assembly during manufacturing. They recognised that the operational workers had no idea about coding and wanted something that was easy to use, mobile and reduced defects. This enabled them to obtain seed funding of over $6 million in Switzerland a few months after being founded. This was on the back of customers knocking their doors down due to the intense demand of their solutions. In spite of not being obvious to end consumers, these defects during manufacturing can cost billions of dollars if they are detected late, resulting in companies having to scrap their entire manufacturing run or being forced to recall their products. A case in point is Cosori, which was forced to recall two million air fryers due to the risk of fire and burn hazards. This is in addition to the risk of being sued by users for millions of dollars. For a publicly quoted company, this can dramatically reduce their market valuation as their customers lose trust in them. For a privately held company or a startup, it can be even worse, as this can put their ability to raise future funding in limbo.

Addressing Pain

The first step is to recognise customer groups that have a pain that your platform will mitigate. Your perception of their pain may be different from their real pain, which is why actual customer feedback is key. Once you recognise the real pain and can address the platform to own these customers, you've taken the first step towards becoming *the* platform.

There is a continental divide between Europe and the USA. Skype is a notable exception, but most other platforms always emerge from the USA. A key reason is the common culture and language across the USA. This facilitates quick replicability across multiple sub verticals once the first beachhead vertically comes onboard. The second reason is the level of comfort of successful entrepreneurs to fund ideas, which may be seen as high risk and devoid of technological uniqueness but capable of disrupting the existing marketplace. Investors in Europe are conservative, focusing on investments in technology with strong IP that emerges from within research institutions. While this ensures technology excellence, the process of emergence results in delay, which often strikes the death knell on wannabe platforms, where speed-to-market is prized beyond anything else.

Tech ≠ Platform

When technologies come out of research, they are exactly that: technologies looking for customers. This does not make them platforms; all they are at this time technologies looking for a market or solutions looking for a problem to solve.

Technologies that have technology excellence attained over decades of effort, combined with conservative investors focussed on IP as a prerequisite for investment, are the ideal combination for companies with tech excellence. Platform companies, by their very nature, are technology-agnostic, which enables them to scale rapidly to address fast-evolving customer needs. Technology then becomes a hurdle, or at the very least, something that simply needs to be managed, preferably off-the-shelf, if not fully outsourced.

In the uncertain world of changing customer requirements, tech-driven startups tend to return to their area of comfort rather than addressing user needs. If, as an entrepreneur, you feel less comfortable talking to customers about their requirements and challenges than about your technology, you have a problem. You also know who you are. For tech-driven startups, this results in a natural selection of tech excellence arising from Continental Europe and platforms from the USA. If platform startups do not recognise themselves for what they are or address technology in a platform world, they very quickly get swept away or leave relevance, scale and money on the table.

Enable a Conversation

By definition, a platform implies a virtual place where people come together to buy or sell goods or services or simply have a conversation if they both swipe right. It is thus imperative that the platform startup identify the two sides that will come together to have a conversation and the reason why.

Rosie Reality was a Swiss startup led by extremely bright software engineers out of ETH Zurich, Europe's leading technology institution. It developed an interactive virtual robot that could help children learn programming via gamification. It was so well designed that when Apple began its Arcade in September 2019, Rosie Reality's app was one of the 100 on the platform and the only one selected from Switzerland.

However, for all its details and intuitive interaction with the player, it missed one key element. There was only one robot that the user could interact with. The team of developers did not realise that for a game to be truly engaging, it needed to have two robots that two people could control, where the virtual robots could interact with one another. 'Social' was not only to drive stickiness but was also imperative to pull in new players. In spite of funding from Silicon Valley investors, the game ultimately shuttered as the team was unable to sustain user interest over time and there was no in-built ability to pull in new users.

The points mentioned above provide some of the cornerstones of a platform startup. With this as a basis, let us delve deeper into platform unicorns.

Unicorns Over the Decades

Unicorn startups seem to be sprinkled with stardust. These are companies that not only become leaders in their chosen fields but also proceed to define their entire category.

Until the late 1980s, it took a generation to create a billion-dollar company. You had to create a manufacturing company, set up a distribution system, aligned your sub-suppliers, provided your customers with not only your product but also the confidence that you would be around to service it if it went south and developed trust of the marketplace for long enough that you became part of the establishment. This was a long and harrowing journey where companies had to innovate each step of the way. Then, approximately 30 years later, something remarkable happened. A slow but growing proliferation of computers, first to corporates, and soon after, to individuals, began. With the computer as the basis, software companies such as Microsoft came into being and were able to grow rapidly using and leveraging the hardware that was now already available. These companies still had to make the software that was ultimately going to be used by users. However, since there was no easy way for the work done using programmes such as Word and PowerPoint to be transferred to others in the ecosystem other than by floppy drives, there was no growth based on the network effect.

At CERN, Tim Berners-Lee was working on creating a platform that could link documents and called it HTTP for the Hypertext Transfer Protocol. The impact of Tim's work is impossible to overestimate. This became the basis of what we know and simply take for granted; the Internet. However, it did one more thing. It provided a platform that could be leveraged to provide any kind of information. This included information not only pertaining to documents but also relating to goods and services that would be transacted. This then provided double leverage and enabled setting up of platforms and converting the original Internet based on HTTP into a super platform. This further reduced the barriers to creating startups that could scale.

To recap, the first startups that made it to unicorn status needed to develop manufacturing, and then the sub-supplier network, create a distributor network and over a generation, finally get there. Then, came the software companies that, with the advent of the computer that they could leverage on, were able to scale faster and get to unicorn status in about a decade or less.

With the advent of the Internet came the companies that were able to make conventional businesses more efficient or even enable new businesses, which then became platforms making the Internet the original super platform. If the original unicorns were based on the capability to grow revenue based on products and services, the subsequent ones only had to become platforms to enable other buyers and sellers to create transactions. Soon thereafter, however, the next generation of startups recognised that the personal information of users had tremendous value, and commerce began to transition increasingly more users online as consumers began to recognise its convenience. Awareness of the personal information of users, including interests, locations and buying patterns, provided enormous insights, which could be converted into focused advertising opportunities based on accurate forecasting of buying behaviour. Companies soon realised that there were enormous monetisation opportunities for this personal information. At approximately this time, mobile devices began to become smart with the advent of Apple's iPhone. This further accelerated the amount of time that users spent on particular platforms, since access to platforms, whether to access information, interact socially or simply as a means to transact products and services, became seamless and mobile and always available thanks to access via smartphones. Adding to this was the increased integration of the social elements into platforms, which further accelerated the acceptance of these companies' solutions. By using and leveraging social networks, companies were able to accelerate the adoption of their platforms across the networks of initial users.

The initial success of companies that used this route to get to unicorn status made this the preferred route for investors to drive these startups to becoming unicorns. This made the world more unipolar, where the only focus of these platform companies was market capture in an all-or-nothing worldview. Investors, many of whom had made their fortune by starting or backing earlier unicorns, in turn fuelled this. In addition, thus was this further perpetuated.

There was a gradual awareness that tracking the time that users could be motivated to spend on their platforms was a good way to identify and monetise value. However, this also had an adverse impact. The availability of the hardware by way of smart devices and the software platforms connecting them gave rise to opportunities that were unparalleled in the history of civilisation in providing the means to young startups to create something that could scale rapidly to the global scale, sometimes in a matter of months. This resulted in the creation of platform startups whose sole purpose was to get users hooked on to them, to the detriment of all other activities, including physical activity by converting large swathes of the population into sedentary lifestyles, resulting in issues such as obesity. Online friend networks in turn created one of the loneliest generations in history while being surrounded by crowds, also composed of other lonely people, which will doubtlessly be looked at as a generation that had the intelligence to develop technology but had yet to evolve the emotional maturity of interacting with it. Our generation will long be remembered as the one that created the technology of the Gods while still being driven by primal instincts of the Neanderthals.

The ability to scale rapidly as a platform resulted in two challenges. The first one was that of new entrants becoming tremendously valuable in capitalisation terms. While this was not by itself a bad thing, what made it different from the past was that the wealth so created was concentrated in the hands of so few. To take a case in point, WhatsApp, a typical social messaging platform, was acquired by Facebook for $19 billion. It had 55 employees at the time (https://www.forbes.com/sites/parmyolson/2014/10/06/facebook-closes-19-billion-whatsapp-deal/?sh=39e50da95c66). At this time, WhatsApp had no sub-suppliers or partners. Effectively, no other entity benefited by being part of the supply chain of WhatsApp. All the money thus went to the founders and employees of WhatsApp. As has been seen historically when individuals suddenly become wealthy, their propensity towards risk evolves. When they do not have substantial wealth, they are willing to undertake substantial risk. However, with wealth, their focus changes towards protecting the wealth so created. This means that they have a greater motivation to put the money into lower-risk areas that provide more consistent returns. In practical terms, much of this wealth created by these newly minted billionaires goes into assets that may benefit the larger ecosystem.

To compare, Ford currently has a valuation of $44 billion at the time of writing, on a turnover of $165 billion for 2022. The company has 190,000 employees and sub-suppliers, which employ more than half a million more people. Ford thus creates a substantial impact on society by way of providing employment, directly or indirectly. The societal impact of platform startups, as observed from this, is not only tremendous but also separates society into the very small and insular group of people who are directly connected or benefit from the ecosystem, including founders, employees and investors. Then, there are others who are users of the platform but do not benefit from it and whose personal information, preferences or weaknesses (such as health challenges) are leveraged or sold to drive the value of the platform.

The second challenge pertains to the perfect scaling of platform startups, which results in one winner. The problem is not for the startup that becomes the winner and ends up owning the platform. In contrast, this is the ideal scenario for this startup; the challenge is more for the many startups who try to address the specific platform but are unable to be the winner of the segment. In turn, the value invested in them is completely lost.

Before we examine the various elements that can make platforms sticky, it is important to recognise that not all platforms can become or sustain their stickiness over a long period of time. Successful entrepreneurs recognise the competitive advantage that has enabled them to convert an idea into a successful startup rather than becoming emotionally attached to the idea of the startup itself. Since not every competitive advantage is sustained over time, these entrepreneurs would also recognise that the competitive advantage of their own startups was likely to erode over time. Alan is one such entrepreneur.

Having started more than 50 startups and failed more often than any other entrepreneur in Switzerland by his own reckoning, Alan Frei started a company to digitally capture stories of those who died, in effect a digital crematorium. Although this idea seemed to have potential, at some point, Alan asked himself if this was what he wanted to do for the rest of his life—be around (digitally) dead people. The answer was clearly no, so he decided to look for ideas that were clearly more fun… and came up with the idea to set up an online store for sex toys. This idea was naturally not new, but Alan realised that being based in Switzerland, toys ordered from one of the larger European websites took 3–4 days to arrive. He thus devised a strategy to deliver within the same day for toys ordered in the morning. He started Amorana together with Lukas, an old friend who had left investment banking to try entrepreneurship. In the beginning, sales lagged, and they were selling 2–3 packages per day. They were effectively selling products without a specific market focus. At some point, Alan realised that all 18-year-old boys were going for their compulsory army training on a specific date, as is mandated in Switzerland, which was to last for several weeks. He put an ad out focussing on these boys providing a same-day delivery, so they could send sex toys for their girl-friends. Suddenly, they had hundreds of orders. The same-day delivery became the competitive advantage of his company Amorana.

However, Alan also recognised that this strategy could not be sustained over time, as international competitors saw opportunities in Switzerland and created their own distribution networks. Back in the spring of 2019, Alan told me over lunch that it would be tricky to maintain a competitive edge and that their plan was to exit within 12–18 months. He turned out to be on the ball, as they finally sold the company to UK competitor LoveHoney in September 2020 for a comfortably undisclosed sum. As an aside, he has now decided to participate in the winter Olympics in curling and became an Uber Eats bicycle driver to ensure fitness.

In certain cases, the winner wins by dint of specific strategies or relationships or pivots that drive market traction. However, in the majority of cases, it is often down to dumb luck, as well as something else. Let's discuss something else.

Understanding what that something else is that enables the one startup to be the winner of the given platform is imperative for the aspirational platform startup to improve its chances of becoming the 'it'. Let us look deeper at the attributes that enable a platform startup to be the ultimate winner, own the platform and become a unicorn (Fig. 8.1).

One of the key attributes of unicorns is the ability to innately recognise when technologies that may enable new capabilities will converge. Although individual technologies may not be able to create a breakthrough capability, their combination can have a multiplier effect.

Startups that end up becoming unicorns often do so by recognising how diverse but complementary tech will converge, creating opportunities to drive new business models and primarily innovative ways of delivering value. There has been a gradual recognition that this value need not be in products or services. In contrast, there is significantly more perceived value in convenience or recognition of preferences. A good example is people who simply go to YouTube or, for the younger generation, Instagram and simply assume that the platform will come up with a few clips from the millions that are there that may be of interest to the user.

Apple has always been able to think innovatively. It begins with a focus on the best possible customer experience and considers the technologies that may be able to combine together to create this customer experience. In the process, it is able to avoid commoditisation as users are willing to pay more for a better user experience.

8 Platform Startups: Foundation

Fig. 8.1 Considerations to transition a platform startup into a unicorn

Leveraging Weaknesses of Incumbents

Incumbent companies are often limited in their ability to leverage or even recognise the convergence of these trends and new technology due to their lock-in into existing systems and processes. Therefore, the playing field for addressing a new and evolving market is relatively equal. One factor that limits the capability of incumbents to leverage new trends and execute on new market opportunities is their existing stakeholder ecosystems.

A few years ago, I was part of a delegation led by the Swiss President to the USA to discuss new ways of generating employment using clean energy technology. At the conclusion of a particularly animated and frustrating roundtable at Capitol Hill with participants that included two US senators, one of the senators saw my frustration at my inability to get my point across relating to the immense opportunities to generate far more employment by using clean energy technology while walking away from coal. His observation was propitious and telling. 'Mr. Sethi', he remarked, 'I was elected by the folks in the coal belt of the USA, principally to not understand the validity of your arguments'.

Another instance was with the head of a global oil major, when I was invited to pitch my startup at an investor forum. At the end of the event, he was walking towards his chauffeur-driven limousine (as one does, if he is the CEO of a large oil company), I finally cornered him (as one does, if one is an entrepreneur and desperate for funding), to inquire about a possible investment in my clean energy company. His statement was equally telling. 'We can't afford to invest in alternative energy solutions, due to our deep relationships with oil-producing countries'. The existing ecosystem had thus become so strong that it limited the capability of these companies to create new business models, which could help identify new revenue streams and do something for the environment in the bargain.

Incumbents are frequently large companies that have institutionalised their value proposition and have developed the efficiencies necessary to identify customer need for their solution, presales team, sales and on-going tech support. Furthermore, to provide confidence to customers, these incumbents also provide some level of guarantees or service level agreements.

Interestingly, it is exactly the things that make their solutions robust that end up becoming the greatest barriers to innovation. Teams often create silos to protect their fiefdoms within large organisations. The level of comfort is inversely proportional to their motivation to embrace change, resulting in inertia or comfort in the status quo. It is exactly this that new entrants can so effectively benefit from, since the status quo assumes tech stability, and as any tech entrepreneur knows, we live in times where ever-accelerating change is the only constant.

Capability to Scale

It doesn't make much sense having an amazing product that customers are knocking your door down for if you can't make enough of it. However, this is the situation that startups often find themselves in when they begin to commercialise. When you begin to get traction with customers, you try and sell what you can. This often includes both products and services. The benefit of this is that providing both of these ensures that you can control the quality of the deliverable, while at the same time doubling your revenue compared to doing only one of these and letting another partner deliver the rest. You also ensure that you can control the IP from potential competitors.

It is this mindset that limits the capability of these startups to scale. To scale, you need to focus on as few areas as possible. These can be selected based on where the value or IP resides. Everything else needs to be outsourced to drive scale and capture value. This is contrary to the focus on customisation.

An example of a soil stabilisation tech illustrates this. A startup developed this, with the potential to strengthen soil prior to construction. The impact of this can scarcely be underestimated since construction enables infrastructure development, which in turn underpins all development activity. The startup, which was a spinoff of EPFL in Switzerland, saw two options. The first option was to simply licence its IP to large construction players. This would result in sustained revenue and provide stability. The second was to provide consulting and either licence the IP for the soil stabilisation material to its clients or to sell it entirely, since manufacturing, after all, was not its core business. The rationale was that consulting would enable the startup to continue growing its revenues and keep it focused on delivering value that clients needed and the team knew it had while being able to maintain and grow its knowledge.

The weakness of the first option was that it was time-limited to the life of the patents and perhaps even shorter if tech evolved. While the revenue stream was likely to be reasonable, at $ 1–5 million annually, it might come with strings attached. For instance, initial customers would want exclusivity since it would provide them with a competitive advantage.

The limitation of the second approach was that the consulting revenue is normally calculated on a per hour basis for the number of hours worked. The team's opportunity to scale would then be limited by the number of man-hours available, and revenue would scale proportionately with hours. The startup knew that it would become progressively difficult to hire more people with the appropriate background of tech excellence. Since consulting has low entry barriers, potential competitors would be able to enter the market, limiting future revenue potential. After all, the team's breakthrough was in new material identification, while the consulting was only to handhold customers to utilise it appropriately.

A third option was needed: something that would enable the team to utilise the IP while at the same time scaling and establishing a platform. To leverage IP, it became obvious that the specific material that was the 'magic sauce' could not be licenced out. This did not mean the startup had to manufacture it. It could get it contract-manufactured but sell under its own name. The consulting was worth some revenue, but by enabling consulting companies to obtain this revenue, the team could get them motivated to push the product to their existing customers, thus creating a network effect. Existing distribution channels could be used to manage logistics. In this way, the team could continue to focus on new innovative material development while driving revenue and minimising resource utilisation, both human (by outsourcing consulting) and capital (by outsourcing manufacture). Furthermore, the team could maintain the secrecy of the material composition by obtaining the different materials made in multiple locations and using a third location to combine them. Combining its capabilities delivered a multiplier effect on revenues. This was done by using existing networks to access customers and leaving enough money on the table to motivate the network to push this solution, providing the team to position itself to scale.

It is obvious from this example that as startups begin to commercialise, they recognise many revenue opportunities, particularly after they initiate customer discussions, since as customers share information about their issues or pains, the startup recognises that it has the necessary skills to address them. It is critical to understand what each of them can lead to. If the startup is not careful, it may find itself doing something that it is impossible to replicate with the next customer and requires an enormous investment in customisation. Alternatively, it may end up doing too many things for different customer verticals, which spreads it too thin and makes it unable to develop efficiencies of scale in any one activity or for any one customer type.

Thus, capability to scale is driven by the recognition of the areas that have a multiplier effect on revenue and the networks that can further accelerate this, as well as awareness of activities that can limit scaling and effective distribution of revenue therefrom with partners that can enable customer access and acquisition.

Cold Start Problem

A platform often struggles to get users onboard since there are no other users on the platform. This is called the cold start problem. Instagram has over 2 billion users, compared to Twitter, which had (on last count), approximately 240 million users, prior to its acquisition by Elon Musk. When Meta started Threads, it was able to get 70 million users to sign up within 2 days. It was able to address the cold start problem. For a startup, it is imperative to reduce the scope of the market to identify one that has the ability to gain traction and enable the startup to pull other users with the same interest and urgency via the original user network. In effect, the initial users need to become the marketing channel of the startup to overcome the cold start.

On Running is a successful shoe company. This was not always the case. Soon after they began in Switzerland, they decided to create a footprint in the USA. They created a relationship with Footlocker in Atlanta in 2011. When the On team visited the store a few months later, they realised that all the shoes had been discounted. Recognising the negative impact of the discounting on the brand, the On team decided to buy back all the shoes. They then realised that they needed to let users feel the experience of using their shoes, since this was what had distinguished them from the competition. The company created an innovative approach in order to transition this experience. When they rolled out their shoes to a store, they began to take the salespeople for a run wearing their shoes. As a result, the salespeople selling On shoes could share their experience on wearing the On shoes, whereas for all other shoe brands, the salespeople simply parroted the technical highlights of the shoes.

Investor Commitment

Becoming a unicorn starts with truly wanting to scale. This requires being comfortable with uncertainty, not only with the tech evolution or with defining innovative ways of identifying and catering to customer needs but also being able to pivot on a dime from when the solution addresses the beachhead market to identifying and capturing progressively larger market segments. However, to do this, ever-larger rounds of funding are needed. The founders often have very little to show for by way of an existing customer base at the beginning of the growth journey, since the essence of such platform markets is that the size of the market grows with the growth of the company catering to it.

Underlying this motivation and capability to scale is the commitment of investors to the vision of the startup. It needs to be recognised that a startup that intends to scale and be perceived as a platform may indeed start as a tech but will not be seen as such. This means there is very little IP, and whatever there is cannot truly be an entry barrier for competitors.

Investors accustomed to investing in tech startups look for tech excellence and IP, together with demonstrable customer traction and a defined market need. This is far more pronounced in Continental Europe, where they themselves may have made their fortunes in traditional tech or old-world manufacturing businesses. The saying 'if you have a hammer, you only look for nails' is apt here. If investors haven't made their own fortunes by creating, being employed by, or investing in platform startups, their propensity to back something that relies on something as fickle as end-user traction driven by 'social' is low.

Investors who have not encountered startups that have scaled rapidly tend to have very little comfort with or appetite to invest ever-larger sums of money, often in the tens of millions of dollars, in pivots based solely on the intuition of the founders, without demonstrable and verifiable data points to back it up. On the other hand, Silicon Valley has a concentration of extremely wealthy investors who have generated incredible wealth by starting or investing in platform startups that have achieved a global scale. There is thus an innate understanding of how this wealth is created. Added to this is the awareness that platform startups create wealth and revenue in ways different from other companies. While most startups have products or services that are sold to customers, resulting in revenue, platform startups often focus on gaining the maximum traction with as large a part of the user community as possible, in the belief that user traction will result in other revenue opportunities. For those that cross a given threshold, the returns are significant and sustained. However, without the support of investors, this often lies unrequited. It is for this reason that Facebook or Snapchat could not have become the global behemoths they are had they begun in Continental Europe or Asia.

Team Alignment

An often underestimated but critical foundation of startups is that scale is driven by the drive and commitment of the founder team. As the startup begins its journey of scaling, the team needs to own and articulate their vision of the global scale. This entails sharing what one might consider wildly optimistic and unrealistic forecasts of market growth until they happen to come true. At the time when the only thing that the market is likely to believe regarding the capability of the startup to grow and ultimately own the given category is to hear the founder evangelise this, it is critical for the founders to be singing off the same hymn sheet. A reflection of this is the value of Tesla, a significant part of which is attributable to the commitment and vision of founder Elon Musk. Steve Jobs was another such visionary, who could bend reality by the sheer force of his vision and had what even his competitors grudgingly referred to as his 'reality distortion field'.

However, as with anything that has a magnified impact, the dissonance of any cofounder to the vision of scale can have an amplified impact on the message. Founders often have very little recognition of their impact in their direct ecosystems because they are so busy with the struggle of managing the day-to-day challenges of getting their startup off the ground. It begins with the difference in perception between the cofounders, since invariably, one will be the visionary who has an idea of how he would like the world to be 5 or 10 years hence due to the impact of the startup, whereas other cofounders will simply focus on the technical development. The dissonance is normal as a visionary is singular rather than a committee, but it's imperative for the founders to be aligned to the definition of scale.

The first time I recognised this was when we decided to have a Christmas celebration for my own startup and include extended families. When I stood up to say a few words of thanks to the gathered crowd, I saw the expectation in not only my team, which had by then grown to approximately 100 people, but their partners, children and parents. I saw them looking at me with hope of being able to deliver a better future for them. I saw who I was now responsible for. Until then, it had always been the cofounders and a gradual increase of the team. However, standing in front of them, I realised that even as many of them did not fully understand the path we were taking, they still believed, in part because they wanted to believe. It's difficult to imagine the hope, expectation and commitment of your fellowman to you and your vision till you have your first 'town hall' with your team, and impossible to ignore it after this.

Some members of the team, however, define success differently. It is the definition of this success that determines 'success' or 'scale' for them. If success is bringing a tech to the market, they will be willing to exit when this first happens, rather than ride out the tornado. It's said that if you sow the wind, you reap the whirlwind. However, this may be too much of a good thing for some founders, since it entails being always visible. It often takes founders far beyond their comfort zone to perpetuate the vision needed to be *the* platform.

Some entrepreneurs thrive on uncertainty since it enables them to control the narrative. For instance, if there is no existing awareness of the potential impact of a new technology, a tech entrepreneur can create his own reference point regarding the possible impact of his technology or business case in creating a new market. This was first seen in the mid-1990s, when all an entrepreneur had to do was convince investors that his idea would be able to get significant 'eyeballs' to get funded. How that would occur was largely left open-ended, and how these 'eyeballs' would subsequently translate to revenue was, at best, only assumed. At that time, at least one UK investor confided to me that investment teams would be recognised based on how many deals of over £1 m they were able to close in a given quarter. The concept of these investments turning an exit at a nice multiple was not even on the radar. This was similar to the US subprime crisis in 2007, with exactly the same result.

Many entrepreneurs or cofounders of a startup are not comfortable sharing a vision of global scale, since this is too much out of their comfort zone. This is particularly pronounced if some of the cofounders have spent their professional lives doing lab research, which is measurable and is defined in terms of 'yes' or 'no'. Thus, team alignment towards the vision of the startup is critical in building confidence within key stakeholders, including investors, whose decision to invest is largely based on trust in the team and its will to achieve, to senior employees, who are often attracted by the grand vision of scale, and critically other companies that build their solutions on the startup's platform with the conviction that this platform will become increasingly robust as it scales.

Early on in the journey of the startup, or even before it is founded, it is imperative for the team to ask itself critical questions that help define the vision of the startup. These questions include alignment, success, exit, scale and control.

Alignment pertains to those cofounders who are not fully engaged with the startup. If some of these continue to work in research, there is an on-going risk of conflict of interest, since the researchers are motivated by publishing new innovations, whereas the startup's focus is to capture innovations in the form of IP. Researchers are motivated by industry collaborations, which can result in knowledge transfer to potential competitors.

Success seems simple. However, for some cofounders, it may mean the ability to continue running the startup, whereas for others, it may imply finding an exit and selling the startup once it scales.

Scale itself may imply different things. For one founder, scale may mean the ability to obtain external funding and roll out aggressively to 15 countries in 5 years, while for another cofounder, it may mean the ability to run the company independently without investors dictating the vision, developing a niche high-value solution for specialised customers.

Exit may also mean different things, right from time to size of the exit. For one founder, exit may imply a firm value of $ 5 million in 3 years, whereas for another cofounder, a firm value of $ 100 million could just be the beginning of future growth. The reason for ensuring alignment is because the startup will reach critical junctures where external entities will try to find and exploit gaps between the team.

Mindmix* (name anonymised) is a Swiss startup with three cofounders. They got a large investor with $ 6 million to create a platform for IOT. The company had used the funds to grow the team to over 20 people and get traction via paid pilots with a number of key strategic customers, including global insurance companies, to help track data. Insurance companies have enormous assets, including often tens of thousands of apartments and buildings that in turn provide a sustained revenue flow. IOT provided an opportunity to track buildings and provide passive cost optimisation, such as reducing heating if a flat was vacant, or active risk management, such as movement-sensitive security or highlighting potential fire or smoke risk by tracking information anomalies when analysing data from thousands of assets. One of the cofounders, who was the CEO, had a disagreement with the other cofounders regarding the strategy going forward. The other two cofounders took this issue with the investor to get the CEO out. The investor suggested that the value of the startup be reduced to $ 1 to provide the next trench of the funding. By doing so, all cofounders would be completely diluted, and the remaining two cofounders would be given new equity once the ex-CEO was out. Sure enough, the valuation was reduced, the ex-CEO's equity was rendered inconsequential, and he was forced to relinquish his equity. The second step, giving back equity to the two remaining cofounders, was not done, as the two remaining cofounders expected. What ended up happening was that instead of the majority that they had before the imbroglio with the ex-CEO, they ended up with stock options. As they had transferred their innovation to their larger team, and in the process, they had relinquished their leverage in the negotiation. In the process of trying to get the founder CEO out of the company, the two remaining cofounders ended up with reverse vesting, where their future equity ownership was now based on the *future* milestones that they now had to achieve, rather than holding on to equity for the milestones they had achieved to bring the company from an idea to a position of relevance.

Ecosystem

The ecosystem is one of the fundamental tenets of scaling up. This, as discussed earlier, is because it takes simply too long to do it alone, as was the case with traditional industry predating the internet (yes, there was such a time).

Companies that aspired to become unicorns had to utilise the existing ecosystem as a springboard to scale and reach a global customer base. This network, so called because of its network effect, where anyone could be connected to over 99% of the world's population via six degrees of separation in the pre-internet world. If you knew 100 people, and they each knew 100, by the fifth level, you could reach 10 billion people. With the advent of the internet and social networks, if each person has 500 people in his social network, the separation decreases to less than 4.

The implications of this are profound. It implies that someone known to someone known to someone known to you could cover over 99% of all human beings on the planet. It would include the president of the US or that of Russia. That said, the motivation of a node in the network to help you was directly proportional to your perceived past credibility with or future value to that node. LinkedIn leveraged this beautifully. Its premise was that you're motivated to connect with someone in the expectation that at some point in the future, that person may be in a position to hire you, give you a reference, give you business or marry you.

Even before the advent of the internet, there was a network that worked, for the most part, flawlessly. Incredulous as the millennials will be, it had over 80 billion nodes (which is over 10 times the number of people in the world), each joining with other nodes to create trillions (such as the US deficit) of connections. It was all in your head.

The network effect underlying the ecosystem is similar to a new fax machine becoming connected to a network of 100 existing fax machines. A benefit to both nodes motivates them both to desire the connection. An immediate or quantifiable benefit puts a specific price on the value of the connection. However, this results in a transactional perspective. There lies its limitation. A future and sustained benefit seems much more significant in comparison, since each node assumes the best possible outcome over a sustained period of time of the relationship for itself.

However, being able to use and maximise the existing network to reach customers rapidly and achieve scale is only the first step. The second step is what truly differentiates true unicorns. True unicorns do not just use the networks within which they exist. They use existing networks to create the foundation of their own ecosystems. In the recognition that the best ideas and user applications may not come from them but from the ecosystem that comes onboard, they provide a platform that is open. Due to this, other solution providers that want to access the same customer base come onboard. By providing pass-through revenue, the platform is able to attract and retain other providers to come onboard to provide value through it. This act of facilitation ensures that every new provider that comes onboard the ecosystem increases the perceived value by increasing the stickiness of users and motivates them to increase the interactions, transactions or time spent by users.

When developing the ecosystem, the startup provides transparency of revenue sharing to their partners who use it as a platform. This motivates the participating startups to strengthen their offerings, further strengthening the ecosystem. Each new partner coming onboard further drives the sustained success of the platform.

Closed ecosystems very seldom evolve, since although the startup owning the ecosystem has technical competence, it can never imagine all the end-user needs possible. If it continues to keep its ecosystem closed, the user offerings weaken, increasing user churn. In the late 90 s, France was not comfortable with the internet being predominantly in English and decided to develop a fully French ecosystem. However, due to low global traction, new evolving technology powering the net continued in English, and the French version languished.

Apple is another example of starting with a closed ecosystem before pivoting. Initially, Apple began its App Store with the intention of keeping it closed. It was fortunate that it had hardware leadership, whereby users simply had no other option. However, in short order, it opened the App Store to external developers, since it recognised that although it had the platform, it could not imagine the possible uses that users (read app developers) might imagine, providing a large global user base and a pass-through revenue to app providers of 70%. In the process, it has become our extension for ever-increasing activities, times spent per day and increasingly mission-critical parts of our lives.

In the following chapters, we look at how startups may be able to identify opportunities for stickiness.

9

Platform startups: Pre-Empting Challenges and Identifying Opportunities

This chapter delves deeper into the issues that limit platform startups from sustaining their value as well as how these startups can begin creating sustainable stickiness.

Tech-Agnostic

For a startup based on technology to be tech-agnostic would seem counterintuitive. As discussed earlier, technology provides a degree of competitive advantage to the startup. The absence of technology would simply put the barrier of entry too low and inundate the field with competition if the market is attractive enough.

However, if the end users do not care about the technology, any proprietary technology would likely delay the rollout. Furthermore, the team would not be able to benefit from the experience of others who have already created the necessary technology. The greater the complexity of the technology created by the startup, the more variables and uncertainty impact the commercialisation timeline. As any entrepreneur attests, uncertainty delays the time to market and negatively impacts cash flow.

If the startup is not careful, it is easy to fall into the trap of self-sufficiency. This implies custom-designing the product, the software and the machine that may be used to create it. Since the team often has the capability to do all of the above, and the available solutions don't quite fit the requirement, designing from scratch seems easiest. It is at this time that the team consciously needs to step back and break down the various components of the solution and which ones of these can be outsourced. The decision is driven by the criticality and value of the given component and whether it may capture any value generated.

The most seamless scaling up entails completely eliminating the custom design and manufacture of not only the product but also its components. Apple has honed this to an art. Every year, the new iPhone comes out with a new design. However, Apple very seldom creates a completely new hardware technology component. More often than not, it simply sources components from suppliers and puts them together to create yet another magical device. This is to mitigate surprises such as the one that it faced with its iPhone 4. The new form factor had not been tested adequately when it was released, with the result that calls would keep dropping. Finally, it accepted that it had a design flaw in the antennas that were on the outside edges so that when the phone was held, it often resulted in calls being dropped. It resolved this by providing free covers.

As technology startups begin scaling up, they identify many revenue opportunities. While the obvious risk of trying to do too many things and thereby becoming distracted is an obvious one to avoid, the more important one is to identify where the value will ultimately reside and ensure that this is kept within the control of the startup. This is far from trivial since the value may transition with time. The example of the telecom sector is telling. Pre-2007, mobile operators were the entities with whom the value in the telecom industry resided. They were able to negotiate with the hardware companies as well as with application development startups since they had access to the last mile and customer information. Then, in 2007, Apple introduced the iPhone. With that, it enabled users to access applications directly via the iTunes store. With this, it forever changed the balance of value and was able to capture value for all activities in the telecom ecosystem. The impact was so dramatic that even voice calls eventually transitioned to apps. Indeed, the transition of value in the hands of the mobile operators has been so stark that in many locations around the world such as Helsinki in Finland, it is possible to use a mobile and all its functionalities including voice calls using apps, without a SIM card, since WLAN is almost ubiquitous, open and free.

However, tech startups often have a specialised product that requires a custom-designed machine to manufacture. The product itself may have downstream application opportunities. A good example of this is Nespresso. Nestle has custom-built factories to make Nespresso capsules for making coffee. These custom machines enable it to make billions of coffee capsules every year. Here, it is important to note that Nespresso does not grow the coffee beans, since that's a commodity, but focuses on the packaging that enables the coffee ground to retain its flavour for the longest possible time. This provides Nespresso with several opportunities to monetise. It can continue to do what it started with, which is to sell its capsules. However, since the capsule design is off-patent, other companies have jumped into the fray, with their own capsules that fit into the Nespresso coffee machines. It can go upstream in the supply chain and evaluate whether their custom-developed capsule-making facility can have relevance in other industries, including packaging of other foods or health supplements or in health-care products. It could also consider going downstream in the supply chain and creating the coffee experience. It can be argued that this has been one of the highest-growth consumer segments of the last couple of decades, as evidenced by the recession-resistant growth of Starbucks worldwide and the virtual explosion of regional brands that offer the coffee experience such as Café Coffee Day, which began in Bangalore in 1996 with one outlet and grew to over 1500 outlets in less than 20 years. In an interesting twist, its founder Siddhartha died by suspected suicide in 2019 and, in his final note, reflected on his inability to create a sustainable business model. His words were propitious, and the company filed for bankruptcy in 2023 (https://en.wikipedia.org/wiki/Café_Coffee_Day).

User Networking Effect

Brand-driven companies rely on users forging a personal bond with their products to the extent where they identify with the persona of the brand. An example of this is in the mechanical watch industry. From the logical point of view, given the proliferation of smart devices, there should be no reason to continue to wear a mechanical watch, which only shows time and that, too, much less accurately than any number of smart watches that profess to do much more than simply show time.

Rolex has had ads in magazines such as *National Geographic* since the past 40 years, where the focus is on extreme achievers, who are then connected with the specific watch sub-brand. For example, the sub-brand Submariner links show advertisements where people in fields relating to scuba diving have achieved greatness in their own fields. By consistent exposure over decades, the readers (and increasingly, viewers on online media) are able to form personal links with the activities they would like to identify with and see themselves in the shoes (or scuba gear or Mount Everest trekking gear as the case may be) of the adventurers in these exotic fields. Clearly, the strategy has worked, since Rolex sells the highest number of watches in the world per year in the luxury watch segment, by some estimates over 8,00,000 (the company does not provide details of the watches sold).

For this reason, Ferrari has regional clubs where members meet and perceive a sense of kinship, which in turn further perpetuates brand loyalty. Beyond this, Ferrari has also recognised an important source of brand loyalty; let's call them the *aspirationals*. Part of the Ferrari cult is perpetuated not only by the buyers but also by the persons who are unable to own it since they are unable to afford it. This in turn reemphasises the perceived value for the owners of Ferrari.

This is perceived even more strongly by the owners of Tesla. The greetings may be different, but invariably, Tesla drivers greet each other when they cross another Tesla on the road. This isn't seen often with drivers of other cars, who consider their cars to be functional or rather a representation and extension of their personal signature.

If users feel a sense of ownership with the brand and what it stands for, this provides a high degree of stickiness with the brand. Someone who owns a Patek Philippe, arguably the most expensive watch in the world, recognises another person who owns this brand. This helps in breaking the ice while providing a secret language, including comparing the different notes of the minute repeater or their experience with the tourbillon.

Increasingly, celebrity endorsements are used to influence potential users of the product or service. Tennis maestro Roger Federer has been the brand ambassador for Rolex, as was golfer Tiger Woods. However, as shown by the marital cheating scandal that engulfed Woods, if a brand is too closely aligned with a sports superstar, it can be at risk of reputational damage if the brand ambassador does something unethical. Reputation nurtured over several decades can be tainted due to an indiscretion by the ambassador, particularly if he is seen as the face of the brand. Another risk of celebrity endorsements is that in the age of social media, the shelf life of an ambassador tends to be tenuous. The startup needs to be aware that if the followers of a social media ambassador are able to switch so easily to the platform solution provided by the startup, it may be just as easy for these users to move away. It is thus imperative for the startup to transition and build traction with the users of the influencer independent from the influencer to sustain this value.

Evolving Business Models

Business models have evolved over time. In the same way that in the dawn of civilisation, land had the maximum value, and anyone who owned land was considered truly wealthy. Then, over time, those who had access to raw materials such as iron or oil were considered wealthy. This further evolved during the industrial revolution, where the ability to convert iron ore into steel was the determinant of value. As the industrial revolution resulted in industrialisation and revenue generation from using machines, the ability to create high-quality mechanical equipment drove wealth. We have grown up in this period. However, the coming future will see the movement of wealth away from simple goods and services. Let us discuss this in more detail, since the more we understand how wealth creation and transition occur, the better positioned we will be to recognise how wealth will transition in the future.

Goods and Services

There was a time, predating the Internet, when the average business model of a company was to sell goods or services and get paid for it. The more forward-thinking companies link assurance of future performance to drive annual service revenues. This was common for car companies and for companies selling home appliances such as air conditioners and refrigerators. The market for these was driven by two elements: assurance for the customers that the products would continue to work and limiting the financial outflow in case of breakdown. For the companies providing these products and services, this provided a very consistent revenue flow and a high gross margin, since the cost of managing these breakdowns was invariably much lower than the aggregated value of the service fee paid by all users.

However, over time, this has evolved from ownership to usage. Companies recognise the benefits of staying nimble and pivot to address fast-changing market needs. Investing in assets limits this flexibility. Hardware asset investment is also not a very effective utilisation of financial resources if the market is expected to continue evolving. Asset acquisition makes sense in three scenarios.

1. If assets have design or process IP, outsourcing manufacturing risks knowledge proliferation, which would then increase competition.

2. When assets are value drivers, or where the perceived value for customers comes from the asset ownership. The latter is rare but in certain cases accentuates brand perception.
3. Finally, creating assets makes sense if these help retain manufacturing skills. The importance of this last point cannot be overstated since countries such as Switzerland and Germany have largely retained their manufacturing skills, whereas the UK has outsourced manufacturing skills for multiple industries. The result for the UK is dependence on all kinds of products, and its purely service-driven economy finds it far more challenging to sustain value in an increasingly flat world where competition for software skills and services that can be provided online is global.

However, over the past few decades, the business models that underpin the value of some of the most valuable companies in the world have evolved. Some of the most valuable companies today do not sell goods or services as understood in the conventional sense. It is thus important to see how business models have evolved to obtain a sense of, and prepare for, how they may continue to evolve in the years to come. This is assuming that the process and pace of change of this evolution will not only continue but also accelerate as facilitating technologies converge.

Eyeballs

In the late 1990s, the dot-com bubble was alive and well and expanded at an exponential pace. At this time, investors saw the dramatic rise of interest of end users towards websites and realised that those who might be able to obtain and sustain traction with users might be able to convert this interest and traction into revenue via commerce or ads. They were partly right.

With hopes of cashing in on the lifetime value of these eyeballs, investors began to invest significant amounts of money into these startups. The eyeball business was to pivot a couple of times over the next 15 years before companies were indeed able to make money with exactly this. However, for a short period of time, this was considered a valid and valuable business model by many investors across the USA and the UK, two of the most evolved markets at the time. Soon, however, the perception of value that the investors expected failed to materialise in the timeline they had expected. This was partly because social networks were nascent and because the commerce that the eyeballs would ultimately drive was only beginning to take shape. This then partly contributed to and perpetuated the dot-com bust in 2000. However, the seeds of what would become viable and sustainable business models in subsequent years had been sown. This would later spawn behemoths such as Google.

Online Personal Info

Over time, some websites enabled and encouraged users to fill in their own personal information to access specific content. The smart ones went further by enabling users to customise the information that was of their interest. This increased traction since users perceived this to be their own personal virtual space. However, for the websites, having access to personal information enabled them to take the initial steps in determining why users came to them and what they wanted to see to keep visiting the websites. This again was one of the triggers that the truly successful websites of later years used to become unicorns. However, at this time, the business concepts were just that—concepts.

Platforms to Enable Business

As companies began to recognise the full extent of how the Internet was going to transform businesses, they realised that this was going to result in dramatic efficiencies in transactions. Beyond this, this had the potential to give rise to new kinds of transactions that could be performed simply on the Internet.

Uber and Didi Chuxing, peer-to-peer ridesharing platforms in the USA and China, respectively, are good examples of platforms. Despite being driven by technology, they are both perceived to be platforms. In spite of not owning a single car, the number of cars on their platforms is greater than cars on any other platform in the world. Being the gorillas in the business with war chests measuring in the tens of billions of dollars, these two are the platforms that define the space. The absolute market ownership of each platform is evidenced from how Uber tried to get a foothold in China, but the local presence of Didi and support from the Chinese government provided financial stability and the slight advantage that makes all the difference that Uber simply did not have. Ultimately, Uber decided to cede its business in China to Didi, which now owns the market for the space in China.

Platform with Its Own Branded Content

The stickiness of a platform with its own branded content is much more compelling than a pure platform enabling other goods, services or simply content provided by users. The quality of the platform's own content can be properly curated and quality assured, resulting in greater trust. However, this simple pivot in the business case entails ensuring that a logistical backend supported the platform, right from ensuring quality to optimising the supply chain. As soon as the brand name is on the product, it extends a guarantee for a certain build and usage quality and can directly impact the reputation of the startup. It also risks dilution of focus and dissipation of energy and funds to create impact, since creating user stickiness and providing relevant content across different verticals is not trivial or cheap, given the options available to the user. The platform thus needs to have a very specific focus, not only on content but also on user background, preferences and geography. The focus of the platform has to be to own the specific vertical, and the only way to do this is to make it adequately narrow and focused.

Ofo is an example of what happens when the focus is not narrow enough. Ofo was a bike-sharing company based in China and was one of the first to roll out its yellow bikes across China. It had deep pockets, having Didi Chuxing, the ridesharing platform, and Alibaba as two of their backers. Flush with funds in early 2018, Ofo decided to aggressively roll out across China, with scant focus on servicing and maintenance. Ease of use was their hallmark, where users could lock and unlock them with their smartphones and did not have to return them to their designated locations. In their rush to roll out, Ofo did not pay enough attention to servicing and maintenance of their bikes, and by spreading themselves thin, they did not have the funds to drive integration across the sector, as user preferences moved to having the same platform for all mobility solutions, from a bike to a scooter to a car. By focusing on one asset class, Ofo did not see the value transitioning out and subsequently became left behind.

The second challenge occurred with their strategic investors Didi Chuxing. In late 2018, Didi Chuxing brought in their competitor Bluegogo and launched their own bike-sharing service. Ofo's error during Didi Chuxing's investment was to not insist on exclusivity, whereby Didi Chuxing was not allowed to invest in a direct competitor. It cost them dearly (https://edition.cnn.com/2018/12/21/tech/ofo-china-bike-sharing-crisis/index.html).

The last nail on the coffin was when their competitors, including Hellobike and Mobike, decided to forego the deposits that users had to pay due to the deep pockets of their investors. Ofo was unable to do this since it needed the deposits to invest in new bikes. When users found that Ofo's stability was not assured, they began asking for a return of their deposits. This further exacerbated Ofo's financial situation, and as a consequence, in a matter of months, it went from a competitive position to bankruptcy.

User Personal Information

One of the most important elements of a unicorn is the ability to obtain the personal information of the user. By itself, this would be considered highly valuable since it provides relevance. However, it is not only the information about users that is the most pertinent in driving stickiness, as the personal info of users can be obtained in multiple ways, both legal and nefarious. For this reason, 'relevance' is so critical.

To ensure relevance, it is imperative that users put in their own personal info. This would not only provide far greater relevance on account of user updates but would also provide traction driven by these very users. It is important to consider that users would only provide their updated personal information if they had the expectation of obtaining specific value from providing this information. This is one of the most important questions that a startup that aspires to be a unicorn has to ask.

Therefore, what exactly is the value provided by a startup that might not only enable but also motivate users to provide their information? Although this appears ephemeral, it spells the distinction between cost-plus and value-added. The cost-plus approach implies that the startup calculates its cost and provides its solutions to customers at a price that incorporates a profit margin on top. In a value-added approach, the startup evaluates the value its solution brings to end users and prices them accordingly.

Startups do have opportunities to veer more towards value vs simply focusing on growing revenue. The following examples illustrate this.

A Swiss startup Micropulse* (name anonymised) created microphones in an array that provided the capability to focus on a particular sound or to pinpoint the source of any sound. By recording using all microphones in a 360° environment, this provided the capability to 'listen' to any sound from any direction up to 50 m and actively ignore all other sounds in the vicinity. A value-added opportunity could have been to use this for sensitive locations such as airports, so that in case of any terrorist attack, the sounds from a specific location could be picked up by microphone triangulation (similar to GPS positioning) and voices just preceding the attack could have been used to gain insights into the attackers and their motives. Future opportunities could have entailed using sound-based data for data mining. What is interesting about addressing this opportunity is that it is economic-cycle agnostic. Since national security is the one area for which countries always have budgets, it could also have provided sustained revenue. Admittedly, addressing this opportunity would have entailed significant relationship-building with government bodies and airport authorities.

The team was approached by another kind of customer, a company transporting natural gas. The focus was to identify gas leaks. It was an easier customer to address, partly driven by the fact that it was the customer that had approached Micropulse. In this case, existing solutions were already able to do this, albeit with machines that were effective only up to 20 m. Micropulse began to focus on addressing the latter market segment. Due to the presence of other solutions, Micropulse's capability of pricing its solutions was limited. Micropulse had the option of going for the moonshot of creating a whole new niche in security solutions and converting sound information collected over time for data mining, as well as opening this as a platform that others might have used to provide their solutions. However, it took the much easier approach but one that limited their super profit potential and forced them to compete on cost and efficiency, rather than competing on value and impact.

Another prime example of addressing the revenue pertaining to personal user information pertains to Nespresso. As discussed earlier, thus far, Nespresso has focused on providing capsules and in the meantime has developed expertise in custom machines as well as the process of high-speed packaging that may have relevance across other industries. In this context, Nespresso's opportunity may lie in providing users with the ability to have coffee on a pay-per-user basis. This has the potential to provide enormous swathes of information about time and volume of consumption. This would also provide deep insights into user behaviour patterns, enabling Nespresso to pre-empt user demand and push complementary products to users.

In the process of doing this, Nespresso would tap the perceived value in the supply chain. At some point in the future, if it is able to integrate this information-gathering capability in its coffee machines, it may well be able to dispense with the making of the capsules and outsource this entirely, since the value may move to estimating and catering to consumption needs and capsules may only be another cost component of the value chain.

Interestingly, this may be the most significant revenue opportunity for incumbent consumer goods companies since they already have last-mile relationships. Even more interestingly, it may be to protect their existing supply chains that they may not capitalise on this emerging opportunity. In addition, that's the real opportunity for startups.

Platform Looking for a Slice of the User's World

Platforms that are able to capture a slice of the user's life are able to create more sustainable revenue streams. These can be done because the platform can not only push advertising to the user but also, over time, obtain insights about the user preferences and behaviour that can enable more targeted marketing. Beyond simply better marketing, the platform can create real impact and, in the process, sustain greater value over longer periods of time.

Platform Productising the User

The shift from having a better user experience is only the first step towards evolving new models of creating revenue. Platforms that enable business simply take a slice of the revenue generated to create their own revenue. Subsequently, platforms that have their own content try to benefit from creating efficiencies in the supply chain to drive further revenues or to convert their platform into a brand extending to their own products on the platform.

The next step in the evolution is to productise the user. This means that the focus of the platform is not to create revenue from the user but to drive revenue primarily from advertising. To do this effectively, the platforms have to obtain personal information from users to create greater stickiness, relevance and, subsequently, impact. Platforms such as Google and Twitter have used this as the basis of their business models.

User-Driven Network

Beyond the time of the user, traction arises if the platform is able to motivate the user to include his network. Facebook and Instagram are excellent examples of user-driven network effects. However, this is not always the case. Let us look at three scenarios to understand how the user drives the network effect, as well as when he does not.

The first scenario is if someone finds that he has ALS, the muscle degeneration disorder, where the motor neurons in your brain and spinal cord degrade. Therefore, the brain cannot send messages to the muscles, resulting in the muscles becoming weak due to lack of use. This results in loss of control of movement of the extremities, including hands and legs. Finally, the patient dies as he is unable to obtain enough oxygen into his blood or remove carbon dioxide due to the reducing efficiency of the lungs. Given this prognosis, if the patient tries a special herbal medicine that miraculously cures him, it is likely that he will actively share this cure with anyone who will listen. He may seek out others who have contracted ALS to get them to try this medicine as well. I consider this an active networking effect.

The second scenario is where the user has persistent health problems. If this user happens to have a persistent back problem (of which your esteemed author is one), which happens to a majority of people over 50, for which there is no obvious cure short of surgery, you're likely to inquire within your network regarding yoga or other exercises that may relieve the pain. You are likely to do this on a passive basis, since it's something you can live with, and it doesn't result in anything worse beyond the pain. This would be considered a passive networking effect, since I wouldn't shout about this from the rooftops, but if someone were to inquire, I would certainly share my treatment that ultimately fixed my back pain.

The third scenario is that of someone who's contracted a sexually transmitted disease (of which your author has not). Due to the social stigma attached to this, the person is very unlikely to share this information in his social network for fear of becoming ostracised. I consider this to have a negative networking effect.

By having a clear understanding of how the user can drive the network and, further, make each new node in the network perceive that he owns it and has his own motivation to propagate it further with as much motivation, the network can indeed work for the startup. As Ruth Bader Ginsburg, one of the most iconic persons to be the US supreme court justice, once said, 'Fight for the things that you care about. However, do it in a way that will lead others to join you.'

Platform Tracking Users' Interest

In 2015, Apple introduced its next multibillion-dollar product, the Apple Watch. There was only one problem: the absence of one killer app. Over time, it transpired that users were using the watch predominantly for one thing more than any other and that was to capture health information. Even simple things such as the pulse, taken continuously over a period of time, provided valuable insights to users. However, by putting in too many apps in the watch,

Apple erred by trying to replicate the iPhone experience. This became a challenge since it severely impacted battery life, to the extent that it needed daily charging. This, however, opened the doors to other companies that decided to address only this need.

Fitbit was one such company. It began by focusing only on two elements: capturing health and fitness information and maximising battery life. This resulted in a watch so minimalistic that its simplest iteration did not even have a screen but only tiny lights. Users could obtain information such as steps walked by checking their Fitbit mobile app. The innovation was its simplicity since it took away the distraction of the ubiquitous screen that we spend an ever-increasing number of hours each day staring into.

As a result of its unrelenting focus on maximising battery life, Fitbit was one of the first companies to have a product that could capture health indicators during sleep, since it could go on without charging for up to 7 days. Not only has this become a key competitive advantage compared to the Apple watch, but it has also resulted in stickiness with those with health risk. The buzz resulting from lives saved by identifying heart challenges during sleep, such as sleep apnoea, which impacts over 5% of all adults and can result in cardiac arrest if left untreated, was powerful advertising. This had a passive network effect since it did not actively encourage users to share information within their network at the time of writing. Eventually, if and when Fitbit enables sharing this, perhaps to encourage weight loss by sharing success stories from the friend network using Fitbit, it will create a passive network effect. This can be converted into an active network effect within his own larger family network if these user data can help identify other critical diseases at an early stage, particularly given his genetic predisposition.

Fitbit's example showcases the increased stickiness over time of a platform, not due to any technology excellence of its own, but ever-increasing relevance and value over time from information provided by the user to track his or her own health.

The User Assumes Platform Ownership

The difference between fitness and health is similar to the difference between weather and climate. While fitness is transactional and can change in short periods of time, overall health is much longer. While your step tracker may track your steps for a given day, you require something entirely different if you're trying to track your cardiovascular issues or a genetic predisposition to cancer. So although you may get a Fitbit or iWatch for the purpose of tracking your daily steps and over time cast it aside, the scenario is very different if you're trying to track the risk of a second stroke, having already suffered one. The reason for the difference is that approximately 13 million people suffer a stroke every year, and 5.5 million die every year as a result. Furthermore, one-third of those who have suffered a stroke suffer a second stroke within 2 years (https://www.world-stroke.org/world-stroke-day-campaign/why-stroke-matters/learn-about-stroke).

The sustainability of the value of a platform depends on its ability to track impact as well as the significance of this impact over time. As the sustainability of the impact increases, so does the increase in relevance of the platform over time.

Pre-Empting Health Conditions Based on Big Data

The emergence and eventual ubiquity of health measurement devices that do continuous tracking and mentoring of health, together with big data crunching capabilities, enable a whole host of new ways to obtain trend information from ever-exploding swathes of data. While Google and Facebook become some of the world's largest companies by showing the relevance of user information, it was companies such as Amazon that truly showcased the impact of using big data analysis. Big data is surprisingly accurate in determining if you're pregnant. Increasingly, it can identify if you're pregnant before even you know it. It does this picking up subtle changes in your browsing patterns like what you look at, how long you're on a particular topic and even what time of the day or night you search. Since these changes are often determined by hormonal changes when a woman becomes pregnant, by analysing data from a few hundred million users, the algorithm becomes increasingly accurate. This accuracy can be converted into profitable business. Young parents tend to become loyal customers of the brands they are exposed to and, depending on income and wealth, prioritise quality over good deals. Early identification of pregnancy by a platform such as Amazon can be profitable, and large companies are able to calculate the revenue opportunity per child. By locking in the first-time parents to a specific brand of diaper, the diaper brand can target selling 4500–5500 diapers for the first 3 years of the child. However, adult diapers are a lesser known but equally profitable business. The difference is that while the diapers for a child are transactional, adult diapers for older people, of 75 years or more, can help to identify specific health challenges early. Sensors in these adult diapers may pick up urinary infections or the presence of pus cells, which may red-flag significant issues based on existing comorbidities. This early identification can result in a very different health outcome or cost of treatment associated with addressing the ailment. With an ageing population, if we are lucky enough to reach a certain age, we may be able to benefit from the impact of what we create.

Amazon's main competitive advantage against its competitors is its ability to identify user needs before users themselves become actively aware of them. However, there are many gaps in the health-care area that are yet to be addressed and those that big data can directly impact. One such area is mental health. Today, most mental health issues are addressed between the psychologist or the psychiatrist and the patient. If this could be institutionalised, it could result in an opportunity to share learning and optimise treatment. However, the real opportunity for impact may be to link this to physical ailments. It is surprising how many diseases are due to mental health issues. For instance, depression, a well-known mental health issue, has been known to directly influence obesity due to binge eating, liver damage due to increased alcohol consumption and lung disease via increased smoking. These, in turn, result in a whole host of other health challenges. Certain cancers are caused by lifestyles, and a mental health issue would almost certainly exacerbate this; red-flagging, pre-empting and ultimately preventing these ailments based on linking mental health issues would not only be in the best interest of the individuals but also for the economy and health-care institutions, which would otherwise have to cover the effort and expense of the treatment. At the very least, society itself is the worst off if any individual moves from contributing to its GDP to being dependent on it. However, beyond this, it is an opportunity for a platform to be far more than simply social. It is the opportunity to address a critical health challenge for which data points do exist but have yet to be linked. This may also be the opportunity to become the platform that creates the next trillion-dollar startup.

Platforms Looking at Genetic Information

Beyond the platforms that use big data and personal information of users to pre-empt the propensity and risk of health ailments, solutions that are able to use personal information, combined with genetic data as well as information of the ethnicity, will provide even more pertinent health predictions. This will not only provide guidance to users regarding health risks with the same external stimuli but, more importantly, become a powerful tool that could have ever-more relevance for future generations.

Argentines have a gene that enables their bodies to process arsenic in quantities that would normally be fatal for anyone else (https://www.smithsonianmag.com/smart-news/centuries-poison-laced-water-gave-these-people-tolerance-arsenic-180954491/#:~:text=As%20a%20new%20study%20indicates,toxic%20form%2C"%20NPR%20reports). Similarly, people in Tibet (https://en.wikipedia.org/wiki/High-altitude_adaptation_in_humans) have evolved over the past 3000 years to survive in altitudes so high that a normal human being would suffer from altitude sickness, resulting in trauma or even death (https://pubmed.ncbi.nlm.nih.gov/16978132/). Companies that are analysing genetic make-up will, over time, have enormous swathes of information about our genetic make-up, abnormalities in our genes and what these abnormalities can lead to. This can guide treatment, pre-empting possible risks of ailments. Angelina Jolie, a well-known Hollywood actor and UN Special Envoy, famously underwent double mastectomy as a preventative measure after she found that she carried a gene mutation that increased the risk of developing breast or ovarian cancer (https://www.health.com/condition/breast-cancer/angelina-jolie-cancer-preventing-surgery).

As seen above, the relevance of identifying trends and potential risks from data for personalised medicine cannot be underestimated. Even in case of disease, the ability to identify treatments to retain or sustain quality of life by better information on the impact of a particular treatment will directly contribute by providing quality to life. For those who suffer from debilitating diseases such as Parkinson's disease, which degrades muscle control, knowing what exercises can help patients retain better motor control DNA can have a life-changing impact.

Beyond this, the real impact will be for the next generation, who would be able to know with far greater clarity, not only what their propensity of risk is of contracting specific diseases, but if this happens, what kind of treatment can have the greatest positive impact, by studying the progression of the disease in their previous generations.

The greatest challenge that any platform or any company faces is retaining relevance over time or over generations. Today's youth consider Facebook to be the social network that their parents' generation uses. Consequently, Facebook's great challenge is the enormous drop-off rate in the youth, estimated at 40% drop-off in the USA in 2018. The fact that over 50% of the companies that were in the Fortune 500 in 2000 no longer exist in 2023 is a testament to the challenges in retaining relevance (https://ryanberman.com/glossary/business-apocalypse/). For all the control it has on social networks, Facebook recognises that this social traction may be largely transactional.

Furthermore, it has always been devoid of hardware that provides end-user ownership. For this reason, it has taken the first step towards hardware that is owned by it and that enables Facebook to obtain health data. This is in the form of an ear device. More about this later.

Private bankers bemoan the fact that when wealth moves from one generation to the next, the new generation often changes advisors including private bankers. In this context, to have a platform that provides information that can enable better health and data on the predisposition of diseases as well as how they progress and the most effective mitigation measures has the greatest chance of providing stickiness.

Platform Looking for a Slice of the User's Time

Access to the time of a user provides opportunities that are far more valuable than product-related revenue. This is because product revenue only occurs during the sale or servicing of products. On the other hand, when a platform is used by a user for a few minutes every day, combined with personal information about the user, including interests, preferences and location, it becomes a powerful means of driving ongoing revenue by pushing user-specific advertising. This also signals an important shift in the relationship between the platform and the user. The user moves from being a customer to becoming a product of the platform. This is because at this point, the platform drives revenue from advertising, using the information provided by the user, and by extension, the user himself, as the product: the platform thus pivots from servicing the user to producing the user.

TikTok, Google and Instagram are progeny of this fundamental premise that your time is the most valuable resource and can be monetised indefinitely. In the early days of the Internet, there were questions about privacy issues, but today, with users increasingly keener to share their own information, including photos, locations and hobbies, one no longer considers social media platforms as a distraction but as an intrinsic extension of life itself. However, it is Netflix that has provided the clearest statement and at the same time the starkest prognosis of how social media companies perceive our time.

Netflix recognises the value of time and the importance of capturing this value. However, beyond this, it is the only company to have articulated this in so many words. In 2017, Netflix CEO audaciously stated, 'When you watch a show from Netflix and you get addicted to it, you stay up late at night. We're competing with sleep.' The reason this was so audacious was not because it made sense for the company to compete for our time and consider monetising it. The real reason was its articulation that it was productising our time and effectively converting us from users to part of its value chain to sustain revenue. This is also the reason it is important to recognise (as if it needs to be said) that what's good for the platform startups is not necessarily what's good for their users (https://www.independent.co.uk/life-style/gadgets-and-tech/news/netflix-downloads-sleep-biggest-competition-video-streaming-ceo-reed-hastings-amazon-prime-sky-go-now-tv-a7690561.html).

Platform Enabling Users to Share Experiences Within the Network

In the age of Insta influencers, young users sometimes recognise that the aspirational world of the influencers is not always easy to relate to or to emulate. Enter BeReal, where the users capture an image of themselves and one of their surroundings using both cameras of the mobile device. The user simply turns the camera on both sides, taking their photo and one of their surroundings. Limiting the photo to one per day motivates the user to have greater discipline to share one every day. The perception of having a limited resource each day provides greater stickiness. In effect, BeReal became a unicorn startup simply by getting users to turn the camera.

Wordle is another example of a simple idea that went viral. Josh Wardle selected a five-letter word every day that users had to guess. The user had six tries to do so, and if you got some alphabets but in the wrong order, they turned yellow. If the alphabets were in the right place, they turned green. The game had two attributes: there was only one word per day, and users could share their success in finding the right word with their network.

He created this game to play with his partner but eventually made it public in October 2021. It went viral when Wardle created the option for players to share their results on social media. By limiting the game to one word per day, users were more disciplined to try it every day. Furthermore, being able to find the right word in fewer tries became an intellectual badge of honour, where it almost did not seem like a game; as users told themselves, it was logic and a way to keep their vocabulary sharp.

Leveraging the User's Leisure

One of the great differences in how users spend money or time is whether they need to or want to. The same consumers who will bargain for a dozen bananas in a tropical destination don't think twice about getting a 5000-dollar deep-sea angling upgrade for their custom sail-boat. Tinder is an excellent example of this since users are willing to pay good money to find their next hook-up. However, even this market can be sliced into submarkets, as I found when discussing the case with my young entrepreneur students. It turned out that there may be specialised dating markets for single parents, or people over 60, who are looking for companionship rather than only a physical relationship. Tinder may have tapped into a broad category of users looking for options for leisure and the willingness to pay for it. However, there are opportunities for new entrants to take ownership of a small slice of this and become the dominant player, which in turn offers sustainability of their own business case. Bumble is one such example.

Bumble was founded by one of the early team members of Tinder, Whitney Wolfe Herd. Although she was a part of Tinder's team and even involved in selecting its name, Herd left after alleging sexual harassment. However, it was exactly this sexual harassment that motivated her to start bumbling, which changed one critical element in relationships. Bumble enabled women to make the first move in dating, compared to Tinder, which was more about letting men find women for one-night stands. By enabling women to make the first move, Herd identified a critical audience that had been underserved but that comprised half the dating population. Bumble was thus able to create and own a critical niche of the dating scene.

Enjoyment Driving User Stickiness

Pinduoduo is most likely one of the world's fastest growing tech startups that you've never heard of. It was founded by Colin Huang, who clearly understood the value of data mining, since after his internship at Microsoft in 2004, he had joined a small tech startup called Google. This sensitised him to the value of data. In 2006, he moved to China to launch Google China, which made him recognise the opportunity to link the burgeoning middle class and its rising consumption due to its income. In 2015, he launched Pinhaohuo, which was a platform to link people who wanted to buy produce directly from farmers. However, he did something more, which became the basis of Pinduoduo. He provided the option for potential buyers to find others in their network interested in buying the same product. In this way, buyers could see the dramatically reduced price if they were to buy as a group. His profound innovation was the gamification of the shopping experience.

Huang recognised the scalability of the model, as it motivated buyers to engage in something that most of us enjoy and that has become the basis of companies such as Amazon and eBay, getting a good deal. However, there was still a drag. This was because Pinduoduo was initially doing an online direct sales model, where it acquired fresh produce and other perishables from suppliers to sell to consumers. Huang decided to forego this, as he realised that consumers were more driven by Pinduoduo's platform of group discounts and transitioned to purely providing online marketplace services to third-party merchants. The company was able to make it scale by focusing on tier 3 and 4 cities, and within these, on women between 25 and 34 years of age, having recognised that these account for a majority of the spending growth while at the same time being highly social and engaged on the platform. The platform also focused on perishables, thereby motivating sellers to have more interest in giving deals if they could sell in bulk. In turn, bulk-buying enabled buyers to get up to a 90% discount if they could buy in groups, which could be as small as two people. By gamifying the experience of buying products that consumers needed on a regular basis and getting their network to join them in buying it, the platform tapped the buyers' network. Moreover, if buyers could get enough people to come onboard to buy the product, they could get the product for free.

The impact of this network effect driven by the combination of pulling the users' networks and gamifying the platform to provide better deals or even being able to get it for free addressed a market that had not yet been tapped. This helped Pinduoduo to scale up from 0 to 750 million users in 3 years, from its founding in 2015. When the company had its IPO in 2018, it was valued at close to 23 billion dollars. At the time of writing, the company had a valuation of close to 200 billion dollars (https://en.wikipedia.org/wiki/Pinduoduo).

Pinduoduo combined gamification of the buying decisions we take for granted for essential consumables and made users feel that they were able to influence pricing. This is driven by the basic human premise that we love to buy but hate to be sold to. Integrating the social element enabled users with common buying interests to meet online. The element of fun is often underrated as a driver of triggering traction. Pinduoduo combined this effectively and was consequently able to scale.

10

Sustaining Platform Value

In this concluding chapter on platform startups, we look at some of the things that are most important to us and how a deeper understanding of these elements can help create the most effective strategies to sustain value for platform startups in the future.

Tapping the User's Emotions or Stay Mad, Stay Tuned

This truly is the theme of our times. Rulers over the ages have been able to create discord within people and leverage this to create anger, which they then used to disrupt existing or incumbent leadership and replace it with themselves.

More recently, this was perfected by ex-US president Donald Trump, who may well be one of the smartest social media operatives on the planet, his other ethical cornerstones notwithstanding. He leveraged his presidency to perpetuate a con for the ages—getting those who voted for him to get mad about the ostensibly 'stolen election', making the entire Republican party complicit. He then transitioned this to get the voters to pay money to *him*, in order to fight for fairness of their votes. In reality, as long as the individual sums paid by them were less than $5000, the majority of the money came to a super PAC set up by Trump to be used at his discretion. After the US presidential election of 2020, which Joe Biden won by a significant margin, Trump continued to spew his lies about election fraud, which his own voters believed. To fight this fraud, Trump said, his voters were requested to pay small amounts.

Although most outsiders could not understand why Trump simply did not concede, he was playing the long game. His game was to rake in the money to build a war chest for future political ambitions of his own or his children, or in the more immediate term following his election loss, to get his own voters who felt disenfranchised to tune in to his new social media channel.

In effect, keeping his voters angry that their votes did not count got them away from their accepted beliefs and fully into his ambit, so that they became pliable to whatever else he wanted to sell. The strategy of 'stay mad, stay tuned' may well have been innovated by Trump. The only element that Trump missed in his social media strategy was control of the pipeline needed to disseminate his views to his believers. For this, Trump was dependent on Twitter as well as other private companies, rather than a government-controlled mechanism. This was a cardinal error, as he found to his detriment. When Trump tweeted encouragement to his followers to sedation, Twitter took this incitement to be the last straw and blocked his account. After all, Twitter recognised that at some point, Trump was going to leverage their platform and his reach to over 77 million followers towards creating his own social media platform. As we have discussed earlier, the vision of a platform startup is to own the entire ecosystem that it has created. It was the one thing that Trump missed that ultimately led to his failure to sustain social media leadership.

Businesses have recognised the opportunity to dramatically increase stickiness and monetise far more effectively and directly by tapping into our anger. This may be to our own detriment as a society, since for this to be truly effective, the anger has to be directed towards someone. Facebook recognised this as a key revenue driver, since its own internal metrics indicated that a post that elicited anger or similar emotions was up to five times more likely to be acted upon as one that was positive. Unless we as entrepreneurs who envision and create the future consciously recognise that our progeny will live in it, we may well create a dystopia where business cases step on the cracks of society to scale.

However, it's not all bad news. Products and platforms that elicit emotion in users drive traction. Trump tapped into anger, which meant there was an 'us' and a 'them', tapping into, and over time, magnifying divisions within society. However, these products and platforms can also elicit positive emotions. This positive emotion can indicate and result in very high loyalty. Apple is a great example.

Way back in the mid-1990s, when Apple was but a rogue outfit, their users loved their products. Incredibly, despite going almost bankrupt in 1997, Jobs' return refocused Apple on creating products that users loved. This emotion that Apple has always elicited in users converted to loyalty. This loyalty in turn converts to a premium. In comparison, IBM's ThinkPad was a workhorse but seldom elicited the love for the device that Apple's laptop frequently did for users. Finally, the ThinkPad became fully commoditised, and IBM finally sold it to Lenovo. Tesla is another example of how a product elicits strong emotions. Stock market short-sellers have always bet against Tesla stock, believing that it was bloated and heading for a crash. However, they did not consider two elements. One is that Tesla buyers love their cars. In fact, the first thing you're supposed to do when you buy the car is to name it. This almost insignificant step personalises the car. The kinship towards the car extends to other Tesla drivers. It is common to wave a greeting to another Tesla driver, which creates a kinship that perpetuates the network, which has been discussed elsewhere in this book. The second is that Tesla created an ecosystem that is effectively the first app that you actually sit in.

Companies that elicit a positive emotion in users provide a basis for brand identity. This can be monetised in multiple ways, as football clubs in the UK and elsewhere know. Fans pay hundreds of dollars per year on merchandise to identify with the specific club.

In 2012, Barnes Foley, who was into fitness, realised that he was far more motivated when he performed coach-assisted workouts than when he worked out in the gym alone. He felt that there had to be a way to bring this experience to other people as well. Although many people had stationary bikes at home, most bikes just sat in the garage after a few uses. At the same time, despite smart devices such as iPads rolling out, apps by themselves did not have stickiness due to the lack of a device that provided the full experience to the user and feedback to the trainer to enable tracking of the calories burned. In addition, so was the idea behind the Peloton born. Foley's vision was to not only create the machine but also integrate the ability to interact with the trainer on video and to have group training sessions. This would be similar to the Zumba and group fitness courses in gyms and health clubs but done from the comfort of your home. His perception that his motivation in doing group fitness would be shared by others was absolutely right. In spite of numerous social media memes about the Peloton bike, or perhaps because of that, a strong community feeling was created between its proponents. This was driven by the kinship of finding others with the same interest. At the same time, since the other people were not from the immediate social network of the users, there was no risk of being judged. By being in the training programme, the user found others who were also believers, which again eliminated the risk of being scorned for using an expensive machine.

Beyond this, there was a very high stickiness when using the machine, since users perceived an emotional connection with other kindred spirits who were also using the machine, without being judged. With the proliferation of COVID-19 in early 2020 and largely driven by the risk of infection in public places, there was increased consciousness of the importance of personal space. This further brought the social component of Peloton to the fore, since in large cities, people were not allowed to leave their apartments for months on end, other than to buy groceries and medicine. Even in places where they were allowed to go out, there was limitation of how many people you could meet. Even when you were out, activities such as running were frowned upon due to the risk of spreading infection when exhaling hard. The same social dissonance that limited outdoor fitness activities provided social cohesion among the online network. This market growth was thus driven by public limitations. Furthermore, Peloton was able to get celebrity fitness trainers onboard to provide personalised training. The data capture from the fitness training enabled the trainers to know about individual progress over time, providing an immediate and sustained feedback loop to users. This was important to sustain stickiness in the user community. Most importantly, as the hardware and software were integrated, the users were locked into the Peloton ecosystem.

The stickiness of the user community was initially reflected by the sustained increase in its share price, with the company being valued at over $50 billion. However, as hubris often overtakes any entity that succeeds because of market trends rather than something of its own making, Peloton made rash business decisions due to the work-from-home phenomenon predicated by COVID. These included a 20-year lease of 300,000-square-foot office in New York. The question regarding the sustainability of the ecosystem created and identifying a user base that had reason to stay due to value, despite cheaper alternatives becoming available, had not been addressed by the company. In addition, this may have been its undoing. At the time of writing, the valuation had come down to $2.2 billion.

Platform Owns User

Over time, the platform increases ownership of the user by making the user dependent on it for various aspects of his time or interests. This incremental dependence gradually shifts the user's personal information or social network on the platform, moving from convenience to dependence.

Partially Closed Loop

Platform stickiness increases progressively from the starting point of getting a few minutes of the user's time by incorporating personal information to ensuring relevance, tapping the user's social network and ensuring relevance over multiple generations by addressing and pre-empting health challenges. However, this addresses one element of the user's life at a time, whether it is social or social with hopes of benefits, to health to fitness.

Let us look at the increasing gaps between evolving user needs and solutions provided by incumbents. These illustrate the opportunities for startups or even how existing players may evolve their offerings to sustain and scale their relevance.

Over time, companies recognise that real value may not reside with products but with owning customer information. As we have discussed, companies such as Facebook, Google and Amazon are classic examples of three simple words: 'pre-empting user preferences'. However, this has thus far been transactional, as knowing what book you may have purchased may simply enable Amazon to recommend other books you might like. Or something more.

Let's delve deeper into something more. If the book you brought was about dating, Amazon knows that you're single and likely looking for someone special. Based on knowing your location (Amazon already knows where you live, since you told them, remember), your working history (I assume you're also on LinkedIn), things that are important to you (thanks to Facebook), Amazon knows you quite well based on how your purchasing habits have evolved. Unless you believe that in spite of being a two-trillion-dollar company, Amazon hasn't figured out how to collate freely available information about you from other social media platforms. How far would Amazon need to travel to begin providing recommendations of someone who shares your interests, since it also knows about other books you may have clicked on but did not purchase. Or, if it were truly nefarious, as Facebook has allegedly been questioned about, its cookie in your computer (of course it has one—that's how it remembers your previous searches) may track everything else you do and all the other websites you visit even when you're not logged into Amazon. This would help Amazon identify risks. Risks that may relate to your health (if you've been searching for Alcoholics Anonymous in your vicinity) or specific preferences (you known what I mean). This would enable Amazon to go from one book you've purchased to carving out a slice of things that matter most.

The underlying pivot for Amazon would be to move from a transactional to a sustained or more long-term relationship. The strength of its business case with you is then based on the criticality of the things that matter to you. The sustainability of its business case with you is driven by how long these things matter.

Apple makes iPhones, among other products. However, over time, the iPhone has become commoditised as other players such as Samsung began making similar smartphones. Apple then locked value via the iTunes store. With this, Apple was able to obtain a slice of revenue from all our app-based transactions. Over time, the Android platform was able to mimic the Apple app store. However, with the sensitive capability of sensors of the iPhone, including its microphone and accelerometer, Apple may be able to identify early signs of impending strokes due to voice modulation or slurring or muscle tremors as you hold the phone. It may also be able to identify early stages of Parkinson's or Alzheimer's by capturing information from the vagus nerve in our ear, since we increasingly consider Apple EarPods ubiquitous. By capturing this information and red-flagging health risks, Apple could make the iPhone (or whatever wearable device replaces it) part of what concerns us most, from being a device that some of us would otherwise consider replacing with a competing smartphone. One device that could replace the iPhone could be spectacles. This product would become a wearable, which would address several challenges that either afflict the iPhone or have resulted in its commoditisation. It would track health by having an inwards facing camera to track eye movements. This may do two things. One would be to see what you look at. The second would be to track your health parameters from your iris as well as from brain waves. The outwards facing camera would help you augment information that you look at, which could be shown on a virtual screen. This may also offer a more complete app immersion experience since this would provide audio via bone conduction and 3D video with depth perception. Of course, this makes many assumptions about what Apple may make. However, given that all these technologies are close to commercial realisation, it is only a matter of putting them together. If Apple does not do this, due to privacy considerations or because they feel there may be much to lose with their existing ecosystems, a startup may do this, capture future value and, in the process, take over the mantle of the most innovative company on the planet that Apple has owned for close to 20 years, at the time of writing. In addition, so the wheel turns.

How about work? LinkedIn knows about your qualifications. It also knows that you may be looking for a new job by how often you click on those job ads. By analysing your clicks, it knows if you're looking for selectively clicking ads for truly senior positions or any position that comes up. This tells LinkedIn how comfortable you are with your existing position. Your posts on LinkedIn and how many people have liked them, as well as their own credibility and professional standing, provide LinkedIn with a pretty good assessment of your skills and their ongoing relevance. On the other hand, LinkedIn has excellent insight into skills relevant for the future and companies receiving funding due to the frequency with which these startups hire people and the quality of the talent hired, scaling revenue and increasing impact. If you're one of the first individuals with this skill, LinkedIn could push plum assignments your way, as lifetime jobs are superseded by the knowledge-driven gig economy. The satisfaction of the companies that use your skill and their feedback could form part of your professional credibility profile. In this way, LinkedIn could transition a part of your work life into its own network.

Weight is a problem in all major developed countries. In the USA, over 40% of adults are obese. This is not simply an image-related issue. The estimated annual medical cost related to obesity in the USA is close to $150 billion and is increasing. This challenge is also an opportunity (https://www.cdc.gov/obesity/data/adult.html).

Weight Watchers is an amazing programme that addresses, as the name suggests, weight. Those who use it swear by it and make it part of their lifestyle. They plan their shopping around what they are allowed to eat. It addresses people who are overweight and want to lose weight without actual exercise, while giving users the option to eat whatever they want to eat, so long as they consume a maximum number of points, since each food item has points based on calories. Users are able to continue being lazy while they indulge in their favourite foods and do not have to create healthy food from raw ingredients. Users stay in the programme over very long periods of time since it keeps them borderline overweight for the most part without actually slipping into obesity. However, the programme is always at risk of becoming old-fashioned if new trends relating to health emerge, such as personalised weight management by identifying the signature of your gut microbiome and make it do the heavy lifting of optimising calorie burn. One way to drive more value from the programme is to focus on the users rather than the programme itself. Since it is clear that the focus audience is overweight, it stands to reason that this same audience is also likely to have other comorbidities resulting from excessive weight. One observation during COVID-19 was that those who were obese had a dramatically increased risk of mortality compared to others. Beyond this, obesity puts stress on organs and significantly increases the risk of cardiovascular diseases, diabetes and hypertension. In fact, a majority of the mortalities due to COVID-19 occurred for those who had at least one of these underlying conditions, which again occurred due to obesity.

Weight Watchers has these people in its network. It has the opportunity to track health issues and may be in a pole position to pre-empt more significant health risks, as well as specific lifestyle changes that may mitigate these risks. By tracking health challenges that these people have, as well as food habits that either help in flagging those that may result in mortalities, Weight Watchers may be able to provide pre-emptive guidance and highlight risks to future users. Further information about the family or cultural background of its users may enable it to personalise possible risks. By using their app to track the user's movements could further enable health tracking beyond simply stating points for different foods. Instead of passively tracking the user's physical activity, Weight Watchers could put daily goals that become motivators for users. Beyond all of this, they could bring together users who have the same background and motivations so that they may form virtual networks to encourage each other towards better health, doing all this using the Weight Watchers platform. Or they may not, in which case, this could be a ripe opportunity for a startup that decides to do just that. In such cases, it is difficult to see how Weight Watchers is able to sustain its super profits based on selling yoghurt with points on it.

These examples illustrate the possibility of transitioning transactional and cost-driven networks to more sustainable value capture driven by the things that sustain us, such as our jobs, or those we cherish most, such as our relationships or our health. With this transition, incumbent players are able to sustain and scale the transition with their customers. Over time, this provides them with the option to provide an ever-widening ecosystem that users enjoy spending time in, or one where they need to spend time as it provides them with the means to earn their livelihood, or give it meaning. The flip side of this opportunity that incumbent players have is that they don't often take it, as it risks cannibalising their existing ecosystem, which over time has become less lean as they spend more and more time building assets to sustain it. This is precisely where new firms find opportunities to build new pockets of value.

Fully Closed Platform

Imagine.

Imagine a solution that knows about your ovulation cycle to maximise your chances of becoming pregnant.

Imagine an app that knows when you're pregnant, even before you know it.

If your unborn child has health issues, imagine being able to identify and fix them.

Imagine an app that helps your child in home schooling based on his or her ability to learn and natural attributes.

Imagine having something that gives your child the ability to meet peers and make friends virtually.

Imagine having a virtual companion for your child.

Imagine being able to pre-empt your child's health risks based on your own genes and being able to have the most effective treatment based on efficacy and allergic risks.

Being able to buy any goods or services online and having them delivered to your doorstep?

Imagine your child being able to find a job and being able to earn a living using an app.

How about being able to find love?

Being able to find online insurance, optimised for the level of fitness tracked by a wearable 24*7?

In old age, how about soulmates who have complementary interests?

And finally, when you die, a digital record of a life well lived, with all important moments captured?

Each of these apps or platforms exists. Perhaps one that does not yet have regulatory approval due to ethical considerations is the option to change the unborn child's genetic make-up to mitigate specific disease risks. However, the technology exists.

Now imagine all of these apps and capabilities being available in one platform. If there's too much of a good thing, this might be it. It would truly be like living in the matrix. Would it give the illusion of access and freedom while controlling everything? Would this then cement full economic extraction, where the time of the user is the ultimate currency for those who control these platforms? These are open questions but ones that are increasingly pertinent. Companies including Alibaba are already in the process of building many parts of the platform. The question for these behemoths is whether governments would allow them to do so, without having oversight on it.

True unicorns know that the greatest value of a platform is not from what it can provide but from what it *enables*. This is also the greatest difference between tech startups that are run by scientists who only speak of what the technology can do and true visionaries who help us all visualise what it can enable and how that impacts all of us. The same input can have different reasons or perspectives, with wildly different results. A software engineering student who wants to find a good job focuses on his grades. However, if the same student realises that he may soon be the manager of others creating software, he tries to understand what can go wrong and perhaps the most efficient way to create software. If he expects to create his startup, his focus shifts to understanding the market need that his software can fulfil and perhaps productise the software to sell it to multiple customers.

In the early days of space travel, government entities demonstrated their capabilities by sending blocks of concrete to showcase the power of their rockets. Then, Elon Musk came along and sent his own Tesla roadster into space. For those of us who waited breathlessly as the countdown to the launch began to when the final stage of the rocket reached space, the vision of the car effortlessly cruising in the vastness of space and the earth casually moving by in the background is so surreal that it may define our entire generation.

Meta, one of the most valuable companies in the world, enables user interaction or the use of information that users happily, nay, and eagerly update. What is interesting is not that users simply feel comfortable sharing information online; they perceive that they own this virtual space. They put up their information. Increasingly, this is where they meet new people, find common interests, make new friends and get to know about news from around the world and what is trending but also what their friends consider relevant. With all of this, Meta has a valuation of over USD 860 billion at the time of writing.

An even more compelling example of how users perceive their ownership of this virtual space and how it translates to the value of the platform is Tencent. Tencent has a presence across a diverse range of businesses, including e-commerce, retail, video gaming, real estate, software, virtual reality, ride-sharing, banking, financial services, fintech, consumer technology, computer technology, automobile, film production, movie ticketing, music production, space technology, natural resources, smartphones, big data, agriculture, medical services, cloud computing, social media, IT, advertising, streaming media, artificial intelligence, robotics, UAVs, food delivery, courier services, e-books, Internet services, education and renewable energy (https://en.wikipedia.org/wiki/Tencent).

What this implies is that Tencent's users are slowly but surely spending more and more time on the site, be it to earn a living, spend their leisure time, buy goods or services and find friends with common interests. If we consider that the individual per capita income is reflected in the time per day that a user spends, the revenue opportunity is the reflection of the per capita income of all the users on the site. Furthermore, if we consider the future relevance of the personal information provided by users, it begins to capture the total value of Tencent. However, not fully. The true approximation of the value of Tencent may be the accumulation of the above plus the knowledge about the *changing* user preferences, since it provides guidance regarding how future preferences of other users who are behind the curve will evolve. The curve could be the age curve, the prosperity curve or indeed the health curve. By better understanding this curve, Tencent may be able to pre-empt the evolving needs and motivations of users and cater to them on a proactive basis, increasing revenue and keeping its profit margins on revenue high and sustained. If Tencent is able to use its network to help its users move in the prosperity curve by enabling them to find work or on the health curve by helping them live longer by pre-empting ailments, it ultimately owns the ecosystems of which the users are a part rather than simply serving them.

If the value of knowing that a user is likely to see the next instalment of Star Wars or be more interested in buying the first edition of a toy from Star Wars series is significant, imagine the value in a user knowing that they may run the risk of getting a preventable ailment, such as some kinds of cancers, and the value of knowing how to mitigate this risk or how to find the most effective treatment from others who have recovered from the ailment.

The true value of the platform seems to be achieved when the user perceives that he or she owns it. In reality, it is precisely the opposite. By going in deep enough down the rabbit hole, the user becomes part of what gives it depth.

R Value

Until 2019, the R value was the stuff taught in universities in statistics or applied mathematics classes. Outside the classroom, this had been used in the determination of how diseases such as EBOLA or SARS were likely to spread. This was used to calculate the transmission of the disease.

EBOLA is one of the most virulent infections in recent memory. It is believed to have begun in Guinea, when a 2-year-old boy, Emile Ouamouno, became infected while playing near a tree that was a roosting place for free-tail bats infected with the virus. It rapidly spread to his family and soon to the entire community. Soon, it spread to Liberia and Sierra Leone. In both of these countries, the virus decimated entire communities, ultimately leading to an official death toll of close to 5000 in Liberia and approximately 4000 in Sierra Leone. Liberia, being one of the least developed countries in the world, had only 50 doctors for a population of 4.3 million at the time. This enabled the spread of the disease to go on unchecked. In Sierra Leone, social involvement during funerals aided the spread of the disease, including rubbing the body with oil, dressing it in fine clothes and hugging prior to burial. This contributed to further spread since dead bodies had particularly high concentrations of the virus (https://en.wikipedia.org/wiki/Ebola_virus_epidemic_in_Liberia).

The mortality rate, as calculated by the WHO, was close to 50%. This meant that 50% of those who were infected died. This was transmitted by direct contact with infected blood, secretions, tissues, organs and other bodily fluids from dead or living infected persons. From this perspective, the virus was partially successful if success was measured by the ability to infect combined with the mortality rate. The only point where the virus failed was that the EBOLA patients became infectious after they began displaying violent symptoms of the disease. At this time, the R value began to find relevance in the medical and WHO community. The R value, or the effective reproduction number, is the rate of infection. This helps to measure an infectious disease's capacity to spread. If this was equal to 1, it implied that an infected person was likely to infect one person. In such cases, the disease was likely to continue spreading in a linear progression. If the R value is 1.1, the infection rate increases dramatically, from 1000 cases to 25,000 in 60 days. For Liberia and Sierra Leone, the R value was more than 1.5. This meant that the rate of infection continued to increase, resulting in a surge in infections in the two countries. The fact that patients with EBOLA became infectious after they started showing violent symptoms was the only reason that it did not become a global pandemic. It thus failed by being unable to sustain its spread.

However, it was only in early 2020 that this R value caught the public imagination. This was when the coronavirus, or COVID-19, which began in Wuhan in China in late 2019, began spreading around the world. Not since the Spanish flu of 1918 had the world seen a pandemic quite like this. The Spanish flu was estimated to have infected approximately 500 million people, or approximately one-third of the world's population at the time, with death toll estimates ranging from 17 million to 100 million (https://en.wikipedia.org/wiki/Spanish_flu). Although COVID-19 had a much lower mortality rate, it was particularly virulent for several other reasons. It was spread by air via droplets from infected persons. The virus survived for several hours on surfaces, including doorknobs. However, worst of all, the infected persons became infectious several days before they began showing symptoms of the disease. It was the last point that resulted in COVID-19 spreading to virtually every country in the world within 90 days. This is also what resulted in the R value of COVID-19 being as high as 8.9 at the peak infection period (https://en.wikipedia.org/wiki/Basic_reproduction_number).

At the time of writing, the jury is still out on whether antibodies may stop the virus from manifesting in the disease. What is still unknown is whether having caught the virus once may preclude another infection, how long the immunity may last and whether the body may remember how to fight it the next time or whether it would be worse the second time.

10 Sustaining Platform Value

Managing a pandemic is about understanding the spread of the disease, the factors increasing the rate of progression and the R value. Furthermore, knowing what ultimately stopped the spread and how comorbidities create an impact on the mortality of the disease can help in pre-empting the risk of a second infection and better treatment options. However, the factors that make the pandemic happen are exactly what makes a platform startup succeed. Let us look at them in more detail.

A baseline assumption of a platform startup is that the R value needs to be over 1. This means that every user of the platform needs to bring more than one new user to the platform. Over time, this provides a substantial group of users. It is important to note that the startup does not need to address all users across all regions. Like a pandemic that creates a stronger footprint in countries where the health tracking system is less developed or where there are structural weaknesses, a startup needs to find a market that is more susceptible or has low entry barriers (Fig. 10.1).

From the visual above, it is clear that even iterative growth can help a startup become the dominant platform. It needs to be kept in mind that the narrower the segment, the easier it is to *initially* scale. Once the users begin to see the platform as the default in the category relevant for them, the platform can expand. Speed of rollout to gain enough of an audience to have a meaningful exchange is imperative.

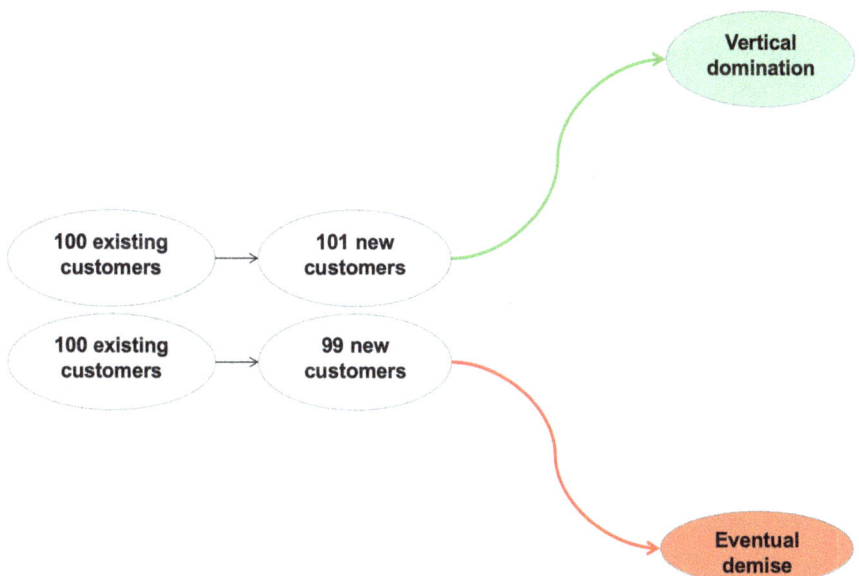

Fig. 10.1 Network effect enabling a platform startup to scale

On Running's understanding of the R value in marketing was one of the factors responsible for their success. As Marc Maurer, co-CEO, told me, '*we began our rollout in the US by going to different cities at random. Very quickly, we realised that it wasn't working. We realised that we needed a certain penetration per 100,000 inhabitants in a geofenced area. As soon as we hit that level of penetration with the runners, the sales would just take off, even if we tapered off our marketing.*' On Running's understanding of peer validation became a key cornerstone for scaling sales successfully.

The USA provided an excellent example of what not to do during COVID-19, which counterintuitively is exactly what you would like your entry strategy with the beachhead market to be if you're the virus. While all other countries were trying to identify those with the infection and tried to provide the best possible treatment, the USA instructed the infected people to stay at home until their fingers began to turn blue. The problem with this was that at this point, the oxygen in the body was so low that the organs of the infected people were beginning to become infected. This in turn made the pandemic more successful in the USA, if its successful traction was determined by the number of people it could infect and the revenue being the number of those who would die from the infection.

In the same way, the best opportunity for a platform startup to make inroads into the market is to identify existing and incumbent ecosystems that simply do not address the evolving needs of customers. Amazon was an excellent example of this. In its early days, Bezos realised that Internet usage was increasing exponentially. He tried to identify the sectors where people could buy things online without adversely impacting the buying experience. Products such as shoes were not viable since customers usually like to experience the shoe and its comfort before buying it. The same was the case with clothes, since people like to try them on before they make the purchase. Books were the one item that people bought simply by selecting the book and possibly reading the review. The online buying experience in the case of books could effectively be better than going into a book shop since a customer would be able to obtain more detailed reviews, and once he brought it, he could obtain other recommendations based on his preferences.

One reason why the COVID-19 infection rate in the USA was so high was the high payment at hospitals, much of which was not covered by insurance. Therefore, those who had the virus with relatively mild symptoms avoided going to hospitals and, in turn, spread it further. This is a very effective way for a platform startup to address customer experiences with incumbent competitors. Thus, if competitors provide products and services for an upfront fee, a platform startup can use this insight to create inroads to customers.

An important element of a pandemic is that it does not spread evenly in the population but creates a maximum impact in the form of mortalities with those with comorbidities. For COVID-19, the mortality of those with other health issues, such as diabetes, hypertension or respiratory diseases, was significantly higher (https://www.ncbi.nlm.nih.gov/pmc/articles/PMC7098485/). Similarly, for a platform startup, it is imperative to find hooks with complementary solutions that potential customers are already using. This provides an easier access point and subsequently provides a beachhead. The startup does need to take care that it does not become locked into the complementary solution. Otherwise, the value risks are captured by the complementary solution rather than by the startup, in addition to limiting the growth of the startup.

A key aspect of COVID-19 is not the infection itself but the risk of another infection once a person has had the infection and has recovered. The risk of contracting the infection, given comorbidities or antibodies, is another important element. Data on past or existing health challenges and how they may impact an individual's risk of getting the infection, or once he gets it, his prognosis, is driven by data. Over time, these data improve the ability to ensure the best scenario: survival and return to good health. In the same way, a platform startup's main advantages over time are the ability to split its market into various target segments and identify the criticality of the information that it may be able to provide to them over time with the data it is able to collate. These help it sustain traction with specific customer groups, since better decision-making over time ensures that customers stay with the platform.

In July 1996, Sabeer Bhatia and Jack Smith created the first free e-mail. This was Hotmail, which was a playful reference to the similar-sounding language used in showing documents on a browser and the basis for the Internet, HTML. For several months, the team was unable to obtain any significant sign-up. Finally, the team, backed by John Doerr, the fabled VC investor based in Silicon Valley, decided to make one small change below the e-mail. Each time the e-mail was sent, the reader saw 'Get your free e-mail at Hotmail'. This simple modification made each e-mail sent by a user a marketing pitch. This was a new way for users to participate in the new world that the Internet had enabled. In effect, this was the first case of viral marketing on the Internet. Within 24 months, they had 12 million users, and they sold the company for close to $400 m to Microsoft (https://en.wikipedia.org/wiki/Outlook.com).

In retrospect, what Hotmail had achieved could have easily been the basis for what Google became. The important learning here is to understand what the market will want to move to. When Hotmail was sold to Microsoft, Hotmail had a total capacity of 2 MB. You thus had to clean your folder if you wanted more space for new emails. This did not change since Microsoft did not see the B2C value of being able to create dependencies with users. Google introduced Gmail in April 2004; it did so with over 10 GB. Hotmail still had 2 MB. Microsoft missed one simple element in its strategy when it saw the cost associated with giving more memory space to its users when it had virtually no competition: what gets users in is very different from what keeps them hooked. What got you to get a Gmail account was the now 15GB capacity. What keeps you on it are the 10 K unread emails. This can provide sustained revenue, even if you continue to provide the e-mail capacity for free. Given what Gmail became and where Hotmail was as a first mover, by selling Hotmail for $400 m, Bhatia may have left approximately $ 1 trillion on the table.

Microsoft's approach shows another factor endemic to large industry leaders. When they become industry behemoths, they become so comfortable with the market they have created that they hesitate to pivot to new markets for fear of jeopardising their existing market. When value transitions out, they lose relevance, leading to the emergence of new players.

The best way to teach students is to help them identify and own their own vision and let the teaching become the enabler to achieve this vision. By the same token, the best way for a platform startup to sustain users is when they feel they own it and obtain actionable intelligence that increases in relevance over time.

Unicorn startups appear to be made of stardust. This may well be the case. This may also be a good time to reflect in the mirror and see if you can find what creates them. It always starts with your vision as an entrepreneur. As nineteenth-century Indian sage Vivekanand observed, 'Your beliefs become your thoughts, your thoughts become your actions, your actions become your habits, your habits become your character, and your character becomes your destiny.' And isn't your destiny worth thinking about?

11

Waves of Value Transition

Breakthrough innovation comes in waves. These are not consistent with the ones that crest on the beach every few seconds. Instead, they are more like the waves generated by a tsunami. These waves do not form in isolation but require an environment where the underlying technological infrastructure is able to support their emergence. They gather strength when a change in user requirements meets an innovative and replicable solution that delivers that. A tiny difference in direction changes everything.

The First Wave: Risk

The creation of wealth and how risk evolves is exemplified by *The Golden Book on Venice*. *The Golden Book*, or *Libro d'Oro*, was compiled between 1297 and 1315 and was made up of the eligible families of Venice. These were the families that had amassed wealth, including from the shipping trade. The families listed in *The Golden Book* were then recognised as royalties. Individuals began with a high-risk mentality in order to try to amass wealth by investing in high-risk ventures such as ships that sailed to new lands for the purpose of trading and importing precious cargo such as spices from the East. As people became wealthy, their focus shifted from high-risk ventures to create wealth to low-risk strategies to sustain this wealth. However, *The Golden Book* limited the investment in these shipping ventures, so only the families listed in it could invest. New individuals who wanted to invest in high-risk ventures were now prohibited from doing so. This resulted in the eventual decline of the wealth of Venice over the following decades.

The Second Wave: Credit

We consider the second wave of value transition to be just one word. It was called 'credit'. During the middle ages, India was divided into many kingdoms ruled by kings. There was often conflict, and the kings who conquered neighbouring kingdoms took the spoils of war, which were mostly in the form of gold and expanded territory. The majority of the value they captured was in turn either stored as gold or used to build new palaces to sustain their lavish lifestyles, with some of the new wealth used to provide patronage to the arts and to create and sustain religious institutions. The wealth distribution reflected the traditional class system, wherein the highest class was the priest class or Brahmins, followed by the warrior class or Kshatriyas. Below this was the trader class or Vaishyas, and the bottom rung was the labourers or the Shudras. The spoils of war and wealth distribution reflected the class system. Thus, very little wealth was distributed to the trader class. Additionally, the upper classes deemed it below their rank to partake in trading.

At about the same time, Europe was seeing the emergence of credit in the form of banking. Individuals would provide funding to someone with a good idea. This was done by way of credit or by partaking in the risk itself by way of having a share of the enterprise.

Sapiens: A Brief History of Humankind illustrates how money can be multiplied elegantly. A building contractor deposits $1 m in a bank. A baker goes to the bank and takes a loan of $1 m to set up a bakery on credit. In turn, the baker pays the building contractor to build the bakery. The building contractor in turn deposits the second $1 m in the bank. Although the bank has $1 m in actual cash, it has given a credit of $1 million, and on paper has $2 m. Due to the banking rules, it is often mandated that the bank needs to hold 10% of the money it gives out as on credit or as loan. The bank is thus able to give a loan of $10 m when it holds $1 m in actual cash.

The concept of credit enabled Europe to steal a march over India and many other Asian countries, which were still feudal with a focus on wealth as a store of value rather than an opportunity to invest in risk.

Banks and financial institutions developed as commercial funding sources to support the development of new enterprises, which in turn created greater relevance for financial institutions, creating a virtuous cycle. The USA institutionalised this in the nineteenth century. However, the concepts of credit and banking further diverged when banking became either a means to create commercial activity or wealth-capturing mechanisms. In 1818, the USA had 338 banks. This increased to close to 28,000 banks by 1914 (*The Wealth of

Nations). The plethora of banks meant that people looking for loans had low-cost loans available due to the intense competition between banks. In Mexico, on the other hand, there were only 42 banks in 1910, of which two controlled over 60% of banking assets. This lack of competition resulted in banks lending only to already wealthy individuals and charging very high interest rates. This suppressed the emergence of new commercial activity since the propensity of risk of wealthy individuals changes from a high-risk entrepreneurial mindset to a low-risk wealth sustainability perspective.

The Third Wave: Extractive

Observe any country that may have a closed and protected economy and begin the process of opening to outside products and investments. As it begins opening up and reducing restrictions, the first international companies that enter the market are often Coca-Cola and McDonald's. This is because the investment needed for these companies to enter a new market is negligible compared to an infrastructure company. The products of these companies are also purely transactional. This implies that consumers do not have to plan to buy these products in advance or have to live with the consequences of these buying decisions, broadly speaking. This does not mean that the companies that provide transactional products do not capture value. In contrast, they consolidate their position over time as first movers, even as their products, for the most part, create no skill base or high-quality employment in the country.

I had the opportunity to visit Myanmar in 2020 as a UN delegate. This country is one of the least developed countries in the world, partially due to the government straitjacketed by the strict military regime. (Author's note: this has now regressed back to being fully controlled by the military.) Despite having partially opened its economy, global companies were loath to enter the country. The first companies that entered the market were companies such as Coca-Cola. The local malls that rapidly proliferated in Yangon all had food courts, where every dish had high sugar and was deep-fried. Although this provided an explosion of flavour compared to the farm-grown food, the health of the population rapidly degraded, resulting in obesity and diabetes, almost before they realised the detrimental impact of these foods. Because the products needed almost no local manufacturing, they provided no benefit to the local economy.

However, we don't need to look thus far. Often, the activities that we take for granted and those that provide us with a degree of convenience are extractive. When you go to YouTube or Instagram, you always seem to find the content that seems to be personalised for you. This is not simply by chance but is based on an algorithm that these companies spend billions of dollars on. We assume it's to provide us with content we'd like to keep us onboard as customers. You're partly right. It's to keep us onboard and motivate us to spend ever-increasing times of our day, day after day, and to keep coming back for more. It is not, however, to keep us onboard as customers. It's important to recognise that if we're not paying for any service (Facebook, Instagram, Google, TikTok, the list goes on), we are not the customers of these platforms, but its products. They extract our data and personal preferences and sell this to *their* customers, the advertising companies that in turn use this information to sell us more goods and services. From buying products, goods and services, we have transitioned to *being* products. This is extractive. (Ref.: *Why Nations Fail*).

The Fourth Wave: Transactional

The activities that we engage in during our leisure time increasingly have to pre-empt our immediate needs and desires or provide us with engagement and the social connections that we now find via apps. Companies providing the digital equivalent of McDonald's and Coca-Cola have already accessed, addressed and staked their claim on this market. Each day, your personal preferences determine what you're exposed to. Meta spends billions of dollars each year on better understanding individual preferences; in effect, what you're likely to like based on what you've liked. Among the youngest companies and those for the youngest of us, Instagram is all about providing specific content tailored to what you've seen and motivating us to follow influencers and topics based on our stated interest or what we've clicked.

Amazon shows you what you're most likely to buy based on the time of year, the season, even the time of day (or night) when you're surfing. YouTube is famous for driving stickiness among those too old to be on Instagram who simply want to while away the time while awaiting inspiration to write something of relevance *and* impact for his audience, your esteemed writer included.

For all practical purposes, and for all new entrants inspiring for a slice of this market, I have bad news; you're late.

However, like a tsunami, the first wave is not the biggest one or the one that creates the greatest impact. The first wave simply heralds what is to come, and it is the next waves that truly bring institutional change that brings about sustainable impact or a long-term lock-in of the user base.

The Fifth Wave: Pre-Emptive

The third wave is that of data captured to enable better decisions. This is by way of billions of IoT devices. The ones in your electricity smart meter help you optimise electricity and provide the opportunity to transact excess electricity generated by your PV modules. Then, there are the IoT devices connected to the sensors that calculate the quantity and quality of hydrocarbons on the ground to determine if it is worth pumping the oil out, given the price of oil in the market or the price of plastic for one-time use and for reducing the proportion of water in the ocean.

Although there are IoT devices all around us, they're trying to make sense of existing ecosystems. The ones that are trying to get smarter or pre-emptive are doing so with the simpler or transactional areas of showcasing value. Examples include sensors that can sense the temperature in a building and can modulate it, given the weather forecast, or where a holiday home temperature can be lowered in case it is expected to be unoccupied for the coming days. Other examples include wearable devices that track your heartbeat and physical activity as well as tracking your steps every day.

This space is beginning to receive traction, particularly the segment dealing with wearables, and key players include Apple's iWatch and Fitbit. However, the sustainability of this segment has yet to be proven.

The Next Wave: Generational

We are beginning to see and live in the period of transition, as the focus moves from transactional to generational. Over time, the value of this increases, since it begins by being a technology but slowly captures information relating to personal health. Now imagine the opportunity to pre-empt certain disease risks for your children if they have a genetic predisposition or if there is an opportunity to mitigate the worse effects of a disease from afflicting them. This is far more likely to have multigenerational traction that increases over time. The ability to convert data into actionable intelligence, the hallmark that began in the first wave, comprising transactional or price-optimisation decision or social networking decisions, now moves to life-enhancing impact or decisions that pre-empt or help mitigate health risks. 'Wellness' will then transition from the lexicon of sauna to mitigating genetic predispositions to specific diseases. This wave will look at energy optimisation in homes but use sensor technology to check ambient carbon monoxide levels, track specific indicators of the occupants, red-flag health risks based on tracking their oxygen levels in the blood and call emergency response if abnormality is found in the resting pulse of the occupants. Alexa would be able to listen to the sounds of snoring and recognise early symptoms of sleep apnoea, which afflicts over 14% of all adults, most of whom are not aware of it, resulting in early mortality while asleep (https://www.ncoa.org/adviser/sleep/sleep-apnea-statistics/).

To better understand the move from transactional to generational, imagine Meta but for health. Interestingly, you're not the only one to imagine this. Meta has already begun to think about it. Not quite generational yet, but it's taken the first step by creating a hardware solution that is able to augment the sounds that the user can hear. There are hiccups along the way, as we saw after Facebook changed its name to Meta, and hired thousands of developers, but as the demand failed to materialise, fired 10,000 people. However, beyond this, it is the first solution that enables Meta to become a wearable for the user, soon followed by their recently announced AR glasses. Ultimately, this step is essential to avoid the risk of getting locked out by the new generation of users or where the most attractive health-driven markets are locked in by competitors (https://about.fb.com/news/2020/09/facebook-reality-labs-research-future-of-audio/).

One of the hallmarks of the next wave will be personalised health. Although this has been spoken of for a long time, even today, insurance companies, whose entire business case depends on paying as little as possible in case the insured person becomes unwell, have very little idea about the specific health conditions of their customers, beyond their height, weight and whether they smoke. Many insurance companies do not even have the contact details of a large portion of their insured persons since this information is kept confidential by their independent agents. Thus, although a whole host of diseases arise from depression, since overeating, excessive smoking and alcohol abuse are often a result of depression, which in turn results in obesity and lung and liver disease, insurance companies have very little idea or ability to track depression.

Interestingly, the cause and effect of depression are well known. Even so, the existing insurance companies do not focus on this since there is a time gap between depression and the onset of diseases. In addition, the agents' compensation is often done from year to year. In Italy, the average time that the insured person stays with an insurance provider is 2 years before he moves to another cheaper provider. There is thus no motivation to track information if the gap between cause and effect (read 'mortality') is likely to be over 2 years.

The Final Wave: Convergence

As we go through the waves, the attributes of technology startups and platform startups begin to converge. While it may be possible to scale for a technology startup if it pre-empts and addresses potential limitations to scale, it is far from trivial to sustain this value.

Take automobile companies. As long as the technology ecosystem was largely stable (read: no breakthroughs underlying ecosystem development and no breakthrough innovation waves), these car companies created and sustained value by highlighting attributes of the car, including its shape and design as well as its acceleration. Then, Tesla entered the market. Predictably, the established care companies began by ignoring it until it began to produce cars that owners loved. They were driven by their existing ecosystems, both internal and external. The internal ecosystems included the employees, who were comfortable with their skills and did not want to leave their comfort zones. The internal ecosystems also included the suppliers who were completely dependent on and had invested heavily to support the existing business. Finally, the distributor agency network, which also provided servicing to cars and had established exclusivities that further drove up the price of cars and by establishing industry networks, was often able to lobby local governments to enact regulations that were beneficial to them, to the detriment of the end customer and for new entrants. All of these factors provided support for the status quo and resisted change since it would impact their own business models.

The external ecosystem was built by multigovernmental systems. On the one hand, the oil and gas companies, closely linked to oil-producing nations, and in some cases, extended proxies of the nations, had a lot at stake by ensuring that traditional car manufacturers did not deviate from producing fuel-consuming vehicles. These governments were in a position to put pressure via governments including the USA and Germany, resulting in subsidies and emission standards that enabled the automobile companies to continue making fuel-guzzling vehicles. In turn, these companies were able to access sops including tax breaks and soft loans. In addition, so the cycle was perpetuated, till Tesla entered the fray.

When the car companies perceived a threat from Tesla's innovation in electric cars and the changing perception of the public towards electric cars, they began to move towards electric mobility, assuming this to be the innovation that they had to address and the competitive threat to their businesses. However, what they failed to address or even recognise was Tesla's other innovation: the network effect. This innovation was for the car to transition from being a product to becoming the networked ecosystem that produced intelligence to the car, enabling it to improve over time due to the data captured from all cars. Tesla also captured the specific personal attributes of each driver to provide a better driving experience. In the same way that users flocked to Gmail for the 10GB data when Hotmail still provided 2 MB but stayed and became locked in due to the thousands of conversations accumulated over time, Tesla's innovation of creating and becoming the ecosystem provided a powerful platform that not only enabled it to scale and capture user value but also to sustain it for the foreseeable future. That charger network provided an opportunity to gain intelligence, and the closed network loop enabled it to actually pre-empt potential issues with the car so that the service engineers knew about it before the driver became aware of it and could come and fix it on the go since they also knew the location of the car. The insights gathered enabled Tesla to easily address multiple new sectors that traditional automobile companies simply could not, including insurance of the car, leasing and taxi networks to compete with Uber, and delivery or logistics, since cars are normally used less than 5% of the time. As autonomous driving rolls out and eventually becomes commonplace, these new segments will open up, and Tesla will have stolen a march on competitors across segments far beyond the automobile sector. Over time, incorporation of health tracking sensors will enable Tesla to track the health of the driver and go into health insurance on a far more personalised basis due to greater awareness of the health of the driver and his movements, as the Tesla app for smartphones is able to track location and movement. Recognition of only a few of these emerging business cases is why Tesla is worth more than many of the traditional car companies combined. Being able to capture the leisure time of the people in the car, particularly when the car is able to drive autonomously, will further enhance and consolidate its lock-in and ability to take a slice of revenue from the like of Netflix. As autonomous driving scales, Tesla will be the first app that you actually sit in, and it will own your time for the duration of your ride.

Google, another company that led and was a product of the first wave, does 'search'. Its challenge is that although it has tried to go into several new business areas, the revenue driver continues to be advertising related to search. As a pure platform, this was a reasonable strategy for riding the first wave, but sustaining relevance in the subsequent waves of moving from transitional to institutional or generational traction, a lock-in via hard assets is imperative. This is because Google's entire business is based on its browser and is the repository for search, including knowing what *you* search for. The catch is that the browser or indeed the search itself requires a device, something that Google has little control over. One could argue that since Google owns the Android platform, which in turn is the operating system for 4 of 5 smartphones, this would ensconce it from competitive risks. It does, so long as people keep using mobile phones. However, over time, the Internet experience will move from being completely open to splitting into specialised verticals, each vertical in turn becoming a walled garden. A walled garden implies a closed ecosystem that limits external access and provides a safer or higher quality experience. Apple, with its iTunes store, is a perfect example of this. In the absence of ownership of a device, Google is always at risk if high-value applications move from smartphones to interfaces locked in by higher-value ecosystems such as Tesla. Apple has recognised the relevance of smart cars as a potential walled garden. In its latest software update, Apple announced that its app will be able to open cars. This is, however, outside looking in, since Tesla recognises its ownership of its own walled garden and would like to have full control over it, exactly like Apple.

TikTok is a prime example of a dominant player that failed to converge. It created a very strong ecosystem by innovating and ultimately owning the platform for sharing short-form videos of up to 1 min. TikTok, in turn, is considered to be under the purview of the Chinese government. Up to this time, it had done incredibly well in getting users to consider its platform their own and create their own videos, which were then shared by an active network. TikTok also used AI to consistently improve the user experience so that over time, users were able to obtain suggestions that were increasingly tuned to their own interests. This also drove traction and time spent by users on the platform.

Due to the perception of national security considerations arising from the over 800 million active users as of mid-2020, the USA felt that TikTok might be able to influence those using the platform. To alleviate this concern, US President Donald Trump stated that TikTok would be banned in the USA unless part of it that addressed US users could be owned by a US-based company. Since TikTok was an app that ran on iPhone and Android platforms, both American-based entities, complying with this regulation meant that all Apple and Google (which had a majority ownership of Android) had to do was to get it off the app store and block this on their servers. TikTok's challenge was that even though it was incredibly popular and created and largely owned its own category, it was an app that ran on hardware that was owned by others. This ultimately became its weakness, since this dependency created confusion in the minds of users and gave an opportunity to companies such as Facebook to attract these users with Reels, a TikTok lookalike. In retrospect, the punitive threat of blockage to TikTok was only a ruse to enable its American competitors to roll out and institutionalise competitive solutions. From its modest beginnings, this was another example of social digital media transitioning to becoming part of geo-politics.

In 1998, the Google founders were looking at the option of selling the company. The potential buyer was a company called Excite. Excite offered $750 K, and the Google founders were looking for $1.25 m. The deal did not go through. Approximately 20 years later, Google had a valuation of close to a trillion dollars and had the opportunity to buy Tesla for less than 30 billion dollars. However, at this time, Google was the leader in the first wave and failed to recognise the possibility that there could be new waves of innovation that could disrupt its business model. It thus saw Tesla as yet another car company, where the only difference Google saw was that it was powered by batteries rather than petroleum, rather than the first app that you sit in, and where Tesla absolutely owns your time and controls what you're able to stream, as well as has absolute ownership of what you do in the car, with the opportunity to monetise information about your interests and social networks, as well as your health parameters. In this, Google really missed out, in the same way that Excite had missed out a mere 20 years earlier.

As mobile devices transition to specialised walled gardens, particularly for more high-value or high-impact customer segments, Google's revenue sources risk migrating away. If the smart device screen transitions into a virtual screen or if information begins to be displayed via a source integrated into the body, Google's business case risks disappearing entirely. This is the essence of the convergence between being a platform and being a technology, and the possible impact on Google illustrates the risk of ignoring the leverage that hardware lock-in provides in ensuring the sustainability of value.

In effect, Google began by capturing transactional value and stayed there. By failing to drive and own the network effect, Google missed the opportunity to put itself in the middle of social networks or their evolving ways to communicate. Contrast this with the strategy of Meta, the product of the first wave. It acquired Instagram and WhatsApp in 2012 and 2014 at what seemed to be unbelievably high valuations. In retrospect, that may have been incredibly cheap since they each have over a billion users. Furthermore, as these apps are hubs between conversations and social interactions, they continue to sustain relevance. Google's strategy of acquiring YouTube was more geared towards seeing content as the point at which value resides. Following the reasoning above, YouTube's content relevance may be transactional, implying that the monetisation may not be sustainable but instead become a way to capture a historical perspective of our time in visual format.

From these examples, it becomes obvious that with waves of innovation, the pecking order of startups that are able to recognise, ride and own the first wave are able to replace the incumbents from even the Fortune 500, or the 500 most valuable companies in the world in the late 1990s. However, what is also pertinent is that most of these behemoths are built on foundations that may be ephemeral and by no means guarantee the sustainability of their value. Unlike companies of the previous generation, be it car manufacturers or electricity utilities, they built expensive physical assets and locked in both the supply and the demand. These companies built manufacturing facilities with funding and support, including tax breaks and subsidies from local authorities, and provided job opportunities to the local communities. The local governments, having invested so much in these companies, had a stake in their ongoing success and provided protection from competitors or exclusivity. This is akin to you getting a loan of $ 1000 dollars—the bank owns you. If you get a loan of $ 100 million, you own the bank. The example of Donald Trump, as illustrated by the book *Too Much and Never Enough*, by Mary trump illustrates this richly.

In mid-1990, Trump had ever-increasing loans on his profligate spending, from his yacht to his three casinos. For the completion of his third casino Taj Mahal, Trump had to issue junk bonds of $700 million carrying a 14% interest rate. The financial liabilities were so high that the three Trump casinos had $94 million in annual debt. However, because the banks had paid much of the money for the construction of the assets that bore Trump's name, they realised that much of the value was linked to Trump's lifestyle. Without the veneer of success that Trump had to exude, the banks realised that they risked losing their money, since gamblers would simply stop coming and people would not buy the Trump bonds that provided future revenue. In effect, the banks knew they had to pay Trump to sustain his lavish lifestyle, including his private jet and Mar-a-Lago. Therefore, in mid-1990, the banks decided to pay Trump $450,000 *per month* to enable him to sustain his lifestyle. In effect, paying him for failing miserably.

The new companies that rode the first wave are extremely asset-lite. This is what has enabled them to scale so rapidly. However, by focusing on their own growth and value capture at the expense of developing the ecosystem, they may have focused too much on the equivalent of pleasure at the expense of happiness. As Dr. Robert Lustig, a feted professor of endocrinology at the University of California, summarised, pleasure is short-lived, and happiness is long-lived. Pleasure is taking; happiness is giving. Pleasure is experienced alone, whereas happiness is experienced in groups.

By failing to develop strong ecosystems that also benefit in an inclusive manner, these players have failed to create stakeholders that also have a vested interest in sustaining their success. However, when we look at the last wave, there is good news and bad news. The good news is that very few companies are clear leaders in this. So in effect, this is an area that will generate startups that will occupy Fortune 500 spots within 20 or even 15 years, but at this time, are in the process of being conceptualised or founded. The bad news is that it is not trivial to find investors who may provide support over the time it may take to create and support startups that recognise the last wave and decide to ride it. However, the good news is that for those who persist because they are driven by an intrinsic belief of the possibility of impact of their work, they will find other stakeholders who are driven by the same ideals. Some of them will survive, and this will make all the difference.

Let us consider an example of how to create relevance and sustainability in an emerging business. An emerging trend is towards nonmeat meat, where brands such as 'Impossible Burger' or 'Beyond Meat' are valued at billions of dollars. Increasingly, there is recognition that meat may not be good for you *and* not good for the environment. If India and China begin consuming meat protein in the same volume that the USA does, we'll soon run out of farming land, or forest cover. Nonmeat protein is thus coming into vogue. Even if you do have a patent relating to the process of extraction of protein from peas, soya or an ever-increasing number of grains or even the waste product from beer production, a competitor could simply use another process. After all, a process patent is not water-tight like a patent on a unique end product such as a molecule. Second, even if a competitor is using your process for their products, you can't ask them to open their machines, so long as your patented process does not leave a signature on the end product. Furthermore, it is increasingly likely that departmental stores may have an advantage if they begin manufacturing this within their own brand, since they own the shelf-space and definitely have more visibility to the end market.

Your strategy then cannot be to simply try to outcompete the stores on volume, since someone may be able to do it cheaper. You could mitigate this by way of locking in brands or store chains into reverse exclusivity. This means they can't sell competing products or their own products, whereas you can sell to others. If you can do the reverse exclusivity, congratulations. However, they're getting smart about this, particularly given proliferation of competition, so they may not agree. Additionally, you truly need to ask yourself if price competition is your competitive advantage, since it's a race to the bottom. You could sell your nonmeat products at a high price in the beginning since someone may try it once. However, for you to continue trying to sell at a high price, you need to know more about your audience. In effect, you're not selling to one audience. If we look closely, it may be possible to segment the buyers into someone who is simply curious about it and is willing to pay once. However, the audience may also include a person who is vegan and is unable to find other alternatives that taste as good. Another user may want to buy for their children, who may have health limitations. A fourth user may be an elderly person who is simply unable to digest meat but does require the protein, and their alternative may be to have medical intervention. Your challenge is to distinguish the needs of each, the criticality of this need, the time for which the need expects to continue, what the other option is, who pays for this and how long this need (or indeed, the patient) expects to last. Over time, if you're able to track specific health challenges (via an app) that are eliminated or mitigated due to your nonmeat product, this provides stickiness with the specific user. Furthermore, this could become an opportunity for addressing other users with the same afflictions. With data points captured over a period of time, you may be able to further customise the portion and specific content, for the user in particular and the specific category in general. If you are able to capture a feedback loop, one user's experience can be shared with other users afflicted with the same health challenge. It then becomes increasingly difficult for a new competitor to take your market since you are not simply selling a product but addressing their specific needs. If the user customises his attributes in the app interface, the stickiness increases further. If the user takes you to his network of others who may have the same afflictions, this network effect further helps you scale, with the stickiness driven by the personalisation made by the primary user, using his credibility to address his network. Having locked in the demand, you are at liberty to optimise or even outsource the supply side. As discussed earlier, heavy investment in manufacturing can risk becoming a drag and dramatically reduces flexibility, in addition to having a far lower multiplier effect in your valuation, if you look for future funding. Once you've identified and secured traction with your target segment based on personalisation-driven dependence, you become a dominant player in the specific category. This then becomes your beachhead market and a springboard towards further expansion.

Notwithstanding the discussions regarding the creation and sustainability of unicorns, a fundamental principle needs to be kept in mind. Decisions made by a startup to scale rapidly enough to become a unicorn at the cost of stable growth and stepwise market traction almost always entail high risk. Sometimes, they work out if everything falls exactly into place. However, more often than not, something doesn't. Then, they suffer the fate of Icarus. In Greek mythology, the father of Icarus made wings of feathers and wax to escape from Crete and warned him of complacency and hubris. Complacency was to warn him not to fly too low, lest the sea's dampness clog his wings, or hubris by flying too high, lest the sun's heat melt them. Icarus ignored his father's advice and flew too close to the sun and tumbled from the sky when the wax in his wings melted and drowned in the sea below. Like Icarus, when these wannabe unicorns scale for the sake of scaling, they often crash and burn (https://en.wikipedia.org/wiki/Icarus).

Pure platform startups, most often from the USA, have a very low survival rate (less than 10%) since their only chance of survival is by scaling rapidly (https://www.failory.com/blog/startup-failure-rate). In comparison, research between 2003 and 2007 for technology startups from ETH Zurich, one of the world's top technology universities, was still approximately 92% of the time after 5 years. Even in the USA, research about technology startups showed that 72% of all startups founded out of MIT starting in 1945 are still around today. This is an incredible survival rate, and by most measures, it may be equal to or higher than the survival rate of large companies across multiple industries. Thus, the balance the startup needs to strive for is scaling enough to create impact as well as to sustain it while creating dominance via dependence of and inclusive value for the ecosystem (https://ethz.ch/content/dam/ethz/main/industry-and-society/entrepreneurship/ETH-spin-offs/dokumente/Performance_of_ETH_spin-offs_2015.pdf; https://innovation.mit.edu/assets/EntrepreneurshipInnovationMIT-8Dec2015-final.pdf).

Closer to our time, those of us who witnessed the moon landing on 20 July 1969 or who saw the terrorist attacks on the Twin Towers on 9/11 remember exactly where they were when they witnessed it. Such events result in a surge of activity, including investment, to address the impact because there is now acute awareness and focus on risks or fallout from the specific event. This awareness and focus in turn drives investment in the sector impacted by or able to deal with such risks in the future. 9/11, for example, resulted in a dramatic spike in investments that addressed or mitigated such attacks, as well as a heightened awareness of transatlantic terrorism-related information networks between security agencies of Europe and the USA, something that would have been unthinkable prior to 9/11.

COVID is one such moment in time. Although the scientific community has been pre-empting this risk and building scenarios for many years, having seen the impact of EBOLA and SARS, there was no consciousness or specific focus by governments because there was no urgency. The prediction of a pandemic did not come to pass thus far, so the argument was that it was unlikely to happen in the immediate future, or more particularly, during their term in office. However, between early 2020 and the middle of the year, nothing was considered more important than addressing this. In fact, for the most part, nothing else happened since everyone other than the health-care community was home-bound. Health-care workers, now suddenly recognised as 'essential workers', could go out to help care for millions of people, both young and old, who became infected around the world. The drop in nonessential activity was indeed so stark in 2021 that the vibration normally felt on Earth due to cumulative industrial activity ceased for the first time since the First World War.

Failing to recognise the last wave and its sustained impact is perilous. This danger is not simply for developed countries, where those with access to or control of data begin to capture more and more value at the expense of the others. However, to an extent, the government and social security systems in developed countries at least provide some level of support for those left behind. The risk is particularly pronounced for developing countries, where entire populations can be at risk due to value extraction. Like the first Spanish Armada that sailed to South America and found silver ore, enslaving and ultimately decimating entire local populations towards its extraction in the process, data, particularly personal data regarding preferences from a transactional perspective, and far more significantly, health data from a generational perspective, may well be the silver ore of our time. As an entrepreneur building a unicorn startup, your ethical dilemma should be how you will enable those who are digging the ore to share in some part of the value created by the silver. In effect, history may ask you one question: how did you behave with those whose destiny was in your hands when no one was looking?

Sustainable competitive advantage is based on mutual benefit or being inclusive, where the relationship with customers is based on a relationship rather than transactional focus. Finally, the most robust competitive advantage is based on customer loyalty and trust.

12

Identifying the Right Investors

One of the main questions for startups driven by first-time entrepreneurs is how to get investors to invest. When you consider starting something, the prospect of investors carrying pots of money trying to knock your door down seems so real you can almost hear the crackle of the fresh currency. Getting millions of dollars seems to be a dream. However, when you look carefully, it appears to be something that's only happening to other people.

However, you notice something else. When you decide to become an entrepreneur, a lot of money appears to have just recently been invested in a whole bunch of other similar startups that seem to have been copied from your business plan documents. This seems so much that you will be forgiven if you think that all the money that was available for your vertical has just been invested. Of course, if you delay for a few months, you realise that what you thought was the entire money a few months ago was only the tip of the iceberg, and now, a whole lot more money has been invested, which puts the earlier amount in the shade.

Once you raise the first round of funding, it does something critically important for first-time entrepreneurs. It provides reality. To put this in perspective, when someone comes up with a breakthrough technology, it seems incredible to him that no one has ever done this before, in the entire history of civilisation. It signals to these entrepreneurs that their technology excellence has global validity and relevance in an increasingly flat world. As an entrepreneur, once you conclude that your technology innovation has some uniqueness, the next step is to identify investors. However, the prospect of getting investors is similar to getting a butterfly to alight on your hand. You do not go after the butterfly; you put flowers on your palm. In the same way, getting investors to invest requires some work. This work begins by defining what makes your idea unique. There could be multiple reasons why this is the case.

The technology itself could be unique. This is often a starting point but is not always an advantage. This is because a unique technology often entails defining and creating everything around it, including the process and the hardware, in turn having an implication on the timelines and financial requirements. A more attractive option is to consider a unique way in which technology components are put together. The advantage of this is that when technology components are available off-the-shelf, the scaling-up becomes more seamless, and the team can focus on other challenges, such as demonstrating solution uniqueness and customer acquisition.

You could also attract investors by going after a specific customer segment rather than simply focusing on technology. Some of the most successful start-ups are driven by existing customer relationships, including companies that have been started by founders who have come out of these very same companies who they now consider their customers. Once a startup has established a hook, which can be any of the above, it needs to consolidate the other components of the value chain. For example, if a startup has showcased its vision to customers, it needs to insource technology, including IP licensing, which enables it to have a value proposition that provides a competitive advantage and a superior solution to customers.

Once the value proposition and customer focus have been established, the process of addressing investors can then commence. Here are some of the things that investors look at when they consider investing.

Obsession

Are you obsessed with the product? Investors do want to see this. There are a couple of good reasons why. The first one is that you will go through rough times. These include getting pressure to hit milestones from investors, market moving faster or in a completely different direction from what you anticipated, team members barking up a completely wrong tree and technology simply not being as easily replicable as you originally thought. You need to be pretty passionate to pivot and pivot again. They are not kidding when they say that entrepreneurship is about jumping off a cliff and assembling a glider on the way down.

Communication

Are you a great communicator? One of the main tasks of the founders (or at least one of them) is to communicate your vision. Investors very seldom, if ever, invest in technology, IP or hardware. They invest in teams and the passion that they demonstrate in achieving the vision, using the technology as a basis. When you are starting up, all you have is your vision. You need to communicate this to the investors, in the hope that one of them recognises that not only do you have the right value proposition but that you are the right team to pull it off. The investors also look for the team's ability to communicate the value proposition since this needs to be done to future team members to attract the best people out there. In spite of the fact that founders of technology startups are often exclusively technology people, they spend an inordinately large percentage of their time communicating their vision to all stakeholders. So communication is more than telling people what you think; it is about elucidating your vision and getting others excited about working towards it.

Can you Sell?

Founders must sell their vision before they have the opportunity to start selling their products. From this perspective, investors look carefully if they are able to sell their business value proposition to them, since their initial sale to customers is slightly more than selling a concept, with perhaps a prototype that may not fully work and where more work may be needed to ensure replicability. Founders also need to sell the future growth and amazing emerging business opportunity to their potential partners and suppliers to obtain attractive terms at the point in the startup's evolution where there is zero clarity about the future market opportunity. You begin by selling what you don't have in order to transition to selling what you do.

Often, founders assume that they will be able to hire people to sell them. Although this works for large companies, a startup relies so heavily on the vision of the founders that it is virtually impossible to outsource this to new outsiders, particularly at a point when the systems are yet to be put in place and the entire vision has yet to be institutionalised. Therefore, for at least one founder, being able to sell is not semantic but is absolutely core to whether investors invest.

Gel

Investor relationships are truly relationships, more than one-time deals. Founders sometimes realise that they spend more time talking to their investors than communicating with their spouses or partners, given how much time they often spend at their startup. On the other hand, investor relationships often last for the life of the startup or at least until a successful liquidity event such as an IPO or company sale. There is no easy exit from an investor relationship, so long as the founder continues to work at the startup. Given this high level of sustained interaction, it makes sense for investors to feel comfortable communicating with founders. The flip side of this is that for founders to have a positive working relationship with their investors, it is imperative that they feel aligned on the vision and see the investors supporting and challenging them rather than a reporting relationship. Investors and founders sit on different sides of the table, resulting in differing perspectives, but this notwithstanding, gelling is key to not only get investors to invest but also to not make it feel like a mistake over the entire life of the startup.

Who Will You Hire to Report to?

The hiring of the first employees beyond the founders is one of the most important decisions for the startup. This is because investors want to know that the founders realise that they often do not have all the right skills needed and will not only have to hire senior people but also often report to them if the need arises. If the startup is technology-driven, it is easier to hire since the requirement is more clearly defined. However, the challenge is for platform startups since the solution is more ephemeral and requires many pivots before it finally becomes aligned with the market need. The first employees then have to be able to relate to what the startup is doing as well as where it expects to go and map out a fast-moving target. The more clarity the founders have regarding the kind of person they expect to hire, the greater the likelihood of the startup being able to scale. In the fast-moving world of platform startups, any error of judgement regarding initial employees risks being the last one. Therefore, investors look particularly at how founders perceive hiring and evolving the reporting mechanism, where an external hire can come in and head the company as CEO.

Bootstrap

A simple piece of advice is: bootstrap as long as you possibly can, but not forever. Bootstrapping helps increase the value of your startup, and with pilot customers coming onboard, it helps you attract investors. More importantly, with pilot customers coming onboard, you are able to not only ask for a better pre-money valuation but get more attractive conditions on the investor documents.

Once you're in the market, you get a chance to road-test your ideas and pivot, so that you're much more confident of your milestone plan with investors. Since delays in achieving milestones are what negatively impacts the relationship with investors and subsequently triggers the more onerous terms of the investment, having the milestones under control provides an enormous boost in the working relationship with the investors. This also positions you more strongly for future rounds of funding at not only progressively higher valuation but also the opportunity to get a partial exit during the next round of funding.

What Is Your Priority?

Investors want to know what your priorities are. Technology entrepreneurs often veer towards working on the technology, even when the need of the hour is to work on transitioning the technology towards manufacture. This is even more pronounced for platform startups, even as the technology entrepreneurs continue to focus on the technology. To investors, this entails a large risk. Platform startups inherently operate in an uncertain environment, far more than technology startups. Being able to deal with and create a platform in this environment where neither customer behaviour exists nor there is clarity around the regulatory environment is not something that most entrepreneurs can deal with.

Investors want to know that not only are you doing things right but that you're doing the right things. It is important to take a step back and recognise what needs to be done, including talking to customers, trying to hire people who are better than you in the areas that need to be covered to take you from technology to product to scale and not hesitating to find people who you may ostensibly report to, in the interest of maximising growth of your startup, before you dive headlong into operational stuff. It is also a great way to send a message to investors that you get it.

What Are You Making Better?

In my first startup, I agonised for weeks on end trying to figure out the colour schemes for my presentation. I veered between different tones of blue and aggressively different and bold colours to strike a balance between mature colours representing the constitution of the team and different colours that just stood out for the visuals and graphs in my slide deck. In retrospect, the impact of the colour schemes was probably zero and negative if you consider the time lost in initiating conversations with potential investors. I would have been far better served if I had spent that time in doing the one thing that would have made us more attractive to investors. It is the same thing that would ultimately make us more relevant for the marketplace—a world-class manufacturing person who would help transition the mindset of technology of the team and focus our attention to converting the tech excellence to manufacturing expertise. As Marc Andreessen, the founder of Netscape, which started it all, once mentioned, 'you're better off making your business better than making your pitch better'.

Being Great

Startups try to do too many things at the same time. That is why investors like to ask what founders want to achieve. It is commonly known that if you have more than three priorities, you do not have any. Even doing one thing well is challenging enough, as seasoned entrepreneurs recognise. That is why when first-time entrepreneurs say that they can address multiple customer segments at the same time, it raises a red flag for investors. Far more effective than being good in multiple things is to be absolutely outstanding in one so that other weaknesses can be ignored. It is the outliers that generate almost all the returns for investors. Bruce Lee said it well: 'I fear not the man who has practiced 10,000 kicks once, but I fear the man who has practiced one kick 10,000 times.'

Examples of startups that became blockbuster successes demonstrate excellence in one thing. Google decided to search at a time when the search was not even considered a core area of focus. In fact, Yahoo outsourced this to Google in the early 2000s, since this was not where the money was. Who would have thought that there could be a real business in convincing people to welcome absolute strangers into their homes. However, this simple yet counterintuitive idea became the basis for Airbnb, which popped during its IPO at $86.5 billion. These are the same outliers that seem crazy to begin with. Investors like to look out for the breakout idea that is crazy enough to work, and in the process, disrupt the entire industry.

Easy Money

During my MBA at the London Business School, my professor used to say that compared to how fast life was going to get in the future, the present was the slowest it was ever going to be. We used to laugh, since life was incredibly hectic. Now, in retrospect, this was before Facebook, LinkedIn and Skype. Today, just keeping up with my social profile is more hectic than I can handle.

In the same way, when you're trying to do a startup, investors like to remind you that getting funding is the easiest thing you'll ever do as an entrepreneur. The tasks that will be far more challenging include getting great people to join your startup when all you have is a vision and a prayer. Getting customers onboard is even harder, getting revenue from these customers is almost impossible and viral growth is another planet. It is perhaps for this reason that investors do not make it easy for entrepreneurs to obtain funding. Those who have the motivation and creativity to get through to investors get through the first hurdle and are much more likely to survive the journey of entrepreneurship. Sometimes, entrepreneurs get easy money due to their technology having the buzz or because of strong networks. This lets many entrepreneurs who would otherwise not be able to handle the stress of dealing with and leading in an uncertain world and set them up for a subsequent fall. For this reason, startups that are founded during recessions have a much better chance of surviving. They are accustomed to working harder for their money and focus on customers, relevance, reference and revenue, rather than projects and awards.

Milestones

Investors invest based on the expectation of being able to exit at a multiple of the original valuation. To do this, the startup has to do many things post-investment, including developing its product, finding new customers, obtaining and consolidating new revenue streams and converting revenue into profit. In this way, investors always have a different view from the founders. Founders look at the things that need to be done in a startup. Investors, on the other hand, look for the result of the things that are done, or milestones. It is when the startup achieves key milestones that the valuation of the startup increases for investors. This results either in new investors willing to invest at a much higher valuation or the opportunity for the existing investors to exit by way of a liquidity event.

However, to become attractive to investors, the startup has to perform some milestone planning. This implies capturing and documenting the key highlights that have been achieved over the past few months to couple of years. This showcases the ability of the team to achieve or overachieve key milestones and demonstrates to the prospective investors that the founders recognise the investor's view and are driven towards doing what needs to be done, rather than just focusing on one area such as technology, since they have the greatest level of comfort in operating in this area.

Technology Risks

Investors evaluate startups based on the risks that still remain. In the early stages of a startup, it is not much more than an idea on a piece of paper. The risks include validation of the business case and to see if it is possible. In the case of a technology startup, it may be only a proof of concept with perhaps only a working prototype. Investors then like to see if this can be replicated, even if it requires specialists with PhDs to do so. As the startups continue to progress, the process of manufacturing the product gets dumbed down so that someone with a much lower degree of specialisation can operate the manufacturing process.

As the startup begins the process of risk elimination, the first risks for technology startups are technology risks. These imply risk that the technology may not be able to deliver what the proof of concept has shown. When this happens, the technology may function perfectly in the lab, and it may even be possible to create product samples in lab machines. However, the transition from lab machines to pre-pilot machines may simply not occur. There can be multiple reasons for this failure. The lab machines may have certain design elements that simply enable sample production that cannot be replicated. Alternatively, there may be certain variables that 'auto error-correct' but that the technology team may not be aware of. These are the highest-risk startups since all the risks lie ahead of them. Investors who come in at this stage are very long-term investors who understand the capability of the technology to completely disrupt the existing marketplace. Often, emerging technologies have the buzz, and this also attracts investors who simply see this as an attractive opportunity to invest. This is extremely dangerous for the startup as well as for the investors since investors expect the startup to live up to the buzz. The startup is closer to reality and eventually ends up making all the mistakes that it is possible to make, based on Murphy's law. It often ends quite badly for both the startup and the investors that are simply investing in the buzz.

Manufacturing Risks

The second kind of risk is manufacturing risk. Once the startup has mitigated technology risks, it needs to eliminate manufacturing risks. This implies scaling the production from the pre-pilot, where each machine is manned by a specialist and the yield and throughput are inconsistent, rather than being over 90%, as is the case with commercial manufacturing. Over a period of time, production and machines evolve, progressing manufacturing towards large-volume commercial output. This progressively reduces risk since the technology is now in the process of transitioning towards volume production, with replicability improving consistently. This is more pertinent with hardware manufacturing, since in software, there is no risk of replicability issues once the startup is able to do it right. This is also one of the key reasons why the barriers to entry for software startups are much lower and why software startups often focus on being platforms.

Investors recognise the level of maturity of the startup based on its ability to manage replicability, yield and throughput in the manufacturing process. This not only results in obtaining far more traction from investors but also positively impacts the ability of the startup to command a higher valuation.

Commercial Risks

The third and final set of risks are commercial risks. At this point, it is much more than a startup and has likely raised a number of funding rounds. When the startup has already addressed the technology and manufacturing risks, it finally has to address commercial risks. These entail optimising production and decisions, including whether to insource or keep the manufacturing outsourced. A key decision also pertains to the size of the manufacturing. The reason size is important because if it is too large and the market has yet to develop fully, machines can lie idle. This translates to higher fixed costs that need to be shared between the smaller amount of output. On the other hand, having smaller machines permanently keeps the variable costs high due to the higher average costs. The startup thus needs to decide between higher volumes and customisation. A smaller facility provides a greater degree of customisation between lot sizes and minimises the total cost impact in case the production is stopped sporadically. Another element that needs to be defined when deciding on the commercial plan is to define the level of automation. Startups that operate in highly specialised areas focus on a lower level of automation and focus more on customisation instead. The trade-off depends on whether the firm operates in a volume-intensive and cost-competitive environment or whether it is more tuned to high-value solutions for niche industries.

Lock-In

It is surprising how many startups take discussions with investors for granted. It is good to keep in mind that if investors agree to certain steps, particularly in meetings or calls, you cannot take this as permanently agreed. This is for two reasons. The first is that investors meet many startups. In fact, other than when investors do due diligence or engage with their investee companies to support or challenge them, they mostly spend their time looking at and having conversations with new startups to identify the next big thing. Thus, they tend to forget specific things that they may agree on. If these pertain to valuation or agreed milestones or stages in funding or salaries or sign-on bonuses for founders (this is rare, but it happens if the tech founder owns the core technology), it is best to document this in an e-mail to confirm understanding. The second reason is that it is also possible that after investors meet your startup, they may meet with another startup that seems more attractive. They may then 'forget' about the agreements with your startup if they have been agreed upon orally. However, once the written document trail is in place, it becomes a reference point, not only for the person responsible within the investor group but also if new individuals pick up the discussion from the investor side.

My own discussions with an angel investor for my first startup is a case in point. We had discussions where the angel investor agreed to invest $ 1.5 million. She also recommended her legal firm as an entity that would be able to help us to incorporate. She also said that she would cover the cost of incorporation. We naturally took that at face value and got them to do the incorporation without any questions regarding the time or cost involved. At the end of the month, when everything was done, we got a bill for close to $50 K. We were not only shocked at the amount, since we had estimated $5 K, based on other startups but also surprised to get the bill in the first place, since we had clearly understood that the angel investor would cover this cost. When we inquired about this to the lawyers, they said it was understood that the incorporation fee was to be paid from the amount the angel was investing in us. Since we had omitted confirming our understanding with the angel investor regarding the cost, we ended up having to pay $50 K, an enormous amount for a young startup.

The second instance was in a subsequent round of funding. We were having conversations with one of Europe's top VC investors, who had backed several global unicorns. At a particular point in the technical due diligence, the VC indicated that they were ready to give us a term sheet. Since we were also in the midst of discussions with strategic investors, we shared this information with the VC, assuming that this would help us during the valuation discussions and that this would provide a long-term perspective and stability, since strategic investors normally have a longer view towards institution-building. As soon as we told them about this strategic investor, the VC told us that they were willing to consider coming with the strategic investor. However, after a couple of months, we realised that the strategic investor was going to take much longer since they operate on very different timelines. We went back to the VC about closing the deal. It was at that point that we realised that the original VC term sheet was no longer on the table. To our chagrin, we realised that by putting an option on the table, we had effectively negated the original offer of the term sheet from the VC. That was a tough lesson; choose your options with care because they become more than options as soon as they are on the table; they are the new normal with no possibility of going back.

Existing Entrepreneurs in the Mix

Most investors recognise the value of having someone in the mix who's done it before. Entrepreneurship is like cycling; you simply have to get on the bike and figure out how to balance the thing. In the same way, the uncertainty of entrepreneurship is challenging for both founders and investors since entrepreneurs are trying to determine not only how to work the environment and to lead in a world of uncertainty but also how they behave and their own reactions to being in this environment. To this extent, the risk for the investors is multiplied by trying to help a startup move forward and at the same time not knowing how the first-time entrepreneurs will deal with the world of crazy. Having someone who's done it before at least mitigates the risk that the entrepreneurs will simply go to pieces halfway through the journey. More importantly, it helps investors recognise that entrepreneurs can see the world through the eyes of the investor and do what needs to be done rather than because it is easy.

Once Investors Are Onboard

An important shift happens when investors come onboard. They are now predisposed to support the startup and effectively market it to future investors. The same investors who may have been very critical about the startup prior to investing now pivot to becoming its messaging channel, since this helps to protect their investment. This is a gift that keeps giving, since the current investors will continue to push up the potential value of the startup, since this helps to push up their equity value. It is for this reason that it is important for a startup to align the founders' exit with that of the investors since this motivation of the investors to talk up the value of the startup only lasts as long as they have skin in the game.

IPO and Implications

For startups that consider an IPO, there is an important consideration relating to the value of the startup that changes. This is far more significant than the dramatic increase in the administration and regulatory formalities consequent to doing an IPO. This pertains to the value of the startup. As long as the startup is a private company, the shares are not liquid, and there are restrictions on being able to sell equity. It is thus in the interest of the owners of the equity, whether they are founders, employees or investors, to talk up the perceived value of the startup. The value of the startup is thus in its potential rather than its revenue. However, as soon as the startup has its IPO, all these equity owners can sell. If they do not see the potential, they do an exit. If those exiting the startup are more than those interested in entering it, the value falls after the IPO.

Furthermore, if the startup needs to raise more money to scale up as a private company, it can simply create a business case that shows the scale opportunity and its ability to capture more of the market or reduce the price of its products further. By doing so, it is not only able to raise more money but also able to do so at incredibly high valuations. A case in point is Uber, which raised about $3.5 billion from investors at a mind-numbing pre-money valuation of $59 billion, prior to going public. However, once it is a public company, its options of raising money dwindle. If it tries to raise money by way of a secondary offering of equity, it is a signal to the existing shareholders that their shares will become diluted since the company is unable to obtain enough revenue to drive further growth. If the company decides to obtain a loan, it becomes highly geared, and the risk to the shareholders increases. Thus, it makes sense for startups to remain private for as long as possible and for founders to try a partial exit along the journey.

First-Time Investors and Their Mistakes

You always remember your first time. This is, however, also the time you are most likely to make mistakes, because you didn't think it through, did it in the heat of the moment, or did not align expectations with the other party.

It may seem strange to talk about investor-related risks in a book meant to help entrepreneurs scale. However, a bad investment does not only risk the money of the entrepreneur. It also makes it challenging for the entrepreneur to take his innovation to the market, get new investors onboard or even exit. In addition, since no investment comes without strings attached, it's important to recognise strings that pull you up or dress you for success from those that risk becoming a noose around your neck or pull you back.

We specifically cover two kinds of investors, since these investors are likely to be first-time investors and, in many cases, the first investors that join the startup's board. These are angels and strategic investors. We have addressed these earlier in the book, but here, we specifically focus on mistakes these investors can make when investing for the first time.

Angels

As discussed earlier, angel investors are those who have an investable income of between $1 and 10 million. They normally invest approximately $100 K–250 K in any given investment. They often make certain errors when they first invest. This results in them losing their investment. Counterintuitively, their investment also results in failure of the startup. Some early errors of first-time angel investors are discussed below.

FOMO

Most first-time angel investors make their first investment in a rush because they fear that they may miss their once-in-a-lifetime opportunity. This is aptly called fear of missing out or FOMO. We've all done this the first time we decided to invest in shares, when we look at a price dip and buy, only realising later that the price had not bottomed out yet. The only difference is that when the angel investor invests in his first startup due to FOMO, he does so without proper due diligence or technology, with very little information about the market and often almost no information about the team or their ethics. Therefore, the angel investor is hooked to the incredible potential of the technology and the hope of the impact, rather than any real timeline of the rollout.

Emotional Investment

Angel investors often invest for the first time because they feel a strong emotional connection to the technology or solution. For instance, an angel investor who has suffered from a health problem may be more inclined towards supporting a startup that is developing a solution to address this. However, what they fail to appreciate is how much time it takes to bring a medical device to the market, and the certification requirements and affiliated expense this entails. The good intent fails to appreciate or compensate for the additional time, effort and expenses towards bringing this to the market. An investment driven by emotion also fails to look at the business case, which entails evaluating if a market exists, how long it may take to get there, and whether the startup has a competitive advantage that will enable it to sustain the market it creates.

Timeline

The first-time angel investor often has an overly optimistic view of the investment and expects to obtain an enormous multiple within a very short period of time. His reference points are the most successful startups that have been able to scale up and become immensely valuable in a short period of time. However, even the best startups take time, and the path is never even. If the angel investor has a specific timeline after which he expects to obtain a return or even his money back, he is likely to be disappointed. If the startup makes the mistake of giving him specific rights in this regard, this may also doom the startup.

Future Funding

More often than not, startups require future funding to hit key milestones. Without these key milestones, the startup is unable to attract new investors.

Even if new investors join, they expect the existing investor to coinvest, as a sign of confidence in the startup. If the angel investor is not ready to do this, there is a risk that the startup simply runs out of money, or new investors do come in, they invest in a distressed startup, reducing its valuation and significantly diluting the angel investor as well as the founders.

Competence

The angel investor often looks at a startup and finds the sector complementary to his own experience. He thus assumes that he may be able to bring value and help in guiding the startup as it progresses. This can be a cardinal error since new startups not only bring new technology but also innovate the business model to capture the transitioning value. The real competitive advantage of a startup is not only its technology but also the fact that it recognises customer trends and is able to position itself accordingly. The angel may bring his experience, which may be more aligned with the incumbent that the startup is trying to replace. This may thus be counterproductive. It can be even more detrimental if the angel also becomes involved in the operational management of the startup since in such cases, he tries to run day-to-day operations with the mindset of the incumbent competitors. This risks moving the startup back rather than taking it forward.

Sole Investor

The angel investor often wants to lock in all the future upside from the startup. With this mindset, he decides to invest greater amounts as and when the startup has a requirement. Due to this open source of funding, the startup does not perceive a need to focus on key milestones necessary for future investors. With this, the angel ends up investing ever-increasing amounts and, in the process, creates increasing dependency on the startup team. With soft funds and no specific pressure on key milestones, the team continues to focus on the technology, rather than addressing the go-to-market, which is necessary to take the technology to the market and attract new investors. With no wisdom from other investors, the angel investor is unable to recognise red flags or protect his investment. This is also why VCs also prefer to invest with other VCs, since having more investors in the mix enables them to identify risks and create a stronger network to help the startup with future funding and market access.

No Clarity

The first-time angel investor often has very little idea about fundamental questions beyond the technology. These questions include what it does, who it does it for and why they should care. He often invests because he knows the team or is aware of the market need. However, these still result in a gap about the time, effort and expertise needed to transition the technology to be ready to the market. This is what finally results in failures of startups, taking the angel investor's investment with it.

Financial Oversight

Since the funds invested by the angel investor are a significant percentage of his total investable capital, he likes to have oversight on where these are spent. However, the startup often has no demonstrable reason why a certain machine needs to be brought or why a specific investment is needed. This is because a lot of what the founders are doing entails creating new value, which implies there is simply no reference available. By requiring proof of value before a specific expense can be made by the founders, the angel investor hinders their work, since their future value is driven by their experience, competence and intuition regarding what may work.

Different Objectives

Different kinds of investors have different objectives. Angels have a lower threshold relating to time for their return as well as the multiple. However, larger investors who invest in future rounds have much higher expectations. For instance, an angel who invests at a pre-money valuation of $2 m may be comfortable with an exit at $15 m. However, a VC investor who comes in at $10 m may have an expectation of $50 to $100 m before considering an exit. If the angel is in a position to influence or veto a decision, such as having a seat on the board, this difference in opinion between the two different investors could result in a decision freeze. This often becomes personal when the egos of the individuals become involved. As with cofounders with different opinions, egos play a key role in bad decisions or blocking a decision and ultimately result in the failure of the startup due to inaction.

First-Time Strategic Investors

Strategic investors are an important source of investment for technology start-ups. This is because they enable the technology to institutionalise and create market impact. Strategic investors also have existing supply chain and manufacturing ecosystems that startups often lack. However, first-time strategic investors make some mistakes, which results in the failure of the startup technology to integrate into the business of the corporation. Worse, these mistakes often doom the startup.

Executive Sponsorship

Strategic investors often invest small amounts of $0.5 m–2 m without executive sponsorship or board oversight into startups. However, as the startup scales and requires more funding, which then requires board approval, the startup could find itself in limbo. The reason for this is that the corporate begins its startup investment being led by the corporate venturing team, which in turn does not require executive confirmation for investments up to a certain size. It is the startups that receive investment below this threshold that fall through the cracks since not all of these early-stage startups become strategic.

Size of Investment

A first-time strategic investor makes a few tentative investments to test the waters. Often, these are small in size. As a consequence, they end up investing in early-stage startups. Early-stage startups frequently have yet to resolve basic technology challenges, including stability, replicability and manufacturability. The strategic investor may never have faced these and has no idea how to deal with them. This expectation gap results in a failure of the startup to integrate. Often, the strategic investor decides not to fund the startup in future rounds, resulting in the startup's demise. This is also a missed opportunity for the investor to roll out a sustained strategy of startup investment.

Future Funding

The investor often does not define future funding for the startup. However, the only time when no future funding is needed is when the startup is unable to hit any milestones or it becomes clear that industrialisation is simply not viable. The funding need is often greater if the startup achieves key milestones. If the investor does not have a strategy to enable this, it again results in the stagnation of the startup. For this reason, the best VCs only invest 40%–60% of their planned investment into any given startup in the first round.

Other Investors in Future Rounds

First-time strategic investors often have not considered the option of having other investors onboard. While the idea of having another investor bring in more money appears appealing, they soon realise that there are strings attached. A financial investor's focus is to multiply its investment. This implies that the strategic investor needs to commit to buying the financial investor's equity at a given point in time. Since the strategic investor may originally have made the investment in order to buy the rest of the startup cheap, this does not fit with the VC's view. If another corporation is invited as a second strategic investor, it also expects a share of the startup's IP. As the strategic investor may want to have exclusivity on the IP of the startup to use as a competitive advantage, it does not want to share this, since it would defeat the purpose of exclusively owning the IP.

Rights and Obligations

Corporates often expect all rights when they first invest in tech startups. What they do not realise is that with rights come obligations. For instance, beyond the funding and exclusivity discussed above, the corporation may want to maintain control over all manufacturing. However, the point of tech innovations is that they bring and require innovations in manufacturing as well as how value is captured there. By keeping control over this, the corporation limits the startup from identifying or indeed creating innovative manufacturing, which may be part of the possible competitive advantage.

Timeline to Scale

Technology startups often have a long timeline to scale. If the technology is truly innovative, it becomes necessary to customise the machinery to build the products. Custom software also needs to be created. However, this results in a very long timeline to stabilise the manufacturing and debug the software. The corporation often expects to integrate the technology into its business and take it to market within months. This expectation gap results in failure to launch for both the startup and the corporate's startup investments.

Future Strategy (Scale or Exit)

A first-time strategic investor often is yet to decide what it would ultimately do with the investment. A fundamental question is whether to treat the investment as a future area of strategic growth or to consider it simply as a financial investment. Microsoft invested in Facebook at a mind-numbing valuation of $15 billion at the time. This was not a strategic investment from the perspective of Microsoft wanting to get into social. It simply was a matter of recognising where value was transitioning and wanting to utilise a part of its oversized war chest to get a nice return. If the investor's strategy is to scale, it actively needs to integrate the startup's technology into its business. However, if the strategy is to exit, it needs to ensure that the startup is capturing, sustaining and monetising value by way of industry rollout and customer references independent of the investor. The best strategy for the investor to exit from the startup is to make the startup's value independent of the investor's business.

Inclusive or Exclusive

Early on, the corporate acquirer needs to define whether the technology of the startup will be only for the corporate or will be provided to the entire ecosystem including the corporate's competitors. This is often not done since the corporate is not sure what to expect. The result is that when the corporate invests, it elicits exclusivities from the startup, including veto, preferences and first right of refusal. It also tries to integrate the startup's technology into its manufacturing and route-to-market. However, the new technology often competes with the existing ecosystem established by the corporate, since people prefer the status quo due to the comfort of familiarity and often have little motivation to learn, particularly if the new technology risks making their old skills or roles obsolete.

Due to the pushback from the line of business, the corporate does not integrate the startup's technology into its business. However, it also balks at rolling back the exclusivities negotiated with the startup. This limits the capability of the startup from new funding as well as its ability to address customers that compete with the corporate. The result is that the startup simply is unable to bring its technology to market and remains a glorified but orphan outsourcing arm of the corporate's R&D. The impact of the decision is on the startup's route-to-market as well as funding.

Reason for Investment

Microsoft used to have a strategy for interaction with partners. If the potential partner was small, acquire. If it did not want to be acquired, kill. If it was too large to be acquired or killed, partner. A first-time corporate investor does not need to have this level of clarity (or aggression) when considering investment. However, it does need to think through whether its investment is to obtain IP, block competitors and ensure freedom to operate or commercialise the technology. This fundamental clarity can then drive decisions including how to get founders onboard and ensure retaining a link with the research institute underlying the startup's technology.

This begs the question that a first-time corporate needs to ask itself: what is the reason for the investment? Based on the three stages that any corporate innovation undergoes, of innovation for competitive advantage, innovation for revenue maximisation or innovation for cost optimisation (covered in more detail elsewhere), the startup's capability and goal need to be aligned with this. Furthermore, it is critical for the corporate to obtain a line-of-business buy-in if the startup's business needs to complement, or potentially replace, it. Failure to do this will not only doom the investment and the startup itself but also risks the status quo with the existing business team. The investment may also be to create a new business line, have IP to obtain freedom to operate, have IP to block competitors or create an option that the corporate may want to evaluate. Since the startup team is the more critical element, particularly for technology startups, it is important for the corporate to ensure alignment with the team to avoid a scenario where the founders simply quit and walk away.

Payment for Buying or Investing and Startup Founder Lock-In

Corporations often fail to consider the additional development needed to complete the startup's product and the critical input, leadership and motivation of its founders to drive this. The technology founders bring about tech innovations, much of which remain limited to their sole competence. The challenge in institutionalising this process know-how cannot be underestimated given the increasing complexity of technology and its accelerating pace of development. The business founders are no less important since they provide a perspective of how value will transition for the industry and perhaps transform the industry itself.

The corporates' failure to appreciate the founders' perspective results in two erroneous decisions. The first is to provide a large upfront exit to the founders when they invest rather than a payment based on fair, transparent and measurable milestones that are within the control of the founders. If the founders have no motivation to remain to develop and transition their innovation, there is a substantial risk that they will leave. In such cases, the corporate is left with a technology that still needs work before it is ready to be commercialised. The second is that the corporate relegates founders to existing roles within its hierarchy. This completely stifles creativity, which normally requires an environment without shackles, corporate hierarchy or office politics to thrive. Steve Jobs recognised this when he created a counter-culture, which attracted individuals with a passion for their work, which in turn was responsible for most of Apple's innovations. The first-time corporate investor needs to recognise the greatest value of the tech startup they invest in; the founders are its most valuable asset since they are the visionaries building the future. By questioning the existing status quo, these are the individuals who can bring a culture of innovation, which in turn can sustain its relevance.

In conclusion, corporates can be a strong and sustained source of investment for a startup as well as support outstanding technologies to reach the market. The benefit for corporates in defining a startup's investment strategy is to future-proof their technology and innovation and thereby sustain relevance and a technology-driven competitive advantage. If done right, the innovation pipeline from investing in startups can help corporates to sustain strong gross profit margins even as their mature businesses become commoditised or outsourced and, in this way, sustain their brand and relevance with their customers.

13

All About Equity

One of the most important considerations in a startup is the equity split. It should be. After all, this finally reflects the value that you get as a founder, out of the value that your startup generates, in case it is sold or does an IPO. Often, co-founders delay having this discussion even when they have been working together for months in the mistaken assumption that this will simply go away and that they will not have to bite the bullet. Unfortunately, this often makes it worse, since by not talking about it, the co-founders overestimate their own value in the startup and underestimate the work done and value created by the others. The uncertainty of how much equity the founders will ultimately get also distracts from the real business of going ahead and making the startup come alive and move from idea to reality.

Like with most important things, the equity split needs to be done at an early stage, preferably when you're discussing the idea. It definitely needs to be done before the prospective founders have put in months and months of effort. The reason for this is that each founder will tend to overestimate the amount of effort he is putting in and underestimate the efforts of the other co-founders. This can result in a misplaced sense of entitlement of each founder and result in friction even as the startup is in the very early stage. The two questions to ask when determining the equity split are the relevant value that a co-founder brings and his skin in the game. If a co-founder is critical to the idea itself, or in the case of a technology startup, the inventor of the technology, he clearly deserves a large stake. However, this needs to be tempered with the founder's loyalty to the startup. If the founder is also fully onboard in the startup, he deserves a large stake in the startup. However, if the inventor of the technology continues to conduct research in a university and the startup is but a spinoff, he deserves a minority position since he is not taking the risk of commercialisation. Furthermore, if he reserves the option to work with other startups that may overlap with the startup's technology, his equity position should reduce further to a mere token.

The visual below shows the possible equity split if there's one lead founder with the idea or the technology that becomes the basis for the startup. In such case, the founder should hold the major portion of the equity. He should also be able to ensure that in case a co-founder leaves, he's not able to walk away with the entire equity agreed to. This is shown by the bucket system. The equity may then be split into four buckets. One bucket of equity opens every 6 months. If a co-founder leaves after 1 year, he would only be able to walk away with 50% of the equity he is entitled to (Fig. 13.1).

While defining the agreement to give shares to co-founders, the founder needs to ensure that he's able to get his equity back if the co-founders do something they're not allowed to do. This can include consulting for a competing company or sharing IP with competitors. It is important to highlight what non-compete means, as without a clear definition, it's impossible to

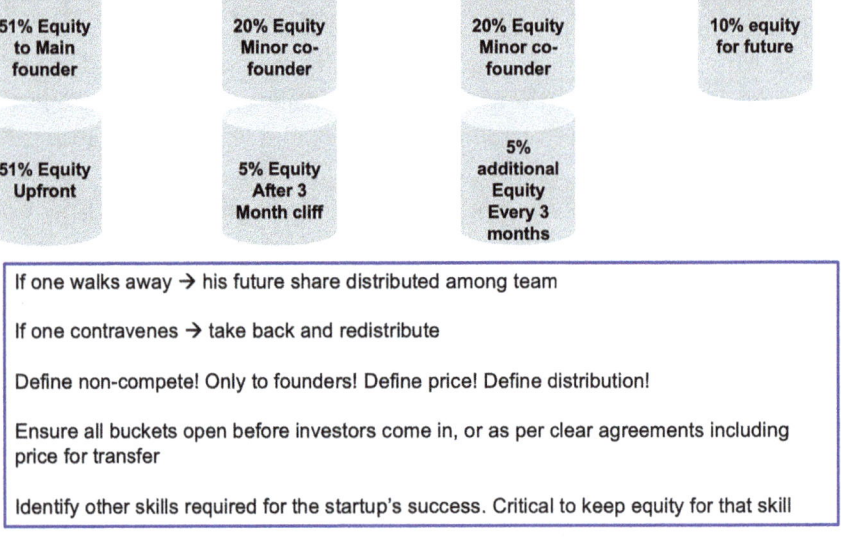

Fig. 13.1 Protecting equity in case of one main founder

enforce this clause. It is also important to ensure that the equity returned from the exiting co-founder comes back to either the founder or to all founders. Finally, the price at which the equity is returned needs to be agreed upon. Otherwise, the exiting co-founder may ask for the market rate for his equity rather than returning it at nominal price. The equity that is returned to the founder reduces with the increase in the time spent by the co-founder. Thus, the exiting co-founder can walk away with a higher proportion of equity to reflect his value added over a longer time spent in the startup.

If there are a number of co-founders with equal equity, the scenario is slightly different. There is no one founder who controls the value. Instead, the equity agreement is equal for every co-founder. Thus, if any co-founder leaves, the remaining co-founders have the right but not the obligation to get the exiting co-founder's equity at nominal price. The visual below shows this. As above, if the departing co-founder exits within a year, he's unable to walk away with the entire equity he would be entitled to. Instead, he leaves with only 10% of the equity. His remaining 10% equity is then distributed to the other four co-founders over the next 12 months (Fig. 13.2).

First-time technology entrepreneurs who have identified or invented a breakthrough technology often have a sense of ownership over the technology. This is reflected in their initial view of ownership in the startup; they expect to have the large majority. After all, without the technology, there wouldn't be anything to commercialise, would there? They fail to recognise the importance of other team members who bring complementary value

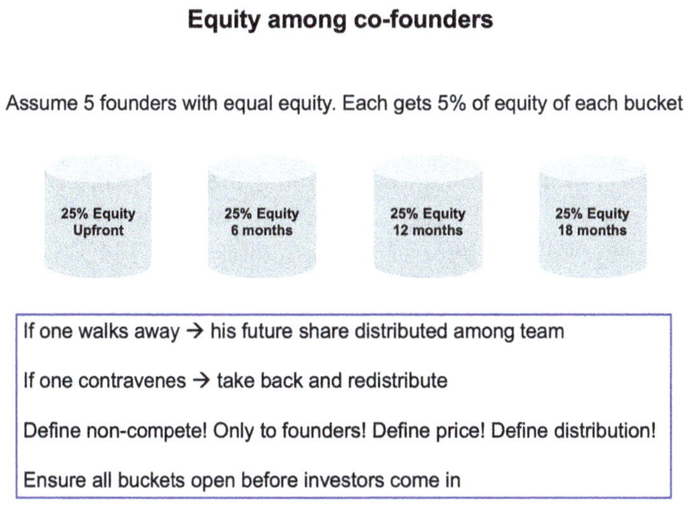

Equity among co-founders

Assume 5 founders with equal equity. Each gets 5% of equity of each bucket

| 25% Equity Upfront | 25% Equity 6 months | 25% Equity 12 months | 25% Equity 18 months |

If one walks away → his future share distributed among team

If one contravenes → take back and redistribute

Define non-compete! Only to founders! Define price! Define distribution!

Ensure all buckets open before investors come in

Fig. 13.2 Protecting equity with several co-founders

towards commercialising the technology. Without the capability to commercialise, the startup is unable to extract and maximise the commercial value of the technology, resulting in commercial irrelevance.

The distribution of equity is tricky in the best of circumstances. Tech teams often completely underestimate the value of go-to-market and manufacturing know-how (particularly if manufacture is a core element of the startup). Therefore, the equity allocation from the tech founders' perspective to the other team members (business and manufacture) tends to be far less than proportional, assuming that all founders come together at the same time to find the startup. However, equity allocation is also a reflection of the importance that founders give to the various elements that are necessary to make the startup a success.

Successful startups require three elements: technology, manufacturing and go-to-market. Without the latter two elements, the technology is simply technology, without any capability of market impact. The earlier that a person with any of the criteria needed joins the team, the greater his entitlement of equity. This is because at the early stages, the core team members are involved in forming the value proposition based on which the startup is founded. Second, the co-founders joining early take higher risk, both financial (e.g. opportunity cost) and reputational. In effect, the startup is built on their shoulders. When a co-founder states that he would only be willing to join the startup when there is some funding available, so that he is able to get a salary on joining, he would be entitled to less equity, even though he may come from the technology team. This is because his risk is far less than those who work on it despite not receiving any compensation since they take the risk to make it happen. This is also something that often distinguishes those who are truly committed from others who are simply there for the ride.

When a founder is looking for skills for his startup, the rarity of the specific skills plays an important role in determining the proportion of equity that they should obtain. I recall a conversation with one of my students who was just finishing his PhD in information technology at ETH Zurich. He had been contacted by a startup that was trying to use breakthrough facial recognition software. He asked me if it was okay if he charged them $150 per hour. I asked him what the relevance of his knowledge was to the software. His response 'that's the basis of the startup'. On my inquiring how many other people globally had the capability to build the software that the startup was interested in, he answered without a trace of irony: 'I believe I'm the only one who can do this'. My suggestion was not only to charge a multiple of what he had originally estimated on a per hour basis but also to request a percentage of equity that would increase if he decided to join the startup full-time. He got both!

When you start a startup, a key question relates not only to the competence and capability of the co-founders but also their loyalty to the idea and determination to make it succeed. You simply don't know how they (or you, for that matter) will behave or what they will decide when the going gets tough. In addition, there are many tough situations and difficult decisions that need to be made on the way to commercialisation, even when things are proceeding according to plan.

Often, tech founders, who are ostensibly the ones who generate the idea behind the startup, tend to be less than loyal to the idea than the business drivers. This is when conflicts of interest occur. This is particularly true when tech founders continue to stay at their research institutes. In my own first startup focusing on flexible solar cells, the tech researchers had worked on the topic for almost two decades. Even then, when we founded the startup, I was the only one to leave my position in a large corporate to lead the startup. To my shock, the technology co-founders were so risk-averse that they declared that they would only transition to the startup only on funding, so that their salaries could be paid. When we did get funding and the time came to transition, they not only wanted equivalent salaries but also wanted to transfer their pending leave at the university.

Often, some of the greatest challenges to the survival of the startup relate to issues with the founder team. One of the most important, and often underestimated, elements of a startup is the team. Most often, the main reason startups fail is because their teams implode. This doesn't just happen in the beginning. In case the team members see the world differently, this implosion and value destruction can happen even when the startup is well on its way to success. Some of the main reasons why startups implode are captured below.

Loyalty to the tech: Tech founders are often more loyal to their tech than to the startup. If they continue to work at their research institutes, the risk for the startup is that their primary focus remains research. One conflict of interest relates to funding opportunities. Technology co-founders who continue to work in research in universities see funding opportunities and have to decide whether the funding should go to the startup or their university department. This is where loyalty to the vision of the startup conflicts with loyalty to the research. Which gets us to our next concern.

Tech ivory tower: In the face of uncertainty, which implies just about everything in a startup (market definition, investors, IP strategy, cost-plus or value-added, initial customer focus and strategy, manufacturing strategy, to name a few), tech team members sometimes return to their zone of comfort, which is tech research. Unfortunately, filling more air in one tyre is not enough to get the car moving if your other wheels are missing.

IP vs *peer reviews*: Tech team members are predisposed to peer reviews. Their first focus is to publish their research. This is contrary to the focus of a startup, where new ideas become the source of IP, a source of competitive advantage.

Size: Different team members have different visions of what constitutes 'big' when defining how the startup will look 5 years down the line. This is the least asked question between founders. One founder may see a 15-man company doing $2 million annually with operations in 3 countries, whereas another founder may visualise operations across 30 countries and a workforce of 500 people.

Funding: Founders tend to be close to their ideas and technologies. In some cases, this proximity tends to be closer than what is strictly in the best interest of the startup. Sometimes, technology founders tend to perceive ownership over the technology where they cannot see an investor coming in and 'taking the technology away from them'. This results in the startup being limited to growing organically, since without investor funding, very few startups can truly scale.

Tech or business: There is often a conflict between how business and technology co-founders see the world. For team members who come from the world of technology, the key priority is often the ongoing improvement of the technology since this is (ostensibly) what the startup is built on. This view becomes a belief and eventually a conviction the longer the tech co-founders are in the world of research, prior to starting the startup. The business co-founders, on the other hand, see the world as customers who have a requirement and try to identify the *minimum viable solution* that can be provided to early adapter customers. This dichotomy results in tech teams over-researching the tech to the point where the startup's solution becomes technically overengineered and commercially obsolete. It is in these cases that the inferior solution becomes the standard.

Boats: Tech team members are accustomed to working on multiple tech simultaneously. This often continues once they transition to the startup and when they continue to work at their university. This not only becomes a critical distraction but also raises ethical questions, particularly when there are decisions that can impact the startup and their research, such as funding questions or questions related to either/or.

Bloat: Some founders grow into their roles as the startup grows. Others bloat to their new positions. Getting founders who are eager to learn and evolve is a very tricky component of the startup team, since there is a real risk of success going to your head, particularly before success happens.

Culture: Culture within any startup percolates down from the startup team. If there is a clash or a laid-back 'large company' culture of 40-h weeks, it is very difficult to change this or become competitive, particularly if your competitors are sleeping in office to make it work.

Hands-on: Tech teams within any startup often come from research. They tend to be more focused on saving money and doing every tech activity themselves. However, this risks creating fully customised equipment that cannot be easily replicated.

Hierarchy: Often, startup founders include those who have been relatively senior in their previous lives. This particularly includes large-company managers or research leaders. These people have likely led teams of younger people. Sometimes, it goes against the grain for them to consider younger startup founders as peers or to report to them. If not aired early, this can fester and strain the fragile balance in a startup.

Exit: What exactly does it mean to get an exit for you as the founder? It is more than likely that your co-founders have a different perception of exit. With large-company valuations and the buzz about unicorns, wannabe entrepreneurs start startups in whatever happens to be the buzz, specifically with a view to selling. By the time the startup starts, the buzz has often passed, and they have to run it. The difference in opinion between co-founders between what constitutes the right time to exit results in friction and destroys value or the company, which may be on the verge of getting to the black.

Rich or king: Different founders have different long-term objectives of how they see themselves in the startup as it evolves. If the objective of a founder is to have a certain position, he could end up becoming the bottleneck that ultimately limits the startup's growth.

Spouse/partner: Startup founders underestimate the importance of having the partner onboard on their vision and aware of the challenges to come. The revenue almost always takes much longer than anticipated, and even after revenue begins, the founder is the last to get any. The partner thus needs to be aware of the financial strain and the fact that the full burden or getting food on the table falls on their shoulders. As they say about holidays, the best ones are when you have a nice home to come back to.

Success: Co-founders have to ask themselves how they would define success? In other words, how rich is rich? The difference in perceptions between the co-founders regarding what rich is has a great impact on whether the startup is sold or becomes a player.

One way to mitigate the risk of co-founders simply giving up part way into the journey is to avoid distributing all the equity to the co-founders in the beginning. Equity could be split and distributed over 3 or 4 years. If the equity distribution is planned over 4 years, the co-founders could distribute 25% of the equity in the agreed-upon proportion when the startup is founded. Then, at the end of every 6-month period, the cofounders become entitled to the same distribution of the second, third and fourth quarters in the agreed-upon proportion. In this way, any co-founder who walks away from the startup after a period of time would only be entitled to the equity distributed until his departure. The excess equity that would otherwise have accrued to him can then be used for other future employees or be distributed among the remaining cofounders. It's also important to separate the equity allocation of founders from future investors, since you don't want the investors to get a larger proportion of the company if any founder loses his allocation. This can do far more than give the investor more shares; it can tilt the balance of ownership and decision-making to the detriment of the founders.

As with any relationship, it is always good to have an exit option so that an unexpected exit of a co-founder at an inopportune time does not impact the survival of the startup. With this in view, in case any co-founder or employee decides to leave the startup and join a competing entity, the shareholders' agreement should clearly force him to sell his shares and the price at which such shares should be sold. This can be at original cost plus interest, rather than at market value. There are two reasons for this. The first is that by leaving the startup, the departing co-founder risks a negative reputational impact on the startup in the eyes of investors and customers. The second is that it is unlikely that the startup's shares are liquid, even though they may have a high paper value. Therefore, in the absence of a market where shares can be traded or sold, the share value is theoretical. In the absence of a clear share price in case a buy-back option has to be exercised by the startup or by the remaining cofounders, the leaving co-founder can state any valuation for him to sell his shares. A clear exit clause can thus mitigate much heartache for the startup at a time when it should be focused on more critical things, such as developing its solution, addressing investors or initiating conversations with pilot customers.

For employees who join the startup, a good option is to have a 1-year cliff after which they begin to obtain stock options. The 1-year timeframe ensures that the employee has a good fit with the ethos of the startup. This is as, if not more, important as the specific skill or capability of the employee. If the employee does not have the right fit, his presence may have a detrimental impact on the morale of other team members, particularly with those who join the startup after him. In case the startup has to let the employee go within the first year, it no longer needs to worry about managing the stock options that may have vested with the employee, in case of the cliff. The 3- or 4-year timeline for vesting of the stock options for the employee can then ensure that he is also focused on the long-term success of the startup.

Many jurisdictions around the world allow startups to hold a percentage of the equity that is issued. This can be converted into stock options. However, this can also be provided to active cofounders. The following example illustrates when this makes sense.

A co-founder of a startup recently approached me with a quandary. He only had 5% equity in a startup that he had co-founded with another person. It transpired that they did a 'founders and friends' round when they founded the company. A few of their friends also invested in the startup. Since his investment was $ 100 K of a total investment of $2 million, he received 5% of the equity, and his co-founder received 15% since he had invested $ 300 K. The method of providing equity to 'friends and family' together with the founders was unusual to the detriment of the co-founders, since each friend also received 10% equity for an investment of $ 200 K. The unfairness was because while the 'friends and family' did not put their future on the line, the two founders took a step back from all their other activities to focus on commercialising the startup. Another important consideration was that the founders did proportional board representation based on equity. This resulted in the founders having minority representation and voice in decisions relating to their startup, despite being all-in.

Given this background, the question was how to make things fair for the co-founders so that they could have a greater stake in the startup. This was not fully biased towards the co-founders, since as any investor knows, it is important to ensure that the co-founders have enough equity to keep them motivated by looking forward to a personal financial upside in case the startup becomes successful. Furthermore, with a 25–40 dilution with each round of funding, the founders expected to have a tiny proportion of equity after 2–3 rounds of funding, putting their motivation in question.

Without diluting the 'friends and family', there were three options to strengthen the equity position of the two co-founders.

1. The first one was to set equity aside for the active co-founders. This would not take any equity away from the equity issued, but over time, would ensure that the equity position of the active co-founders was bolstered and provided motivation to continue making their efforts in the best interest of

the startup. There are ample examples of this in large companies as well, and it is well recognised as an effective technique to align the motivation of senior management to the long-term success of the company.
2. The second was to provide a stock option pool that could be topped up sporadically and could be used in lieu of bonuses for the co-founders. The difference between the first and the second options was the time when the equity would be transferred to the co-founders. In the first option, the equity would be transferred as it was issued. In the second, the equity would be put into a stock option bucket and would vest over time, with a risk of tax implications by being treated as income equivalent during vesting.
3. The third and final option to strengthen the equity position of the co-founders was to provide non-dilutable equity to the two cofounders. This would ensure that the two co-founders did not become diluted when new equity was issued to new investors. In effect, the two founders would receive additional equity when new investors came in so that their equity in percentage remained the same.

It is important to keep in mind that these do not include co-founders who may not join the startup on a salaried capacity but have relevant knowledge and expertise that can help drive the startup towards successful commercialisation. For all practical purposes, these are considered part of the active management team.

In summary, equity is your opportunity to share in the success of your startup, as it achieves your vision. It is also your opportunity to gain an incredible amount of wealth. Finalising it crystallises the joint foundation of what the team members are trying to create and focuses their energy on the real challenges that lie ahead.

Startup Valuation

One of the greatest quandaries of you as an entrepreneur is how to value your startup. This question becomes relevant fairly early on in the life of a startup. This is because unless your startup can survive the early period or tech evolution or platform development using organic funds, you do need investors to come onboard. How you value your startup *prior* to the investors coming in with funds determines how much equity you give them for their money. This impact of this is that you may end up giving them too much equity for their funding, which may be one of many rounds that you may require as your startup evolves. It is important to keep in mind that the money you make when the startup is sold for a billion dollars is not actually a billion dollars. It is equal to the equity you hold as a percentage of the total equity when the startup is sold.

The dilution of founders is shown below. It is critical to understand how this happens, since each investment round reduces their ownership of the startup. Furthermore, onerous conditions imposed by investors dilute founder equity further. This is also why founders need to maximise the multiplier effect of money (Fig. 13.3).

Since no entrepreneur got rich on the meagre salary that his investors allowed him to earn, your only option to get seriously wealthy is to ensure that you give away as little equity as possible to investors for their investment. For those entrepreneurs who argue that your main focus is not to get wealthy but to do something good for humanity, keep in mind that your investors may or may not think that way, but would be quite happy to have yet another 1% equity in case you happen to be the next Facebook. In addition, you always have the option to give it away once you have it, and your slice of equity (which hopefully will equate to incredible wealth) is only a fair reflection of the value you have created for a segment of society.

A good way to go about this is to understand how investors like to value startups as well as how they finalise pre-money valuation for closing an investment round. The two are different.

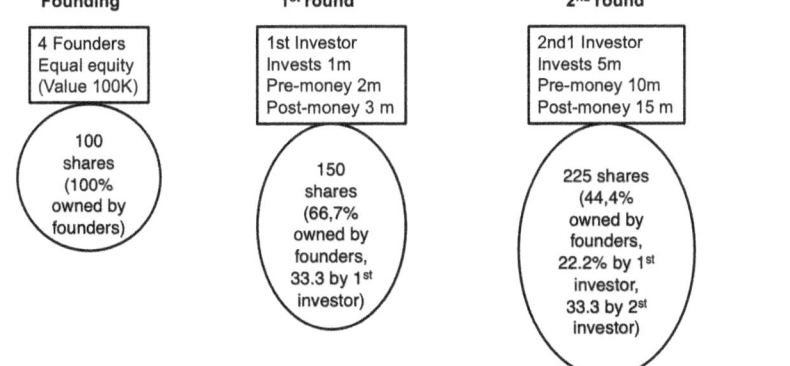

Fig. 13.3 Evolution of percentage ownership by founders after investment rounds

Looking Inwards

Investors often look at the details of the numbers that the startup provides. This is not to say that they necessarily believe the numbers. American president Eisenhower once said, 'In preparing for battle, I have always found that plans are useless, but planning is indispensable.' Investors like to see the numbers prepared by the startup, since this shows the discipline that the startup has used to keep the financial needs as close to reality as possible. This does not imply that they believe in it but is an opportunity for them to verify if the startup has captured all possible financial elements over reasonable periods of time. Startups often underestimate the time taken for certain operational steps. Investors are more aware of the time needed for these, including legal, IP, machine ordering and delivery as well as assumptions underlying initial and sustained revenue. They simply compare the numbers provided by the startup against common data points based on experience to see variance. With the revenue numbers, startups often provide metrics including NPV and IRR. More often than not, these tend to be irrelevant since they only make sense in the case of a mature company operating on standard growth in a stable industry with an industry-standard gross margin. Intrinsically, startups are anything but, since the stars among them may end up defining an entire industry and capture super profits for a fairly sustained period of time into the future. Startups often assume that NPV forecasts enable them to demonstrate the value of their value proposition to investors to obtain an attractive pre-money valuation. They do not realise that they do themselves a disservice, since without realising it, they underestimate the future growth that their startup may be able to achieve. Since investors are often far more familiar with these numbers and the sensitivities underlying them (such as terminal value and its capitalisation, which can often contribute up to 80% of the value of the company), the startup often undervalues its own future growth and value generation.

Investors like to discuss valuation based on internal metrics that startups provide. This helps them cap the valuation by finding flaws in the startup's internal numbers of growth, whereas their main motivation while investing is to check how the startup will stack up against its global competitors. So while they're salivating about the prospect of the startup taking a leadership position in the global market and the multiple returns they would then expect to make by investing in this opportunity, they are able to pull the startup's valuation down by simply challenging it on the things they know best, rather than the reality of the business potential. Whatever its valuation based on internal metrics, investors will always pull it down since it is easier to shoot holes in assumptions rather than based on valuations of the startup's competitors or other investor deals.

Valuation to Close Deals

This brings us to how investors finalise valuations for the purpose of closing an investment round. If the startup is savvy enough to have multiple parallel investor discussions running with the same endgame timeline and has enough liquidity to see the process through, investors realise that they are in the sellers' market where they are the buyers. The startup then needs to use this leverage to address not only a valuation that is attractive for them but also other terms that are most fair to all parties concerned, rather than leaning heavily towards the investors (which is normally the case).

At the same time, the startup should consider a valuation of the way investors consider it by comparisons with the industry. If there have been investments in competing startups (as is invariably the case), this method of defining a pre-money valuation is far more relevant, since it tells the investors that you are not only aware of their metrics, but have the same focus, which is outwardly bound. Investors are likely to say that the other competitors are better funded and therefore have a higher valuation to counter the startup's argument of comparable valuations. However, if the startup is tech-driven in a technology marketplace, this needn't cut ice, since the raison d'être of a tech startup is to leverage its tech excellence. Additionally, unlike in a platform startup, the first-mover advantage for a tech startup has less impact since manufacturability still needs to be addressed. Additionally, some manner of discounting is always possible, so long as the starting point is the valuation of other competing startups.

There are several elements that are often more important than valuation per se. These are discussed below.

Anti-Dilution

Investors often come in at valuation terms that seem attractive to startups. They provide a great pre-money valuation, agree to the milestone plan and provide a little cash bonus for the founders to boot. The legality, of course, is done by their lawyers and is as per standard norms of the industry. Therein lies the nub. There are very few norms of the industry, with one exception; in case of doubt or uncertainty, the equity of the investors is protected.

One of the most innocuous points in the investor documents relates to anti-dilution. This implies that in the case of future fundraising, investors will not become diluted. The founders often feel that there is no reason to push back on this, since they have confidence that there may not be a need for a future fundraising round and that they will be able to reach the black with the current round. What they do not realise is that you always need more money, and often a lot more if you're overachieving on your milestones. They often gloss over potential challenges and completely miss out on some elements related to bringing a technology to market. This is similar to dieting, where you always remember the things that you have not eaten, but often forget the things you have.

Come the next round of funding, as it invariably does, the legal documents that have been signed are legally binding. Thus, the investors hold on to their equity as a percentage of the company, and the founders get extra dilution.

Veto

Investors often have the right of veto on strategic decisions of the startup, including the salaries of founders and large unexpected expenses as well as pivots. More importantly, they can have an option to veto new investors by stating in the transaction documents that any new investors have to be aligned to the interest of the startup as well as those of the existing investors. This is so broad that it effectively becomes a catch-all phrase. This then provides existing investors with the flexibility to stop or delay any investor from coming in and enables them to have a right on future rounds of investment. More importantly, by discouraging new investors from coming in, the existing investors are able to suppress the valuation of the startup. With dwindling investment options, the startup continues to be dependent on additional funding from existing investors. This enables investors to maximise the equity that they are able to obtain in future rounds of funding. This can become even more insidious when used by strategic investors, since the rationale behind their original investment is not to multiply the value of their investment but to acquire the startup and convert it into their future competitive advantage or an area of future growth. This is discussed in more detail in the chapter 'Scale or sale'.

Initial Funding Size

Entrepreneurs often focus on closing the round of funding that enables them to work on commercialisation. However, if this does not cover 18–24 months of runway, it may not be adequate for achieving key demonstrable milestones. This implies that the startup does not have enough to show and has to fall back on the existing investors. Without specific milestones, there is no chance of obtaining higher valuation, and the founders end up giving up more equity at a low valuation. The only exception is the angel investment round, where the founders get investment in exchange for simple equity or even convertible loans. In the case of simple equity, which is similar to the equity held by the founders, the funding size is smaller, but the investors do not have any special rights, giving the startup complete flexibility to look at future investment options without encumbrances.

Convertible Loans

In case the angel investors are granted convertible loans, it can reduce the administration and legal expenses since it is a very standard process with minimal legal steps. The investors are protected, as the conversion of the loan into equity can occur at a discount to the valuation in the next round of funding. The longer the time taken to the next round of funding, the larger the discount provided to the angel investors on converting their loan into equity. Thus, if the next round is closed within 3 months, the angels' loan is converted into equity at the same valuation as the new investor. If the new investors come in 6 months, the angels may receive a 10% discount. If the new investors come in 12 or 18 months, the angels would receive 15% and 20% discounts, respectively. This provides a benefit to angels, who take a larger risk by coming in early. Furthermore, there is an option to have a cap and floor for investors. In case the next round of funding happens at a very high valuation, the angels would still be converted at a reasonable maximum valuation. For instance, if the next round of funding happens at $20 m valuation, the $200 K to $500 K angel funding provided would give them very little equity on conversion. The cap could then limit the maximum valuation of the startup to $10 m so that they still obtain a reasonable percentage of the startup's equity. The floor protects the founders, since it implies that in case there is no future round of funding, the loan is converted at a minimum valuation of the startup, so that the founders still maintain a significant majority of ownership of the startup.

Priority Rights

If the investors that the startup gets onboard in its first round of funding happen to be strategic investors, they invariably incorporate priority rights on the material needed for the product, the product, route-to-market or manufacturing, which may not be fully developed. The view of strategic investors is to consider the startup as an outsourcing of its R&D function. Therefore, the investor expects to have priority rights on everything that may be of strategic interest. For instance, if the startup uses chemicals, the investor would expect to provide the necessary chemicals, rather than letting the startup obtain them at more market-competitive prices. If the investor is in a business aligned with the business of the startup, which is most often the case since this tends to be a precondition for strategic investment, the investor will consider buying the products of the startup. Although this appears to resolve the issue relating to finding customers for the startup, it often results in lower prices for products. In practice, the strategic investor would bind the startup in an agreement where the startup is forced to sell their products to the strategic investor at a predefined price, and the investor then sells them at the market price, which is significantly higher. This transfer pricing, which is often done to mitigate international taxes for large companies, can dramatically reduce the super profits of the startup. In the event that the startup is able to attract new investors to the table for future rounds of funding, it needs to be kept in mind that strategic investors are also notorious for not giving the same rights on future commercialisation to new strategic investors. This then defeats the purpose of new strategic investors coming onboard. Even financial investors are not motivated to join in future rounds since their main focus is to maximise the return on their investment and exit in a reasonable period of time. The initial strategic investor is likely to cap future valuation since this provides an option to buy the remaining equity of the startup. By having the veto on new investors coming in as well as access to the products of the startup, the investor hinders the future value of the startup and limits founders from their exit. With this level of control over the products of the startup, the strategic investor does not even need to buy the equity of the founders. In such cases, the founders remain locked into the strategic investor with no option to exit.

Valuation with Future Funding for Strategic Investors

Startups often take equity from strategic investors with onerous conditions such as veto, as discussed above. However, if the startup is unable to obtain any external funding once the strategic investor invests, its only option to obtain funding is from the strategic investor. A critical element that needs to be discussed is the valuation of the startup for future funding rounds. If this is not done, the investor may simply decide to keep the valuation static. For example, if the startup receives initial funding of $1 m from the investor at a pre-money valuation of $4 m. The strategic investor receives 20%, as the post-money valuation is $5 m. However, if the startup requires $10 m in the next round of funding, the investor may keep the valuation static at $5 m. In such cases, the investor would acquire another 2/3rd of the startup. If the startup does not mitigate this risk before getting into exclusivity for the first round of funding, it becomes very difficult to do so at a later stage. Over a couple of rounds of funding from the investor, the founders lose majority and are unable to capture any upside from their value created.

Earn-Up

Often, investors will seem to agree to the startup's valuation or even seem to agree to a slightly higher valuation. However, this is done with a caveat. The founders start with a low pre-money valuation and earn up as they achieve milestones. What the founders do not is realise that you always get delayed in achieving milestones. This is for three reasons. The first one is that you under-estimate what can go wrong as you try to commercialise your innovation. This is particularly for external dependencies of the startup, where the startup needs to outsource components but does not have control on the quality, logistics or how they would work together. The second is that you simply do not know what else may be needed as you commercialise, since you have never been there before. The final one is that since the investors are likely also on your board, they may change the milestones or priorities, but may still measure you based on the original signed agreement.

The result of this is that looking back, you realise that you have slipped on a few milestones along the way. It may be that some of the said milestones are no longer relevant since the market has moved on or the startup has pivoted. However, if the founders slip up on achieving milestones, the end result is that you are unable to earn up the equity, which would have given you a comfortable majority and a very nice valuation. You then end up with giving up a large chunk of equity to early-stage investors who know from experience that if things can go wrong, they will.

For example, the startup may receive a pre-money valuation of $10 m but starts with a $1 m valuation and needs to hit 9 key milestones, each of which contributes a million to achieve $10 m. Invariably, the startup will only manage to hit 2–4 milestones, resulting in a final pre-money of $3 m to 5 million, a discount of 50–70% on the startup's expectation.

Participating Preferred

One of the most onerous conditions of investors is participation. When investors invest, they like to do so with preferred shares. This means that in the case of liquidation, they are paid first. This is not unfair, as the founders have not been able to deliver, resulting in the liquidation. However, the participation preference enables the investors to double-dip or obtain an exit twice. In such cases, if the investor invests $1 m for 20% equity, in case of liquidation or trade sale, the investor would get his $1 m back and then get 20% of the remaining money.

A Swiss startup doing biotech was able to receive pre-seed and seed rounds funded with angels. However, having received close to $4 million thus far, it needed to obtain more funding and approached a large private investor. Since the angels were maxed out at this time and had no more appetite to invest, the private investor invested $5 m with aggressive conditions linked to his investment. One of these was a 3X participation preference. Soon thereafter, the startup was sold to a large pharma player for $20 m. The private investor received $15 m (3X of his investment) and then participated again on a pro rata basis for the $5 m that was left. The founders were left with hardly anything, simply because they did not push back on the 3× participation preference.

Drawing Them In

Investors will often ask founders what their pre-money valuation is. As the entrepreneur, you have to ensure that they are interested in the startup before you start discussions on the valuation. A valuation cannot and is never the starting point for negotiations, since if investors are looking only at this metric, you can be certain that they themselves are unlikely to bring much other than money. You would never negotiate salary with a potential employee till you determine whether he's a good fit for your company. A good option is to simply state the money you're looking for and draw them in. If you do not know what their sweet spot is, you can simply provide a set of milestones that you would like to achieve, and if you have more money, you would be able to significantly outcompete your competitors and get to the market faster. This often gets the investors to show their cards regarding how much they can invest, either themselves or by leading a consortium.

In conclusion, there are only two things that are important for founders other than transitioning their idea or technology to create market impact: the ability to have the option but not the obligation to exit by selling their shares and to ensure fairness in equity ownership with their startup eventually going towards IPO or being sold. The points above help entrepreneurs ensure fairness, even as they focus on creating value for the future.

14

Scale or Sale

As a startup, one of the questions that you're always facing is whether to raise future funding to continue growing your company or to sell it. These two options become more tangible once you've raised some funding in order to bring your idea to life, captured your idea with IP, built the manufacturability to demonstrate replicability of your product and got some degree of traction with strategic or beachhead customers.

The visual provides an overview of the options to scale or sell your startup. We also discuss how to maximise exit valuation and minimise lock-in (Fig. 14.1).

Factors That Help Decide Whether to Scale or Sell

Scaling or selling the startup is not easy to define but depends on several factors. Clarity about these factors can help the startup make the best decision, since the founders need to live with the consequences of these decisions for some time to come. Additionally, many founders consider these two in isolation, whereas the focus on selling the company implies that you know what a potential buyer will buy. This in turn can help all strategic decisions, since not every part of the company will drive its sale value. You can then focus on building the value that someone would buy in the future and thus maximise the exit value of each dollar invested in growing the appropriate value within the company.

Founders

The first element to consider is the founders themselves. If some of the founders clearly desire an exit or if there is a conflict between the founders, it would be reasonable to choose exit. In case the investors agree, this is an opportunity to provide an exit to the dissenting co-founders and clean up the capitalisation table. It is important to note that this is more likely to happen if there are new investors, since if only existing investors are investing in the new round, they would have no motivation to provide an exit to some of the founders or even to bump up the valuation of the company with the new round of funding. For any founder who wants to exit at this time, this may also be an opportunity to negotiate a specific technology that he can take in exchange for a noncompete on the main areas of the company's business. In this way, the departing founder is able to create a new startup or address a new market.

Technology

The next element is the technology. If the technology is unique and new or if the market is only beginning to open up and grow and the startup is in a leadership role in capturing more value over time, it is a better option to choose scale rather than sale, as the future upside is likely to be larger. An easy way to know if the technology is still considered unique is if customers ask for exclusivity. This implies that customers want to be the only ones to have this technology and consider this to become their competitive advantage. While this is a good sign, the startup needs to be particularly careful regarding how it deals with exclusivity, since it can restrict it from selling to other customers. There are several ways to deal with exclusivity. The startup can make it time-dependent, region-dependent or market-sector dependent. Time-dependent implies that the exclusivity is given for a specific period of time, e.g. 2–3 years. Region-dependent implies that the startup could provide it for regions where it does not expect to expand its own operations. Here, it is important to limit the customer from exporting to the regions where the startup wants to focus. Sector dependence is more relevant for technologies that may have relevance across multiple sectors. An example is 3D nano printing, which may have relevance in touch screens, health monitoring and security applications. By slicing the exclusivity, the startup may be able to restrict the scope of the exclusivity while still being able to benefit from the large payout in exchange for granting such exclusivity. Once this is done to the advantage of the startup, it may be able to exploit the growth of the market. It's critical that the startup gets good legal advice, rather than trying to wing it to save money. Any contract performed incorrectly may lock the startup for the life of the technology. There's nothing quite as expensive as a cheap lawyer.

Funding to Scale

Let us delve deeper into the specifics of scale vs sale of the startup. If you consider scaling up, you have two main options regarding funding, as well as some ancillary options. The first option is to obtain funding from financial investors, and the second is to obtain funding from strategic investors. These options are shown in the visual below (Fig. 14.2).

Financial Investors

Financial investors have certain advantages that make them attractive. There are also some concerns with financial investors that the startup needs to recognise upfront (Fig. 14.3).

The main advantage is that they are looking at a high return on their investment, which happens with an increase in the value of the startup after they invest. This directly benefits the founders since the value of their equity also

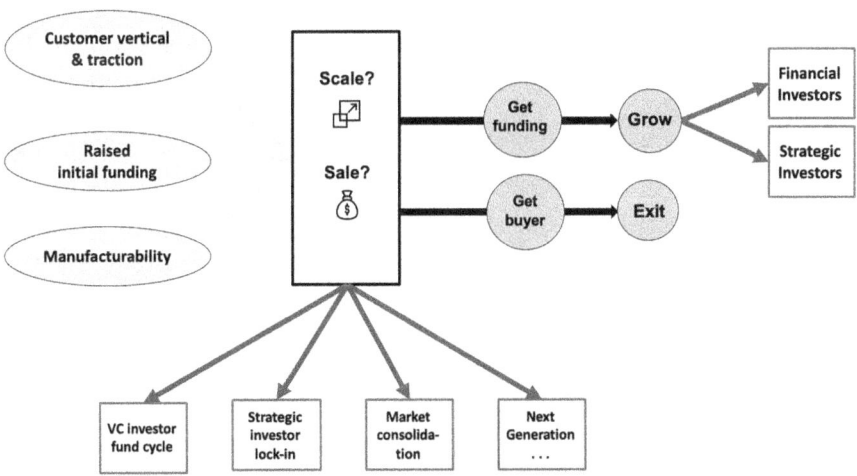

Fig. 14.1 Factors influencing whether to scale or sell

increases. Furthermore, financial investors are very focused on their exit, so founders are also protected from adverse conditions from customers or future investors who try to limit their exit. These investors also have a relatively fast timeline from evaluating the investment to the money flowing into the startup. This still averages approximately 6 months, so it is important for the startup to plan accordingly, since if the startup's cash situation becomes critical, the financial investors can negotiate the valuation down.

However, there are some risks that the startup needs to be aware of with financial investors. These investors sometimes have a portfolio strategy, so that they invest in multiple startups focusing on the same market segment, using slightly different route-to-market approaches or technologies. This means that if one of the startups seems to be moving ahead faster than the others, the investors may cannibalise the others to focus on the first one. This is particularly common in US-based financial investors since they have a transactional approach. Since financial investors are keenly focused on multiplying their investment, they can be predatory with equity. For a startup, this implies that if you miss your milestones and you go back to your existing investors as you're not yet ready to approach new investors at a higher valuation for the next round of funding, the existing investors can only agree to provide bridge funding at a lower valuation. Missed milestones thus result in founder dilution. Another point that startups need to be aware of is that financial investors have funding cycles. These tend to be up to 10 years, at the end of which they liquidate their investments and return the money to *their* investors. This means that if a startup receives an investment from a financial investor's fund that is 5 years old, the investor will already want to plan an exit within three to 4 years. In case the startup's timeline for future funding or exit is not aligned with the investor's exit, the investor can simply write off the investment. This is a bad signal for other investors, and the startup simply becomes untouchable for new investors.

To mitigate the risks of early exit associated with financial investors, the startup can consider obtaining strategic co-investors since they have a longer perspective. This can also enable the startup to create a potential exit to the strategic investor, since every startup cannot have an IPO or a trade sale with an unrelated buyer. The startup can also consider actively getting new investors onboard to mitigate the risks of missed milestones and equity dilution. Getting new investors is also an opportunity for the co-founders to obtain a partial exit, which can be up to 20–25% of the funding raised. Although existing investors would never suggest this, it enables the co-founders to sell part of their equity in a larger funding round. This exit is often tax-free, given the legal jurisdiction of the startup. This partial exit is a sound option, since slightly lower equity holding by the co-founders does not change their rights or future upside dramatically in case of the startup's success, while at the same time reducing their financial risk in case the startup fails.

Strategic Investors

The second kind of investor is strategic investors. These can be customers, suppliers or even competitors. They do not invest because they want a 10X return on their investment. They invest because they see the startup as providing a competitive advantage or future area of growth to them. The visual below shows the advantages and risks of strategic investors, as well as how to mitigate the risks of getting them onboard (Fig. 14.4).

There are several advantages of strategic investors. One is that these investors do not invest from a closed fund but rather from their R&D or innovation budget, so the startup does not have a strict timeline before the investors require an exit. The second is that strategic investors are often large companies with hundreds of millions of dollars of funding available. Since strategic investors are also most likely customers, they can also become the initial reference market or provide the route-to-market. This initial customer traction is otherwise difficult for a startup and often is the major hurdle between innovative technology and market rollout. Strategic investors also have deep manufacturing expertise, a large area of weakness for technology startups that often struggle with commercial manufacturing due to the high capex involved. Together with logistics and supply chain expertise, the startup can benefit from tapping manufacturing to plan its scale-up more effectively.

Risks with Strategic Investors

However, there are challenges with strategic investors. The main challenge that directly pertains to the co-founders is that strategic investors invest with a view towards buying the rest of the startup. With this aim, the strategic investors have no motivation to increase the value of the startup after they invest but want to pay as little as possible for the rest of it. The second challenge is that although the strategic investor is open to paying more in future funding rounds, there is often no clarity regarding how to value the startup. Since the strategic investor is likely sitting on the board of the startup with

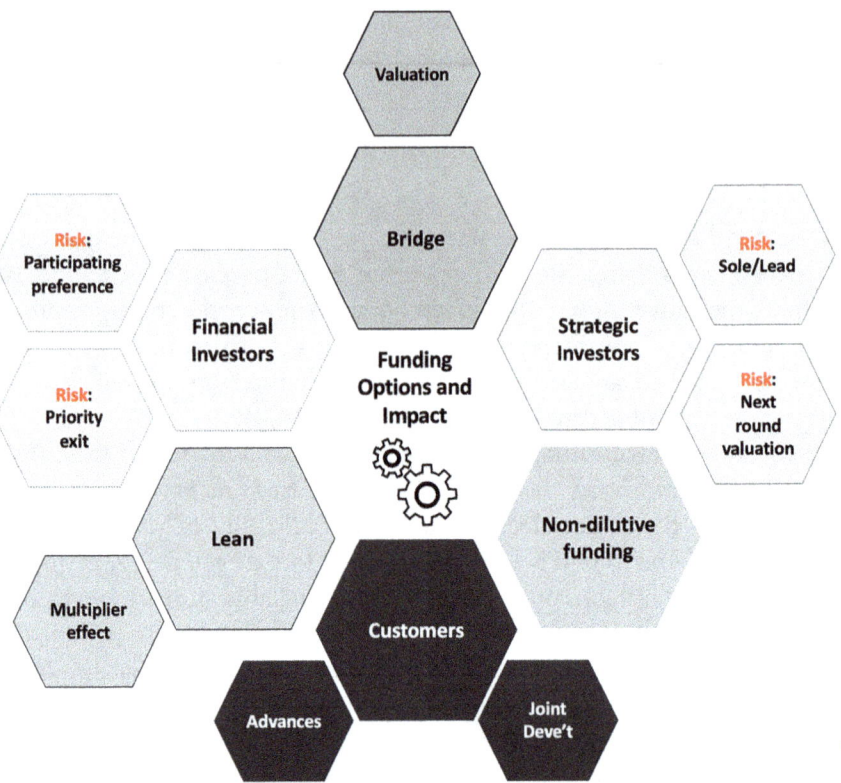

Fig. 14.2 Different funding options and risks

veto rights, the strategic investor can dramatically reduce the valuation to own a majority of the startup with a funding round. As the startup commercialises, the investor becomes its main, if not only, customer, and the startup often uses the supply chain and route-to-market of its investor, as discussed above. However, this results in a risk of transfer pricing, where the startup sells its products to the investor/customer at cost, and the investor subsequently sells at an enormous mark-up. However, the main challenge is regarding the founder exit. If the investor has no motivation to buy the startup since they already have all the know-how and rights, there is no obvious route for the founders. They then run the risk of becoming a glorified external R&D arm of the investor.

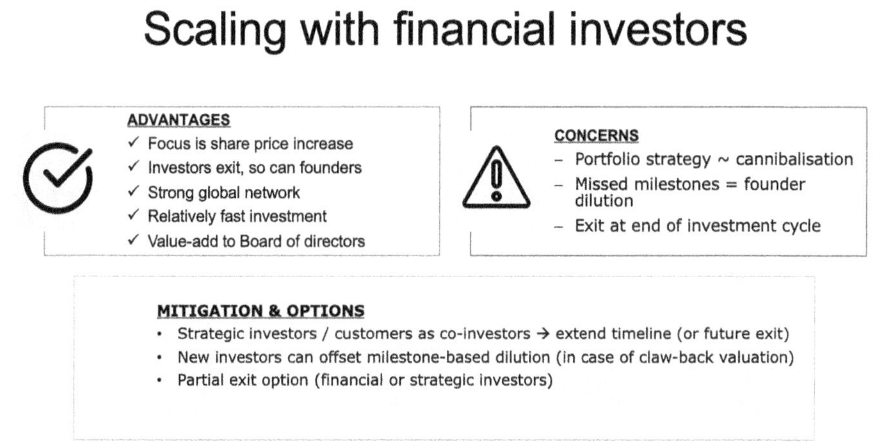

Scaling with financial investors

ADVANTAGES
- ✓ Focus is share price increase
- ✓ Investors exit, so can founders
- ✓ Strong global network
- ✓ Relatively fast investment
- ✓ Value-add to Board of directors

CONCERNS
- − Portfolio strategy ~ cannibalisation
- − Missed milestones = founder dilution
- − Exit at end of investment cycle

MITIGATION & OPTIONS
- Strategic investors / customers as co-investors → extend timeline (or future exit)
- New investors can offset milestone-based dilution (in case of claw-back valuation)
- Partial exit option (financial or strategic investors)

Fig. 14.3 Advantages and risks of scaling with financial investors

Risk Mitigation

The startup's co-founders can mitigate these risks with specific actions. The only thing to keep in mind is that these actions need to be taken before signing the legal agreements with the strategic investor, in the same way that the prenup needs to be signed before the wedding.

When negotiating with strategic investors, it is valuable to remember that everything takes longer. It is not uncommon for funding to take between 9 months and 3 years. This means that the startup needs to plan for bridge funding. The startup also needs to avoid business integration and lock-in before funding is in place. Having multiple co-investors (financial or strategic) provides an option for the co-founders to their own exit. The startup also has the option of doing a reverse exclusivity with the strategic investor. This is a counterintuitive strategy to lock in the strategic investor. From personal experience, I know it can be done!

Reverse exclusivity means the strategic investor agrees not to use or invest in any other similar technology to address their internal requirement or external market. Normally, it is the strategic investor that asks the startup for exclusivity. This means that the startup is not allowed to sell to any other customer. This results in the startup being completely dependent on the investor and dramatically limits exit options for co-founders, since the startup is unable to create independent value. However, if the strategic investor recognises the future value of the startup's technology towards sustaining its competitive advantage and gross profit margins, it is possible for the startup to negotiate this in the investment. With reverse exclusivity, the startup makes the investor dependent on its technology. This enables the startup to capture value linked to the market created or identified by the investor. With my first company Flisom, we were able to get a reverse exclusivity with our global strategic investor as part of the terms of their investment. Subsequently, when they were approached by our competitor Nanosolar, which had raised over $960 million including a large part from the US government as soft loans, they had to decline the opportunity to invest, although their investment in us at the time was in the low tens of millions of dollars. This reverse exclusivity can become a bargaining chip for co-founders of the startup during negotiations with the strategic investor to negotiate an exit or a partial exit.

Given the risk of lock-in, it is wise for the co-founders of the startup to define the terms and valuation of their exit. The terms should ideally be based on elements that the investor cannot change, such as time rather than revenue. This is because the investor can reduce the startup's revenue by way of transfer pricing. The co-founders also need to have a backup plan in case the investor decides not to proceed with additional funding and transitions the manufacturing from the startup to itself to insource the startup's technology.

A good example of a startup that received a strategic investor onboard that subsequently lost interest is Skyva. Skyva was an early mover in providing enabling software for collaborative commerce. In September 2000, ABB decided to invest $130 million in Skyva. This was at the height of the dot-com boom, and a month before it would come crashing down. ABB itself was soon fighting its demons and was hit by lawsuits relating to asbestos, as its link with lung cancer became known. ABB, which had acquired the US company

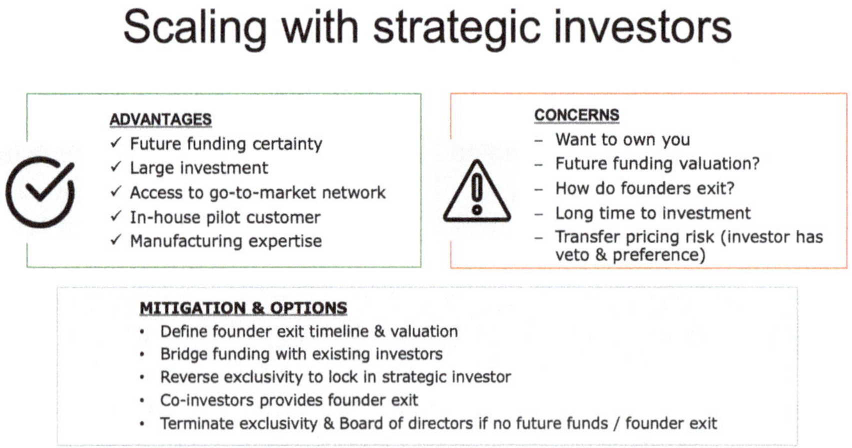

Scaling with strategic investors

ADVANTAGES
- ✓ Future funding certainty
- ✓ Large investment
- ✓ Access to go-to-market network
- ✓ In-house pilot customer
- ✓ Manufacturing expertise

CONCERNS
- Want to own you
- Future funding valuation?
- How do founders exit?
- Long time to investment
- Transfer pricing risk (investor has veto & preference)

MITIGATION & OPTIONS
- Define founder exit timeline & valuation
- Bridge funding with existing investors
- Reverse exclusivity to lock in strategic investor
- Co-investors provides founder exit
- Terminate exclusivity & Board of directors if no future funds / founder exit

Fig. 14.4 Advantages and risks of scaling with strategic investors

Combustion Engineering, a manufacturer of asbestos, did not even see this liability coming. Combined with its governance crisis, where it emerged that the CEOs had been paid too much and were asked to refund this money, ABB was in PR hell in late 2000. Its share price crashed from over CHF 56 to CHF 1.4 from June 2000 to October 2002.

Soon after, the CEO of ABB changed, and the new management decided that Skyva's technology was not strategically aligned with ABB's strategy of going back to the basics. Skyva's management wanted additional funding to continue developing their business. ABB also did not agree to let Skyva's team perform a management buy-out since it was still reflected in their balance sheet. At this time, Skyva was doing revenue and already had approximately 70 people on its rolls. Skyva was caught between a rock and a hard place since they could not obtain additional funding from with ABB to grow their business and were not permitted to obtain funding from outside sources due to the terms of their agreement. The founders did not receive any payout since there was no one to buy them out due to the ABB lock-in. Ultimately, Skyva could not sustain this impasse and finally folded (https://www.edlundconsulting.com/abb-from-almost-bizarre-bravado-to-all-back-to-basics; https://www.theengineer.co.uk/abb-to-invest-130-million-in-skyva/).

Bridge Funding

When planning a new round of funding with either financial or strategic investors, the startup needs to recognise that it always takes longer than anticipated. In such case, it is imperative that the startup plans for a bridge funding round with existing investors. If this is done early enough, the existing investors have the opportunity to set aside their own funds. The startup is also able to manage expectations of its existing investors by highlighting the achievement of key milestones and showcase additional milestones that the bridge funding round will achieve. The additional milestones can then be shown to further increase the pre-money value of the startup, giving more confidence to existing investors. This mitigates the risk of the bridge funding becoming a down round.

If the startup fails to indicate the need for a bridge funding round sufficiently in advance, there is a risk that the existing investors either force the startup to reduce the valuation or ask for onerous conditions that protect the valuation for the investors, while increasing the dilution for the founders.

Non-dilutive Funding

The value of non-dilutive funding in providing a bridge without strings can never be underestimated. This is available in most developed countries, including in the EU in the form of Horizon Future grants, in Switzerland in the form of Innosuisse startup innovation project grants and in the USA from DARPA and other government programmes. Joint projects with universities increase the chance of getting such grants, since most universities in Europe generate IP without having a clear route-to-commercialisation. Although the European grants are often limited to €2–2.5 million, it can provide a valuable few months of runway and significantly improve the startup's negotiation capability with the new round of investors.

Lean

This is not so much a funding option for the startup but an opportunity for the startup to evaluate what activities will help it to increase its own value. Instead of asking itself what activities it can do in-house, if the startup asks itself why any particular activity should not be outsourced, it begins to focus. This focus is only towards the value-added activities and those that create customer dependence. Ultimately, this does not only reduce the reliance on funding but ensures minimisation of dilution of the founders' equity.

Funding from Customers

Startups often ignore the option of getting funding from customers. Since this is not in the form of equity investment, it offers startups the benefit of minimising dilution. This funding also adds to the startup's credibility during investor negotiations.

There are two options for getting funding from customers. The first one is joint development. It needs to be kept in mind that this is not the same as joint R&D. This is because in case of joint R&D, the customer may ask for rights on any IP arising from the R&D efforts. Joint development, on the other hand, would only provide shared IP for the front-end or specific product design, rather than the technology that enables it. The second option is to get an advance from the customer for future deliverables. The risk with getting an advance is that the startup needs to ensure delivery of the product within the stipulated time and with the necessary service guarantees. In case of delay, the customer may take legal action against the startup, which in turn drives away investors. Joint development provides the startup with far more flexibility with regard to its timeline and also provides access to manufacturing capabilities of the customer.

Sale

The sale of the startup is an opportunity for the co-founders to sell what they have built and monetise.

Before the co-founders think about sale, it is important to know what the acquirer is buying and whether the acquirer is a competitor or customer. While a customer may be buying a technology that enables them to sustain their competitive advantage for longer, a competitor often buys market access, customer ownership or a monopolistic position in the marketplace. In the sale of Amorana, Lovehoney brought access to the Swiss market and customer preferences, which remain stable even as competitors may develop similar logistics capabilities of quick delivery of sex toys. In essence, the competitor is unlikely to simply relinquish their own technology for the sake of the startup's innovation. Additionally, over time, technology always runs the risk of being copied, in spite of IP, commoditisation or automation, as discussed earlier. Information about what the buyer is buying helps the startup to obtain the maximum price possible and minimise the risk of not being able to obtain the earn-out paid by the seller over the following years.

The three most important questions that a founder needs to ask of his startup are as follows:

1. Who is the customer?
2. What will he buy?
3. How is the startup putting all its resources in capturing this value?

The startup can then identify the highest perceived-value market segments, create dependencies and move to where the value is in the supply chain. Some risks that the startup needs to be aware of when negotiating an exit as well as how to mitigate them are discussed below.

Risks

However, selling the startup means the co-founders of the startup can simply decide to sell the technology and the market potential, since it's easier than scaling up and addressing the challenges of manufacturing and market traction, right? Not quite. Very seldom does a sale result in the founders getting the full cash upfront and simply walking away. Unless the technology is completely institutionalised and the founders are no longer needed for driving the innovation, the buyer most often mandates that the co-founders get a small proportion upfront and the remaining amount as a payout based on milestones. This implies that the founders are locked in for a period of 2–3 years so that the buyer is able to ensure that the founders take responsibility for the manufacturability and customer traction and revenue that they had promised to the buyer when they sold the startup. Only when these targets are met do the founders obtain the rest of the money from the acquisition. However, this payout becomes a problem, particularly since the operational control and IP now vests with the buyer. This is because since the buyer already owns the IP and route-to-market, there is very less motivation to pay, and the buyer now has the control to delay or even limit the payment.

Furthermore, the buyer may decide to pay the co-founders with equity rather than with cash. In case the buyer is a privately held company, this means that if the company decides not to go to the stock market or get sold, the founders of the startup may end up holding equity that is illiquid with no recourse of exit.

Mitigation

There are certain mitigation measures that the selling co-founders can take to maximise their chance of exiting. The first is to ensure that the milestone payments are fixed and within their control. They can negotiate for time-based payouts since the buyer is unable to influence them. They can also ask for milestones that are within their capability, rather than those within the control of the buyer. These include patents, which can help bolster the buyer's IP and future competitive advantage. The co-founders must ensure that they are given the resources to create IP. However, in case the buyer changes strategy, the co-founders should negotiate that all conditions precedent to payouts have been met so that they receive their payouts. In addition, the co-founders can negotiate for the right to take their technology out if the buyer does not provide the payout. It is wise for the startup to avoid business integration and exclusivity before the final signature and initial cash-out. To ensure that the co-founders are still receiving their final payout, they can consider postponing the transition of their IP to the buyer until there is absolute clarity about their final payout.

Beyond this, the co-founders can also negotiate taking out the nonstrategic technologies and to be excluded from the noncompete, which limits what they can do so that they have the option to start a new startup. In this way, they can use their experience to start the next big thing.

A startup's journey is considered complete when the founders not only commercialise it successfully but are also able to convert this value into monetisation. This happens when they have the option to sell their equity. Where you end up is largely determined by your plan when you start. It is very seldom that you get there by luck, in spite of what successful entrepreneurs would have you believe.

Takeaway: *Find and develop outstanding individuals to be your successors. You can't scale or exit if you're indispensable.*

Irrelevance

One of the most important points for the founders of any startup is to have the option to exit. It is thus imperative that the founders ensure their own exit when they consider the sale of their startup. This is not a default, as most buyers consider the founders to be core to the acquisition and consider locking them in. Since founders find the corporate environment post-acquisition stifling, they are seldom able to endure the full period of lock-in. They thus leave after 1–1.5 years, leaving a significant amount of the acquisition value on the table.

For founders to ensure a clean exit, it is important for the founders to become irrelevant and relinquish executive roles. If the founders are only active via the board, it is difficult for the acquirer to mandate an operational lock-in. An operational lock-in would imply that the founders are unable to pursue any activity for the period of the lock-in, normally 3–4 years. Becoming irrelevant enables the founders to walk away with the money and pursue other entrepreneurial ventures.

As a founder, there are a number of options to plan your exit. These are shown in the visual below (Fig. 14.5).

These are discussed below, including risks and how to mitigate them (Fig. 14.6).

1. *Sale to strategic buyers*

This is the most common outcome for a majority of startups. It is important to reiterate that technology startups are most often acquired for their

Exit routes for early growth stage startups

| Strategic Investors | Private Equity | Initial Public Offering |

Fig. 14.5 Exit options for startups

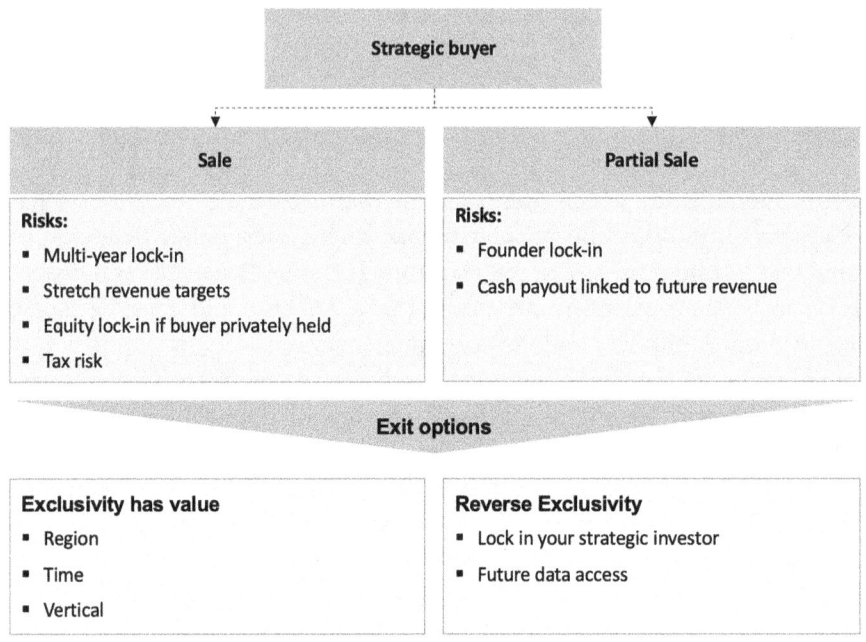

Fig. 14.6 Considerations when planning an exit to a strategic buyer

technology, whereas platform startups are acquired for their user base. For technology startups, the acquisition is often performed by customers since the technology provides an option to sustain their gross profit margins. It may also be done onboard the founders. The latter is risky, since instead of getting a clean exit, the founders may find themselves locked in, with an uncertain timeline for monetisation or exit. In this option, it is important to align all terms, including valuation and timeline for ongoing payments after acquisition, *before* signing any exclusivity. To the extent possible, the milestones that trigger subsequent payments should be driven by time, rather than technical targets, since the former are fixed, whereas the latter can be changed at the discretion of the acquirer.

Trade sales can also be made to suppliers to enable them to extend their value propositions and go forward in the supply chain. The third option for a trade sale is to competitors, and this may be done if the startup's technology is superior or if the competitor simply wants to mitigate competitive risk.

Risks
When selling to strategic buyers, the startup has certain risks. The major one is that of payout for the sale. This is because only approximately 10–25% of the total agreed price is paid upfront, with the remaining price payable over the following years. This implies that the entrepreneurs need to earn the majority of the money payable by the acquirer for their startup, and this is normally a percentage of the revenue generated by them. Since the revenue projection of the startup is often optimistic or subject to optimal market conditions, they are unable to reach all of these milestones, resulting in a significantly reduced payout. Another risk is that the acquirer pays by way of equity. There is often a lock-in with this equity, but the challenge is far more critical if the acquirer is a privately held company. In such cases, the founders of the acquired startup may realise that they have ceded control and now hold much smaller equity that is also not liquid and cannot be sold for an uncertain period of time. Furthermore, if the acquirer still requires VC funding before it has its IPO, the founders of the startup may end up becoming further diluted. Finally, when the founders get their payout over future years, they may not be able to benefit from the money being considered as capital gain and instead have to show this as regular income. Since capital gain often has lower or no tax, this needs to be considered before the transaction is finalised.

Mitigation
Once founders recognise the risks in selling their startup, it becomes easier to take mitigation measures. The first step is to try and obtain the maximum amount upfront since they are then less dependent on anything that happens to their acquirer. Since a significant amount of the sale price will be paid over the next few years, they should align the milestones to things that the acquirer cannot change to ensure that the acquirer is unable to move the goal post after the acquisition is done. For instance, founders should link future payouts to time rather than revenue. In this way, they would be able to get a part of the payout every few months, and the buyer has no ability to change this.

In case the buyer is only interested in one part of the business, the founders could also consider selling only that part of the business, enabling a partial exit. This can also be done by selling rights to specific geographies that the startup does not want to focus on. If a technology has multiple uses, the startup may also be able to sell the rights to a specific vertical that it does not want to focus on. This is quite common with technology companies, as a new technology such as nano printing may have uses in creating sensors, touchscreens and personal medicine. Since even investors prefer that the startup focus on a specific area, it could be an opportunity to sell the rights to the other market segments. While selling the technology for the noncore areas, the startup could create a revenue stream by mandating that the buyer needs to buy the specific nanomaterial to ensure quality. This could then be sold like Nespresso capsules or printer ink.

A UK-based founder of a luxury goods company that he had co-founded with his wife decided that he did not want to continue running the company as he was getting divorced from his wife. Since the only investor, who was also on the board, was keen to continue building the company, he was locked in in an uncomfortable working situation. Since the startup was already in the black and showing strong growth, he decided to sell exclusivity to the Middle East market to a company based in that region and take that as an exit. Since the Middle East was not a strategic area for the startup, this ended up being mutually suitable and provided an exit from a difficult situation.

2. *Sale to Private Equity*

A small number of startups also exit to private equity. There is an important distinction between strategic buyers and private equity. Whereas strategic buyers acquire startups because they want to have access to the technology or the user base and because they see this as an extension of their business, private equity acquires companies to flip them. With startups, their strategy often is to buy a number of startups that may cover a significant part of the supply chain and package them together with the view of selling them within 2–3 years. Knowing the value drivers of private equity can help startups price their startup very differently. They are likely to be far less interested in long-term scalability than the perception of value and the potential for dominance.

A Swiss startup created a platform for dynamic pricing for airline services. They found a private equity acquirer and made the deal in single-digit millions. Once they sold their company, they realised two things. The first was that the private equity acquirer purchased five more companies in complementary areas for similar valuations. They then packaged all six companies and sold them for over 300 million dollars. This was performed within 12 months of the first acquisition. The second was that the private equity acquirer made the acquisition via a shell entity and only made part of the payment for the startup. Ultimately, the final buyer did not find the startup strategy and decided to not pay the remaining amount. Although the startup got the technology back, the passage of almost a year meant that their technology was no longer relevant (Fig. 14.7).

Since a private equity acquirer only has a limited timeframe and a narrow area of focus, the founders can negotiate a carve-out option that is outside the area of focus for the acquirer. In this way, the founders can continue building the other areas as a second startup, even as they negotiate an exit from the acquirer.

3. *IPO*

Initial public offerings, or IPOs, are the most visible kind of exit for startups. That said, they are comparatively rare for most startups, particularly for technology startups. This is because the startup needs to have a certain revenue as well as the capability to scale after raising money during the IPO. However, founders often do not realise that they are not automatically allowed to sell their equity after the IPO. They often have a lock-in of a few months to a year, and it is the investors who have the preference to sell their equity first, after the IPO. Even within investors, there is a certain hierarchy, and the last investors who may have come at the highest valuation have the first right to sell their shares at the IPO. Thus, if the share price goes down post-IPO, the founders get much less by way of exit than anticipated.

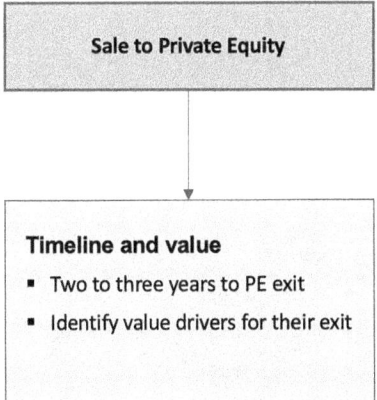

Fig. 14.7 Considerations in case of sale of startup to private equity

Another important element to consider is that after the IPO, founders have very little opportunity to raise more funding unless the company has strong revenue to begin with. The reason is that as long as the startup is private, the investors are locked in and talk up the value of the company to attract new investors. However, once the company is public, the investors are no longer locked in and simply sell their shares if they consider the prospects uncertain. This is an important reason why privately held startups are able to raise billions of dollars, but their valuation often dips immediately after their IPO. Finally, post-IPO, the startup faces dramatically increased scrutiny, both from regulators and from research analysts. This is often underestimated by founders and can become a significant distraction from business-as-usual, risking their short-term market focus (Fig. 14.8).

When founders consider an IPO, they assume that they may be able to control the timeline. However, geo-politics can play a strong role in ensuring a suitable market environment for an IPO. It is thus important for founders to consider a bridge funding round in case the IPO needs to be postponed. Finally, given that the investors may have the first right to exit during an IPO, the founders should consider a partial exit in the last round prior to the IPO. In such cases, if the startup gets $100 m, the founders can take up to 20% of this as their own minority exit, mitigating their own financial and market risk linked to the IPO.

SPAC

A very small number of startups find their exit via SPACs. SPAC, or special purpose acquisition company, is a company with no commercial operations

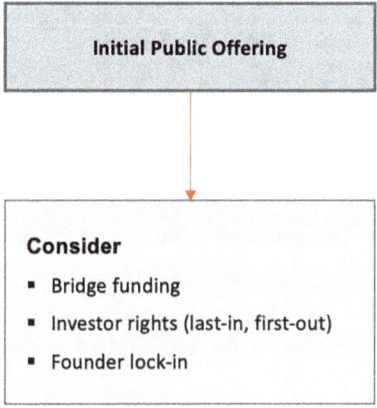

Fig. 14.8 Considerations if startup plans to IPO

but is formed with the sole purpose of raising capital by way of an IPO to acquire an existing company. They are often called blank cheque companies since their investors do not know what company the money will be used to acquire. Although they had been around for a long time, they came into vogue in the late 2020s as a way for a startup to have a soft IPO without having to go through all the red tape normally associated with an IPO. However, as with ICOs (or initial coin offerings) or crowdfunding, which caught the public imagination in the recent past but subsequently turned out to be akin to Ponzi schemes, it is not clear at the time of writing if SPACs will suffer the same fate by providing an opportunity for unscrupulous entities to flip suboptimal assets for a fee, as this was what led to the subprime housing crisis in 2007.

As seen, there are a number of options for startups to monetise the value created by them. However, this end game is not a given, and the vision of the entrepreneurs needs to be aligned from the time before the first round of funding is finalised. Your decision to go for organic growth based on pumping profits back into the business, or get an angel investor who may be conservative about risk, or a VC investor whose rush to exit may leave your product less than mature, or even a strategic investor who may want exclusivity of products or technology, will all get you to very different end points. Although end points are not easy to define since the commercialisation of a startup is an evolution, for this purpose, it becomes much clearer if the startup recognises this at each decision point with investor rounds and customer agreements.

Specifically, the end game in the case of an organic growth scenario or technology licensing will create a tiny niche, with revenue topping off at approximately USD 2–five million in the case of a technology startup. A risk-averse angel investor coming in may not only limit the flexibility of the team to 'go with their gut' but also limit them from getting new investors, since the angel investor may not be comfortable giving up some of his rights when new investors come in. A VC in a rush is someone who normally invests in software startups or platforms and has now invested in a technology startup. He would normally want to exit fast, and in case the technology has yet to demonstrate stability, manufacturability or route to scale, this may actually destroy value by sending an adverse message to incoming investors. A strategic investor's insistence on exclusivity is a sound strategy for the investor since it provides a new potential source of competitive advantage. Not so much for the startup.

How Can You Maximise Exit Valuation?

Given all these scenarios, is it indeed possible to maximise exit valuation for founders? Let us explore how this can be done.

There are some factors within the control of the co-founders that determine exit valuation, and some that are not. The factors that are in control of the co-founders revolve around the decision of whether to do it alone. If you decide to not get investors, your ability to scale effectively and compete globally will be hampered by your limited financial resources. Another element is the definition of what exit means and what success implies. Different co-founders often define these terms differently. This gives rise to conflict, which results in decision paralysis.

The factors that founders can control until they sign the first agreement and have a large impact on the exit valuation are discussed below.

Standard

Perhaps the greatest contributor of sustained value is when the solution of the startup becomes the next standard. This ensures that it becomes a core part of the funnel through which all value flows, putting it in pole position to capture some of it. To become the standard, it is imperative that it be adopted by as many users as possible. Thus, no one company has the exclusivity to use the solution. Since strategic investors normally like exclusivity, as it provides them with future competitive advantage, it is important to ensure that this is not provided by the startup since it can risk value transfer from the startup to the strategic investor.

Startups born out of research often are part of the new wave of innovation that disrupts existing industry and brings forth a new set of standards. We have seen this across multiple industries. An example is nuclear waste. We have used nuclear fuels over the past few decades, but only is now the challenge of proper disposal of nuclear waste coming to the fore. Countries including Canada, Germany, China and the USA are trying to address this. Since nuclear waste is supposed to be secure for hundreds of millions of years, the gestation period of the new technology wave is longer as well. Switzerland is planning tunnels that may be over 30 km long and have a diameter of 10 m. In France, the tunnels are likely to be four times as large. This technology has only matured to the necessary extent now, and the window of opportunity for new evolving technologies to become the next standard for safe disposal of nuclear waste has opened up. Because the technologies have a very long-term impact, with a stated disposal stability in the thousands of millions of years, the window for reversing the disposal is also long. In the case of Switzerland, the disposal done for the next 200 years should be capable of being reversed in case a new technology for disposal comes up. In the case of France, the reversal period is 400 years. Concrete and the technology to create it that may remain stable over millennia may have a unique opportunity to address this market, even at very high price points, since the need is driven by the perception of risk. As this example demonstrates, any change in technology driven by awareness of market needs or perceived risk provides a unique opportunity to become the next standard. Incumbent competitors have no specific advantage since all old references pertain to the previous technology, which has no relevance. This is also an opportunity for the startup to capture value, since the old ecosystems, to the extent relevant, remain part of the supply chain but not always where the value transitions.

Platform

If the solution has the capability to be perceived as a platform, it provides the opportunity to get other stakeholders onboard, who then build their ecosystems on top of the solution. Each new ecosystem strengthens the platform further since failure would imply the failure of revenue streams of the ecosystems. In geographic terms, although China began holding the US dollar as a hedge against its own currency devaluation, it is now in the interest of China to prop up the US dollar, since it holds over three trillion dollars. Devaluation would result in the real value of the dollars held by China to go down as well.

Transitioning Value

Value transitions over time. Even in an industry where the end product is commoditised, there is always an opportunity to identify where the value resides in the value chain. An example of this is Nespresso machine suppliers. Since Nestle's strategy is to focus on the capsules, it has provided the standards and machine specifications across the industry. As a result, many companies make coffee machines. They all have a profit margin ranging between 10 and 20%. There is no opportunity to make super profits since there is no sustainable competitive advantage. In this case, Nespresso is able to capture the super profits, since it owns the funnel and owns the brand that sells.

Contrast this with brands such as watch companies, say Rolex. In this case, since Rolex is the brand that people buy and pay for, the value belongs to Rolex. It would thus be able to squeeze part suppliers for the most sensitive part, the movement, which is the heart of the mechanical watch. Of course, unlike most other watchmakers, Rolex also makes this part in-house, which further helps consolidate its reputation by addressing any possible risks of commoditisation and dilution of value therefrom. For a startup, it is important to recognise where the value will transition to and ensure that it does not give up some of these. User attributes, whether they are buying behaviour and preferences or health attributes, challenges and limitations, will over time become critical cornerstones where value transitions occur. It is important for startups to recognise this, particularly in the context of big data and its ability to extract invaluable trends for the future. This will continue to play an ever-increasing role in how exit value is recognised.

Stakes of Stakeholders

The reputation of stakeholders is a less understood but critical factor in the success of startups. If partners and customers are ambivalent about the startup's solution, they are unlikely to push to ensure the buy-in within their own organisations. However, as soon as they buy in fully, they put their own reputation behind the solution. They then become extremely powerful spokespersons of the solution, particularly because they are not considered to have a vested interest in the startup. In a sense, when the potential stakeholders put a stake in the ground showcasing their belief in the value and efficacy of the solution, it becomes a powerful reference point that helps build credibility. This in turn provides an opportunity for the startup to reach the stakeholders' networks, keeping them as a market beachhead.

Strategic Investors

These are extremely valuable since they provide an internal reference point for the startup's solution and provide a soft launch opportunity, where the impact of failures or pivots can be minimised on the market. For the startup to maximise its exit valuation, it needs to ensure that the strategic investors do not have any exclusivity for use of technology or transfer pricing in place, since this would hinder the option for other customers to access the solution under the same conditions.

Reverse Exclusivity

If the startup is able to get strategic investors or customers to state that they will only use its solutions, it provides a reverse exclusivity that helps them capture a market without limiting their own growth opportunities with other customers. This converts strategic customers into stakeholders without limiting the future business opportunities of the startup and can be a powerful tool in maximising exit valuation.

Investment Rounds

As the startup commercialises, it requires additional rounds of funding to facilitate growth and scale. It is important to ensure that the rights and conditions given to previous rounds of investors in no way limit the valuation for all future investors (including the previous investors). Rights to investors to use the startup's solutions should not limit the startup from accessing new customers.

Own Vertical

It is far more valuable for a startup to own a specific vertical than to try to provide some technology capability across multiple verticals. In the former case, there is an opportunity to be the reference point and the default solution that the vertical veers towards. In the latter, the presence of strong competitors implies the risk of the solution being selected based on the lowest cost, rather than for its specific value or credibility. To maximise exit valuation, it is important to recognise what prospective buyers value most since, in many cases, these are large strategic players. If these buyers are already operating in a particular area of the market where they recognise the value and want to expand their offering, it is far easier for them to buy a niche player than to develop the market organically. The important word is 'market', not "markets'. Thus, if a startup focuses on developing and dominating a market segment, the payoff is likely to be far more than simply providing some of its technology across multiple sectors. While the latter strategy mitigates sector risk, it is far less likely to bring you sector leadership, and this makes you that much less attractive for the buyer looking at buying leadership across a sector. The example of IMDb illustrates this. In the mid-1980s, Colin Needham posted on Usenet about actresses with beautiful eyes. Soon thereafter, others with similar interests responded with additions or lists of their own. Over time, this list expanded to include both active and retired actors and directors. By late 1990, the list had information for over 10,000 movies and television series. In 1990, Needham incorporated the option to search this database, and IMDb, or Internet Movie Database, was born. In 1993, it was moved to the web, which was then in its infancy. In 1996, Amazon made overtures towards the database, and it was incorporated as a company in that year. Finally, Amazon bought it for approximately $55 m in Amazon stock in 1998. Interestingly, when Amazon expressed interest, the database was being managed by a group of volunteers, some active and others partially involved. Several of these were based in Switzerland and did it as a hobby. They all got equity. Many of them held on to the Amazon equity and did very well indeed, as it increased multiple times over the next few years. What was interesting was that although the technology evolved, the value continued to reside with the database, which, over a period of time, became the reference point for all movie-related information. The continued relevance of IMDb is reflected in the fact that over 20 years after Needham created this database, it continues to be one of the most visited websites on the Internet.

Long-Term Contracts

Startups live and die by their customer traction. It is important to mitigate the variations, whether they are daily, quarterly or annually. An effective way of doing this is by having multiyear contracts. This provides stability of revenue and helps in planning the investment in further development and rollout. Long-term contracts also mitigate economic cycles since investors always look out for revenue opportunities that continue in tough economic times. While some revenue streams are countercyclical, it is not easy to find them or incorporate them into a large business.

A startup based in Zurich performs radiation testing to ensure that no radioactive materials are taken across borders for the purpose of terrorist activity or to make dirty bombs. This company has deployed its solutions in multiple countries across Europe at borders and international airports as well as in the USA. The revenue of the company is countercyclical. This implies that when the markets are subdued on account of political uncertainty and the risk of international conflict, the company's solution has ever more relevance. Additionally, since the budgets of any country always have an ever-growing component dedicated to national security, there is no negative impact of economic cycles. Finally, national security is never determined based on the cheapest solution but rather by the more secure solution. As a result, the revenue of the startup is always driven by perceived value rather than cost-plus. Since many larger companies look for stable revenue during bad times, having stable revenue provides a strong basis to plan an exit.

Multiyear Service Agreements

One of the most sustainable revenue opportunities involves servicing and maintenance. This provides comfort for the customer and at the same time provides a small but sustained revenue flow for the startup.

Mettler Toledo is a company based in the outskirts of Zurich in Switzerland. The company provides weighing scales, with precision starting at micrograms. Its products are used in research labs around the world as well as entities such as your local grocer. The company has built a high degree of trust with customers over the years. One of its revenue streams is servicing and certification revenue. The company sends service technicians every year to customers to recertify the weighting scale. If the scales pass the test, the technician sticks a sticker that certifies them for another year. This provides comfort to the customer and a very healthy revenue stream to the company. This revenue is consistent over time and ensconces the company from any economic slowdown in a given year.

If this is planned well by a technology startup, it can provide an opportunity to become the reference point for measurement in an evolving standard. This can extend the revenue opportunity for a company and lock in customers further, without diluting its core value proposition. Even if the startup's solution enters a more competitive environment in the future with the entry of competitors, the need for customers to certify the startup's solution annually by the startup enables it to capture revenue for a very long time by becoming the measurement standard. Since value evolves over time, having multiple value points provides the startup with multiple opportunities to capture value and monetise.

Ecosystems

As the startup progresses, support systems around the startup's solution, or ecosystems, develop around it to take its solution to the market. Although the startup may have the capability to address all customer requirements, many of which may relate to customisation, it is tremendously valuable to let other players perform this customisation. This does two things: it enables the other players to create their own revenue, and this motivates them to support the startup's solution and actively market it to customers, and it also enables the startup to focus on scaling up, since it does not have to focus on customisation, which hinders scale.

Exclusivity with Strategic Customers

Strategic customers provide very powerful hooks to accessing the market since they have relationships and credibility built over decades with their end customers. These strategic entities also consider a startup's technology relevant to drive future growth. The difficulty begins when these entities look for the startup's solution as a source of competitive advantage, since this implies that they prefer exclusivity. This is contrary to the startup's goal of having as wide a footprint as possible. It is thus important for the startup to begin by obtaining traction from the ultimate end users and use this as leverage to gain better conditions from the strategic entities. Traction from the ultimate end users validates the startup's solution as a source of value, and this validation is critical for driving and sustaining super profits, as well as obtaining a better deal from the strategic entities.

As seen from the above, maximising exit valuation begins before the startup signs the first investor or customer deal. Once the startup signs off a component of the value to customers or provides a future right to investor, it's gone, as is the potential for value capture for the startup and wealth creation for its founders.

Partial Exit

This is a very effective way for founders to minimise their lock-in and the possible risk of being unable to extract value, whether the startup is sold to a strategic buyer, to a PE or in case of an IPO. The visual illustrates the possible reasons for a partial exit, as well as how this can be done (Fig. 14.9).

Partial exit is when founders sell part of the value they have created by their startup. The benefit of doing this is that it enables founders to diversify their value outside their startup. This is also done because the timeline to exit may still take a number of years and because founders are often locked in even after their startup is sold.

Partial exit

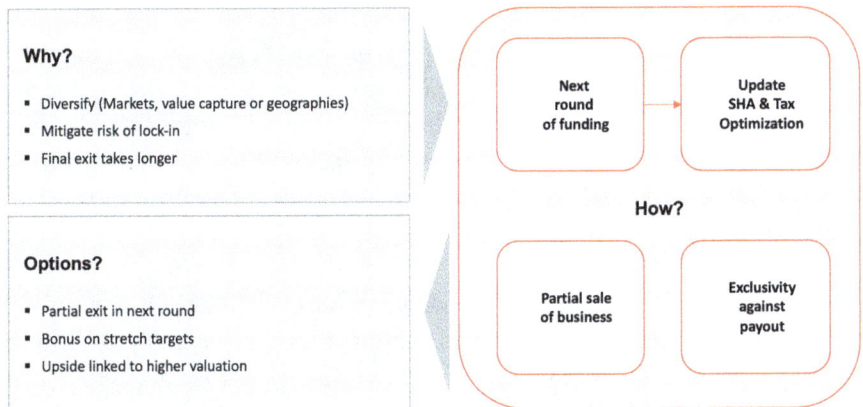

Fig. 14.9 Considerations and options for partial exit of founders

Partial exits can be done in several ways. The most common way to do this is to sell part of the equity during the next round of funding. This requires agreement from existing investors as they have to relinquish their tag-along right and is possible if the new investors come in at a higher valuation. The benefit of selling their equity is that for many jurisdictions, sale of shares is tax-exempt as it is considered capital gain. Further, in case the founders want to reduce their dilution, they can always get some equity from the stock option pool after the new funding round.

Another way of getting an exit is by selling part of the business. In case of technology startups, the technology may have relevance in multiple areas. If the founders agree to focus on one particular sector, the noncore sector can be licensed out for a one-time payment. The startup can also do this for a geography that it does not want to actively roll out to, by providing a licence to another entity to operate. It is important to ensure that the licence is only for a given geography, as otherwise there is a risk that the entity getting such licence may begin competing on the startup's geography.

The founders can also agree with their investors that if they hit stretch targets, they will have the option to sell part of their equity at a pre-defined valuation. This is often done if the startup has strategic investors, as the presence of strategic investors makes it difficult to attract new investors.

Institutionalisation: Why Startups Need to Institutionalise

'Beyond all the frustrations and challenges, the sense of fulfilment comes from knowing that you have self-worth that is not dependent on belonging to a large corporate entity, but in the knowledge that the next large game-changing company or, indeed, an entire industry may spring from your guts, wisdom and conviction.' (*From Science to Startup*, published by Springer in 2016, author Anil Sethi).

As an entrepreneur, you always begin with a vision; to bring a new idea to the world, and see it fly, to hold it like a newborn, then help it take its first steps with chosen customers. You then support it as you watch it grow into an independent being able to and capable of standing up for itself, till such time that it is supported by and supports its own ecosystem. In other words, institutionalise. There is one key difference between entrepreneurs and their employees.

Institutionalisation is most often linked to giant lumbering old dinosaurs, which are public institutions. These are, more than anything, unencumbered by their own weight and the burden of history, policy and procedure of how it's always been done, which takes precedence over change. However, there is a positive aspect to institutionalisation. It is to ensure that best practices are provided to the entire market that can benefit from them. Even very traditional professions can benefit from this. The medical profession, to name one, is where doctors diagnose aliments by way of eliminating those for which the patient does not have symptoms. However, beyond the obvious diseases that can be diagnosed by objective tests, diagnosis and treatment tend to be subjective. You may have experienced this if you've had a health problem for which a second medical opinion seems completely at odds with the first one. For this reason, the institutionalisation of organic knowledge can bring value and quality to life. Knowledge, accumulated over decades of experience, can then be captured in the form of machine learning and be used as a foundation to enable future health-care advances.

Institutionalisation is far from trivial. This is because companies are often established in the image of the visionary entrepreneur. Therefore, although they ostensibly provide a product or solution, this is seldom the starting point of the founder's thinking. Rather, it can be argued that the product is but the output or end result of the vision of the visionary. That's why they are called visionaries. Entrepreneurs sell what they do not have, and employees sell more of what they have. Transitioning from selling the vision to selling the actual product is a key pivot and the first step towards institutionalisation to magnify your impact and scale. Institutionalisation is to ensure best practices, originally in the DNA of the entrepreneur. This is what gives the startup its mojo in the first place. If this vision of the entrepreneur is properly institutionalised, it becomes ingrained in the entire company and enables it to survive as an entity independent of the founder.

Take Dell. Michael Dell built his entire company with a simple premise of being able to make computers cheaper by keeping inventory low and bringing incredible efficiencies into computer manufacturing. Dell was in fact the first company in the world to be in negative inventory into the lexicon, and it did so by taking orders and payment from customers before ordering components from its suppliers. When I first met him in London in the late 1990s, I was a starry-eyed MBA student. He was the master of his universe, where his company was growing faster than virtually any other company at the time, with him at the helm. This was some feat, given the explosive growth of new companies powered by the explosive usage of the Internet at the time. We all looked up to him as an example of what was possible, since he was a self-made billionaire by the time he turned 25.

Fast-forward for approximately 10 years, he was now entrenched, as one of those had succeeded not only in institutionalising his vision but also in enabling his company to hold its position in a fast-evolving ecosystem. This was at the time when other players such as IBM were evolving their strategy of computer manufacture in the face of competition from China in ever-increasing commoditisation. However, the ground was shifting. Some, such as IBM, recognised it early and moved from hardware to services. Others, such as HP, remained entrenched in what slowly became a quagmire and saw their market capitalisation dissipate like the morning dew. Fast-forward another decade and having extricated himself from the company he had founded to focus on his foundation in the hope that his vision had been institutionalised, Michael Dell found that it had not. Dell had begun to lose market share in the market that was no longer driven by high growth and high margins driven by better computers but was more at risk of evolving out with the advent of smartphones, tablets and the cloud. There was a real risk of computers moving into pockets, wrists and spectacles. From simply being efficiency enhancing tools, the future of computing capability was increasingly being looked at as drivers of intelligence argumentation and better decisions passed on pre-emption. The greatest challenges when Dell began revolved around bringing affordable computers to the greatest number of people. Fast-forward two decades, the discussion had evolved to such an extent that one of the greatest challenges of today deals with the risk of artificial intelligence becoming superior to human intelligence and how to ensconce ourselves from what we've created. The fact that some of the smartest minds of our age, including Stephen Hawkins and Bill Gates, took opposite sides in this argument is telling. Companies that are now driving value include Neuralink, which is focusing on augmenting human intelligence by developing brain–machine interfaces, and Life-log, which provides a camera that takes a photo every 30 s to capture each moment of the user's life, in a surreal instance of science following science fiction as depicted in films including *Minority Report* and *Total Recall*.

However, back at Dell, Michael Dell had recognised that his vision had not been institutionalised enough to ensure the sustainability of leadership of his company. With a group of private investors, he decided to take his company private in 2013. For a 30-year-old company with over 10,000 employees and a multibillion-dollar market capitalisation to be taken private by the founder for not having institutionalised, his vision was telling. However, despite how incredible it initially seemed, it was not remarkable. Apple, one of the biggest companies of our time, continues to struggle to find the next big thing replace the eponymous iPhone, which was the vision of founder and visionary architect Steve Jobs. Arguably, it is more than a little challenging to innovate a new market segment that ultimately needs to grow to have annual revenues of more than a hundred billion dollars. Keep in mind that this is Apple's second coming, after it almost went bust in the late 1990s after the ouster of Jobs from the company. At that time, it only managed to claw its way back from close to bankruptcy after Jobs returned in 1997 to lead its resurgence by moving it back to its roots of product excellence and redefining the customer experience.

The question then is whether institutionalisation is ephemeral. In fact, institutionalisation is perhaps the greatest legacy that an entrepreneur can leave behind since it implies that the company and the foundation on which it was established continue to live and thrive long after the entrepreneur leaves. It is also the most challenging. This is because the positive impact as visualised by the entrepreneur can only occur over the long term if the company continues to deliver value and evolve long after the entrepreneur has departed.

To become institutionalised, the company needs to provide direct and sustained benefits for everyone in the ecosystem. This begins with customers but also includes suppliers, partners and employees. Only then does part of this benefit percolate to its shareholders. This makes sense from the revenue perspective since revenue sustainability for the foreseeable future enables the entrepreneur to exit and convert his equity into wealth. Institutionalisation also enables the company to attract outstanding people who then become instrumental in driving its destiny in a virtuous cycle. It enables the company to become a global standard if it attains global relevance. Becoming a standard ensures greater sustainability of relevance, since other companies who build products based on the company standard prop it up, which is the basis for their survival. This then becomes one of the most effective sources of competitive advantage and normally lasts for as long as the business vertical remains relevant.

The latter case can be demonstrated with the example of the US car industry, which has inefficiencies built in, in the form of dealership under the dealer franchise law. The law was put in place in the 1920s and 1930s to let the Big Three (Ford, GM and Chrysler) to do what they were good at, which was making the best cars possible. The independent dealers were licensed the rights to sell the cars to end users and focused on establishing a strong link into the local communities (https://www.ecowatch.com/states-cant-buy-tesla-2278638949.html).

In the 1930s, when automobiles were becoming commonplace in the USA, distributor networks sprang up and became the link between car manufacturing companies and buyers. These distributors were locked into specific brands or automobile companies. Since their destiny was now locked into the destiny of the respective car companies, they did whatever they could to ensure the survival of the car companies. Since distributors provided the only opportunity for customers to interact with the new car and determine its features, distributors provided a location-based competitive advantage to car companies. This went on for several decades, and car companies with distributorships had a competitive advantage on account of their presence. This business vertical of distributorships remained relevant all the way through to the point when Tesla began to use the Internet to reach customers directly. Over the past decade, Tesla introduced not only a new kind of car but also a new kind of customer relationship; one that no longer needed a distributor network. The existing distributors see this as a risk to their relevance and have gone to court in multiple states in the USA to stop Tesla from selling its car directly to customers. This naturally benefits existing car manufacturers but may ultimately be to the detriment of prospective customers. What started as a way to build efficiency in the system ultimately became self-serving and unable to pivot to continue serving the ultimate value generators: the car buyers. But ultimately, if you have to go to the government to stop a more competitive company to enter the market or to stop a new business case that your end customers want, the writing is on the wall. You have now become a protected business ecosystem that stops other more competitive and better products from getting to the customers. This is what India was until 1991, when it only had one television channel, two car brands with no design change for over 30 years and no consumer choice. Superior value in the eyes of end users is reflected in Tesla's valuation, which at the time of writing is more than the valuation of the next six car companies *combined* and is now considered to be among the most valuable companies in the world.

It is in the process of becoming institutionalised that a company can not only become a billion-dollar company but also sustain its value over time.

However, when you start thinking about entrepreneurship, one of the thoughts that undoubtedly crosses your mind is whether you might be able to achieve what the greatest entrepreneurs of our generation have done. Might you be worthy of aspiring to the heights of those entrepreneurs who have not simply started successful startups, but startups that have defined or even created entire industries?

As an entrepreneur, one of your greatest challenges is to understand how to survive long enough to succeed. For this reason, it is good to keep in mind that doing a startup is not a sprint but a marathon. The best startups are the ones where the entrepreneurs focus on sustainability beyond their lifetimes. This question forces the entrepreneur to think in terms of value creation and a value-based system focusing on people as their core assets, rather than simply a 'scale-to-flip' mentality. Changing the question elicits very different responses. In the same way that asking yourself where you want to be in 5 years takes you on a very different path from asking what you'd like to be written in your obituary. As a teacher of entrepreneurs, I often begin by asking the question about a 2- to 5-year timeline and where these entrepreneurs see themselves. Once they prepare a write-up, I ask them to put it in an envelope and seal it. I then ask them to write an obituary that someone may have written about them after their death. Their perspective changes completely, as they recognise what is truly important, and what matters.

15

Why Entrepreneurs Fail

Entrepreneurs wear failure on their sleeve. This failure is not only in getting the product out or selling the company but also at each step, right from getting co-founders onboard to getting the first investor to getting the next investor and so forth. When only one out of 10 startups succeed, failure is no longer a statistic. However, even for the startups that succeed, success is not without bruises and hurdles. However, it's important to recognise failure for what it is. It's an entrepreneur's greatest competitive advantage. Failure occurs when the customer does not confirm the product need that the entrepreneur expects or when the product cannot be manufactured reliably in line with the prototype developed in the lab. The advantage for the entrepreneur is to recognise this failure early and pivot. The incumbents are unable to pivot in line with changing customer needs since the cost of doing so is prohibitive. Flexibility is the entrepreneur's competitive advantage by recognising failure early.

A startup's survival is determined by the number of pivots it can make with the funding available to find the correct product market fit. To know why failure occurs beforehand can offer these entrepreneurs an opportunity to change their destiny. This is particularly pertinent since in most cases, failure is not on account of the technology not delivering. From my own personal experience as well as that of those entrepreneurs I have helped in their journey, the main reasons why entrepreneurs fail are discussed below.

Options

One of the main reasons that entrepreneurs fail is because they still have the umbilical cord to their research institution or to the day job. The reason is that entrepreneurship is about forging a new path and doing something that is not even done before. It thus entails stepping into a world of uncertainty and becoming the constant element that provides a semblance of certainty to members of one's team.

To ensure that you as an entrepreneur can be that immovable rock that others can count on, you need to feel that sense of belief and sense of purpose that makes other people believe as well, not because they can see your vision but that they know that you see it and are willing to follow you.

If you have options that are more certain, it gives you an immediate fallback and comparison with the crazy stuff you have to go through as an unpaid and unappreciated entrepreneur. This also implies that you do not have the full unwavering commitment that makes you walk on water, which, among other things like doing the impossible, is what you will have to do to make the startup work. It only sounds easy when you see others who have made it.

As the driver and visionary of the startup, the one thing you cannot afford is 'options'.

Equity Split

It is shocking how many founders assume that the equity discussion relating to who gets what percentage of the startup can be postponed and will simply be resolved with time. More often than not, as co-founders continue to work on the startup, each one assumes that he is doing more of the work than the others. Each co-founder also assumes that the value of his work is more than the work done by the others. Therefore, their idea of how much equity they deserve compared to everyone else becomes increasingly out of whack.

At some random point in time, closer to when they commence initial discussions with investors, this misalignment not so much surfaces but explodes. This is the time when otherwise good team members depart, leaving the startup weaker as a result. However, it can be worse. This happens if the departing founders start a competing startup, doing exactly what the original startup intends to do. You then end up in a situation where both teams co-own the IP and have similar ideas regarding commercialisation. In turn, if customers see similar messaging, they consider delaying the pilot. Furthermore, investors get scared away as they don't want to be involved in a legal dispute with the result that neither startup gets funded.

Tech Affair

It is always a surprise to non-tech co-founders how much tech co-founders are in love with their technology. It does not seem a means to an end; rather, it seems to be an end in itself. Normally, this would be a good thing. However, in an age where one of the strongest attributes of a startup is to recognise the value to customers and provide what these customers want, a focus on technology can become a serious limitation.

A focus on technology also hinders tech co-founders from pivoting and ignoring messages that customers provide regarding what is relevant for them. It is important to keep in mind that customers only pay for things that bring perceived value for them, rather than for the technology itself. Seeing the world through the lens of the tech ignores these often sublime messages from customers at the startup's peril.

Differing Vision

Co-founders often do not take a step back from the operational work of creating the company to define what they actually expect. This results in a scenario where one co-founder may consider creating a fully owned company that performs specialised solutions for a tiny and high-value niche segment. Another co-founder considers it logical to scale up to address the larger market by going high-volume and low-cost. When the time comes to define the strategy, the vision of the various co-founders is so different that it is impossible to reconcile it, since one automatically excludes the other. At the same time, there is often no arbitration mechanism in place to decide one way or another. This results in the issue becoming personal and based on ego. This is the beginning of the end, unless there is an option to buy off one founder or ensure his exit and continue the firm.

Friends Onboard

You're starting to think about an idea and you get people you know onboard, since it seems easy to build a team this way. What could go wrong?

The team members you get when you start are often likely to be from your area of expertise. In a best case, this duplicates skills rather than getting complementary skills to cover the various elements needed. In the worst case, this sets up parallel power and authority structures. While in a 3-person startup, this does not have an impact, the fissures become more visible as you get your first employees. The reporting structure results in a power play between the overlapping authorities of the co-founders. The employees are often casualties since it is extremely frustrating to report to two bosses who have different expectations. Ultimately, unless the startup can manage this, it quickly spirals out of control and spells its demise.

Not Firing Fast Enough

You hire your first employees, and you're still pretty emotional about the romantic notion of the team being a big family. The employees have the same vision of greatness and of changing the world and making it a better place as you and the other founders… or not.

Often, these employees are truly good at their work. That is why you hire them. You slowly realise that with the work excellence comes pride in their work (which is good) and an ego (which is not). Often, the ego transitions to wanting to control and have the final oversight on decisions. This can impinge on other team members, who are operating more like a team. It is clear that this attitude has a negative impact on the morale of the rest of the team. You have to make a decision regarding the excellence of the employee (or indeed, the co-founder) is valuable enough to continue having him on the team.

The decision can be precipitated by checking if the employee can work in a silo, where his work is completely independent and he has very little interaction with the team. This is possible, but not common. If there's an option of him working in a basement where he only communicates by e-mail or by providing updates on the tech/design/IP, it may be worth keeping him. However, you do this at your own risk. Additionally, the idea of startups is to take excellence to market and institutionalise it. To have a person working in a silo goes against the grain of institutionalising excellence, where more people help to scale.

If your startup will absolutely not work or truly needs the IP/tech excellence or will not get funding in absence of this, fire him. Failure will likely doom your startup.

Do Not Dream Big Enough

Technical entrepreneurs often focus on what they can deliver and only plan delivery of what they can actually manufacture. This is typical in Continental Europe, since US-based startups are much more in tune with expectation management and a clear focus on scale.

The challenge of promising only what you currently have the capability to deliver is that you only consider organic growth. This is far too conservative for most investors, since their view of investing in startups is to reach scale and own the market that is created. These investors are thus simply not able to justify a return on their investment, since the 10% annual growth is more in line with mature companies than startups, where they like to see a hockey stick curve. For customers, a modest delivery capability based only on what the tech team is able to deliver on lab equipment (rather than on commercial manufacturing) means the volume is tiny and the cost per device is truly high. An example is a Swiss technology startup. The team was creating prototypes of sensor solutions. During customer discussions, they quoted the price based on the cost of doing approximately 50 pieces a month. Incidentally, these were done on 3-D printing, rather than using mould-based injection manufacturing. Naturally, the price was several multiples higher. The team did not mention to the customer that with increasing volumes, the price would drop dramatically. Since the price was out of line with the customer's price expectation, the startup missed the opportunity to obtain development funding from the customer to show the product-market fit, which would have enabled a more compelling story for investors.

Geek-Speak

Technology founders often speak to investors and customers about what the tech can do. While this geek-speak is akin to red-hot gossip in the scientific community, it simply is tech for both investors and customers.

Tech entrepreneurs often struggle to relate to investors, whose only motivation is to obtain a return of a multiple of the amount invested. Where the investors are looking at market size, growth, current solutions, IP situation and exit at a nice healthy multiple based on scaling up and providing value-added solutions, the tech entrepreneurs focus on the tech and how it is the best in class in whatever esoteric scientific area it pertains to.

On the other hand, customers look for the perceived value of the solution to help them either increase revenue, reduce costs or preferentially provide a sustainable competitive advantage via the perceived value of the solution. In summary, tech entrepreneurs focus on what the tech can do, whereas the market is looking at what it can *enable*.

Between what the tech can do and what it can enable lies the valley of death, strewn with the pitch decks of technologies that could have been.

Fear of Uncertainty

Scientists and researchers from the world of technology often foster visions of becoming entrepreneurs.

However, the world from which they come is built around certainty. Although the research is built around building something new and the process of doing so is evolutionary, the environment around the research is very stable.

Compared to this stable environment, the one thing that the world of entrepreneurship is defined by is uncertainty. This begins from the business idea itself, where the raison d'être of the startup is to provide value where it does not yet exist. This does not simply entail stepping into a world of uncertainty but to take the customer into that world as well.

Each day, as soon as the entrepreneur steps into his office (or more likely, opens his eyes each morning), he has a clean slate ahead of him. Rather, he has a bunch of priorities, which includes looking for funding, managing investors and their expectations, looking after the slipping timelines for milestones, determining what the milestones should be, managing expectations of the team (which cannot seem to get the big picture), determining the social media strategy (do you have one yet?), define IP and strategy and look at the product's relevance and the value perception for customers. There's no right or wrong on where he should be spending his time; that becomes clear in retrospect.

Compared to everyone else who has a job or works in research, an entrepreneur literally has to earn his own salary. This either comes from money from investors or by sales to customers, and he only gets it once he pays his people. Things do not get much more certain with time.

Some entrepreneurs find themselves when they are faced with such uncertainty and thrive on it. However, ever so often, when tech entrepreneurs are faced with uncertainty, they go back to tech, since this is where they find their level of comfort. This is when the startup regresses to become a research entity… until the money runs out.

Going for Perfection

Scientists do research in the elusive search for perfection. Isaac Newton spent a majority of his working life doing alchemy and on his quest to convert metals such as lead into gold. The vision of scientists working on photovoltaic technology is to ultimately convert 100% of sunlight into electricity, and superconductivity is approximately zero electrical resistance in a conductor of electricity at room temperature. Although the research helps in pushing forward the boundaries of scientific knowledge, with practical applications so vast that they often give rise to entire new industries, scientists are very seldom the ones who commercialise their innovations.

The reason is that the things that drive science are the opposite of what drives startups that can ultimately scale. Science is all about striving for perfection. Startups, on the other hand, focus on linking research with market relevance and freezing the research to replicate the 'minimum viable product' to get it to customers at the most cost-competitive level in the shortest time possible. The startups that behave like research and strive for perfection most often run out of money, and even if they are indeed able to create technology excellence, they risk commercial obsolescence due to the excessively long period of time taken to get there. In summary, perfect is good, but fast time-to-market and customer revenue is better.

Two Boats

People from the world of technology often take their initial steps towards becoming entrepreneurs by doing this on weekends. The point where they expect to transition fully into the startup always seems to be somewhere in the future. The longer researchers stay in technology institutions, the further the time to transition appears. This clearly has to do with risk propensity, since the longer you stay in the world of tech, the more time you invest towards a tenure-track professorial position, and the more you have to lose.

The problem occurs when these scientists fashion themselves to be tech entrepreneurs and decide to continue with one step in research and another in the startup. This results in two problems for the startup. The first one is that the investors do not quite see the entrepreneurs' skin in the game that they like to, by way of being fully committed. After all, the investors are putting their money on the vision of the entrepreneurs since the business plan always pivots when it makes first contact with customer expectations. The second is that the members of the team that go to the startup fully get short thrift, since they are putting their entire time on the line for the startup, whereas the most senior technology members of the startup continue to be there only sporadically, treating it as a hobby. Ultimately, this results in milestones slipping since with two boats, the prioritisation given to the milestones also becomes lower.

Another risk is that the senior researchers start more than one startup while continuing to work full-time in the area of research. Not only is the time spent by the researcher at a premium, but knowledge-related conflicts occur ever more frequently. This puts the efforts of the team members working full-time in jeopardy. Ultimately, this conflict does not bode well during investor discussions, or if early-stage investors have invested, it can result in acrimonious disputes. The requirement of a level of comfort of a key tech co-founder has doomed more than one promising startup.

Save Money, Not Time

Researchers always have a paucity of funding, whether this funding comes from their own departments, their university or a national authority with oversight on national R&D. At the same time, due to the inherent uncertainty that new research entails, the timeline of deliverables cannot be predicted. There is thus a propensity towards acceptance of delays when looking at project milestones. This focus on saving money at the expense of time becomes ingrained in their work.

Researchers optimise by a frugal innovation by building the equipment needed for their research. This saves significant money since commercial equipment can frequently cost 4–5 times the cost of the components. This gives researchers a false sense of priorities when they commercialise their research. Since they recognise that they do have the capability to construct equipment, they simply go ahead and do so.

The investors' focus could not be different. Since the competitive advantage of a startup is driven by being first to the market, investors put far more weight on the commercial acquisition of equipment. However, there is a more important element driving the commercial acquisition of building equipment. As the startup scales, it becomes imperative for it to focus on product and customer acquisition. If it needs to build all the equipment, this becomes an enormous bottleneck, on account of the logistics needed to manufacture equipment as well as the guarantees needed in commercially procured equipment. This skill is very different from simply being able to make a breakthrough device in the lab. Insourcing equipment manufacture, if this is not the startup's core business, can negatively impact milestones, delaying time-to-market and time-driven competitive advantage. This often results in dilution of the founders' equity.

In markets where time-to-market is key, being second to market forces the startup to 'catch-up' and address a commoditising market and becomes a lingering path to perishing.

Try to Do Everything (HW and SW)

Tech startups, like most startups, start with an overpowering desire to change the world in their given field and make it a better place. In addition, to make money. These are the right reasons.

The challenge occurs when you confuse the solution that needs to be provided to the customer with your core competence. Since you have always been able to accomplish everything needed to showcase your innovations as a tech 'guru', the logical implication is that everything that the startup needs to do can be done by you.

The result of this is that the startup tries to bring the technical innovation to market, prepare the software and the strategy underlying it onboard and do the logistics of manufacturing the hardware as well. This takes the startup out of its area of excellence relating to its innovation and into the far more competitive area of manufacturing. As a result, the startup is limited by its weaknesses rather than being driven by its strengths. However, on the cost front, the startup's solution becomes far more expensive on account of having to work a suboptimal manufacturing facility to do the hardware.

By keeping its focus on software and customer relevance instead of hardware, the startup is able to align with industry partners who are already involved in manufacturing and are keen to move from a commoditised existing business to new areas of growth, with commensurately healthier margins. Having these partners onboard also has the effect of reflecting their credibility into that of the startup. This is a magic bullet for investors, who look for certainty in the route-to-market as a core challenge.

If the startup does not appreciate the value of focusing on its core value and onboard complementary stakeholders, it risks being relegated to a very expensive solution that grows organically and eventually gets overtaken by the lower-cost solutions that are able to improve quality on account of ever-deeper pockets resulting from market dominance.

Technology vs Investor Documents

As the startup progresses towards the first step in getting investors onboard, they realise that investor documents need to be prepared before they can initiate investor discussions. In case the startup is driven by only the technology team, there is often a tendency to postpone working on the investor docs, since this implies that the team has to delve into the uncertain world of making assumptions about the future. Creating investor documents implies finding the product-market fit, which means the team needs to initiate conversations with different market segments to find a monetisable need for the technology. To avoid this uncertainty, the team often resorts to go back to working on the technology.

The impact of this is that the initial cash that the startup has begun with continues to see a small but steady decline. Eventually, this results in the cash simply drying up, and time runs out for the team. When the startup only has 3–4 months left, investors can smell the desperation, and unless discussions have already started early on, the only recourse is to sell IP, if any, at nominal cost, and the founders simply move to working as employees of the acquirer.

Different Levels of Risk

Technologists who aspire to become entrepreneurs often think that the main challenges come from investors. However, in reality, the challenges begin much earlier. In the life of every startup comes a time when money is low. I mean, really low. This not only drives some tech entrepreneurs but also defines them. With other technology people in the founding team, this becomes the last straw in a world which is far removed from the one they are in the process of leaving, where the boundaries were clear and the funding and career progressions comfortably defined all the way through to a pension plan.

Funding issues multiply the uncertainty of the startup, where not only are the day-to-day activities not clearly defined, but the stuff that is on fire needs to be prioritised over others that are merely extremely urgent, but the future seems dark, interspersed with faint light at the far end of the tunnel, which may well be that of an incoming train. This is when some founders break and recognise that the entrepreneur's life is not the one for them. In doing so, they often take the startup with them.

This risk can be mitigated if there is a clear shareholder agreement between the founders of the modus operandi in case some founders want to exit. The equity transfer to the remaining shareholders while still retaining some future upside in the startup offers the most suitable step forward for all parties, so that even the founders that walk away retain some opportunity to re-join the startup in the future as well as some equity. This plays another important role: ensuring that some co-founders do not start a competing startup in the future since their future upside (and noncompete) is linked to the first startup.

Assume Tech Superiority in Manufacturing Play

Technology founders frequently have global technology excellence underpinning their startup. If this has already been translated into IP, it provides an unassailable advantage with investors that challenge the startup on IP as well as ensuring freedom-to-operate. However, for hardware manufacture, tech founders often underestimate the relevance and importance of the capability to not only manufacture in high quantities but also to have a manufacturing mindset. This has become even more pertinent in the post-COVID world, where we moved from 'just in time' to 'just in case', even as the supply chains that we had taken for granted over the past few decades turned out to be far more fragile than we had assumed, and supply times for even basic chips extended to up to a year.

Streamlined manufacturing is particularly pertinent in high-volume industries, since your competitors focus on volume and often already come from manufacturing industries into the technology, compared to your strategy as a startup of moving from the technology to manufacturing. Margins in volume manufacturing tend to veer towards the lowest common denominator, and your capability to extract all extraneous costs from the manufacturing defines your profitability. Startups that do not prioritise manufacturing and instead focus on taking the technology approach to scaling become their own stumbling blocks. There are only two ways to survive: to slice a very high-value niche that puts the same perceived value in your product as the value arrived at by piecemeal manufacture and a super profit to boot. The other is to become a brand and price accordingly.

Most tech startups in a manufacturing play are neither able to carve out a high perceived-value niche nor become a brand. As a startup, your best-case strategy is to sell as soon as possible since perceived value degrades rapidly. Otherwise, you risk being able to only get the price per kilo of your hardware equipment at junk rates when the fat lady sings.

Tech Excellence in Platform Play

Technical founders take great pride in their technology. Rightly so, since they have forged a path that has resulted in something never before seen or done in all of human existence. This is not the problem.

The problem occurs if the startup is focusing on a platform play rather than a technology-driven market. A platform play implies that the value provided to users is technology-agnostic. Thus, there is no technology IP, and the technology components, to the extent they exist, are largely off-the-shelf. Facebook is a great example of a platform company since the main drive is the user interface and convenience of personal and social network information access.

If the startup operating in a platform play does not recognise this critical aspect, the technical team continues to focus on its core competence, viz., the technology. This is particularly common for startups that have a preponderance of technology. The tech team focuses on perfecting the technology instead of going to customers to obtain feedback on the relevance of the solution and the value of the technology in enabling this. The other disadvantage is that a technology-driven solution in a platform space risks delaying the time-to-market. Since this is absolutely critical to the mind-space of users, this delay results in other startups going ahead and owning the platform. The best-case scenario for the startup is then to own a tiny niche vertical or a sub-segment of the platform that desires additional bells and whistles. However, more often than not, a platform has relevance because it is driven by one entity. As a startup, if you do not own the entire platform, you own nothing.

Organic Growth

Technology founders often bring forth breakthrough technology into their startups. However, they often have a degree of reticence in regard to getting investors onboard, since this entails giving up the freedom of decision-making and stepping back from hands-on interaction with customers.

The great risk of organic growth for a technology startup is that you always have a paucity of funds for buying additional equipment to streamline processes. This is because the revenue always comes in with a delay, whereas costs have to be paid upfront. Additionally, the fact that technology co-founders are fully involved in dealing with the operational challenges of providing solutions for their customers implies that they have little bandwidth to consider strategic challenges towards reaching scale, or where the value will transition to, over time. Finally, manufacturing in organic growth often continues to be fully customisable, limiting the ability of founders to replicate and provide a similar solution to other customers.

A startup developed a set of microphones designed like a sphere. Due to the sensitivity and configuration of the microphones, it provided the capability to record ambient sounds from all directions. However, the remarkable element of the solution was the capability of being able to replay sounds from up to 40 m for any direction by specifically focusing the recording of the appropriate set of microphones and ignoring the rest. This was similar to a GPS, which identifies your location by triangulating based on locking into the signals of a number of satellites. This startup, based in Switzerland, had already secured some contracts with military entities for providing microphones when I first came across them over several years ago. Fast-forward a few years, I expected to have heard about them in the media, due to the immense value of their solution being deployed in locations such as airports and public locations, to evaluate voice information prior to a terrorist attack. When I met them again, I inquired about their progress. Their response was typical of technology founders. 'We wanted to have full control of the solution and were not sure if investors would provide restrictions on us or take our technology away from us.' The status of the startup was three full-time members (including the two co-founders), providing a few solutions priced at over $50 K per year. Most likely a good revenue stream, from their perspective, but they had completely missed the larger global market, which was desperate for a solution for homeland security. It is noteworthy that for any country, whether in peacetime or during conflict, the only budget that never goes down is the military budget.

By focusing on organic growth rather than scaling, the startup missed creating and owning a massive market and ultimately is likely to be absorbed by a larger player as a technical extension, unless competitors get there faster, in which case, it may ultimately disappear in the footnotes of history.

Value vs Volume

Technology founders of startups start by focusing on their innovation. What they do not easily recognise are the market dynamics of the given (and fast-evolving) market segment. Therefore, they often tend to focus on high-value-based customers for their solution. The larger the market and the higher the rate of growth, the more likely it is for volume-focused competitors to jump in to address this market. It is important for young startups to recognise that while they are mostly the ones that perform breakthrough innovations and new business models, larger companies have the manufacturing capability and market credibility to drive scale.

If the technology startups are able to recognise this as an opportunity and transition their technological edge to grow volumes, they have the opportunity to become significant players. However, to enable this, the innovations go beyond technology and extend to manufacturing as well as logistics. Since it is not possible for young startups to develop all these capabilities in-house in parallel, a viable approach is to address volume while keeping some money on the table for industry players who already have the logistics capability to deliver the solution to the market. Another approach is to focus on keeping the innovation in-house and outsource the manufacturing as well as logistics to industry players. It is important to keep in mind that this is not the same as becoming an IP licensing company but a company that proactively has oversight on end-customer requirements and innovates to address this need. Therefore, although the outsourcing of manufacturing and distribution is done to existing players, the core value in the supply chain continues to reside with the technology startup.

Most technology startups are unable to make this transition from value to volume manufacturing. The high-growth industry continues to evolve, and profit margins move from value-added to cost-plus as larger players enter the fray. When this happens, the only opportunities for survival are ownership of a tiny high-value subsegment, being brought over by a volume player or returning to their origins and focusing on technology licensing.

Wrong Investors

There's a shocking number of startups that see investors as simply money. The reality could not be further from this notion.

When the startup is looking for funding, any money looks real since it provides a validation to the team that there is real value for their vision. It also provides an opportunity for the team to transition their ideas into specific milestones that take their ideas into reality.

The challenge occurs if the team tries to align their milestones to the far more aggressive milestones needed by the investors. If the investor does not impose any penalty clauses (such as founder dilution, X times conversion of preference shares or veto rights), this is still manageable. However, the real trouble begins when the founders try to make their milestones aligned to that requested by the investor, at costs documented in the investment agreement. In the reality of startups, one tenet is that milestones are always delayed. This is due to a combination of factors that the founders are overoptimistic about, as well as those they do not even consider. A penalty aligned to slipping milestones directly impacts the founders' ability to operate or dilutes them at a very early stage in the startup's evolution. From the universe of investors, if the startup does not select investors who are aligned to a realistic milestone timeline (read 'flexible'), it stymies the startup's capability in multiple elements, including acquiring equipment, hiring people and product definition.

With misaligned investors, the startup is plagued by friction and, more often than not, the only value for the founders as the startup folds is clarity about the right kind of investors and its importance in the evolution of a startup.

Failure to Pivot

A startup inherently has to pivot when the founders' ideological visions of commercialisation related to the desperation of prospective customers to acquire anything provided by the founders come in contact with the harsh reality of customer requirements. The successful startups pivot and pivot again, and in fact, continue to do so until they find a product, the route-to-market, the packaging or payment systems, or part thereof, that the customers are willing to pay for. Once the startup discovers this, it focuses on scaling up and replicating whatever the customer wants to buy.

Unfortunately, most startups are so wedded to their technology that they initially consider it an affront if customers do not appreciate it or ask them to modify the core technology. Reality comes to bite fairly quickly. Even so, a majority of technology startups continue to push their technology to customers after modifications necessary to capture value. Only the tiniest sliver of technology startups has the courage to set aside a majority of their core technology if customers provide feedback stating that their requirement is ancillary to the technology or simply a process or component used in the technology. These are the ones that make it big.

The above challenges pertain to technology startups. In the case of platform startups, the ability to pivot on a dime is even more indispensable in order to find their raison d'être. This is because if they do not provide exactly what customers want and the customers move on, they have lost them for ever. Additionally, the survival of platform startups depends on each set of 100 customers receiving an additional 101 rather than 99 new customers, as discussed above. The keenness of customers to not only use the platform but also to motivate new customers to board is critical. If the startup is unable to pivot, it very quickly becomes a white elephant before disappearing altogether. In the long term, the survival of startups is not driven by how strong they are but by how fast they are able to adapt to changing market needs.

Long-Term Liabilities Tracking Short-Term Revenue

Adam Neumann set up WeWork as a new paradigm of work. It was less a place for short-term office space rentals and more a new lifestyle and a way to be. Along the way, Neumann was able to get over $13 billion, including from Japanese investor Softbank. Its valuation skyrocketed to $47 billion at its peak.

The cardinal error of WeWork was to get real estate on long-term leases for short-term rentals. When it filed for its IPO in mid-2019, it turned out that it had over $47 billion in future lease obligations and only $4 billion in future lease commitments. Questionable dealings between Neumann and WeWork did not help investor confidence. With COVID-19, the concept of working from a common working space ceased to exist for 2 years, as 'work-from-home' became the default.

In spite of this hype, the ongoing interest of $2.7 billion annually by early 2023, which comprised 80% of its total revenue, simply eliminated the flexibility of WeWork to pivot. Finally, the company folded as reality caught up (https://en.wikipedia.org/wiki/WeWork).

No Beachhead in Platform Startup

Platform startups scale rapidly not only to become globally dominant players but also to eventually own the entire platform. However, they need to begin with a small beachhead market. This ensures that the initial users know exactly what they should expect when they visit the platform. In other words, the startup needs to bridge the expectation gap. Facebook began at Harvard, and over the coming months, it only rolled out to six other universities. Airbnb began in San Francisco and focused on ensuring that users who visited their site always had a few options of places to stay in San Francisco. Pebble aspired to become the platform to replace X (formerly Twitter). Why they could not provide a cautionary tale.

Gabor Cselle was a serial entrepreneur, having founded two startups that were acquired by Google and Twitter. In early 2022, he left Google and decided to try and find the next big thing. As it happened, Twitter was acquired by Elon Musk soon after, and Gabor found the angst of the Twitter users who were bereft of a neutral platform to be his calling. He founded T2 as the next platform to be more inclusive. He soon renamed it Pebble, reflecting the waves that spread outwards. He and his team began dropping invites on Twitter and other platforms as their own platform stabilised with increasing users. However, this already took several months, and Twitter's turbulence normalised in the meantime. Pebble also tried to be a place for all conversations for users from everywhere. Perhaps this was their cardinal error, since if I was the only beekeeper sharing insights, this did not turn into a conversation. As discussed earlier, conversations are the lifeblood of platform stickiness. Over time, they were simply unable to demonstrate growth to their investors and closed their doors in October 2023 (https://en.wikipedia.org/wiki/Pebble_(social_network)).

R&D Mindset

Typically, technology co-founders of startups have spent their entire working lives in labs doing research. This is typical in Continental Europe but less so in the USA due to the prevalent culture of commercialising ideas. Even after they set up the startup, the co-founders have the propensity to continue working in the research of the product they hope to commercialise. This tinkering is perfect for research, but a dangerous slope to go down for a startup, where the manufacturing mindset dictates that the product specifications be frozen at the earliest as soon as it can be considered the 'minimum viable product' that can be taken to early adapter customers.

If the manufacturing mindset does not have oversight on the go-to-market and the manufacturing and replicability-related process and logistic capability that need to be developed are considered subservient to the will of the technology co-founders, this will reflect on the priorities of the startup. For a startup that considers a unique hardware product made on a proprietary manufacturing process using customised equipment to be its core competence, the subservience of manufacturing to technology spells the death knell of the startup.

Research Projects

Technology entrepreneurs often come out of research institutions with no commercial experience. Therefore, they consider their startups extensions of their research projects.

If there is no business entrepreneur in the mix and the startup has yet to receive any investor funding, the focus of the startup becomes winning government funding grants. The startup's efforts often go more towards enabling the main research entity to obtain more government funding, and the focus becomes more 'research' than 'development'. As a result, far more efforts go towards R&D than prototyping, process standardisation for commercial machines and replication.

At this stage, early-stage investors such as angels often invest as 'dumb money' since they have very little knowledge regarding the steps needed to commercialise the technology. This further consolidates the focus on technology research rather than its commercialisation. The startup continues to obtain drip-feed funding from projects and becomes a hobby of the key technology driver.

For other co-founders of such startups, it is a tough way to go since they see the market evolving and not being a part of it, while their competitors have founders sleeping in offices to make it happen. Their own startup lives and dies a research project.

Family

Some founders of technology startups start by considering it their family business. Towards this end, they provide equity to family members and incorporate them as managers or administrative staff. This can be extremely disconcerting for other co-founders and future employees since it is not easy to know how to deal with an administrative person whose spouse happens to be the main founder.

The intentions of the founder whose spouse comes in as an administrative person may be perfectly honourable. However, this creates friction within the team since the founder always pushes the team to overachieve and set seemingly unrealistic milestones. However, from the team's perspective, the spouse appears to be someone sent to spy on them. Even investors often consider this an underhand tactic of the founder to try and suck up more funds from the cash available in the form of an additional salary. Other than in cases where there is only one founder (who can then hire whoever he wants), this mostly ends badly for co-founders of otherwise good technologies, since any distraction is a distraction too much.

No Visibility (They Do not Know You)

Technology entrepreneurs are often reticent about talking about their vision, since this appears to imply that they are trying to make future 'probables' appear concrete. This often goes against the grain of how they perceive reality, which from the researcher's perspective is either black or white. When they do talk about their startup, they simply talk about what they have done and the immediate things that they expect the technology to do.

On the other hand, investors like to hear about what the technology will *enable*, rather than simply what it will *do*. This is because customers do not pay for technology, but how it can make a positive impact on them. When there is an opportunity to talk about the vision and opportunity to change the world, technology entrepreneurs often limit themselves to the black and white of the technology. Journalists like to write human-interest stories. Since technology inherently is an extremely dry subject unless its impact can be visualised in human terms, most tech-driven startups often fail to generate buzz due to the lack of human interest. Eventually, they simply disappear from the public consciousness and return to the research domain.

When it is time to raise funding, whatever the round may be, a public profile is key. If the investors do not know you, it simply does not matter what your achievements are. For young startups, credibility is a factor of achievement and visibility. Even if they have investible funds and they cannot find you, you're not getting their money. The investors that these startups approach try and find information that is in the public domain. If there is nothing, the investors (rightly) assume that the startup is too tech-focused and early-stage. This is the dilemma of otherwise outstanding technologies that never make it to market. They simply do not know you!

16

Does Geography Matter?

There is a recognition that entrepreneurship is different between the USA, Europe and Asia. However, what entrepreneurs fail to appreciate is how this impacts their time-to-market, route-to-market and level of technology readiness or relevance of technology innovation for successful commercialisation. Even with regard to investors, investor readiness to fund, investor expectations after investment and future investment are driven by geography. These reasons impact not only the risk of the startup's ability to scale but also the entrepreneur's option to monetise and create personal wealth.

The US Perspective

In the USA, the degree of comfort with risk is high. This is driven by how wealth was created in the first place. For the most part, wealth in the USA in recent decades has been a result of platform startups that have scaled to become behemoths, owning the entire market they have created. These include Amazon, Google, Facebook and others. These companies converted tens of thousands of employees into millionaires, with the resultant explosion in value of their stock options. These same individuals are increasingly comfortable investing in high-risk platform startups where the winner takes all. This makes the USA a fertile ground to try new ideas. This works well for business cases that are more dependent upon creating platforms where the value is created by the platform's ecosystem. However, this does not augur well for commercialising technology, which requires a certain incubation period before it has achieved the degree of maturity necessary to ensure replicability and stability to bring it to market.

Platform startups require far less technological insight and often use off-the-shelf technology. Thus, the entrepreneur's time investment to develop the idea is often in months rather than in years. As a result, in case things don't work, there's always this opportunity to try something else and get funding to try it all over again. On the other hand, the incremental increase in the upside by sticking with the first idea all the way through, combined with the increasing risk of not being able to make it happen, results in the decision to try different ideas rather than staying the journey with just one idea. How failure is seen by investors also plays an important role in determining the risk that the entrepreneur is willing to take, and this failure is often seen as a badge of honour in the USA.

The recent president of the USA Donald Trump epitomised this transactional view. He spurned traditional allies such as France and Germany and cosied up to adversaries such as North Korea and Saudi Arabia. His view was that there was more immediate upside to working with them with the far more pragmatic if misguided 'what's in it for me' mindset.

View from Europe

Continental Europe has a whole different set of factors underpinning its technology and entrepreneurship ecosystem. Due to a historical lack of comfort with risk linked to entrepreneurship, combined with state support for higher education, the focus on research in Europe has been strong in recent decades. Access to free higher education, which is considered a right rather than a privilege, has also enabled Europe to tap into the collective academic potential for excellence. This is different from the USA, where you have to be able to afford to go to university before you ever get the chance to excel. This is also reflected in university funding in Europe, which is normally provided by the national government or even directly by the EU without any expectation of a payback, compared to the USA, where universities need to operate like businesses and cover their own costs with revenue or corpus funded by wealthy donors, who are often alumni.

Technology takes a number of years before it is able to transition from the lab to prototype. This is only half the journey since it then needs to look for potential market relevance. Therefore, it takes a certain degree of ownership of the vision by the entrepreneur that goes beyond the technology itself. This has to be sustained over several years before it achieves fruition. However, even at this time, questions relating to whether the value is in the machine, the process, the IP or the products downstream still need to be answered.

The case of Christophe Chautems illustrates this. Christophe was my student in autumn 2017 in my entrepreneurship course at ETH Zurich during his PhD. Prior to his PhD, he worked for another startup that developed a robotic system to address cardiac arrhythmia, which is an irregular heartbeat. For reference, the heartbeat is a result of electrical impulses alternating between the auricles and the ventricle. Irregular heartbeats occur when the electrical impulses develop a slight short circuit, resulting in a small electrical impulse to the ventricle when the actual electrical impulse connects with the auricle, or vice versa. This results in a weaker pulse and lower oxygen supply to the body. His solution was a flexible robotic catheter that went to the heart via the femoral vein in the thigh and neutralised the electrical leak via ablation. However, even if the robotic system did obtain the necessary certifications to be used in humans for the first time, the startup did not succeed in obtaining market traction. It took further research of over 5 years to improve the technology, build an IP portfolio, build a team and refine the business case. The result of those efforts is the startup Nanoflex Robotics, which develops a robotic platform to steer the flexible catheter from the femoral artery to remove blood clots in the brain and with an initial funding of over $12 m in 2023. In essence, it took 10 years of fundamental research at ETH Zurich, 5 years of development in a prior commercialisation tentative and 6 additional years to prepare a second commercialisation of a technology that can have the potential to save thousands of lives and dramatically drive down health-care costs in the process. This is indicative of the time and effort it often takes to commercialise a technology, even after many years of developing research excellence. This is also why tech-driven startups of the kind that emerge from Europe would often be impossible to imagine in the USA.

Second, the investor community in Europe has most likely created their wealth in traditional industries, due to which their greatest level of comfort is in investing in areas they can relate to. They thus look at IP, technology and manufacturing innovation and articulated market needs as prerequisites when investing. Finally, customer acquisition is much easier with technology that relates to the B2B sector relating to technology, be it material technology or healthcare. On the other hand, the conservative customer environment in the B2C space in Europe results in greater hurdles in customer acquisition, limiting scaling. For all of these reasons, there is a focus on treating entrepreneurship as institutional.

Europe, after Russia's war on Ukraine, has become much closer. It has recognised that inclusive entrepreneurship on a broader regional level can provide a geographic competitive advantage against Asia or the USA, whether it is on account of supply chains breaking down, as was illustrated during the COVID crisis, or geo-political risks underlying business decisions, such as the squeeze on natural gas as a mode of retaliation by Russia on Europe for supporting Ukraine. Putin's threat to limit natural gas supplies to Europe may in retrospect be the most significant factor driving the transition to renewables. Furthermore, his imperialist ambitions may then go down in history as the ramblings of a demagogue even as Europe reclaims a united front to strengthen support for technologies and their commercialisation as a strategic imperative. In a curious twist of fate, Putin's main legacy may be Europe's transition to energy sustainability.

The Asian Perspective

The view from Asia does not fit in either of these two scenarios. For the most part, family ties run deep, and there is a shared responsibility towards assets, where entrepreneurs consider themselves custodians of wealth for the next generation. Therefore, access to funds is easier for scions of families, which often results in a motley group of unrelated businesses being owned and run as family businesses. This mindset is rapidly changing for a small but growing segment of startups emerging from premier technology institutions in countries such as India. Finally, India is producing close to a dozen unicorn startups per year. However, many of them are transactional platforms and copycats of similar platforms that already exist in the USA, including food delivery and online transactions of goods and services, which also proliferated in China in the last decade.

The different perspectives of entrepreneurship in different geographies discussed above have certain systemic implications for the development of the broader ecosystem over time. The US model of entrepreneurship as transactional results in opportunities of very high value creation for entrepreneurs, with a proportionately higher risk. However, the lower timeline between idea generation and value extraction is responsible for the fact that most startups from the USA are platform based. These include Uber, WhatsApp, Facebook and Amazon. In this case, the value comes from the traction with the user base, which populates and drives the platform. The problem is not that immense value is created by the founders; it is that it is concentrated solely in their hands. This implies a complete absence of any ecosystems around the platform startup. To the extent that the ecosystem does develop, it is cost-based rather than value driven, in the same way that Uber is able to capture value from the personalisation and end-user relevance, while the taxi drivers, who are an integral part of their service delivery, are compensated only based on cost, which is often the minimum cost mandated by different jurisdictions where they operate. Once Uber gains monopoly in local taxi services, it is able to begin extracting a greater percentage of revenue even as the drivers have to work more to cover costs. In my recent trip to London, I paid about £50 for a taxi trip from the airport to the hotel. On inquiring, the taxi driver told me that he's only getting about £25. This means Uber receives 50% of the total fee, even as the taxi fare has increased due to the reduction of competition. Facebook, on the other hand, ostensibly provides a networking platform for free but in reality captures user info to sell to its advertisers. Amazon facilitates the sale of products by users, but since the platform is driven by price competitiveness rather than product uniqueness, transactions are driven based on the lowest price.

From these examples, it becomes clear how entrepreneurship, when seen from the transactional perspective, becomes an extractive industry. Value is thus concentrated in the hands of the startup, to the detriment of everyone else involved. Although this bodes well for the startup itself, its impact on the larger ecosystem is not only adverse but sustained. As an example, if core manufacturing is only considered to have customer relevance based on its cost, rather than its value, manufacturing will develop only based on this yardstick, and over time, all innovation and excellence in manufacturing will cease. Additionally, newly skilled people move to fields other than core manufacturing as attractive career options, further depleting the future talent pool of new minds and fresh perspectives and weakening the country's manufacturing-based competitive advantage.

View from the UK

We have seen the impact of outsourcing manufacturing over the past three decades in the UK. Since the time of Margaret Thatcher, the policy of the UK was to focus on services. It was in fact stated that the UK was driven by services, and manufacturing was seen as cost-driven rather than value-adding for the end customer. On account of this, the UK government deprioritised investments in manufacturing. As a result, three things happened. Young people did not take manufacturing as a focus, instead moving into other fields such as social sciences instead. Second, the manufacturing base that existed did not keep up with innovations that would have resulted from ongoing investments and new talent flowing in. Third, the experience in manufacturing was eventually lost over a period of time, as the most experienced people retired. Due to a cumulation of these factors, entire ecosystems were lost, and there was no subsequent creation of new sub-supplier networks since base manufacturing eventually moved out of the country. Today, the UK is completely dependent on Continental Europe and other countries for a majority of its products, from toilet paper to radioactive materials to treat breast cancer.

Today, if someone wants to set up a manufacturing startup, it is unlikely that they would choose the UK, even if the financial capital were to be available. This is because they are unlikely to find high-end manufacturing skills, which play a significant role in creating and sustaining manufacturing-related IP. In turn, the absence of this IP does not augur well for the UK's ability to sustain its competitive advantage, since these companies would likely set up their manufacturing out of the UK when they scale due to the paucity of local manufacturing talent. The funding for university research that may have led to future innovations was also reflected in how dramatically it reduced after Brexit. Oxford and Cambridge, which received over a billion dollars in funding in the 7 years ending in 2020, only received approximately $2 million post-Brexit in 2021 and 2022 from the EU's Horizon research funding. This will further create dependencies in the UK for the import of finished products, which in turn may further drive value out of the UK and may risk an ongoing downward spiral. Thus, the vicious cycle may continue and become self-perpetuating.

These examples show the different approaches of countries and how this can have an impact on deciding the location of the startup.

The Continental European model of institutionalising entrepreneurship takes a much more long-term perspective of creating and sustaining value since the time investment is far greater. It is imperative that the risks of failure be proportionately lower. This is a natural result in the case of tech-driven startups since tech excellence creates its own layer of protection via IP and process know-how. Although achieving unicorn status is much more challenging than for platform startups, tech startups require other capabilities, including manufacturing excellence and go-to-market capabilities. This results in boosting the supplier and strategic partner ecosystem. The ecosystem serves two valuable purposes. First, it attracts other tech startups since they find the ecosystem in a state of readiness to help transition tech to the market. Second, a value-driven ecosystem encourages investment in innovation and attracts smart people to join and drive further development. This long-term perspective of institutional entrepreneurship enables startups to create solutions that are not topical but have relevance and value that is sustained over a long period of time.

The Swiss Perspective

Switzerland is on the other end of the scale compared to the UK due to its deep focus on developing manufacturing skills, which have been fine-tuned with an education system that encourages students to choose their vocation early on. As a consequence, only approximately 20% of all school students proceed towards a university education. Eighty percent move towards a vocation, and by the time they are 18 years old, they are able to earn their own living. They are then equipped to be the best in one narrow field, whether it is pipe-laying or micromanufacturing. I recall when we did an extension to our house and called the plumber to extend the pipes. He came with a complex set of tools, and on my inquiring about them, explained (in Swiss German) that they enabled the pipe to be fused on the molecular level. I inquired how long he expected them to last. He seemed to not understand my question. Finally, I got a friend to ask him this question in the local dialect. The worker could still not understand why I assumed it would begin leaking. On my insistence, he finally said it would be good for at least 75 years. The quality of work on the pipes was so high that the worker found it inconceivable that it would not work perfectly. However, good work does not come cheap, as we found since the cost of skilled workers per hour was close to $150. For this reason, companies doing high-end manufacturing find Switzerland attractive, particularly if their customers pay for value rather than cost.

When you start a startup, you do not often look at the location as a variable, since where you are is often where you start. However, location, or geography, plays a significant role, right from idea generation, how you start, how you get funding and how you scale. Clarity regarding what these factors are and how they influence the ecosystem and how they are influenced can play a pivotal role in maximising the chance of success of a startup.

Technology

If your geography does not have high-end research institutions or universities that provide funding to research or are able to attract international researchers, your opportunity to spin off world-class technology from such research institutions is unlikely. One way of identifying whether the technology is world class is to see the peer-reviewed articles that have emanated from such universities in top research journals. In parallel, it is important to have a look at the patent portfolio and the patents that you may want to license from the research institution. If the technology ecosystem is weak, there will not be much by way of patents and articles with strong peer reviews. This makes your value proposition of starting a technology startup that much weaker.

Incubators

Incubators provide valuable support to tech teams trying to transition to become startups and teams with ideas or technology trying to figure their way to the market. These incubators not only provide some funding but also, more importantly, provide access to like-minded people trying to bring their own ideas to market. With several startups under one roof, good incubators also cultivate relationships with advisors and successful entrepreneurs, who then become angel investors. This is critical in changing the mindset of the team from tech excellence to market relevance. For a young startup, this is an excellent opportunity to tap the network that an incubator brings. Angel investors or successful entrepreneurs who support the incubator by way of providing advice or guidance then see the startups more as fragile entities that need to be carefully nurtured rather than harshly evaluated to decide whether to invest.

Inclusive Environment

An environment that not only tolerates but also celebrates entrepreneurship is conducive in many ways, which often complement each other. One of the most important elements in a startup is the team. The strongest teams, in turn, are composed of people who complement each other's skills. This not only means complementary skills but also includes international experience. Those with international experience, who most often are on some kind of residence and work permit, need to feel comfortable about a seamless work permit transfer from a corporate job or a research-related permit to a permit enabling them to start or work in a startup. More importantly, people with international experience need to feel secure about being able to stay in the country in case the startup goes belly up. While this is not something that citizens of a given country ponder on, expats to that country worry about a few things more than the uncertainty relating to their being asked by national authorities to leave.

Open Ecosystem

An ecosystem that is open is the basis for new ideas to thrive. Only when people are able to challenge conventional wisdom are they truly able to innovate and develop new ideas. This ability to challenge conventional wisdom and existing ideas, solutions and incumbent businesses also extends beyond business to politics. This is because for new business models to thrive, they have to challenge the large existing incumbents, and the repercussions extend to the political powers that be as well.

This also goes down to the fundamentals of how startups come into existence. When ecosystems are closed, external ideas are normally restricted, as are the opportunities for global investors to invest. In such cases, the only entities that are given the de facto right to address opportunities are the large incumbents. As a result, the environment itself becomes static due to a combination of low motivation to innovate as the market is protected and legacy assets that only allow incremental changes that are fully aligned with these assets. If assets remain in an ecosystem for long enough, they become liabilities in that they restrict the flexibility of the organisation from innovating out of that ecosystem. This is seen when the organisation spends more time and effort to safeguard its own downstream servicing capability than innovating the customer experience itself. Efficiency then supersedes effectiveness. This is only good when the innovative ecosystem is static. However, when the ecosystem experiences rapidly change due to evolving customer expectations or new technological breakthroughs such as machine learning or social networks, it results in rapid innovation. Incumbents that continue to focus on sustaining their existing ecosystems then become prime targets for new startups and then see their market relevance erode, as they begin competing on cost rather than on value driven by innovation. Countries such as China create limitations on external entities to access the local market. This then results in barriers enabling the local players to thrive and create customer dependencies. Open economies, on the other hand, do not have these limitations. A good example of an open economy is the USA, where simply the opportunity to have a conversation with like-minded individuals can result in innovation.

The latest example of this is Clubhouse. Clubhouse began in early 2021, partly due to the COVID-19 pandemic, as a result of which people could no longer meet due to global restrictions on movement to the extent that in many cities around the world, people had to obtain police permission to travel more than a few kilometres from their place of residence. Clubhouse thus began as a way to have a conversation with a small number of individuals who shared a common interest and to do this in the old-fashioned way by having a conversation. This was not text-driven or visual but just a conversation using voice. The remarkable thing about this was that in the age of social media and networks of hundreds of thousands of people, many of us did miss the opportunity to simply talk to individuals who shared a common interest. The second interesting thing about Clubhouse was the network effect. By limiting the network to a small number of people, there was a feeling of exclusivity about it. Each person wanting to join needed to be invited by an existing member. The feeling of exclusivity was further perpetuated by the limited invites. Each existing member could only invite two new members in any given time period. This made the invitation relatively sought-after. Furthermore, the profile of every member showed the person who invited them. This meant that members had to be careful who they invited since their reputation could be besmirched if their invited members did something untoward.

Clubhouse began its pivot to becoming mainstream-cool when Elon Musk invited Russian President Putin for a conversation on the platform. This could have made it a serious player, and there were indications from representations of both that they would be willing to participate. However, the messaging was lost, and as a result, the rumoured conversation never took place. Based partly on the buzz, Clubhouse also had the opportunity to be acquired by Twitter for a rumoured $4 billion. Instead, they decided to raise funding at a valuation of $4 billion. However, in their rush to capture all the interest and stop any other platform from coming into their space, Clubhouse dramatically increased the frequency with which existing users could invite new users, as well as the number of new users that existing users could invite. This resulted in the loss of exclusivity since anyone who wanted to become a user could easily do so. Scale was at the cost of loss of exclusivity and commoditisation. As a result, Clubhouse lost an incredible opportunity to become the next viral platform and became a footnote in the annals of time.

Manufacturing Skills

Even if there is outstanding technology and research in a given ecosystem, due to historical strengths in high-quality universities and learning institutions, it is very difficult to commercialise technology if there is no manufacturing skill available. This is due to three reasons. The first is that if the country focus is towards a service economy, existing manufacturing capabilities either move into other sectors or simply disappear as people with the right capabilities retire and are not replaced by younger people. The second is that with a lower focus on manufacturing, manufacturing capabilities become obsolete since they are not replaced by new technologies that may provide competitive advantage. The third reason is that education institutions focus more on developing skills that relate to service industries rather than providing training and internships relating to skilling and manufacturing activities. While in the short term, the focus on outsourcing of manufacturing activities can be good for the balance sheets of corporate entities, the long-term depletion of these capabilities weakens the underlying stability of entire ecosystems, since service skills are far easier to outsource and compete in a global environment, where the earning opportunities are limited due to opportunities to outsource to a lower-cost environment. The UK example discussed above is a case in point.

Hiring Good People

A startup needs people who are able to think independently. More importantly, a startup is defined by people who are able to find creative solutions to problems. In fact, a good startup team recognises that the other side of any problem is opportunity. Beyond the mindset, startups also require skills and relevant capabilities dealing with the manufacturability of technology or software capabilities.

Exceptional startups spend weeks or even months to hire their first employees. They recognise that these early employees, together with the founders, set the tone for the ethical cornerstones of the startup. This is because a startup often grows much faster than the capability of the organisational structure to keep up. Thus, any friction within the work styles of the early team members can send mixed signals to those who come later. Geographies where the focus on deliverables is missing due to a more procedure-driven attitude or one driven strictly towards following regulations are far more challenging for startups to thrive.

Funding and Investors

The initial phase of a startup begins much before the startup is actually created. For tech-driven startups, the funding needs to be available for the research teams for testing the value proposition and creating the first prototype and showcasing the physical manifestation of the results suggested by the theoretical science. However, this is not enough. Creating a second prototype showcases replicability. Beyond this, funding is needed to invest in developing equipment on which the replicability and the actual working of the hardware are showcased with the integrated software. These elements are expensive and, more importantly, require consistent investment before the technology becomes 'investible', from the perspective of angel investors, assuming an articulated need by a customer. Government support via incubators, combined with bank loans to showcase the proof of concept, is instrumental in helping startups take their first steps towards commercialisation.

With investors, startups need to be sensitive to the expectation gap when they consider investors from a different geography. This is similar to the expectation gap between financial and strategic investors, where financial investors look for a return on their investment and strategic investors want to have access (read 'exclusive access') to the technology, market or data.

American investors are relatively more comfortable with investing in startups that entail higher risk, since most of them, particularly in Silicon Valley, have created wealth with platform startups such as Google or Facebook by being founders, early employees or angel investors. However, given that most platform startups scale to 50X or 100X within a short period of time, often in months, their timelines are incredibly short. Startups that emanate from the USA are often platform startups since the ability to scale 50X in a matter of months is far easier to achieve with a platform backed by enormous marketing effort (and investment) but where the technology is already commoditised. These platform startups in turn entail very high risk, since you can't aspire to 50X growth without risk, and quite often, platform startups in the USA have failure rates of over 90% in the first couple of years.

Compare this with traditional investors in Continental Europe, who have often made their fortunes in traditional industries. They consider far more traditional capabilities such as patents, manufacturing capability and sustainability to be of primary importance. For a deep-tech startup emanating from Europe, where the founders have invested several years in developing their technology, the risk mindset of an American investor may be too high. At the same time, a technology-driven startup is unlikely to achieve 5X growth in a year. Time is also defined differently by investors between Silicon Valley and Europe. 'Short term' is less than 3 months in Silicon Valley, whereas in Europe, it is approximately 2 years. 'Mid-term' is 6–9 months in the Valley compared to up to 5 years for technology startups in Europe. 'Long term' in Europe can easily be over 10–15 years. Investors in the Valley cannot even relate to this timeframe. If the startup gets investors from different geographies and gives them board seats, board meetings can very quickly devolve to a shouting match due to the different perspectives and end up in a decision freeze due to the very different reference points on marketing, risk, scale, growth and exit.

In summary, failure is largely a result of the gap between technology excellence and market relevance, the expectation gap within teams, technologies looking for a problem to solve and whether investors are aligned with the vision of the team. If any of these variables are out of alignment, it can significantly derail the success of the startup and the ability of the founders to exit and monetise on the value they have created.

17

Purpose

Countries such as the USA and Switzerland recognise the value of innovation and entrepreneurship: it helps create new businesses that generate value and revenue and help create high-paying jobs. This percolates into the economy and helps sustain a high quality of life. However, the two countries have very different approaches. The USA has a top-down approach, where companies receive financial support and other tax subsidies to sustain their business. This results in maximising the wealth of those who are already wealthy at the expense of the workers in the lower rungs of the ladder. Switzerland, being completely devoid of natural resources, has taken the approach of skilling everyone. Those with an academic bent of mind go to university and constitute approximately 20%. The remaining 80% focus on building a specific skill based on the needs of the market and their own inclinations. Since Switzerland considers education an investment in the sustainability of the ecosystem for the future, education is free. In the USA, on the other hand, only the wealthy can even afford to go to the best universities, since higher education is considered a for-profit business. The end result of the two approaches is that the USA creates a two-class system, whereas Switzerland is far more egalitarian. In a knowledge-driven society, it is imperative that those most suited to academics go into it, not just those who can afford to do so. If the sustainable competitive advantage of a country is the result of per-capita innovation, the USA may struggle to find the best people from a much smaller pool of those who are wealthy enough to send their kids for higher education, since the majority have not had the opportunity to even go to university. Furthermore, if sustainable development in a country is based on not only the incredible wealth of its wealthiest 0.1% but also the average living standards of its 25% least affluent citizens, the US model would need to be re-evaluated. This is particularly given the increasing hurdles for immigrants coming to the USA. This plays an important role, as over a third of all companies founded in Silicon Valley in recent decades have been founded by immigrants or their children. If those at the bottom of the ladder have nothing, they will have nothing to lose by taking to a path of crime or resorting to violence. As many developed nations from the Nordics, Japan and Switzerland have demonstrated, stability is an essential tenet of sustained development.

We began with examples of how certain events result in a positive impact on all of society and are considered inclusive. We also discussed other examples that benefit certain segments of society due to control of value and are considered extractive since they result in value being at the expense of, or being extracted by, those in power from those without. When the first person walked the earth on her legs, leaving her hands to forage or hunt with tools, all mankind benefited since these were the first tentative steps towards civilisation. On the other hand, when the Spanish Armada began to explore South America in search of precious metals, entire populations of these countries were decimated. The first was inclusive because everyone benefitted as a result of the individual action, while the second was extractive since the Spanish Armada benefitted at the cost of the native population of South America.

For a long time, decisions that impacted large swathes of humanity were largely in the hands of governments. Countries that had easy access to natural resources such as oil invariably resulted in those in power increasing the scope of this power to encompass exclusive access to these natural resources. Over time, this state control became less democratic and more autocratic. Those without access to these natural resources became less relevant. Countries in the Middle East have seen the ruling elites gain control over oil and placate the remaining population by way of incomes without working and free sops such as access to free healthcare. Since those in power had access to revenue from the sale of natural resources, they saw no need to develop any other sector or drive skill development in the rest of the population. The only focus of those in power was to hold on to this power.

With the industrial revolution beginning in the twentieth century, large companies employing thousands or tens of thousands of employees took over the responsibility of supporting their employees as well as being responsible to their customers. They had to be responsible to their customers, since the latter paid for the products, which in turn ensured the survival of the companies. However, towards the end of the twentieth century, with the advent of the Internet, the balance began to change. There was no longer a need to hire thousands of people and have gigantic factories in order to have revenue of billions of dollars. If you created a software that became the industry standard, you could replicate it unlimited times, without needing thousands of employees to manufacture it each time you had to sell it. However, the Internet also created new industries, including social networks. These did two things. First, they were able to create very powerful ecosystems largely from personal information, services or goods transacted by the people in the network. Second, and more nefariously, the people putting such personal information on the platform were able to do this without payment to the platform. Therefore, the platforms were monetised by sharing the personal information of the users. In effect, the platform users became the *products* of the platforms. As a result, the platforms, which had become incredibly powerful due to the power of the global network effect, had all this personal information of billions of individuals but with no oversight whatsoever, were in a position to create powerful influence. The influence of companies including Facebook or Amazon is not only valuable in motivating a user to buy a specific brand of perfume based on the comments of his or her celebrity crushes. This influence can also distort truth or make people question it. At a time when elections in which hundreds of millions of people vote can be decided by less than a few thousand votes, this power to influence and move the needle a tiny fraction can be hugely consequential.

It needs to be kept in mind that the above examples all relate to the transactional wave, discussed earlier in the chapter 'waves of value transition'. The good news is that few enterprises address the 'pre-emptive' wave, and even fewer address the 'generational' wave. The reason is simple. Doing so would compete with existing business ecosystems that have been built over decades. However, as today's startups that address the next wave of institutional, multigenerational and pre-emptive impact emerge, the impact of these startups and entrepreneurs is likely to be far more sustained for a much longer period of time. For this reason, it is imperative that those technology researchers who expect to become entrepreneurs in the era of the next wave recognise their power of impact as well as how this can be made inclusive, since it is likely to become more pervasive for future generations.

This perspective is important for one reason. This is that if you've come this far in this book and as a researcher can relate to your own technology's relevance in addressing challenges that have long-term impact, and thus may be part of the third wave, you need to take the leap towards becoming an entrepreneur. Going forth into the uncertain future to create your own is what defines an entrepreneur. In addition, as an entrepreneur, your learning curve begins at the edge of your comfort zone. Creating multigenerational impact may indeed be your purpose.

Once you've established your purpose by recognising the power of the platform, *your* platform, you can get a better sense of your capability to create inclusive or extractive networks. Your early recognition that your startup idea of today may become the basis of tomorrow's Fortune 500 behemoth, one that becomes more valuable and relevant over time due to multigenerational relevance, may help you in defining your own purpose as a responsibility. Here, we are no longer talking about your own capability to amass wealth. As they say, after the first billion dollars, wealth is just a number.

If as a tech researcher or scientist you have come this far, this book is a gentle reminder to ask yourself about the purpose of your research, and more specifically, what your own purpose is. Is it limited to doing breakthrough research in the lab, where it may at best see publication in a top scientific journal? Or does tech excellence deserve something more, such as the opportunity to create real-world impact by bridging tech excellence with tomorrow's market need? By asking the last question, you may find it easier to define and recognise your own purpose.

In conclusion, a billion-dollar startup is nothing if it is unable to sustain its value over time. A billion-dollar startup that sustains its value over time is nothing unless it uplifts, includes and shares value with all stakeholders in its ecosystem. A sustainable billion-dollar startup that is inclusive may not happen unless you create it. We all hope for a better tomorrow and for someone to make it so. What if we're the ones we've been waiting for?

GPSR Compliance

The European Union's (EU) General Product Safety Regulation (GPSR) is a set of rules that requires consumer products to be safe and our obligations to ensure this.

If you have any concerns about our products, you can contact us on

ProductSafety@springernature.com

In case Publisher is established outside the EU, the EU authorized representative is:

Springer Nature Customer Service Center GmbH
Europaplatz 3
69115 Heidelberg, Germany

www.ingramcontent.com/pod-product-compliance
Lightning Source LLC
LaVergne TN
LVHW010336260326
834688LV00036B/728